Philosophie antique

Problèmes, Renaissances, Usages

Numéro 24 2024

Philosophie de l'action

Revue publiée avec le soutien de
l'InSHS du Centre National de la Recherche Scientifique

Librairie philosophique J. Vrin
6, place de la Sorbonne, 75005 Paris
http://www.vrin.fr

http://www.vrin.fr

ISBN : 978-2-7116-3204-6
ISSN : 1634-4561

Livre imprimé en France

Table des matières

PHILOSOPHIE DE L'ACTION

Dossier coordonné par
Thomas Bénatouïl et Charlotte Murgier

HERACLITUS' IMPLICIT THEORY OF ACTION

Zoë Audra
University of Cambridge
za274@cantab.ac.uk

ABSTRACT. *I argue that Heraclitus has an implicit theory of action: successful intentional action is dependent on a grasp of* logos *which is a causal account of all things in the cosmos. My analysis of Heraclitus hinges on the concept of* gnōmē, *which I will show is a manifestation of the juncture between understanding* logos *and intentional action.* Gnōmē, *which allows divine fire to steer 'everything through everything' in B41, consists of three parts: the capacity for forming a plan, the plan, and the delivery. I will illustrate how failure to perform successful action comes from a lack of* gnōmē *by focusing on two parts in particular — delivery and the plan. I will look at the relationship between understanding and control and how (a lack of) physical control impacts the delivery of a plan for the drunken man in B117, as well as how knowledge can influence the suitability of the plan itself by examining Heraclitus' fragments on religion.*

RÉSUMÉ. Je soutiens qu'Héraclite développe une théorie implicite de l'action : l'accomplissement réussi d'une action intentionnelle dépend de la compréhension du *logos*, qui constitue une explication causale de toutes les choses dans le cosmos. Mon analyse d'Héraclite repose principalement sur le concept de *gnome*, qui, comme j'entends le montrer, est une manifestation de la convergence entre la compréhension du *logos* et l'action intentionnelle. *Gnome*, qui permet au feu divin de guider « tout à travers tout » en B41, se compose de trois éléments : la capacité à élaborer un plan, le plan lui-même, et son exécution. J'illustre comment l'échec à accomplir une action réussie résulte d'un déficit de *gnome* en mettant l'accent sur deux aspects particuliers : l'exécution et le plan. J'examine la relation entre la compréhension et le contrôle, ainsi que la manière dont le (manque de) contrôle physique affecte l'exécution d'un plan pour l'homme ivre en B117. J'étudie en outre comment la connaissance peut influencer la pertinence du plan lui-même en examinant les fragments d'Héraclite sur la religion.

Philosophie antique, n°24 (2024), 9-36

Heraclitus' doctrine is centred on teaching the audience how to grasp *logos* by reflecting on their own experiences. As Johnstone persuasively argues, Heraclitus' *logos* is not just a cosmic principle; it is an account of a cosmic principle which can be heard, understood to a greater or lesser degree, and can be listened to.[1] That being said, very few scholars have moved beyond a purely theoretical analysis of the subject's experience.[2] Much of the available scholarship focuses on how a subject can grasp *logos*, and not what they can *do* with a grasp of *logos*. For this reason, in this paper I ask: what does it mean to act according to an understanding of *logos*?

There is, however, one area of practical action explored already by scholarship on Heraclitus, ethics. Sider, Bolton and Johnstone all establish a strong connection between ethics and physics, and argue that knowing physics provides a foundation for ethical action. Bolton offers a rudimentary study which explains that *logos* provides an 'unvarying and uniform' moral standard which, by being common, provides an easy justification for ethical action.[3] Sider and Johnstone provide a more detailed discussion of what it means to grasp *logos*. Sider offers an intellectualist reading, arguing that ethics is inextricably linked to epistemology and politics, and that a greater understanding of *logos* makes someone a better leader by teaching them about the best way of living.[4] Johnstone establishes that there is a two-way causal relationship between the physiological state of the soul and psychological well-being: a dry soul is wise and prospers, and a wet soul is ignorant and suffers.[5] A proper understanding of *logos* will thus improve the quality of our souls and allow for living well. God, he explains, is a perfect example

1. Johnstone 2020, p. 1-29.

2. One notable exception is Long 2009, p. 87-109 who places practical value on understanding *logos* in terms of *metron*, measure, and with respect to B112, argues that acting truthfully means performing properly measured actions.

3. Bolton 1989, p. 212-264.

4. Sider 2013, p. 321-334.

5. Johnstone 2020, p. 1-29.

of what intelligent understanding is, towards which a subject should aim. Two scholars, Fattal and Rosella-Schluderer, also try to interpret what ethical action would look like more specifically. Fattal also argues for the strong relationship between ethics and physics, according to which physics informs the wise agent how to act in accordance with the unity of opposites. He describes this as not overstepping natural order, citing B94 as an example of the consequences of injustice.[6] Likewise, Rosella Schluderer uses B112 to build an ethical model in Heraclitus. She explains that speaking and acting in accordance with *logos* means that performing actions in certain ways, *i.e.* in accordance with *logos*, can signify a mental grasp of *logos*. This, she speculates, might mean understanding the triviality of things beyond *logos*, much like the Stoic sage.[7]

This ethical discussion is an excellent starting point for thinking about practical action in Heraclitus, especially the recognition of the strong connection between physics and ethics. I agree that there are evaluative undertones to Heraclitus' epistemology insofar as he insists that virtue comes from wisdom. Moreover, I agree with Johnstone that god is an example of perfect intelligent understanding in Heraclitus.[8] However, none of these accounts explore the relationship between wisdom and successfully performing ethical action. I want to know how a grasp of *logos* is useful, not just that it is useful. Another way of putting it is I am interested not in the *subject* who grasps *logos*, but the *agent* who uses *logos*. How does *logos* inform an agent's decision to act as well as their ability to act? In order to do this, I will look for instances when different cognitive states inform actions through levels of access to *logos*. The scale of the action will vary from the individual-human to the cosmic-divine. However, the relationship between cognitive states, actions and efficacy of actions should be positively correlated: the more knowledge, the more power and control, the better the chances of successful action. This means any instance in the fragments of a cognitive state influencing action will be relevant to building a broader picture of the relationship.

I will direct my analysis of Heraclitus by searching for successful intentional action. What I mean by this is I am interested in the actions of an agent, what they hoped to achieve by their actions, and whether or not they do achieve what they set out to achieve. As I will show, successful action comes from a grasp of *logos*, knowledge which provides a causal explanation

6. Fattal 2011, p. 24-53.

7. Schluderer 2017, p. 1-19.

8. I hold no opinion on whether a human can achieve divine understanding or not. I merely maintain that Heraclitus argues that divine understanding is the greatest form of understanding, and it allows the divine certain actions. Furthermore, humans derive their ability to act more successfully from understanding, of which the divine has the greatest. Whether a human can close the gap between these two levels of understanding lies beyond the scope of this paper.

for everything within the cosmos. This knowledge takes the active form of *gnōmē*, an inherently successful plan through which divine intelligence acts. On a more individual scale, for whom divine understanding may not be attainable, some grasp of *logos* also proves essential for successful action. Either because *logos* impacts how much control an agent has over their ability to deliver their actions or by providing information to contextualise what sort of action they should choose to attain their goals.

1. Forming an Outline

The focus of this paper revolves around developing a comprehensive model that explores the relationship between Heraclitus' epistemology and the achievement of successful intentional action. My first task is to establish that there is reasonable evidence to read action into Heraclitus' epistemology. Already in support of this are the discussions of Heraclitus' ethics which begin from the observation that Heraclitus is concerned with individual and civic questions of how to live.[9] However, I will argue for a general theory of action which includes ethical questions concerning how best to live. I will begin, therefore, by arguing that B1, as the 'proem', sets the groundwork connecting successful intentional action to a grasp of *logos*. B1, which introduces *logos* as a cosmic principle, offers two contrary examples of actions: those which are performed successfully with a grasp of *logos* and those which fail due to a lack of *logos*.

1a. General Principle: B1

Heraclitus DK B1: τοῦ δὲ λόγου τοῦδ' ἐόντος ἀεὶ ἀξύνετοι γίνονται ἄνθρωποι καὶ πρόσθεν ἢ ἀκοῦσαι καὶ ἀκούσαντες τὸ πρῶτον· γινομένων γὰρ πάντων κατὰ τὸν λόγον τόνδε ἀπείροισιν ἐοίκασι, πειρώμενοι καὶ ἐπέων καὶ ἔργων τοιούτων, ὁκοίων ἐγὼ διηγεῦμαι κατὰ φύσιν διαιρέων ἕκαστον καὶ φράζων ὅκως ἔχει. τοὺς δὲ ἄλλους ἀνθρώπους λανθάνει ὁκόσα ἐγερθέντες ποιοῦσιν, ὅκωσπερ ὁκόσα εὕδοντες ἐπιλανθάνονται.

This *logos*, which is ever holding, people always fail to comprehend, both before and after they have heard it. Although all things come to be in accordance with this *logos*, men are like the inexperienced when they undertake such words and actions, the sort which I explain, distinguishing each thing according to (its) nature and saying how it is. But other people are oblivious of what they are doing awake, just as they are forgetful of what they are doing while asleep.

B1 connects successful intentional action to proper understanding and a grasp of *logos* and, if Aristotle and Sextus Empiricus are right about the position of B1, it also provides a framework that can be applied to the rest of

9. Sider 2013, p. 324 gives B43 as an example of individual action, and B44 of civic action.

Heraclitus' philosophy.[10] There are three mentions of action or things occurring in relation to *logos* worth raising:

– γινομένων γὰρ πάντων κατὰ τὸν λόγον: while this is not a reference to action *per se*, this claim is significant as it qualifies the scope of *logos* in terms of its explanatory range. The first sentence in B1 has already described the *logos* as temporally unrestricted (ἐόντος ἀεί), and the second sentence is now expressing the implications of *logos*' eternal presence. The statement is 'all things that come to be (γινομένων... πάντων) have something to do with the *logos*'. The phrase of interest here is κατὰ τὸν λόγον, which expresses the relationship between things which happen in the cosmos and *logos*. There are two possible readings here: i) a weaker claim that *logos* is just a descriptive account in a non-causal sense — all things happen in a way that is described by *logos* — or ii) a stronger claim that *logos* could have causal power by being a prescriptive account — all things must happen according to *logos*, which *logos* can also describe. Unfortunately, it is not possible to discern from the extant fragments whether *logos* is prescriptive or descriptive here, *i.e.* is there another causal power which *logos* describes or is *logos* a causal power in itself.[11] That being said, it is the descriptive and explanatory power of *logos* which is important here: if *logos* describes all things which happen within the cosmos, then understanding *logos* should provide an agent with a causal understanding of how things happen or have to happen. This should be taken in a cosmological context. What I mean by this is that *logos* explains the physical goings on in the cosmos, the cosmological states of affair, which may also provide explanatory context for actions but do not dictate individual actions.[12] This sets up the following general principle: when changes occur, these changes can be explained through an understanding of *logos*.

–(πειρώμενοι) καὶ ἐπέων καὶ ἔργων: here Heraclitus introduces agency. This example is what I will refer to as a 'failure' example, an example of what happens when an action or actions are done wrong or unsuccessfully, that is, the agent does not do the action right or they do not achieve the goal of their action. In this case, the error comes from speaking and acting in an unexperienced manner (ἀπείροισιν ἐοίκασι). This is shortly clarified by a 'solution' example which resolves that a successful subject (ἐγώ) does these things by

10. Aristotle *Rhet.* 3.5 1407b14 and Sextus Empiricus *Adv. Math.* 7.132. I am working with an understanding that *logos* here is a cosmic law as well as Heraclitus' account, *contra* Burnet 1948, p. 133; West 1971, p. 124-129; von Fritz 1974, p. 42; Barnes 2001, p. 59.

11. We will see later that nature is a causal power which *logos* describes.

12. *Logos* governs human actions insofar as they happen in a physical world, and in some contexts such as ethics and politics, *logos* does determine the direction an action should take to be successful, but this is different from saying that *logos* prescribes how each individual acts. See below on ethics and politics.

'distinguishing each thing according to (its) nature and saying how it is'.[13] This introduces a curious connection between speech, action and knowledge. Here φράζων means to show or display through speech, a speaking which carries a purpose of identification.[14] Success in action for Heraclitus (ἐγώ) has something to do with how and what he expresses through language. When paired also with *logos*, which is a linguistic concept cognitively linked with *legein*, there is a sense of some understanding which can be heard.[15] In other words 'distinguishing each thing according to (its) nature and saying how it is' is another way of saying, doing these things with a grasp of *logos*; *logos* is an understanding of nature expressed in language. The implications of Heraclitus' successful grasp of *logos* are his being able to succeed where others have failed, in speaking and acting. The failure example is of people failing at speaking and acting because they lack understanding of *logos* — they do not know what they are talking about. Here we start to see why it is relevant for intentional action that all things happen according to *logos*, as *logos* now becomes the knowledge on which success and failure are dependent.

– ποιοῦσιν: the final sentence provides further qualification of failure in action. In contrast to Heraclitus (ἐγώ) who acts informed by a grasp of *logos*, the rest (τοὺς... ἄλλους ἀνθρώπους) act in a state of oblivion (λανθάνει). What does it mean to act in oblivion? Oblivion implies that there is something the subject does not know or understand. This means the agent is acting without knowing what they are doing or something relevant to what they are doing. However, all things come to be according to *logos* whether or not men understand *logos*.[16] As a result, those who are ignorant of *logos* still act according to *logos*, oblivious to the fact they are acting according to *logos* and oblivious to what *logos* is. Their actions still take place in a world described/prescribed by *logos* whether or not they know about *logos*; these agents do not possess a causal understanding of their actions or what they are doing.

In B1, Heraclitus has already clearly indicated that successful intentional action is informed by an understanding of *logos*. The first mention establishes the cosmic scope of *logos* as a framework which everything can be explained

13. I have translated κατὰ φύσιν here as '(its) nature' to maintain the ambiguity of φύσις without a genitive: both a general overarching nature and the specific nature of a thing. Furthermore, I agree with Marcovich 1967, p. 10 that ὅκως ἔχει does not mean the 'essence' of something, although I disagree that φύσις here is not the same as in B123.

14. Svenbro 1993, p. 15: showing something expressed through speech but without emphasis on the vocalisation, *contra eipeīn* in Homer or *legein* post-Homer.

15. This is why *logos* is common in B2: communication cannot be private.

16. Here *logos* parallels the defence of medicine as a *technē* in Hippocrates *De Arte* 5: *logos* always has explanatory power whether or not men understand it, just as people may recover from illness in a way that can be explained according to medical principles whether or not the patient believes in them. In other words, *logos* and medicine are both independent of belief.

elaboration of the terms 'common' and 'private'? The waking-sleeping comparison also explains *how logos* works. A reflection on the sleeping experience will be useful here as this will illuminate the epistemological differences between waking and sleeping, and, in particular, those which pertain to action: dreams. In short, it will show why it is impossible to have knowledge in a private world, and the impact this has on successful intentional action.

There are three major epistemological problems with a dream experience: first, a dream world is inconsistent, chaotic and disordered. Storylines, people and places morph into each other seamlessly, inexplicably, and without regard for physics or any natural laws. Everything is in flux, and there is no *logos* to unite and give structure to it. This makes it unknowable and epistemologically useless, as it cannot constitute an experience which illustrates *logos*.[25] Second, without an external comparison, a dreamer can have no idea that their dreams are incoherent and inconsistent.[26] Because dreamers are forgetful of previous waking experiences, they act in an unexperienced manner. Third, dreams are private and individual to the dreamer, whereas people awake can have the same, or at least similar experiences. As a result, dream experience can never truly be shared or made common.[27]

This is where the epistemic distinction between ἐπιλανθάνονται and λανθάνει comes to the fore: whereas the awake-agent is oblivious to *logos*, the sleeping-agent has no access to *logos* at all, since there is no *logos* in the dream world at all.[28] This puts the sleeping-agent in an intensified state of oblivion towards *logos*: ἐπιλανθάνονται. The epistemic states are comparable but distinct because the awake-agent acts as if there were no *logos*, despite everything happening according to *logos*. In practical terms, this translates into a combination of the agent acting without proper situational grounding, that is an understanding of what they are doing, and the agent acting with a lack of control, they cannot do what they set out to do. This has consequences for action because the sleeping-agent cannot perform successful intentional

25. Granger 2000, p. 264-265 argues that a dream has no epistemic value because we forget it. I disagree, as people often remember dreams and this is what highlights their absurdity. A memory of a dream is what shows it has no epistemic value.

26. As Kirk 1949, p. 391 puts it: this means '*he* [the sleeping-agent] *sees things peculiar to himself alone*'.

27. See also Holton 2022, p. 66-70 who draws on B66 to make a persuasive argument for the epistemological limitation of sleep in physiological terms, and how a sleeper's soul does not have the necessary capacity to grasp *logos*.

28. The psychological causes of dreams may well be explainable and governed by *logos*, but the content as it appears to a dreamer is not governed by *logos* in the same way that its counterpart, being-awake, is. This is where the comparison lies, and to the best of my knowledge Heraclitus does not discuss the psychological or even physiological causes of dreams in the extant fragments.

action without *logos*. In a dream, not only does the dreaming-agent typically lack self-awareness and intention, but the dream world is not stable enough to make informed plans. In terms of types of knowledge, the dreaming-agent cannot understand what things are (διαιρέων ἕκαστον καὶ φράζων ὅκως ἔχει) without *logos* providing a unifying framework to explain the world in which they act. Therefore, to act like those asleep means to act without *logos* and an understanding of the causal framework which explains how things come to be.

Therefore, there is a clear connection in Heraclitus' thought between a grasp of *logos* and the performance of actions. B1 has shown that a grasp of *logos* impacts an agent's ability to perform actions because a grasp of *logos* provides a causal understanding of the cosmos, and B89 and B2 have shown what actions would look like without *logos*, and why it is so important that *logos* is common.

2. Practical Implementation

I outlined a connection between grasping *logos* and successful intentional action by way of a comparison between the epistemic state of a sleeping-agent, who has no access to *logos*, and an oblivious-agent, who despite being awake, treats the world as if there were no *logos*. This outline captures a general trend in Heraclitus where knowledge enables successful intentional action. Now I want to focus on exactly how this relationship manifests, and for this I will introduce a new concept, '*gnōmē*', which roughly translates to mean 'successful plan'.

2a. Intellectual Functions: B112 and B114

First, I need to add more support for reading *logos* as practically relevant by exploring B112 and B114; B112 and B114 both express the role of certain intellectual functions in practical terms:

> Heraclitus DK 112: σωφρονεῖν ἀρετὴ μεγίστη, καὶ σοφίη ἀληθέα λέγειν καὶ ποιεῖν κατὰ φύσιν ἐπαΐοντας.[29]
>
> Being wise is the greatest virtue, and wisdom is saying and doing what is true, understanding things according to nature.
>
> Heraclitus DK B114: ξὺν νόῳ λέγοντας ἰσχυρίζεσθαι χρὴ τῷ ξυνῷ πάντων, ὅκωσπερ νόμῳ πόλις, καὶ πολὺ ἰσχυροτέρως. τρέφονται γὰρ πάντες οἱ ἀνθρώπειοι νόμοι ὑπὸ ἑνὸς τοῦ θείου· κρατεῖ γὰρ τοσοῦτον ὁκόσον ἐθέλει καὶ ἐξαρκεῖ πᾶσι καὶ περιγίνεται.
>
> Those speaking with intellectual understanding must put firm trust in what is common to all, just as the city in the law, and with much more firmness.

29. I follow Diels-Kranz in placing the comma after μεγίστη rather than Kahn 1979, p. 42 after σοφίη, as does Conche 1986, p. 234, Robinson 1987, p. 64 and Laks & Most 2016, p. 194-196 to name a few.

For all human laws are nourished by one divine law. For it controls to the extent it wishes and it is enough for all and it prevails.

B112 defines wise action as something informed by some kind of intellectual function, and the language used here maps onto the language of B1: speaking (λέγειν), acting (ποιεῖν), according to nature (κατὰ φύσιν) and understanding (ἐπαΐοντας).[30] However, the fragment proves difficult to translate as the range of the second καί remains unclear: i) is wisdom saying what is true *and* acting according to an understanding of nature or ii) is wisdom saying *and* doing what is true, understanding things according to nature (as above)? This is important as it determines whether ἀληθέα is also the object of ποιεῖν and whether κατὰ φύσιν ἐπαΐοντας also qualifies λέγειν. I will opt for the second option, as given in my translation above for the following reasons: first, taking λέγειν καὶ ποιεῖν as a phrase mirrors καὶ ἐπέων καὶ ἔργων in B1.[31] Second, B1 qualifies a form of speaking, διηγεῦμαι, with the same phrase κατὰ φύσιν. Third, it allows ἀληθέα, truth, to be the object of the verbs qualified by κατὰ φύσιν ἐπαΐοντας.[32] This gives the fragment a prescriptive tone; it states that not only wisdom is to be sought, wisdom is achieved by speaking and acting in accordance with *logos*. This is what it means to speak and act 'truly'; to speak and act according to a grasp of nature. This action is also an expression of an agent's excellence (ἀρετή), there is a certain positive value to acting according to a firm theoretical grounding, it is 'excellence' to express wisdom through properly informed action.

What is nature, and what does it mean to act according to an understanding of nature? Two things are worth noting: first, Heraclitus is not using φύσις with an additional noun in the genitive, which suggests this is a more general, overarching principle which somehow governs the individual nature of things. Second, φύσις, as captured by Hippocratic medical treatises which seek understanding of human nature, suggests a causal understanding of what something is and how it has come about.[33] While much of Hippocratic medicine was making intentional strides to distance itself from philosophy, the notion of nature as a causal explanation is telling here.[34] Taking these two

30. I agree with Schluderer 2017, p. 9 that B112 is the positive counterpart to B1.

31. Kirk 1962, p. 390-391.

32. One concern here might be how to make sense of ἀληθῆ ποιεῖν, which is an unprecedented expression, Kahn 1979, p. 122 finds no parallel examples, Schluderer 2017, p. 9 n. 53 finds one parallel in *John* 1.6. However, the phrase fits easily into my reading of *logos* as action based and Heraclitus is well-known for manipulating language to reflect his own philosophy (Vieira 2013), so this concern can be dismissed.

33. For example, *On Regimen* 1.2; *Ancient Medicine* 20. According to Hadot 2006, p. 20 nature means '*the natural process or the working of things, in general, the relation between cause and effect, or the analysis of causality*'. See also Hadot 2006 on the development of the term '*physis*', especially chapter 4.

34. Most notable *Ancient Medicine* 20's criticism of Empedocles.

observations into account, nature is not just the coming to be of an individual thing, it must also mean nature in a more general sense: the cause of how things come to be in the world. This is the nature that 'nourishes' all individual natures, it is what determines individual natures in a systematic, measured (μέτρα) way. There is a parallel in B114 with the relationship human laws have to the divine law, which is why I use the term 'nourish'. The laws of the city are nourished by a divine law, in the sense that there is a systematic, non-contradictory, and directed relationship between them. Furthermore, according to B123, nature is elusive: φύσις δὲ καθ' Ἡράκλειτον κρύπτεσθαι φιλεῖ: '*according to Heraclitus nature loves to hide*'. The difficulty people have in grasping *logos* is a recurrent theme. For example, in B1 people are struggling to grasp *logos* despite hearing it and in B40, understanding (νόον) is something above and beyond lots of learning (πολυμαθή). Acting according to an understanding of nature, therefore, is another way of saying and grasping *logos*. More to the point, nature is the causal power which *logos* describes; to understand nature is to understand the causal principles determining how things come to be. This is why wisdom is acting with an intellectual grasp of nature.

I want to look at this idea of *noos* as understanding in more detail, as it comes up in B114 as well.[35] In B114, speaking with understanding means speaking according to an understanding of *logos*. Intellectual understanding plays the same role as the law does in the city, as emphasised by the word play between νόῳ and νόμῳ. An intellectual understanding provides a strong foundation for acting, and in this case the action is speaking. The city's laws are a strong foundation because all human laws have a common source, the divine law. The same is true of intellectual understanding: it is a strong foundation for action because it is based on something common, something which is communicated and heard: *logos*. The linguistic component to understanding is also evident in the idea of a barbarian soul in B107: κακοὶ μάρτυρες ἀνθρώποισιν ὀφθαλμοὶ καὶ ὦτα βαρβάρους ψυχὰς ἐχόντων: '*bad witnesses for men are eyes and ears for those with barbarian souls*'. Just as barbarians cannot understand Greek, a language which many have in common, barbarian souls cannot understand their senses because they do not have any grasp of *logos*. An ordinary soul would apply a grasp of *logos* to sensory perceptions in order to contextualise them. On the contrary, a barbarian soul, cannot understand that their experiences are governed by and can lead to a grasp of *logos*. This makes sensory perceptions bad witnesses, as they are unintelligible without *logos*. Thus, a barbarian soul, is one which acts without an intellectual unders-

35. I have translated *noos* as intellectual understanding, which may seem tautologous, because I want to capture both the process of intellectually or critically using one's intellectual capacity and the successful act of understanding what their *noos* is engaging with. On the multifaceted range of *nous* see von Fritz 1974.

tanding, and to put this idea into the terms of B112, without sound thinking and without excellence.

2b. Gnōmē*: B41 and B78*

B112 and B114 have shown that intellectual functions are expressible as actions, but what is it that makes actions happen? This is the role of *gnōmē*:

> Heraclitus DK B41: εἶναι γὰρ ἓν τὸ σοφόν, ἐπίστασθαι γνώμην, ὁτέη ἐκυβέρνησε πάντα διὰ πάντων.
> Wisdom is one thing, to know *gnōmē*, which helms all things through all.

B41 associates wisdom with knowledge of *gnōmē*. What is interesting is the relative clause: *gnōmē* is what steers things. The steering is described as a type of planned navigation, ἐκυβέρνησε, the helming of a ship, which may be taken as a gnomic aorist to give it an air of omni-temporality.[36] Furthermore, the object, πάντα, is steered spatially, as indicated by διά with the genitive; *gnōmē* has the power to move things, all things. This fragment should be contrasted with the role of *logos* in B1, in particular, the phrase γινομένων γὰρ πάντων κατὰ τὸν λόγον. In B1 *logos* is involved tangentially as an adverbial qualification explaining how things come to be, in B41 *gnōmē* is the subject of a finite verb, ἐκυβέρνησε and so *gnōmē* is actively steering and moving things. However, they both have the same scope of influence, πάντα. This reveals an interesting nuance to Heraclitus' conception of knowledge. There is the passive grasp of *logos*, the account which describes or prescribes how all things come to be, and there is the active grasp of *gnōmē*, which controls all things, making them come to be. The question is: does knowledge of *gnōmē* allow an agent to act and control things?

Simply put, yes. There are two ways to look at this. One is to think about divine control, and who has access to the wisdom. The other is to look at plural *gnōmai*, and how plans help less knowledgeable agents control things. I will look at divine control when I look at successful delivery, and focus on *gnōmai* now:

> Heraclitus DK B78: ἦθος γὰρ ἀνθρώπειον μὲν οὐκ ἔχει γνώμας, θεῖον δὲ ἔχει.
> The human character is to not have *gnōmai*, divine (character) is to have them.

If *gnōmē* controls everything, what are *gnōmai*? I claim that they are the manifestations of knowledge on a smaller scale. This is another example of a relationship of nourishment; *gnōmē* nourishes *gnōmai* in the sense that *gnōmai* must be in keeping with the *gnōmē*, and *gnōmai* are successful by virtue of doing this. In this case, it also corresponds with wisdom. In B41 it is *the* wisdom (τὸ σοφόν) to know *gnōmē*, in B112 wisdom (σοφίη) is action according to an understanding of nature, which as discussed is acting with a

36. Which is common for Heraclitus, for example B53 ἔδειξε and ἐποίησε; B79 ἤκουσε; and B101 ἐδιζησάμην: Kahn 1979, p. 170-171.

grasp of *logos*, and in B78 it is divine character to have *gnōmai.* It seems then that *the* wisdom is knowing *the* plan, but wisdom in general is just informed action. If informed action is informed by *logos*, and *gnōmē* is the practical manifestation of knowledge, then wisdom is performing actions according to *gnōmai.* The nourishment works in much the same way as nature nourishes individual natures, and the divine law nourishes the laws of the city; it is possible to act with plural *gnōmai* in a way that is nourished by the single divine *gnōmē*. One way of thinking about it is to imagine that *gnōmai* cannot contradict the *gnōmē.* This requires a certain amount of understanding; the agent must understand what *gnōmē* is, and how their *gnōmai* will be actualised.

What are humans' relationship or access to *gnōmai*? If *gnōmai* are responsible for successful action, and human character is not to have *gnōmai*, then we are left with the question of whether humans can do any successful action at all. In the context of action, we might think of an individual's character (ἦθος) as a collection of traits or habits and therefore a tendency to act in a certain way.[37] Humans tend to have human tendencies and not to be able to plan, and this reflects the message of human ignorance towards *logos* in B1; humans struggle to grasp *logos* (if they can ever fully grasp *logos* or be divine) and therefore tend not to have *gnōmai*. However, a person can acquire a greater grasp on *logos* (through sound thinking: B116) and acquire a divine character. Equally, a human can have some *gnōmai* in the sense that, even without learning about *logos,* they still do complete actions successfully, it is just a matter of not being successful as often.

There is also a connection between having *gnōmē*, which is inherently successful, and correct desires. A grasp of *logos* has implications for desires, and desires will have an impact on the selection of the goal of an action. What is it that makes a *gnōmē* better or worse? What makes the best *gnōmē*? This is where a prescriptive element is relevant: a good *gnōmē* must be motivated by the right sort of desire. In B114 the divine law controls as much as it wishes, ἐθέλει, as much as it needs to fulfil what it wishes to fulfil. On an individual level, there are hints of ethical considerations. People also have desires in B110: ἀνθρώποις γίνεσθαι ὁκόσα θέλουσιν οὐκ ἄμεινον: '*it is not better for people to have what they want*'. If it is bad for people to get what they want, then their desire for it must be wrong, bad in some way, or at least worse than divine desire. The implication here is that a person would not choose to act on something if it was bad unless they did not have adequate knowledge to

37. For example: Hesiod *WD* 67, 78, Pandora is given ἐπίκλοπον ἦθος, '*a thievish character*' which accounts for her later actions: 94-95; Sophocles *Ant.* 746, Creon critiques Haemon's actions by critiquing his character: μιαρὸν ἦθος καὶ γυναικὸς ὕστερον.

know what desires are good and bad.[38] This is why human character is 'not to have *gnōmai*', whereas divine character is 'to have *gnōmai*'. It is a common trait of human character not to have the right sort of desires.

When I call *gnōmē* a manifestation of knowledge as action, what I mean is that it consists of three parts: capacity for planning, the plan itself, and the delivery of the action. Each of these parts is dependent on knowledge, and all together they allow an agent to perform actions successfully. The agent can enact a desire by constructing *gnōmai* using their knowledge, and then implementing them. The better a grasp of *logos* the agent has, the better the agent's desires, and therefore the more appropriate the *gnōmai*. In this way a *gnōmē* differs from *logos* by being active. If *logos* is an account of the relationship between knowledge and action, *gnōmē* is its active counterpart: an instantiation of that knowledge.

3. The Delivery

In the remainder of the paper, I will explore *gnōmē* through examples of unsuccessful and successful action. *Gnōmē* consists of three interrelated parts, which can be influenced by knowledge: the capacity to form a plan, the plan itself and the delivery of the plan. I will look at how two of these parts can fail and how this failure comes from a lack of access to knowledge. This is important as it will reveal what successful and failed actions look like for agents without a full grasp of *logos*. First, I will explore the relationship between understanding and control: how (a lack of) physical control impacts the delivery of a plan, the third part of *gnōmē*. Then I will look at how knowledge can influence the suitability of the plan itself by examining Heraclitus' fragments on religion.

3a. Drunkenness: B117 and B79

Drunkenness impairs rationality in B117:

> Heraclitus DK B117: ἀνὴρ ὁκόταν μεθυσθῇ, ἄγεται ὑπὸ παιδὸς ἀνήβου σφαλλόμενος, οὐκ ἐπαΐων ὅκη βαίνει, ὑγρὴν τὴν ψυχὴν ἔχων.
> Whenever a man is drunk, he is led by a beardless boy while stumbling, not understanding where he is going, for he has a wet soul.

I am interested in what is special about the actions of a drunk man. The man's drunkenness leads to uncontrolled movement both in the sense that he cannot control *how* he moves nor *where* he moves. I first want to look at what causes this lack of control and then look at the implications of the lack of control. What is it about drunkenness that causes this lack of control? There are a few things to note: the boy (παιδός), not understanding (οὐκ

38. Not necessarily ethically good or bad, but also achievable or not achievable. My desire to fly is bad because it is not achievable.

ἐπαΐων) and the wet soul (ὑγρὴν τὴν ψυχήν). These all suggest a particular kind of ignorance which causes lack of foresight. In the case of the mention of a boy, B79 gives it context, and is the only other fragment containing both ἀνήρ and παῖς: ἀνὴρ νήπιος ἤκουσε πρὸς δαίμονος ὅκωσπερ παῖς πρὸς ἀνδρός: '*a man hears himself called childlike by a god, just as a child by man*'. B79 portrays the relationship and distinction between god, man and child as one of relative perspective and foresight. Νήπιος literally means 'childlike', which takes on the metaphorical meaning of 'lack of foresight' due to a child's lack of experience.[39] This adjective is interesting when thinking about the drunk man following a child. According to B79, the child who leads him should not ordinarily be a better guide. This suggests the drunk man is regressing into such a state of ignorance that even a child has more understanding than him, and his understanding is so compromised that he lacks the capacity to act on his own. This is further emphasised by the status of divine wisdom. The man, who would call the child childish, would be considered childish from a divine perspective. The drunk man therefore has even less understanding than an ordinarily incapable man.

The verb used for 'understanding' is the same verb as in B112, ἐπαΐω (κατὰ φύσιν). The two fragments illustrate a pair of opposite states. In B112, the wise action, which is the best action, happens according to an understanding (of nature), whereas, for the drunk man, his actions happen without a personal understanding (of where he is going). This suggests that ἐπαΐειν is expressing a particular kind of understanding: an understanding of the information required for both parties to make and act on judgements, an understanding which comes from *logos*. This shows how understanding and physical movement are related. The drunk man's error stems from his directional choice, or lack of it; his inability to decide where he is going and go there. This allows us to make an interesting point about movement and *gnōmē*. The drunk man suffers in all components of *gnōmē*: the capacity, the planning and the delivery. The drunk man is described in passive terms which removes some agency from him, and with it his passive capacity for following a plan. It is not that the drunk man chooses to follow; rather, it is that he is led (ἄγεται). This much is clear from the fact that he cannot even understand the boy's plan. The drunk man also lacks the knowledge required for constructing a plan. A plan needs a firm grasp on the world and an individual's place in it. In this case, an understanding of where the drunk man is and how to get to where he wants to be. Last of all, he lacks the physical control required to get somewhere. Even if he knew where to go and how to get there, he is moving in an inefficient, hindered manner. He cannot deliver a plan because it is beyond his bodily control. The capabilities of the drunk man are similar

39. LSJ entry on νήπιος.

to the sleeping-agents' capabilities in B1. Just as the sleeping-agents act in an ill-informed way while asleep, with nothing stable in their private worlds to justify their actions, the drunk man understands so little that he could not justify his actions, even if he wanted to. He has less memory of his previous experiences than a child, thus he acts like those forgetful of what they are doing. In this way the drunk man is an example of how a lack of knowledge removes self-control.

3b. Cosmic Control: B64 and B32

The drunk man's actions suffer due to a lack of control caused by a lack of understanding. In contrast, the excellent actions in B112 are motivated by wisdom and wise thinking. What this shows is that understanding enables excellence. But excellence in what sense? In light of the discussion on control, the best way to render what it means to have ἀρετή μεγίστη is in terms of success. Such an understanding highlights the clear connection between more knowledge, greater control and successful actions. What is interesting, however, is how this connection relates to the description in B117 of the drunk man's 'wet soul'. This suggests that knowledge and actions can be placed on a continuous scale from those people who are drunk and in a state of sleep to those who are fully informed, and this continuum correlates with another continuum, namely the wetness or dryness of the soul.

To be drunk is to have wet soul. But what is the soul? For Heraclitus the soul is the part of an agent with the power of reasoning and language. This is why the wetness and drunkenness of B117 are shameful, because they are a '*a loss of self-direction, self-awareness, self-control*' from something which is supposed to unite the whole body and all its faculties, in a rational way.[40] This image of the soul is interesting because it depicts it as some kind of driver in varying control of the body as a vehicle. When the soul is wet, it cannot control the body, and this leads to stumbling. What about a drier soul? In conjunction with B41, B64 and B32 express the relationship between divine knowledge and divine control and a hot and dry agent:

> Heraclitus DK B64: τὰ δὲ πάντα οἰακίζει κεραυνός.
> The thunderbolt steers everything.
>
> Heraclitus DK B32: ἓν τὸ σοφὸν μοῦνον λέγεσθαι οὐκ ἐθέλει καὶ ἐθέλει Ζηνὸς ὄνομα.
> The one thing, the only wise thing is unwilling and willing to be called the name of Zeus.

Like B41, B64 describes a subject steering an object in the manner of a ship; in B41, *gnōmē* is the *kubernētēs*, the pilot of everything, and in B64

40. Nussbaum 1972, p. 159-160.

the thunderbolt steers by manner of an '*oiax*', a ship's tiller. Both steer equally large ships, and the size of the ship reflects the power and control of the steerer; the bigger the ship the harder it is to control, and the more impressive it is to have full control. Who is this steerer? In B64 the agent is the thunderbolt. This is both a manifestation of cosmic fire and a symbol of Zeus' divine power. This is relevant because in B32 the wise thing (τὸ σοφόν) is willing and unwilling to be called Zeus. This is the same wise thing, or 'the wisdom' as in B41 which helms the cosmos. This makes the divine steerer both something wise and something which manifests itself as fire.

The notion of divine fire is especially significant because of how elemental fire interacts with the cosmos. Unlike Anaxagoras' *Nous* there is no reason to assume that for Heraclitus the divine agent, cosmic fire, is not included in 'everything'.[41] Fire is the cosmic principle steering everything in B41 in the form of a thunderbolt, and also in B66 fire has judicial control over everything (πάντα). However, B31a-b shows that fire is proportionally equivalent to other cosmic regions: sea (θάλασσα) and earth (γῆ); B76a-c that fire sequentially transforms into three other elements: earth (γῆ), air (ἀήρ) and water (ὕδωρ); and B90 that fire is exchangeable for everything (τὰ πάντα). What this means is fire as a principle is a form which everything can become, and despite being a particular elemental form among 'everything', somehow controls everything; in other words, fire also controls itself. It also means that the extent of the power must correspond to the dryness of the agent. This is reflected in B36, which uses a similar exchange between elements as B31a-c, but substitutes 'fire' for 'soul' and depicts the transition as the soul 'dying': ψυχῇσιν θάνατος ὕδωρ γενέσθαι, ὕδατι δὲ θάνατος γῆν γενέσθαι, ἐκ γῆς δὲ ὕδωρ γίνεται, ἐξ ὕδατος δὲ ψυχή: '*for souls it is dying to become water, for water it is dying to become earth, from earth comes water, from water comes soul*'.[42] Just as with the passages above, water can transform, dry out, into soul, which is fire. Describing the transformation as dying also adds a prescriptive tone, a defamation of the wet, which makes sense when a wetter soul has less control. The drier soul is better because it is more fiery and has more control, and the driest soul is the self-controlling cosmic fire. This is where the continuum becomes apparent, the agent remains the same, the soul, but the control increases with the dryness of the fire. A cosmic fire can control the whole cosmos and itself.

41. Anaxagoras B12: this is where *Nous* gets its power. Its distinctness from 'everything' allows it to know more and have *gnōmē*, whereas Heraclitus' cosmic fire also gains power from knowledge, but it steers from within through self-control to implement *gnōmē*. See Lesher 1995; Laks 1993, 2002 for discussion on *Nous*'s power and control.

42. I follow Betegh 2007, p. 3-32 in taking 'soul' as a continuum of exhalations. With respect to B26, where dying and sleeping are adjacent, this also explains why the sleeping-agent has no grasp of *logos*. See Holton 2022 on the connection between sleep and death, in particular 66-70, where she discusses B26.

To return to the relationship between drunkenness and control, the examples of successful control and planning highlight the problems that the drunk man faces. They show the scale of control possible with different amounts of knowledge as a range from a wet soul struggling to control a stumbling body to an all-encompassing dry soul steering the cosmos. With full understanding comes full control and with full control comes the ability to deliver successful actions. In this way, knowledge of *logos* influences an agent's success at action by determining the control an agent has and whether they can deliver a plan.

4. The Plan

I will turn now to the implications of acting with and without a plan, how understanding feeds into making a plan and how a good plan contributes to successful delivery. For this I will look at religion, in particular the practice of religion through worship in B5, B14 and B15. This is especially important because Heraclitus focuses on religious practices rather than religious beliefs. His criticism of Homer and Hesiod is not about their depictions of gods in the same way that other Presocratic authors criticise them.[43] Instead, his fragments construct a non-overlapping list of religious practices which focus on the performance of religion rather than the doctrine.[44] As Most puts it '*the gods that interest him are not those of the poets but those of the city and the mysteries*'.[45] This raises an interesting point about how religious worship is an asymmetric relationship between mortals and the divine. The asymmetry of the relationship here is important because it foregrounds how practice can go wrong for non-divine agents, what happens when mortals without full access to *logos* attempt to worship the divine without full or proper understanding. The following discussion will be on impious religious practice; all of these fragments identify some kind of common error made by people in the action of prayer or sacrifice. What I intend to show is that this error is caused by a lack of understanding of *logos* which then results in agents making decisions on false or improper information. This means the presiding question will be whether it is the performance of the action itself which is a problem, or what the agent understands as the motivation for performing the action which is the problem.

43. Most 2013, p. 165-166.
44. Adoménas 1999, p. 89-90.
45. Most 2013, p. 159.

4a. Impious Worship: B5 and B14

> Heraclitus DK B5: καθαίρονται δ' ἄλλως αἵματι μιαινόμενοι οἷον εἴ τις εἰς πηλὸν ἐμβὰς πηλῷ ἀπονίζοιο. μαίνεσθαι δ' ἂν δοκοίη, εἴ τις αὐτὸν ἀνθρώπων ἐπιφράσαιτο οὕτω ποιέοντα. καὶ τοῖς ἀγάλμασι δὲ οὐτέοισιν εὔχονται, ὁκοῖον εἴ τις δόμοισι λεσχηνεύοιτο, οὔ τι γινώσκων θεοὺς οὐδ' ἥρωας οἵτινές εἰσι.
>
> They purify themselves in vain with blood, those who are polluted with blood, as if someone who has stepped in mud washed his feet with mud. He would seem to be mad, if any person noticed him doing this. And they pray to these statues of gods, as if they were chatting to houses, not realising who gods or heroes really are.

B5 is concerned with two common actions of worship: purification and prayer. It also provides a similar kind of general explanation as B1 and B117 which we can summarise roughly as: 'on the whole, people act like this and this is a problem'. In the first half of the fragment, Heraclitus compares two processes of cleaning, washing mud and purifying blood, and places a value judgement on the second example to indicate a perceived absurdity. The question is, what is supposed to be absurd? This depends on where the stress is placed: Adoménas wants to put stress on the ἂν δοκοίη arguing that this fragment presents the audience with an absurdity which can be resolved through a comprehension of the unity of opposites. He suggests that much like how the doctor inflicts pain to heal in B58, the polluted spills more blood in order to purify, and the muddy person washes with more mud to clean. The absurdity then is in not realising that this is how a unity of opposites works; more of one thing can indeed banish it. Thus, if the action *seems* absurd, then the agent has not understood the aphorism as it is not.[46] Rowett also places the stress on how it seems but suggests that the nuance depends upon the context contingent on how ἄλλως is translated. For the common person, this act is absurd and 'in vain', but in the context of religion, the act is performed 'differently'. In the latter case, especially when read with B15 which ostensibly specifies that the actions performed during Bacchic ritual are not shameful because of their Bacchic context, the purification with blood loses its absurdity by virtue of being religious. Washing mud with mud is absurd, but blood with blood works because that is how religious practice works.[47]

I agree in part with both interpretations, with Adoménas that unity of opposites will reveal a deeper understanding and with Rowett that context does determine the appropriateness of a practice. However, *contra* both, I maintain that this parallel is designed to show the common person how religious purification is absurd in all contexts because the agents go about it in

46. Adoménas 1999, p. 94-98.
47. Osborne 1997, p. 90-91.

the wrong manner. Purification is a process of dividing the contamination (*miasma*) from the contaminate in order to return to a clean state, just as for example we wash away mud with water.[48] To the uninformed, this may seem to be what purification with blood is: washing away a pollution with blood. However, the parallel reveals that the contamination is actually caused by blood. The secret contaminant is 'revealed' through a slight modification in the construction in the parallel example. At first glance, αἵματι only seems to be modifying καθαίρονται, but the comparison places πηλῷ in the same role as αἵματι while revealing that the thing being cleaned with mud is caused by stepping in mud. By repeating πηλὸν... πηλῷ, Heraclitus draws attention to the fact that αἵματι is also the cause of μιαινόμενοι. This is where the absurdity lies. When αἵματι is revealed as a *zeugma*, it means that the blood now performs the roles of both contaminant and purifier, and the action will not achieve its desired ends. Hence the absurdity is in the action itself not the perception of the action.

In both halves of the fragment the error comes from the manner in which the action is performed rather than the intention behind the action. Another way of putting this is to say that the agent acts on false information about what constitutes an appropriate decontaminant. In the first half, it is not wrong to want to purify yourself, it is wrong to purify yourself *with* blood. The error stems from ignorance. If people knew the irony of purifying blood with blood, then they would not try to do it because they would know that they would just be increasing the *miasma*; they would feel as mad as the hypothetical mud-washer. This means the purifier does not know the real nature of their means; this is a consequence of acting without proper knowledge. The second half of B5 directly references ignorance (οὔ... γινώσκων). Once again, the emphasis is not placed on the intentions motivating the action but rather on the manner in which it is performed. In this case, the praying to statues (τοῖς ἀγάλμασι) in such a way that it resembles 'chatting to houses' (εἴ τις δόμοισι λεσχηνεύοιτο). The source of this error comes from, in some way, the subject's ignorance towards gods and heroes. If the subject knew who the gods and heroes were they would not make the mistake of praying in this way because they would know it was ineffective. The issue is not praying itself, it is praying in this manner.[49]

There is not enough information in these fragments to know what the gods and heroes are really like, which makes determining the precise mistake

48. On purification as division, see Parker 1996, p. 18-31.

49. It is also feasible that knowledge of the divine would prevent an agent from praying entirely, if, for example, this knowledge revealed that gods cannot be influenced through prayer. In response, one could argue that religious practice need not involve practical input from the divine, *i.e.*, religious practice provides a cultural benefit, but then it is hard to see why praying to statues is ineffective insofar as gods are not inside them.

difficult. However, as the mistake has something to do with the domestic settings of gods, it is probably that it comes from a false anthropomorphism of gods.[50] Common people are mistaken in treating statues and temples as homes for the gods to inhabit. When they pray to the statues, they are assuming that there are gods in them listening to their prayers. However, gods do not inhabit space in this 'human' way and there is no one home.[51] The mistake is not in trying to communicate with gods; rather, it is thinking that they can communicate with them by talking to statues. Thus, it is an error because it is an ill-informed pursuit; it is an error of manner caused by a lack of knowledge.

> Heraclitus DK B14 τὰ γὰρ νομιζόμενα κατ' ἀνθρώπους μυστήρια ἀνιερωστὶ μυεῦνται.
> The customary mysteries amongst men initiate them into impiety.

B14 is another example of an impious action typically committed by common people. The reference is to humans as a collective as indicated by ἀνθρώπους;[52] τὰ... νομιζόμενα also carries a sense of custom or typical practice. 'Customs' is another way of saying 'traditions', and Heraclitus criticises the unquestioning following of tradition by mocking those who listen to and learn from Hesiod and Homer, perpetrators of tradition. In fact, in B57, a general criticism is made against Hesiod that he does not recognise simple unities such as day and night, which makes anything learnt from Hesiod uninformed by *logos*. Hesiod's lack of recognition (οὐκ ἐγίνωσκεν) is the same as the worshippers in the second half of B5, so it is quite clear that, even though Hesiod is not discussing the mysteries, listening to him still encourages bad 'understanding'. In B14, then, it is plausible that the impiety comes from following customary practices without knowing anything about the customary practices beyond that everyone else follows them. The same can be said about B104 which criticises the intellectual capacity (νόος ἢ φρήν) of people who take popular bards as trustworthy authorities. The people listen to tradition and the ignorant crowds because they do not know (οὐκ εἰδότες) that the many are bad. This could mean that the error in B14 is in unquestionably following tradition. This does not answer whether it is the content or the process that is the issue. Although, a bad tradition would still result in performing problematic actions, nevertheless it still shows the same missing link caused by misinformation between intention, action and results. Whether the process being initiated is misguided, or whether cults are misguided, this still suggest that the individual has pious intentions, pious intentions disrupted by ignorance.

50. Marcovich 1967, p. 462-463; Kahn 1979, p. 266-267; Conche 1986, p. 175.
51. Most 2013, p. 160.
52. Compare with B1.

4b. Shame and Tradition: B15

Heraclitus DK B15· εἰ μὴ γὰρ Διονύσῳ πομπὴν ἐποιοῦντο καὶ ὕμνεον ᾆσμα αἰδοίοισιν, ἀναιδέστατα εἴργαστ' ἄν· ὡυτὸς δὲ Ἀίδης καὶ Διόνυσος, ὅτεῳ μαίνονται καὶ ληναΐζουσιν.
If they did not make the procession and sing a song to genitalia for Dionysus, they would perform the most shameful act. But the same are Hades and Dionysus, for whom they rave and celebrate Bacchic rites.

B15 contains a conditional which shows that there are requirements which make certain religious actions pious, or at least seem pious. At first glance this seems to be a straightforward claim that if an agent acts with the correct intentions, the actions are pious. In this case, performing the actions with the intention of honouring Dionysus. Nevertheless, just as B5 and B14 were about acting according to knowledge rather than intention, so is this fragment in my interpretation. It is a criticism of listening to the many and acting according to a misunderstanding made by the many. This is because the observation is not about the action being impious, it is about it being shameful. There is a subtle but important difference. Impiety is about an agent's relationship with the divine, for example unholy behaviour (ἀνίερος) or being polluted (μιαινόμενος); whereas shame is about how a person's pious action is perceived and then commented on by other humans.[53] Something the many calls shameful is not necessarily impious. The many might wrongly think something is impious and then wrongly accuse people of acting shamefully. For example, we can assume that the masses would call a phallic procession for Hades shameful, but this would be wrong because Dionysus and Hades are the same and so it would be equally shameful not to have the procession; the masses would err because they do not understand the nature of the gods. Listening to shame and acting out of fear of being shamed is thus the equivalent to acting on a judgement made by the many; acting not on your own understanding but on what the many understands. The error is not about context or intention, it is about acting on bad information coming from a lack of understanding.

It is still worth thinking about the significance of identifying Dionysus with Hades (ὡυτός). What does it mean to perform Bacchic rites for Hades, and why this pairing of gods? Kahn suggests that this identification lies in the notion of ritual madness. Dionysus should be identified with life in the form of procreation and Hades with death. This is because in B62 and B88 life and death are seen as interchangeable, reversals of each other, and hence, the same. On account of this, it is clear that ritual madness is actually a form of psychic death, as it takes the agent further away from sound thinking

53. For a comprehensive discussion of shame in Ancient Greece see Konstan 2003, p. 1031-1060.

(σωφρονεῖν).[54] Oddly, despite this theory and mentioning drunkenness, Kahn still disputes the significance of Dionysus as a god of wine, because only ritual madness is mentioned. This seems unnecessary; a drunk soul *is* a wet soul. Surely drinking at a festival also provokes the dying of a soul. Of course, just because the soul is wet and less perceptive, does not mean it is not enjoying itself: ὅθεν καὶ Ἡράκλειτον ψυχῇσι φάναι τέρψιν ἢ θάνατον ὑγρῇσι γενέσθαι: '*which is why Heraclitus said that it is joy or death to become wet for souls*'.[55] Knowing the identity relationship between Dionysus and Hades should therefore teach people that the many are wrong to shame those participating in the procession for this sort of action. They should not fear shame and act out of fear of shame because they should not always trust the many. Furthermore, it shows that there can be action and result without knowing how or why. The agent wants to celebrate Dionysus but through their ignorance their actions unwittingly celebrate Hades as well.

These three fragments reveal an interesting relationship between intention and action, and ultimately the consequences of misinformation. It is the equivalent to acting without a plan. In B5 and B14 the failure to understand *logos* results in impiety. In B15, fear of shame informed by tradition results in not seeking full knowledge and fully understanding an action performed. In all three examples a lack of understanding means the agents' intended actions do not achieve their goals because they do the wrong thing due to misinformation because of lack of *logos*. In this way, having less understanding of *logos* is detrimental to an agent's success in action.

Conclusion

In this paper I have outlined a connection between understanding *logos* and performing actions as intended by an agent. In the first half of the paper, I argued that a grasp of *logos* is expressed through actions as words and deeds, and that knowledge of *logos* takes the form of its active counterpart *gnōmē*. *Gnōmē* represents an agent's understanding of how to use *logos* to make plans and achieve their desired goals by directing what they should seek, how they should do it, and how much control over their actions they have. *Gnōmē* which is singular, is successful and belongs only to the divine, but lower levels of successful planning, *gnōmai* are accessible to mortals if they learn about *logos*. In the second half of this paper, I have explored how two of the three interrelated aspects of *gnōmē* are informed or limited by access to *logos*: *logos* provides them with a causal knowledge which describes nature. The discussion of drunkenness and control illustrates the physical control associated with knowledge of *logos*. The divine agent with a fiery soul has

54. Kahn 1979, p. 264. The same is true with sleep in B26, Holton 2022, p. 66-70.
55. B77.1-2.

more control over their vessel than the drunk agent with a wet soul. While it is hard to comprehend how the physics works in real terms, *i.e.* why the damp agent cannot control themselves, there is a strong connection between the composition of the soul as fiery and its physical power in terms of control. When an agent lacks *logos* this impacts their soul and their control over their actions, and thus they are unable to do as they wish. Furthermore, the religion fragments show how *logos* provides a framework for shaping a plan and determines the kind of actions an agent will take dependent on their broader causal knowledge. For example, in the case of speaking to empty houses, a grasp of *logos* would show that the divine action is steering, and not dwelling in shrines. Here the less knowledgeable agent fails at achieving what they seek because they try to do things in the wrong manner, be it purifying with blood or worshiping gods in the wrong way. Thus, the discussion throws up interesting relationships between access to knowledge of *logos* and success in terms of how knowledge shapes what an agent tries to achieve and how they try to achieve it. A greater access to knowledge will undoubtedly influence the kinds of plans an agent has, both allowing them to adapt their plans minimally or change their actions entirely as their understanding of the world changes.

Heraclitus therefore has an implicit theory of action according to which successful intentional action is dependent on a grasp of *logos* insofar as this knowledge allows an agent to construct *gnōmai* which aim at the right sort of goal, are performed in the right manner and have the control required to deliver it. Furthermore, due to the correlation between knowledge and success, this interpretation of Heraclitus' epistemology produces several very interesting implications. First, as knowledge is instantiated in action, action is always a key part of Heraclitus' epistemology. Unfortunately, there are only snippets of individual accounts of Heraclitus' conception of decision-making, some of which I have touched on in terms of ethical decision-making. This makes it hard to envision what some of these kinds of actions would look like practically. Nevertheless, I firmly believe a more thorough account of particular actions in Heraclitus can be made. Second, it provides a framework for contextualising the ethical dimension of Heraclitus and understanding how it is instantiated as actions. By virtue of this, my interpretation makes progress towards understanding what exactly it means to act in an ethical way, in accordance with *logos* and with understanding.

BIBLIOGRAPHY

ADOMÉNAS, M. 1999 : « Heraclitus on Religion », *Phronesis*, 44/2, p. 87-113. URL: https://www.jstor.org/stable/4182610

BARNES, J. 2001 : *The Presocratic Philosophers*, London-New York.

BETEGH, G. 2007 : « On the Physical Aspect of Heraclitus' Psychology », *Phronesis*, 52/1, p. 3-32. URL : https://www.jstor.org/stable/4182822

BOLTON, R. 1989 : « Nature and the Human Good in Heraclitus », dans K. J. Boudouris (éd.), *Ionian Philosophy*, Athens (International Association for Greek Philosophy), p. 49-57.

BURNET, J. 1948 : *Early Greek Philosophy*, 3rd Edition, London.

CONCHE, M. 1986 (éd.) : Héraclite. *Fragments*, Paris.

DIELS, H. & W. KRANZ, 1974 (éd.) : *Die Fragmente der Vorsokratiker I: Griechisch und Deutsch*, Zürich.

FATTAL, M. 2011 : *Paroles et Actes chez Héraclite : sur les fondements théoriques de l'action morale*, Paris.

GRANGER, H. 2000 : « Death's Other Kingdom : Heraclitus on the Life of the Foolish and the Wise », *Classical Philology*, 95/3, p. 260-281. URL : https://www.jstor.org/stable/270378

HADOT, P. 2006 : *The Veil of Isis : an Essay on the History of the Idea of Nature*, Cambridge.

HOLTON, S. 2022 : *Sleep and Dreams in Early Greek Thought : Presocratic and Hippocratic approaches*, London-New York.

HUSSEY, E. 1991 : « Heraclitus on Living and Dying », *The Monist*, 74/4, p. 517-530. URL :https://www.jstor.org/stable/27903260

JOHNSTONE, M. A. 2020 : « On the Ethical Dimension of Heraclitus' Thought », dans D. C. Worfsdorf (éd.), *Early Greek Ethics*, Oxford, p. 37-53.

KAHN, C. 1979 : *The Art and Thought of Heraclitus*, Cambridge.

KIRK, G. S. 1949 : « Heraclitus and Death in Battle (FR. 24D) », *The American Journal of Philology*, 70/4, p. 384-393. DOI : 10.2307/291104

KIRK, G. S. 1962 (éd.) : *Heraclitus: The Cosmic Fragments* [Reprinted with corrections], Cambridge.

KONSTAN, D. 2003 : « Shame in Ancient Greece », *Social Research*, 70/4, p. 1031-1060. DOI : 10.1353/sor.2003.0007

LAKS, A. 1993 : « Mind's Crisis. On Anaxagoras' Νοῦς », *The Southern Journal of Philosophy*, 31/5 Supp., p. 19-38.

LAKS, A. 2002 : « Les fonctions de l'intellect : à propos, derechef, du *nous* d'Anaxagore », *Methodos*, 2, en ligne. DOI : 10.4000/methodos.224

LAKS, A. & G. W. MOST 2016 (éd.) : *Early Greek Philosophy: Later Ionian and Athenian Thinkers*, vol. VII, part. 2, Cambridge (Mass.)-London.

LESHER, J. H. 1995 : « Minds Knowledge and Powers of Control in Anaxagoras DK B12 », *Phronesis*, 40/2, p. 125-142. URL : https://www.jstor.org/stable/4182494

LONG, A. A. 2009 : « Heraclitus on Measure and the Explicit Emergence of Rationality », dans D. Frede/B. Reis (éd.), *Body and Soul in Ancient Philosophy*, Berlin, p. 87-109.

MARCOVICH, M. 1967 (éd.) : *Heraclitus: Greek Text with a Short Commentary*, Los Andes University Press.

MIKEŠ, V. 2007 : « Obraz snu a Spánku u Hérakleita a Platóna a jeho Filosofické Souvislosti », *Listy Filologické / Folia Philologica*, 130/3-4, p. 229-249. URL : https://www.jstor.org/stable/23468518

MOST, G. 2013 : « Heraclitus on Religion », *Rhizomata*, 1/2, p. 153-167.

MUTSCHMANN, H. 1914 (éd.) : *Sexti Empirici Opera*, Leipzig.

NUSSBAUM, M. 1972 : « Ψυχή in Heraclitus, II », *Phronesis*, 17/2, p. 153-170. URL : https://www.jstor.org/stable/4181882

OSBORNE, C. 1997 : « Heraclitus », dans C. C. W. Taylor (éd.), *Routledge History of Philosophy Volume I. From the Beginning to Plato*, London, p. 80-116.

PARKER, R. 1996 : *Miasma: Pollution and Purification in Early Greek Religion*, Oxford University Press.

ROBINSON, T. M. 1987 (éd.) : *Heraclitus, Fragments*, University of Toronto Press.

SCHLUDERER, L. R. 2017 : « Speaking and Acting the Truth: The Ethics of Heraclitus », *Méthexis*, 29/1, p. 1-19. URL : https://www.jstor.org/stable/26414174

SIDER, D. 2013 : « Heraclitus' Ethics », dans D. Sider & D. Obbink (éd.), *Doctrine and Doxography: Studies on Heraclitus and Pythagoras*, Berlin-Boston (Mass.), p. 321-334.

SVENBRO, J. 1993 : Phrasikleia: *An Anthropology of Reading in Ancient Greece*, Ithaca (Myth and Poetics).

TARÁN, L. 1986 : « The First Fragment of Heraclitus », *Illinois Classical Studies*, 11/1-2, p. 1-15. URL : https://www.jstor.org/stable/23064057

VIEIRA, C. 2013 : « Heraclitus' Bow Composition », *Classical Quarterly*, 63/2, p. 473-490. URL : https://www.jstor.org/stable/43905983

VON FRITZ, K. 1974 : « *Nous, Noein* and their Derivatives », dans A. P. D. Mourelatos (éd.), *The Pre-Socratics : a collection of critical essays*, Garden City (N.Y.), p. 23-85.

WEST, M. L. 1971 : *Early Greek Philosophy and the Orient*, Oxford.

QUAND COMMENCE LA VIE MORALE

Le statut moral des actions préparatoires à la vertu *Éthique à Nicomaque*, II 3

Alice de FORNEL

Université Paris 1
Alice.De-Fornel@etu.univ-paris1.fr

RÉSUMÉ. Dans les premiers chapitres du livre II de l'*Éthique à Nicomaque*, Aristote affirme l'origine habituelle des vertus éthiques. L'excellence du désir est donc une disposition habituelle, acquise à travers une répétition d'actions semblables. Cependant, au chapitre 3 du livre II, Aristote formule le problème du cercle que pose sa théorie des habitudes vertueuses. En effet, ne faut-il pas être déjà vertueux pour agir vertueusement ? Si les actions par lesquelles sont acquises les dispositions présupposent déjà ces dernières pour être accomplies, le progrès moral est alors impossible et inutile, à moins de distinguer les actions préparatoires des actions accomplies selon la vertu. Cependant, considérer à l'inverse que des actions non vertueuses conduisent à des dispositions vertueuses semble contraire au principe de l'habitude ; en outre, cela conduit à exclure de la vie morale les actions par lesquelles on acquiert les vertus, parce qu'elles ne sont pas accomplies selon une vertu durablement acquise. Cet article se propose d'envisager ces problèmes herméneutiques à partir de la typologie des actions qu'offre la réponse d'Aristote à cette aporie du commencement en *EN* II 3, qui fait écho à d'autres passages de l'*EN* notamment ceux qui envisagent la question de la responsabilité à travers le rapport des agents et de leur caractère aux actions qu'ils commettent (V 10). Une telle typologie des actions semble être féconde à deux niveaux d'interprétation. D'une part, elle permet d'envisager des actions qui sont qualifiables moralement sans être encore accomplies vertueusement : en ce sens, les actions préparatoires à la vertu font partie de la vie morale, sans toutefois être accomplies selon la vertu. D'autre part, cette typologie permet d'envisager différentes phases de la vie morale, et notamment de distinguer une première phase de pratiques propédeutiques à la vertu d'une seconde phase plus active, qui fait partie de la vie pratique, et par laquelle l'agent moral forge son caractère par ses propres actions.

ABSTRACT : *In the opening chapters of Book II of the* Nicomachean Ethics, *Aristotle asserts the habits-based origin of ethical virtues. The excellence of desire is therefore a habits-based disposition, acquired through repetition of similar actions. However, in chapter 3 of Book II, Aristotle formulates the problem of the circularity involved*

Philosophie antique, n°24 (2024), 37-63

in his theory of virtuous habits. After all, don't you have to already be virtuous to act virtuously? If the actions by which dispositions are acquired already presuppose the latter in order to be accomplished, then moral progress is impossible and useless, unless we distinguish preparatory actions from actions accomplished according to virtue. Conversely, however, to consider that non-virtuous actions lead to virtuous dispositions seems contrary to the principle of habit; moreover, it leads to the exclusion from the moral life of actions through which virtues are acquired, because they are not performed according to a virtue that has been durably acquired. This article proposes to consider these hermeneutical problems on the basis of the typology of actions offered by Aristotle's response to this aporia of the beginning in NE *II 3, which echoes other passages in* NN, *notably those that consider the question of responsibility through the relationship of agents and their character to the actions they commit (V 10). Such a typology of actions seems to be fruitful at two levels of interpretation. On the one hand, it allows us to consider actions that are morally qualifiable without yet being performed virtuously: in this sense, actions preparatory to virtue are part of the moral life, without however being performed according to virtue. On the other hand, this typology enables us to consider different phases of the moral life, and in particular to distinguish a first phase of practices propaedeutic to virtue from a second, more active phase, which is part of the practical life, and through which the moral agent forges his character by his own actions.*

Dans le chapitre 3 du livre II de *l'Éthique à Nicomaque**[1], Aristote formule une objection possible à sa théorie de l'origine habituelle des dispositions vertueuses. Selon celle-ci, la répétition d'actions conduit à acquérir des dispositions correspondantes[2]. L'habitude implique une identité entre les actions par lesquelles les dispositions vertueuses sont acquises, et celles qui résultent de leur exercice[3]. Cette identité est d'une part générique, et concerne le champ d'action : jouer de la flûte rend flûtiste, agir courageusement courageux[4]. D'autre part, du point de vue axiologique, elle est une équivalence : les bonnes actions conduisent à de bonnes dispositions, les mauvaises actions à des dispositions mauvaises[5]. C'est le gain théorique des deux chapitres précédents :

* Je tiens à remercier Charlotte Murgier et Pierre-Marie Morel, ainsi que mes deux relecteur·ices anonymes, dont les précieuses remarques m'ont permis de clarifier ma pensée et d'avancer dans mes réflexions.

1. Selon le découpage indiqué en caractères arabes de Bywater 1894, là où Tricot 1994 [1959] suit le découpage de l'édition Susemihl 1880, revue par O. Apelt 1912 (qui fait commencer le chapitre par le paragraphe précédent).

2. « [...] les dispositions morales proviennent d'actes qui leur sont semblables » (καὶ ἑνὶ δὴ λόγῳ ἐκ τῶν ὁμοίων ἐνεργειῶν αἱ ἕξεις γίνονται, *EN* II 1, 1103b21-22, traduction Tricot 1994).

3. « [...] non seulement les vertus ont pour origine et pour source de leur production et de leur croissance les mêmes actions qui président d'autre part à leur disparition, mais encore leur activité se déploiera dans l'accomplissement de ces mêmes actions » (οὐ μόνον αἱ γενέσεις καὶ αὐξήσεις καὶ αἱ φθοραὶ ἐκ τῶν αὐτῶν καὶ ὑπὸ τῶν αὐτῶν γίνονται, ἀλλὰ καὶ αἱ ἐνέργειαι ἐν τοῖς αὐτοῖς ἔσονται, *EN* II 2, 1104a27-29).

4. « Pour les vertus, au contraire, leur possession suppose un exercice antérieur, comme c'est aussi le cas pour les autres arts. En effet, les choses qu'il faut avoir apprises pour les faire, c'est en les faisant que nous les apprenons : par exemple, c'est en construisant qu'on devient constructeur, et en jouant de la cithare qu'on devient cithariste ; ainsi encore, c'est en pratiquant les actions justes que nous devenons justes, les actions modérées que nous devenons modérés, et les actions courageuses que nous devenons courageux » (τὰς δ' ἀρετὰς λαμβάνομεν ἐνεργήσαντες πρότερον, ὥσπερ καὶ ἐπὶ τῶν ἄλλων τεχνῶν· ἃ γὰρ δεῖ μαθόντας ποιεῖν, ταῦτα ποιοῦντες μανθάνομεν, οἷον οἰκοδομοῦντες οἰκοδόμοι γίνονται καὶ κιθαρίζοντες κιθαρισταί· οὕτω δὴ καὶ τὰ μὲν δίκαια πράττοντες δίκαιοι γινόμεθα, τὰ δὲ σώφρονα σώφρονες, τὰ δ' ἀνδρεῖα ἀνδρεῖοι, *EN* II 2, 1103a3-b2).

5. « [...] le fait de bien construire donnera de bons constructeurs, et le fait de mal construire, de mauvais. » (ἐκ μὲν γὰρ τοῦ εὖ οἰκοδομεῖν ἀγαθοὶ οἰκοδόμοι ἔσονται, ἐκ δὲ τοῦ κακῶς κακοί, *EN* II 1, 1103b10-12).

> […] que les actions qui la produisent soient aussi celles qui la font croître ou, quand elles ont lieu d'une autre façon, la font disparaître ; qu'enfin les actions dont elle est la résultante soient celles mêmes où son activité s'exerce ensuite, – tout cela, considérons-le comme dit. (ὅτι ἐξ ὧν γίνεται, ὑπὸ τούτων καὶ αὔξεται καὶ φθείρεται μὴ ὡσαύτως γινομένων, καὶ ὅτι ἐξ ὧν ἐγένετο, περὶ ταῦτα καὶ ἐνεργεῖ, εἰρήσθω, *EN* II 2, 1105b14-16).

L'habitude est donc un facteur de cohérence pratique : mieux on a agi dans le passé, plus on se rend capable de bien agir dans l'avenir. En ce sens, les dispositions vertueuses sont des puissances exercées par des actions pour lesquelles elles s'exercent également lorsqu'elles sont pleinement acquises. Aristote semble assumer cette circularité, parce qu'elle peut être vertueuse. En effet, l'habitude comme processus d'acquisition des dispositions est moralement neutre, puisque ces dispositions peuvent être vertueuses ou vicieuses. Elle permet cependant, quand ce sont de bonnes actions qui sont répétées, de les accomplir plus fréquemment et mieux. Elles peuvent alors former le tissu d'une vie accomplie jusqu'à son terme, d'un bonheur qui se constitue dans la durée.

L'objection qu'Aristote envisage au chapitre 3 implique cependant de poser cette circularité entre les actions et les dispositions vertueuses comme un problème. En effet, si les dispositions vertueuses s'acquièrent par l'habitude, c'est-à-dire par la répétition d'actions vertueuses, ces actions préparatoires ne supposent-elles pas que l'on soit déjà vertueux ? D'un côté, la disposition suppose des actions antérieures, puisqu'elle s'acquiert par l'exercice : or cet exercice semble impossible s'il doit déjà consister en de bonnes actions. D'un autre côté l'action, pour être bonne et réussie, doit être accomplie « selon la vertu » (κατ'ἀρετὴν) de celui qui agit, témoignant ainsi de son état vertueux[6]. Les actions qui rendent vertueux seraient ainsi déjà accomplies par vertu, dont l'acquisition serait de ce fait inutile.

C'est pourquoi les lectures traditionnelles de l'aporie consistent à interroger la possibilité et l'utilité du progrès moral. Ainsi, comme le résume M. Jimenez dans un état récent de la question[7], la question qui se pose est celle de savoir comment le vertueux en devenir peut s'habituer à bien agir, si pour ce faire il doit déjà accomplir des actions vertueuses. Le problème est donc celui de la nécessité apparente d'une vertu acquise pour accomplir des actions vertueuses. Ceci implique de distinguer les actions préparatoires et les actions accomplies vertueusement, par une disposition acquise. En effet, on a vu que lorsqu'il envisage l'origine habituelle des dispositions vertueuses,

6. « […] quand il s'agira de la justice et des autres vertus (à propos desquelles on dit ouvertement que leurs possesseurs sont plus ou moins dans cet état, et leurs actions plus ou moins conformes à ces vertus) » (καὶ περὶ τὴν δικαιοσύνην καὶ τὰς ἄλλας ἀρετάς, καθ'ἃς ἐναργῶς φασὶ μᾶλλον καὶ ἧττον τοὺς ποιοὺς ὑπάρχειν καὶ πράττειν κατὰ τὰς ἀρετάς, *EN* X 2, 1173a18-20).

7. Jimenez 2016, p. 37.

Aristote pose que les actions préparatoires et les actions vertueuses sont semblables et équivalentes. Pourtant, le progrès moral du vertueux en devenir implique, pour être mesuré, de distinguer les actions qui ne sont pas accomplies selon une vertu pleinement acquise de celles qui le sont. Un nouveau problème se pose donc, celui de la continuité : en effet, on peut se demander comment on peut devenir vertueux par des actes non vertueux. La réponse d'Aristote au problème du cercle pose donc un problème de continuité entre les actions préparatoires et les actions réussies[8], mis en lumière par l'article fondateur de M. Burnyeat[9]. Ainsi, N. Sherman[10] considère que si la vertu pleinement acquise doit répondre à certaines conditions, celles-ci doivent aussi se refléter dans le progrès moral lui-même. On peut alors se demander jusqu'où les actions préparatoires sont qualifiables moralement sans toutefois s'identifier totalement aux actions accomplies une fois la vertu acquise.

La question de la continuité du progrès moral est d'autant plus complexe qu'Aristote ne donne pas de ligne de démarcation claire entre le processus d'acquisition et son achèvement[11] : elle n'est pas explicitement thématisée et semble à reconstituer, que ce soit comme postulat de la doctrine ou comme moment précis dans la vie personnelle. Ceci peut s'expliquer notamment par le fait que l'acquisition d'une vertu n'est pas seulement un changement, mais le perfectionnement et l'accomplissement des facultés psychologiques de l'agent vertueux en devenir, immanents aux actions qui le constituent[12]. C'est pourquoi la solution du problème est souvent envisagée selon une perspective modale, à partir de la distinction entre l'exercice ou le développement d'une faculté et la réalisation d'une disposition vertueuse. Une telle

8. Ainsi Broadie 1991, p. 104 se pose la question du rapport entre la simple exécution des actions et le développement du bon caractère. Curzer 2012, p. 318-319 note qu'une conception des habitudes vertueuses comme réflexe quasi mécanique ne permet pas de comprendre en quoi la vertu implique la capacité intellectuelle d'identifier les actions vertueuses et les raisons d'agir, et de choisir les actions vertueuses pour elles-mêmes.

9. Burnyeat 1980, p. 69-92.

10. Sherman 1989, p. 159, suivie par S. Broadie 1993, p. 103-110. Suivant cette ligne interprétative, Jimenez 2016, p. 332 développe une lecture de II 3 critique de la conception dite « mécanique » de l'habitude, selon laquelle le processus d'acquisition des dispositions habituelles serait « neutre » du point de vue des facultés psychiques de l'agent.

11. Voir notamment : Kraut 2012, p. 538-539, et Burnyeat 1980, p. 70 : en outre, il est très difficile d'établir une vue synoptique du progrès moral à partir de lieux textuels et problématiques différents : ainsi, dans les éthiques, Aristote insiste sur la dimension active de l'acquisition des habitudes vertueuses, tandis que dans les *Politiques*, il insiste davantage sur sa dimension plus passive, liée à l'œuvre des lois et au rôle de l'imitation (*Pol.* VII 13-15, 17 ; VIII, 17).

12. Dans la *Physique*, VII 3, la disposition vertueuse est considérée comme une sorte d'achèvement (τελείωσίς τις), au sens où elle n'est pas une qualité accidentelle, résultat d'une altération, mais le perfectionnement d'une puissance essentielle : en développant ses facultés psychiques en vertus, l'animal humain devient davantage lui-même qu'il n'est changé : Verbeke 1971, p. 560, Coope 2011, p. 64-71. On peut cependant noter que l'intégration de *Physique* VII à ce dossier est une question complexe et controversée, que nous ne traiterons pas ici.

perspective permet en effet de concilier la priorité de l'activité par rapport à la disposition et le double problème de la continuité et de la distinction entre les actions préparatoires et les actions réussies : ce sont les mêmes puissances qui s'exercent, mais à des niveaux différents d'élaboration. Une perspective complémentaire est envisagée par M. Hampson[13] : la distinction entre faire des actions vertueuses et agir vertueusement ne concerne pas le fait qu'il faudrait ou non agir vertueusement pour être vertueux, mais plutôt le fait qu'agir vertueusement ne suffit pas à être déjà (ἤδη)[14] vertueux[15]. C'est pourquoi Aristote affirme à la fin du chapitre la nécessité de l'exercice, tout en spécifiant la manière dont on peut identifier un agent par ses actions. En effet, il faut envisager la manière dont il agit, et non seulement ce qu'il fait. Dans cette perspective, il est moins question de la possibilité d'accomplir des bonnes actions chez le vertueux en devenir, que de la nécessité de l'exercice, grâce auquel il élabore sa capacité d'agir[16]. Cette lecture pose donc également la question de « l'engagement pratique »[17] du vertueux en devenir pour acquérir des dispositions vertueuses, et donc celle du statut moral de ses actions.

En ce sens, ces différentes interprétations questionnent un aspect important de la réponse d'Aristote à l'aporie d'*EN* II 3 : le fait qu'elle consiste en une typologie des actions. Aristote distingue en effet les actions accomplies vertueusement, c'est-à-dire à la fois volontaires et accomplies selon une disposition acquise, des actions antérieures à cette acquisition, qui peuvent avoir lieu « par hasard » (ἀπὸ τύχης) ou « sous l'indication d'un tiers » (ἄλλου ὑποθεμένου). De ce fait, le problème de la circularité entre les actions et les dispositions implique un changement de perspective par rapport aux chapitres précédents, où la question de l'acquisition des dispositions vertueuses est développée à travers l'articulation entre la vertu en acte et la vertu en puissance. C'est pourquoi on peut s'intéresser à cette spécificité d'*EN* II 3, dans la mesure où elle permet d'envisager le progrès moral selon le type d'action qu'il implique[18]. En effet, ce chapitre invite à affiner l'opposition structurante dans la caractérisation des actions morales qu'est celle du volontaire et de l'involontaire (ἕκων ou ἑκουσίως, de plein

13. Hampson 2021 ; voir notamment p. 14-16.

14. *EN* II 3, 1105a20.

15. Et ce, même si on loue les hommes vertueux pour leurs actions : *EN* I 11, 1101b14-16. En ce sens, comme le souligne Hampson *ibid.*, p. 15, Aristote prend en compte l'opinion selon laquelle ce que l'on fait révèle ce que l'on est, et qu'on peut ainsi supposer que quelqu'un qui accomplit des actions vertueuses est vertueux.

16. *Ibid.* p. 17-24.

17. *Ibid.* p. 24.

18. Le progrès moral peut en effet être envisagé à travers l'habitude, comme un processus sur la nature duquel on peut s'interroger (voir notamment l'analyse du texte de *Physique*, VII 3 évoqué *supra* par Leunissen 2017, p. 110-115) ; cet aspect sera moins développé ici.

gré, par opposition à ἄκων ou ἀκουσίως, contre son gré), et donc entre ce qui est susceptible de louange ou de blâme, ou seulement de pitié, c'est-à-dire ce qui est moralement significatif ou non. *EN* II, 3 permet d'envisager des cas plus subtils qui ne recoupent pas tout à fait cette opposition, et qui déplacent la perspective et les critères d'identification des actions. Ainsi, faire quelque chose de grammatical (γραμματικόν τι) se distingue du fait de le faire de façon grammaticale (γραμματικῶς). En outre, faire quelque chose par hasard et sous l'indication d'un tiers (ἀπὸ τύχης καὶ ἄλλου ὑποθεμένου) c'est-à-dire agir sans disposition correspondante, semblent renvoyer à deux types d'action différents, tous deux distincts de l'action accomplie vertueusement. On peut envisager ces différents cas selon une double perspective : d'une part, en tant qu'ils révèlent que l'habitude est un processus qui implique le désir et la pensée de l'agent moral. D'autre part, on peut envisager cette typologie de manière diachronique, et faire l'hypothèse qu'elle recoupe, au moins en partie, différentes phases du développement moral.

La distinction des actions préparatoires et des actions vertueuses invite ainsi à s'interroger sur la manière dont l'ensemble des actions accomplies forme le tissu de la vie pratique, puisque le bonheur se trouve dans l'action et dans l'ensemble des actions bonnes et réussies[19]. En effet, la question du statut moral des actions préparatoires implique aussi celle de la place de l'éducation morale dans la vie heureuse. Quand commence-t-on à bien agir, quand commence la vie morale ? Faut-il attendre d'avoir acquis un caractère vertueux, ou bien le fait de s'exercer à la vertu avant d'être pleinement vertueux a-t-il déjà une valeur morale ? Autrement dit, la vie morale ne concerne-t-elle que l'ensemble des actions réussies et accomplies une fois la vertu pleinement acquise[20], ou englobe-t-elle aussi ce qui compte moralement dans l'existence de l'individu, comme la juste mesure des passions et les actions qui rendent vertueux ? En ce sens, un horizon problématique de ces questions est celui des âges de la vie et de leur valeur morale, et notamment la place dans la vie morale de l'enfance et de l'adolescence, âges pendant lesquels le caractère et la raison ne sont pas pleinement développés.

19. Voir *EN* I, 6, 1098a20 ; I 11, 1101a12-16. Pour une analyse des problèmes pratiques que pose la notion de bonheur comme εὐπραξία (fait de bien agir, bonne conduite), c'est-à-dire immanente aux actions ou à la vie pratique, voir Petit 2002, p. 58-72 : la question qui se pose est celle de concilier l'autotélie de l'action et son insuffisance, le bonheur ne s'accomplissant pleinement que dans l'ensemble d'une vie pratique. Plutôt qu'un étagement et une hiérarchie des fins, il propose d'envisager l'*eupraxia* comme une fin « focale », qui s'accomplit dans la fin immanente de chaque action, sans toutefois se réduire à la fin particulière d'aucune d'entre elles.

20. La vie morale serait ainsi comprise au sens de vie pratique et ensemble d'actions bonnes et accomplies (*EN* I 11 ; IX 7, 1168a6), impliqué dans la définition de l'excellence de la vie humaine comme œuvre ou activité en accord avec la vertu (*EN* I 6, 1097b26-29) et du bonheur comme fait de bien vivre et de bien agir (*EN* X 8, 18-21).

L'hypothèse que nous suivrons pour lire *EN* II 3 est donc la suivante : le problème du cercle et celui de l'identité des actions vertueuses et des actions préparatoires à la vertu offrent une perspective intéressante pour envisager la question de l'unité et la continuité temporelle de la vie heureuse. Nous suivrons d'abord l'ordre du texte en distinguant deux moments distincts de la réponse d'Aristote : d'une part, la possibilité minimale d'agir sans disposition correspondante, développée à partir d'un parallèle avec les habitudes techniques (1104b21-26) ; d'autre part, la manière dont Aristote distingue le cas des arts et celui des vertus, en donnant trois critères de l'action proprement vertueuse (1105a26-33). La première phase invite à distinguer fortement les actions accomplies selon une disposition habituelle de celles qui ne le sont pas (1). La seconde, cependant, invite plutôt à se demander dans quelle mesure les actions préparatoires doivent répondre aux critères de l'action pleinement vertueuse pour que l'agent progresse moralement par ses actions (2). C'est pourquoi on peut enfin envisager l'articulation entre ces deux phases. En effet, elle permet d'envisager la dissemblance et la ressemblance entre les actions préparatoires et les actions vertueuses à travers une typologie des actions, qui trouve des échos dans d'autres passages de l'*EN* et par laquelle on peut reconstituer différentes phases du progrès moral (3).

1. Faire avec art : le cas des techniques (*EN* II, 3, 1104b21-26)

L'objection du cercle concerne les dispositions habituelles en ce qu'elles concernent le domaine moral, mais aussi le domaine technique :

> Mais on pourrait se demander ce que nous entendons signifier quand nous disons qu'on ne devient juste qu'en faisant des actions justes, et modéré qu'en faisant des actions modérées : car enfin, si on fait des actions justes et des actions modérées, c'est qu'on est déjà juste et modéré, de même qu'en faisant des actes ressortissant à la grammaire et à la musique on est grammairien et musicien (ἀπορήσειε δ' ἄν τις πῶς λέγομεν ὅτι δεῖ τὰ μὲν δίκαια πράττοντας δικαίους γίνεσθαι, τὰ δὲ σώφρονα σώφρονας· εἰ γὰρ πράττουσι τὰ δίκαια καὶ σώφρονα, ἤδη εἰσὶ δίκαιοι καὶ σώφρονες, ὥσπερ εἰ τὰ γραμματικὰ καὶ τὰ μουσικά, γραμματικοὶ καὶ μουσικοί, *EN* II 3, 1105a17-21).

De ce point de vue, on le verra, c'est plutôt la réponse à l'objection qui pose la question de la différence entre les deux cas. C'est pourquoi Aristote répond d'abord par la possibilité évidente d'agir sans disposition correspondante à partir du cas des techniques, et semble sous-entendre qu'elle concerne le rapport entre les actions et les dispositions en général, qu'elles soient techniques ou vertueuses :

> Mais ne peut-on pas dire plutôt que cela n'est pas exact, même dans le cas des arts ? C'est qu'il est possible, en effet, qu'on fasse une chose ressortissant à la grammaire soit par chance, soit sous l'indication d'autrui : on ne sera donc grammairien que si, à la fois, on a fait quelque chose de grammatical, et si on l'a fait d'une façon grammaticale, à savoir conformément à la science

> grammaticale qu'on possède en soi-même (ἢ οὐδ' ἐπὶ τῶν τεχνῶν οὕτως ἔχει; ἐνδέχεται γὰρ γραμματικόν τι ποιῆσαι καὶ ἀπὸ τύχης καὶ ἄλλου ὑποθεμένου. τότε οὖν ἔσται γραμματικός, ἐὰν καὶ γραμματικόν τι ποιήσῃ καὶ γραμματικῶς: τοῦτο δ' ἐστὶ τὸ κατὰ τὴν ἐν αὑτῷ γραμματικήν, *EN* II, 3, 1105b21-26).

Aristote commence donc par présenter l'objection à travers un parallèle avec les dispositions techniques, auquel il avait déjà recours dans le chapitre précédent, comme le relève T. Angier[21]. En effet, dans les premiers chapitres du livre II de l'*Éthique à Nicomaque*, comme ailleurs dans le corpus aristotélicien[22], Aristote considère l'acquisition des habitudes vertueuses à travers un parallèle avec le savoir-faire technique. Dans la mesure où les techniques témoignent du fait qu'il faut agir pour acquérir une disposition correspondante, les deux types de disposition, morale et technique, sont également concernées par le problème du cercle car elles ont besoin d'exercice et d'habitude, contrairement aux puissances naturelles[23] :

> De plus, dans toutes les capacités et tous les arts il y a des <éléments> qu'il faut avoir appris au préalable et s'être assimilés pour l'exercice de chacun d'eux, de sorte que c'est évidemment la même chose pour les activités vertueuses (ἔτι δὲ πρὸς πάσας δυνάμεις καὶ τέχνας ἔστιν ἃ δεῖ προπαιδεύεσθαι καὶ προεθίζεσθαι πρὸς τὰς ἑκάστων ἐργασίας, ὥστε δῆλον ὅτι καὶ πρὸς τὰς τῆς ἀρετῆς πράξεις, *Politiques,* VIII 1, 1337a18-21, traduction de P. Pellegrin).

De fait, le premier volet de sa réponse porte d'abord sur les techniques : on peut faire quelque chose de grammatical (γραμματικόν τι) par hasard (ἀπὸ τύχης) ou sous l'indication d'autrui (ἄλλου ὑποθεμένου). Ces deux éventualités sont convoquées parce qu'elles n'impliquent pas l'exercice d'une disposition habituelle, mais elles ne semblent pas éthiquement équivalentes. Ainsi, le fait de faire quelque chose de vertueux ou de grammatical par hasard semble renvoyer aux cas de justice et d'injustice accidentelles que l'on trouve au chapitre 10 du livre V de l'*EN* :

> Mais dans les actes justes ou injustes, la justice ou l'injustice peuvent pareillement être quelque chose d'accidentel : si un homme restitue un dépôt malgré lui et par crainte, on ne doit pas dire qu'il fait une action juste, ni qu'il agit justement, sinon par accident. (ἔστι δ' ὁμοίως ἐπὶ τῶν ἀδίκων καὶ τῶν

21. Angier 2012, p. 107.

22. Voir par exemple *Pol.* VIII 1, 1337a18-21, *Métaphysique*, Θ 8, 1049b30-32 : le cas de l'acquisition des techniques étant considéré comme un exemple paradigmatique de la priorité de l'acte sur la puissance.

23. Les puissances naturelles n'ont besoin que de l'acte antérieur qu'est l'âme, entéléchie première, pour s'exercer, ce qui n'est pas le cas de certaines virtualités, qui ont besoin de l'habitude et de l'apprentissage pour passer à l'acte : *EN* II 1, 1103a26-b2 ; *Traité de l'âme*, II 5, 417b12-18. Sur le rapport des puissances exercées aux puissances naturelles, voir Morel 1997, p. 131-148, et Farina 2019, p. 31-45. Sur la dimension modale des dispositions vertueuses, « degré supérieur de la puissance et degré inférieur de l'acte », voir Rodier 1900, p. 255 et Monteils-Laeng 2014, p. 237-254.

δικαίων καὶ τὸ κατὰ συμβεβηκός: καὶ γὰρ ἂν τὴν παρακαταθήκην ἀποδοίη τις ἄκων καὶ διὰ φόβον, ὃν οὔτε δίκαια πράττειν οὔτε δικαιοπραγεῖν φατέον ἀλλ' ἢ κατὰ συμβεβηκός, *EN* V 10, 1135b2-6).

Le caractère non volontaire de l'acte implique qu'il ne soit juste que par accident (κατὰ συμβεβηκός), et concerne aussi le cas où l'on agit par hasard (ἀπὸ τύχης) : par exemple en allant au marché, on rencontre par hasard son débiteur, et on récupère ainsi son argent sans l'avoir prévu ni voulu[24]. On peut donc faire quelque chose de juste ou d'injuste sans être soi-même juste ou injuste. Sans être désiré en connaissance de cause, ce qui est fait n'a qu'une conformité extérieure à ce qui est bon ou mauvais, et n'est pas objet de louange ou de blâme. Ceci recoupe le problème qui se pose dans l'ensemble d'*EN* V 10, où il est question des actions dont l'existence factuelle ne fait pas question, mais dont il s'agit de juger l'auteur[25].

C'est pour cette raison qu'Aristote distingue différents cas, et que ce chapitre offre une typologie des actions qui fait écho à celle d'*EN* II 3. Dans un premier cas, on peut faire quelque chose d'injuste par accident, parce que l'action résulte d'une contrainte extérieure ou d'une méprise – dans ce dernier cas, elle produit des résultats contre toute attente[26]. Ce qui est intéressant ici, c'est que l'injustice semble rester de l'ordre du fait, et non de l'action, si elle ne peut pas être attribuée à un agent responsable, c'est-à-dire qui veut et comprend ce qu'il fait :

> [...] par conséquent, il est possible pour une chose d'être injuste, tout en n'étant pas encore un acte injuste si la qualification de volontaire ne vient pas s'y ajouter (ὥστ' ἔσται τι ἄδικον μὲν ἀδίκημα δ' οὔπω, ἂν μὴ τὸ ἑκούσιον προσῇ, *EN* V 10, 1135a2023).

Il semble que c'est d'abord en ce sens qu'on peut faire quelque chose d'injuste ou de juste sans être injuste ou juste, comme on peut faire quelque chose de grammatical, tracer des lettres sans être lettré. Cependant, on peut distinguer faire ce qui est prescrit par les lois « malgré lui, par ignorance, ou pour tout autre motif »[27] du fait accidentel, qui n'implique pas les facultés psychiques de l'agent, sa raison et son désir, sinon par accident : dans le cas de la méprise qui caractérise le fait accidentel, il voulait autre chose, il pensait agir autrement[28]. Dans le premier cas, la conformité à la loi peut avoir une

24. *Physique*, II 5, 196b33-197a5.

25. C'est pourquoi le contexte implique la possibilité que ces actions soient jugées malgré tout, ce qui pose la question du rôle du jugement lui-même dans le progrès moral des individus. Dans cette mesure, il éclaire un enjeu important d'*EN* II 3, qui est la question de savoir si une action suffit pour caractériser moralement un individu. Cette question peut être éclairée par les travaux récents de Curzer 2012 et de Jimenez 2020 sur le rôle de passions comme la honte dans le processus de socialisation et le développement moral.

26. *EN* V 10, 1135b16-17.

27. *EN* VI 13, 1144a15-16.

28. *EN* V 10, 1135b12-16.

dimension propédeutique, parce qu'elle offre une première occasion de respecter les règles morales et d'agir correctement : les agents ne sont pas justes mais font « ce qu'il faut faire, et ce que l'homme vertueux est tenu de faire »[29]. Ce n'est pas le cas du fait accidentel, dont il paraît plus discutable de louer ou blâmer l'auteur, et qui ne semble pas non plus engagé dans un progrès moral[30].

Dans un second cas cependant, on peut agir par emportement ou par erreur, comme dans les cas d'intempérance par impétuosité et par ignorance fautive. Ces cas se distinguent du vice, cas où on agit mal par choix délibéré. Cependant, contrairement à une situation de contrainte ou d'ignorance factuelle, on aurait pu bien faire : on aurait pu désirer le contraire, ou bien on aurait pu prévoir les conséquences que telle action aurait. Autrement dit, ce cas intermédiaire est déjà plus révélateur des capacités de l'agent à bien agir ou non. C'est pourquoi le cas des actions fautives de l'intempérant semble plus intéressant du point de vue du développement moral. En effet, elles sont susceptibles de louange ou de blâme, sans que l'intempérant ne soit pour autant considéré comme un vicieux invétéré :

> Quand l'acte est fait en pleine connaissance, mais sans délibération préalable, c'est un acte injuste, par exemple tout ce qu'on fait par colère, ou par quelque autre de ces passions qui sont irrésistibles ou qui sont la conséquence de l'humaine nature (car en commettant ces torts et ces fautes les hommes agissent injustement, et leurs actions sont des actions injustes, bien qu'ils ne soient pas pour autant des êtres injustes ni pervers, le tort n'étant pas causé par méchanceté) (ὅταν δὲ εἰδὼς μὲν μὴ προβουλεύσας δέ, ἀδίκημα, οἷον ὅσα τε διὰ θυμὸν καὶ ἄλλα πάθη, ὅσα ἀναγκαῖα ἢ φυσικὰ συμβαίνει τοῖς ἀνθρώποις· ταῦτα γὰρ βλάπτοντες καὶ ἁμαρτάνοντες ἀδικοῦσι μέν, καὶ ἀδικήματά ἐστιν, οὐ μέντοι πω ἄδικοι διὰ ταῦτα οὐδὲ πονηροί· οὐ γὰρ διὰ μοχθηρίαν ἡ βλάβη, *EN* V 10, 1135b19-24).

Ces actions peuvent être qualifiées moralement sans que cette qualification soit accidentelle. Toutefois, elles ne sont pas pour autant causées par une disposition vertueuse ou vicieuse. Ceci correspond au cas de l'intempérant, dont les actions sont mauvaises, sans qu'il n'ait encore définitivement acquis un caractère vicieux, l'intempérance étant un mal intermittent[31]. À l'inverse,

29. *EN* VI 13, 1144a16-17.

30. On peut ainsi se demander si l'on peut distinguer le cas d'*EN* V 10, 1135b28, et celui d'*EN* VI 13, 1144a13-20, dans la mesure où la conformité à la loi en *EN* VI semble avoir une valeur morale, ce qui n'est pas le cas des faits de justice et d'injustice accidentels envisagés en *EN* V.

31. *EN* VII 9, 1150b35. Aristote ne fait pas mention explicite de l'agent intempérant en *EN* V 10 ; cependant, la question des actions dues à l'emportement et aux passions semble inclure les actions dues à l'intempérance. En outre, l'intempérance est une situation morale qui peut éclairer ce passage, parce qu'elle pose également la question de savoir dans quelle mesure les actions témoignent du caractère, vertueux ou vicieux, des agents moraux. Cependant, on peut distinguer deux niveaux problématiques entre les livres V et VII, qui sont d'une

on peut envisager des actions courageuses ou tempérantes attribuées à un agent responsable, et donc moralement significatives, qui ne soient pas causées par une habitude vertueuse pleinement acquise[32]. Cela pourrait correspondre au fait d'agir sur les conseils d'un tiers, qui semble renvoyer davantage à une situation d'apprentissage qui pourrait s'appliquer à l'éducation morale. On peut acquérir une disposition en commençant volontairement par produire selon une règle technique que l'on intériorise progressivement, ce qui pose la question du rapport entre le fait de suivre un modèle extérieur comme celui du pédagogue et le développement des facultés psychiques de l'agent.

En effet, le développement des vertus morales, mais également des compétences techniques ne semble pas pouvoir être réduit à un ensemble de règles que l'on peut simplement suivre sans les comprendre. C'est pourquoi la typologie des actions que l'on peut esquisser à partir des textes d'*EN* II, 3 et *EN* V, 10 pose la question de l'implication des facultés psychiques de l'agent dans les actions qui permettent d'acquérir les dispositions habituelles. À propos des habitudes techniques, C. C. W. Taylor distingue ainsi l'application irrationnelle de règles prescrites par une technique du fait de s'exercer à une capacité technique. En effet, Aristote semble ici poser le problème de l'acquisition des dispositions en envisageant que les capacités techniques sont acquises par des actes non techniques, mais prescrites par des règles techniques. Ceci se distingue de la manière dont il avait procédé précédemment, à savoir que l'acquisition des dispositions morales et techniques est cumulative, et implique l'élaboration et le raffinement progressifs de capacités déjà existantes à un niveau « plus primitif ». L'opposition entre les actions préparatoires et les actions accomplies selon une disposition acquise apparaît ainsi dans un écart avec la définition modale des dispositions, selon laquelle l'apprenti constructeur, par exemple, construit conformément à une capacité qui lui est propre, même si elle n'est pas pleinement élaborée et rationalisée[33]. Le problème posé par C. C. W. Taylor est donc celui de savoir comment on peut acquérir une technique par des actes « non techniques », et, de manière analogue, comment on peut acquérir une capacité morale sans agir vertueusement, mais seulement par accident ou conformité extérieure à la vertu. En effet, les capacités psychiques impliquées

part le fait qu'un acte puisse être jugé ou non, et d'autre part le fait qu'il témoigne d'une défaillance provisoire ou bien d'un caractère invétéré.

32. On peut envisager ainsi les actions de l'endurant (καρτερικός), qui résiste à ses peines sans être courageux (ἀνδρεῖος), ou du tempérant (ἐγκρατής), qui maîtrise ses plaisirs sans être modéré (σώφρων) : en ce sens, leurs actions sont moralement significatives, mais témoignent d'états moraux intermédiaires par rapport à la vertu, comme le sont la mollesse (μαλακία) et l'intempérance (ἀκρασία) par rapport au vice (*EN* VII 8, 1150a13-15). Ces états intermédiaires peuvent ainsi être considérés d'un point de vue temporel : voir notamment Burnyeat 1980.

33. Taylor 2006, p. 82-83.

dans l'action morale ne sont pas exercées dans de telles actions, parce qu'elles ne requièrent ni la compréhension ni le désir de l'agent. Autrement dit, on ne peut pas caractériser les actions préparatoires à la vertu comme des actions accomplies par accident, ou selon une conformité extérieure à la règle. En effet, l'acquisition des dispositions vertueuses semble impliquer une continuité dans l'exercice des capacités psychiques de l'agent, entre la phase d'acquisition où elles sont exercées et développées, et le moment où les habitudes sont acquises et s'exercent dans les actions. Le fait d'exercer une disposition (ἐνεργεῖν) implique ainsi le double sens de la développer et de la faire passer à l'acte :

> [...] que les actions dont [la vertu] est la résultante soient celles mêmes où son activité s'exerce ensuite [...] (καὶ ὅτι ἐξ ὧν ἐγένετο, περὶ ταῦτα καὶ ἐνεργεῖ, *EN* II, 3, 1105a15-16).

En ce sens, les actions préparatoires et les actions pleinement vertueuses ont en partage d'être l'exercice de la même capacité à des niveaux différents de détermination et de perfectionnement. C'est pourquoi la question du développement des facultés psychiques implique la manière dont les actions sont accomplies. C'est particulièrement le cas des habitudes vertueuses ou vicieuses par rapport aux dispositions habituelles en général. En effet, la valeur d'une production peut être jugée par l'œuvre seule :

> Les productions de l'art ont leur valeur en elles-mêmes ; il suffit donc que la production leur confère certains caractères. (τὰ μὲν γὰρ ὑπὸ τῶν τεχνῶν γινόμενα τὸ εὖ ἔχει ἐν αὑτοῖς: ἀρκεῖ οὖν ταῦτά πως ἔχοντα γενέσθαι, *EN* II 3, 1105a27-28.)

Les actions morales au contraire, pour être accomplies vertueusement, requièrent un critère supplémentaire, qui est l'orientation cohérente et durable du désir. Pour bien agir, il faut aussi bien vouloir, tandis que la valeur de l'œuvre produite n'implique pas le désir et le choix de l'artisan. À la question de la continuité entre les actions préparatoires et les actions vertueuses s'ajoute celle de l'implication du désir de l'agent dans les actions préparatoires, comme l'a récemment montré M. Jimenez[34] : en agissant, on donne une direction stable et déterminée à son désir, dont les vertus du caractère constituent l'excellence[35]. En outre, le désir n'est pas en lui-même rationnel,

34. Jimenez 2016, p. 332 : Le problème de la continuité du progrès moral invite non seulement à abandonner une conception instrumentale de l'habitude, selon laquelle le processus d'habituation est un conditionnement qui n'implique pas la rationalité de l'agent, mais également une conception du progrès moral comme étant neutre du point de vue des motivations de l'agent, c'est-à-dire comme n'impliquant pas son désir. Elle défend ainsi l'idée selon laquelle l'exercice qui mène aux habitudes vertueuses implique à la fois les facultés cognitives et le désir du vertueux en devenir.

35. Angier 2012, p. 118 relève le problème qui consiste à séparer le développement cognitif de l'agent moral de celui de ses motivations, dans la mesure où cette séparation ne

en ce qu'il est distinct de la pensée en tant que puissance (δύναμις) ; cependant, il peut non seulement être soumis à la raison, mais également être rationnel ou rationalisé, c'est-à-dire impliquer une représentation rationnelle du bien et s'accorder à des raisons d'agir[36]. C'est pourquoi les commentateurs analysent le rapport entre le développement du caractère et celui de l'intelligence pratique[37] et la conception aristotélicienne des facultés psychiques, en ce qu'elle semble impliquer un codéveloppement des facultés cognitives et désidératives de l'agent moral[38].

Le problème de la continuité entre les actions préparatoires et les actions vertueuses révèle ainsi que l'habitude ne peut pas se réduire à une routine inconsciente, surtout lorsqu'il s'agit des habitudes vertueuses. En effet, une action vertueuse n'est pas une exécution, où l'on peut procéder selon un même protocole quelle que soit la situation : une situation pratique donnée implique une mesure différente des passions et de l'action. C'est pourquoi, comme le formule R. Kraut :

> devenir juste en faisant de façon répétée ce qui est juste implique de rencontrer beaucoup de situations dans lesquelles on doit en arriver à décider de ce qui est juste, et, de cette manière, de développer une expérience et une lucidité suffisantes concernant de telles affaires[39].

En ce sens, l'identité des actions vertueuses est celle d'une mesure qu'il faut à chaque fois pondérer dans une situation donnée, pour faire un choix préférentiel (προαίρεσις) qui implique à la fois une compréhension de la situation et une mesure des désirs et des passions. La qualité morale des actions préparatoires aux actions vertueuses semble fondamentale à cet égard. En effet, l'habitude est un mode d'acquisition axiologiquement neutre par lequel une disposition est acquise par la répétition des mêmes actions, et ne suffit pas en elle-même à déterminer, dans le cas des habitudes vertueuses, le

tient pas compte de la distinction entre l'œuvre et l'action : cette dernière implique le désir, bien ou mal dirigé, de l'agent. C'est pourquoi il attribue à une influence platonicienne (et notamment la *République*) le fait qu'Aristote associe souvent l'acquisition des habitudes vertueuses à la technique, et donc à un conditionnement mécanique apparemment extérieur aux raisons d'agir (p. 121-125).

36. Monteils-Laeng 2013, p. 441-457.

37. Contre cette conception de l'habitude comme conditionnement irrationnel, voir aussi Burnyeat 1980, p. 69-92, Sorabji 1980, p. 201-219, Donini, 2014, p. 66-67 : la pratique qui forme les habitudes implique aussi une forme d'expérience et d'apprentissage sur le plan intellectuel.

38. Gottlieb 2009, p. 99-102 distingue le fait d'être en accord avec la règle et le fait de l'impliquer, à partir de l'exemple technique d'*EN* II 3, 1105b21-26 : ainsi, le second cas implique une intériorisation de la règle, qui détermine l'action et non seulement une simple coïncidence entre la règle et le comportement. Ainsi, dans le cas de l'action morale, les raisons et les motivations, la pensée et le désir doivent être « pleinement intégrés » les uns aux autres (p. 102-106). Voir aussi Vasiliou 1996, p. 771-797 : ce sont les mêmes activités par lesquelles le vertueux en devenir développe ses tendances motivationnelles et ses facultés cognitives (p. 780).

39. Passage traduit en français de Kraut 2012, p. 538.

caractère moral du progrès. C'est pourquoi il s'agit à présent d'envisager une gradation dans l'exercice des facultés psychiques de l'agent et dans l'état de ses facultés à partir des critères de l'action pleinement vertueuse, pour saisir à la fois la continuité des actions dans le progrès moral, et ce qui distingue les actions préparatoires des actions réussies[40].

2. Y mettre du sien : le cas des actions vertueuses (*EN* II, 3, 1105a26-33)

Dans un second temps de sa réponse, Aristote distingue le cas des œuvres et celui des actions morales, dans la mesure où ces dernières ne sont pas identifiées comme vertueuses selon un ensemble de caractéristiques extérieures, comme c'est le cas de l'objet produit, mais plutôt selon l'état de l'agent qui les accomplit[41]. L'habitude et l'exercice ont ainsi une plus grande importance dans le domaine moral que dans le domaine technique, où la maîtrise technique se manifeste moins dans la manière d'agir que dans le résultat produit. Il faut faire et refaire les actions morales, parce que cela change la manière dont on agit : en répétant les actions vertueuses, on acquiert d'une part de l'expérience pratique et une meilleure perception des situations ; d'autre part, on oriente son désir vers une juste mesure des actions et des passions[42]. Autrement dit, les trois critères de l'action vertueuse permettent à Aristote non seulement de la distinguer de la production technique, mais également d'expliquer que l'habitude et l'exercice ont une plus grande importance pour l'acquisition des vertus que pour les dispositions techniques[43]. Aristote donne ainsi trois critères de l'action à la fois vertueuse et accomplie vertueusement :

40. En effet, comme le note Hampson 2019, p. 293-294, le travail critique contre la conception « mécanique » de l'habitude, et les tentatives d'élucidation des problèmes liés à la continuité du progrès moral peuvent tendre, à l'inverse, à faire perdre de vue une perspective dynamique selon laquelle les actions préparatoires ne témoignent pas d'une vertu pleinement acquise, et sont à cet égard imparfaites et distinctes des actions pleinement vertueuses.

41. En ce sens, le juste milieu dans l'action, qui distingue l'action vertueuse de l'action vicieuse, qui penche vers l'excès ou le défaut, ne constitue pas un ensemble de caractéristiques extérieures à l'action : il concerne le choix de l'agent, mais aussi ses passions : voir notamment *EN* II 2, 1106b16-18. Pour un état récent de cette question, voir Morel 2020, p. 183-197.

42. « Or c'est ce qui se passe pour les vertus : c'est en nous abstenant des plaisirs que nous devenons modérés, et une fois que nous le sommes devenus, c'est alors que nous sommes le plus capables de pratiquer cette abstention. Il en est de même au sujet du courage : en nous habituant à mépriser le danger et à lui tenir tête, nous devenons courageux, et une fois que nous le sommes devenus, c'est alors que nous serons le plus capables d'affronter le danger » (οὕτω δ' ἔχει καὶ ἐπὶ τῶν ἀρετῶν· ἔκ τε γὰρ τοῦ ἀπέχεσθαι τῶν ἡδονῶν γινόμεθα σώφρονες, καὶ γενόμενοι μάλιστα δυνάμεθα ἀπέχεσθαι· αὐτῶν· ὁμοίως δὲ καὶ ἐπὶ τῆς ἀνδρείας· ἐθιζόμενοι γὰρ καταφρονεῖν τῶν φοβερῶν καὶ ὑπομένειν αὐτὰ γινόμεθα ἀνδρεῖοι, καὶ γενόμενοι μάλιστα δυνησόμεθα ὑπομένειν τὰ φοβερά, *EN* II 2, 1104a33-b3).

43. « Or ces conditions n'entrent pas en ligne de compte pour la possession d'un art quel qu'il soit, à l'exception du savoir lui-même, alors que, pour la possession des vertus, le savoir ne joue qu'un rôle minime ou même nul, à la différence des autres conditions, lesquelles ont une influence non pas médiocre, mais totale, en tant précisément que la possession de la vertu naît de l'accomplissement répété des actes justes et modérés » (ταῦτα δὲ πρὸς μὲν τὸ τὰς ἄλλας τέχνας ἔχειν οὐ συναριθμεῖται, πλὴν αὐτὸ τὸ εἰδέναι· πρὸς δὲ τὸ τὰς ἀρετὰς τὸ μὲν εἰδέναι οὐδὲν ἢ

> [...] Il faut encore que l'agent lui-même soit dans une certaine disposition quand il les accomplit : en premier lieu, il doit savoir ce qu'il fait ; ensuite, choisir librement l'acte en question et le choisir en vue de cet acte lui-même ; et en troisième lieu, l'accomplir dans une disposition d'esprit ferme et inébranlable (ἀλλὰ καὶ ἐὰν ὁ πράττων πῶς ἔχων πράττῃ, πρῶτον μὲν ἐὰν εἰδώς, ἔπειτ' ἐὰν προαιρούμενος, καὶ προαιρούμενος δι' αὐτά, τὸ δὲ τρίτον ἐὰν καὶ βεβαίως καὶ ἀμετακινήτως ἔχων πράττῃ, *EN* II, 3, 1105a30-33).

La première condition est une condition minimale pour que l'action soit qualifiée de volontaire et s'applique aussi aux productions[44]. En effet, l'ignorance des circonstances particulières de l'action la rend involontaire, comme le sont les choses faites par méprise ou par accident (ce qui n'est pas le cas d'un état général d'ignorance, dont on peut être responsable comme on l'est d'un état d'ébriété : voir *EN* III 2, 1110b24-1111a1). La seconde distingue proprement les productions des actions moralement significatives, qui requièrent le choix de l'agent (προαίρεσις), et sont choisies pour elles-mêmes (δι' αὐτά)[45], et non en vue de l'œuvre et de son usage[46]. La dernière condition implique les habitudes vertueuses en ce qu'elles sont des dispositions stables, par lesquelles le désir de l'agent est orienté durablement. Autrement dit, l'action vertueuse et accomplie vertueusement n'est pas « une velléité passagère ou un acte isolé »[47]. Ces trois conditions ne semblent pas indépendantes les unes des autres, mais constituent plutôt une gradation, d'une condition minimale de l'action volontaire à une action pleinement conforme à une délibération rationnelle et à un caractère acquis. Ainsi, selon S. Broadie et C. Rowe, la deuxième implique la première, et la troisième les deux premières, mais cet ordre d'implication ne peut pas s'inverser[48]. En outre, seules les actions qui résultent des dispositions acquises semblent satisfaire l'ensemble de ces conditions, et donc pouvoir être dites vertueuses à proprement parler. Ces critères impliquent l'état de l'agent vertueux chaque fois qu'il les accomplit (ἐὰν πράττῃ) : la répétition dans le présent semble donner à ces conditions une perspective statique, qui ne semble pas prendre en compte le progrès moral. C'est pourquoi ces critères semblent d'abord distinguer la bonne action de la bonne œuvre, dont, comme on l'a vu, la valeur se trouve en elle-même (τὸ εὖ ἔχει ἐν αὐτοῖς) indépendamment de son auteur. Cependant,

μικρὸν ἰσχύει, τὰ δ' ἄλλα οὐ μικρὸν ἀλλὰ τὸ πᾶν δύναται, ἅπερ ἐκ τοῦ πολλάκις πράττειν τὰ δίκαια καὶ σώφρονα περιγίνεται, *EN* II 3, 1105a33-b5).

44. Bodéüs 2004, p. 109.

45. Ce qui n'exclut pas une subordination des fins pratiques particulières à la vie heureuse dans son ensemble, ni n'implique, comme le note Tricot 1994, p. 99, que la vertu doive être seulement pratiquée pour elle-même, et non parce qu'elle permet d'agir bien (εὖ πράττειν), et rend les actions et la vie dans son ensemble heureuses et réussies.

46. Taylor 2006, p. 7.

47. Tricot 1994, p. 99.

48. Broadie & Rowe 2002 (éd.), p. 115.

elle permet également, dans la suite du texte, de distinguer la possession (τὸ ἔχειν) d'un savoir-faire[49] de celle d'une habitude vertueuse. Ainsi, il semble que ces conditions peuvent être aussi envisagées relativement au progrès moral et aux actions préparatoires. La question qui se pose alors est celle de savoir si les actions préparatoires, par lesquelles on s'habitue et acquiert des vertus requièrent les deux premiers critères, ou seulement le premier.

En effet, la première condition fait de l'action une action volontaire, au sens minimal d'action qui n'est ni forcée ni inconsciente. Elle semble suffire à rendre les vertus volontaires au sens où elles sont acquises par des actions volontaires, dont le principe (ἀρχὴ) est en soi (ἐν αὐτῷ)[50], sans toutefois faire l'objet d'un choix préférentiel (προαίρεσις). Ce dernier implique un niveau d'élaboration supérieur du désir et de la pensée, mais également une gradation dans l'action délibérée, qui est d'une part choisie, et d'autre part choisie pour elle-même. On peut ainsi envisager une phase où on agit volontairement, mais par conseil et en imitant les actions vertueuses, dans la mesure où agir de la sorte peut être distingué d'agir par hasard, mais également sous la contrainte ou par ignorance, et implique déjà l'exercice des facultés psychiques du vertueux en devenir. M. Burnyeat envisage ainsi l'habitude en ce qu'elle rend plus désirables les bonnes actions, parce qu'elle les rend plaisantes à celui qui suivait d'abord ses désirs immédiats : la répétition des actions implique donc une intériorisation de leur motif et de leur valeur, qui permet qu'à terme, on désire les actions pour elles-mêmes et non par crainte du châtiment ou désir de la récompense[51]. Les conseils et l'imitation impliquent ainsi les facultés psychiques de l'agent, et notamment son désir. C'est ce que montre M. Hampson à propos de l'imitation[52] : pour être impliquée dans le progrès moral, elle ne saurait se réduire à l'imitation de l'apparence extérieure de la vertu. Elle donne plutôt une direction à l'exercice du désir et de la pensée de l'agent moral en devenir. L'acquisition de la vertu, même à ce stade, implique ainsi des actions qui peuvent être jugées moralement en tant qu'elles sont volontaires. De plus, elles ne sauraient avoir seulement l'apparence extérieure de la vertu, comme les actions des hommes qui deviennent dédaigneux et insolents par la richesse, et imitent seulement l'apparence extérieure de la magnanimité sans en saisir les raisons et la mesure[53] ; ou encore celles des téméraires, qui imitent seulement l'apparence du courage, sans exercer leur désir à la juste mesure, ni leur pensée au bon

49. *EN* II 3, 1105a33.

50. *EN* III 7, 1114a19.

51. Burnyeat 1980.

52. Hampson 2019, p. 292-320, distingue l'imitation du comportement extérieur de l'imitation proprement propédeutique, qui transforme son agent par son aspect à la fois actif et réflexif, et le conduit à adopter progressivement les fins pratiques du vertueux exemplaire.

53. *EN* IV, 8, 1124b2-3.

calcul des risques et des chances[54]. En ce sens, les actions préparatoires, comme les actions vertueuses, impliquent l'état de l'agent tandis que l'acquisition d'un savoir-faire technique apparaît immédiatement dans la qualité de l'œuvre produite. Autrement dit, même si l'action préparatoire n'est pas encore choisie pour elle-même et conformément à une disposition stabilisée du caractère, elle semble se distinguer de l'action qui n'imite qu'un résultat extérieur.

Ainsi, ce progrès peut être dit moral, dès lors que les actions qui le constituent sont volontaires – et donc louables ou blâmables. Faut-il faire un pas de plus et considérer que les actions exercées dans l'habitude impliquent le deuxième critère ? Cela recoupe partiellement la manière dont on interprète le fait qu'Aristote caractérise la vertu morale comme une disposition concernant le choix (ἕξις προαιρετική)[55]. Selon l'interprétation dominante, cette caractérisation de la vertu concerne la vertu morale pleinement acquise et développée, en tant qu'elle s'exerce conjointement aux facultés rationnelles dans la délibération et dans le choix qui en résulte[56]. En ce sens, les actions préparatoires sont susceptibles de louange ou de blâme sans toutefois impliquer de choix préférentiel, qui requiert un état supérieur d'excellence et de synthèse des facultés psychiques, et par lequel les actions sont non seulement vertueuses, mais accomplies vertueusement. Ainsi, la vertu s'exerce dans un choix préférentiel, mais n'est pas forcément acquise par des choix préférentiels, ni par des actions voulues pour elles-mêmes. Cependant, tout choix n'est pas vertueux ni prudent. De plus, une action peut impliquer un choix sans que l'action soit vertueuse ou choisie pour elle-même : le choix du vertueux accompli atteint bien ce degré de perfection, mais ce n'est pas le cas du vicieux, qui agit également par choix. En outre, l'intempérant aussi peut agir contre son choix[57], ce qui implique que le choix peut être impliqué dans des états intermédiaires entre le vice et la vertu. Dans cette perspective, les choix impliqués dans l'acquisition des vertus morales n'impliquent pas forcément un état de perfection des vertus pratiques et intellectuelles,

54. *EN* III, 10, 1115b31.

55. *EN* II, 6, 1106b36.

56. Voir notamment Broadie 1993, p. 78-82, sur les difficultés que pose cette qualification de la vertu morale. Ainsi, toute réponse moralement significative n'implique pas forcément un choix au sens de ce qui vient au terme de la délibération (*EN* III, 1113a2, VI, 1, 1139a23). En ce sens, la délibération et le choix, en tant qu'ils constituent la réponse la plus moralement aboutie, impliquent un état avancé des dispositions éthiques et intellectuelles. Réciproquement, l'implication du choix dans les vertus éthiques caractérise le choix délibéré : il n'est pas seulement le résultat d'un calcul, mais témoigne d'une implication passionnelle et d'une bonne orientation du désir dans chaque situation. *Contra*, voir l'interprétation de Aubenque 2004, p. 119-121 et Frede 2020, p. 420, selon lesquels Aristote fait usage de la notion de choix en *EN* II au sens large d'intention ou de résolution, c'est-à-dire en un sens plus général et moins technique que le résultat de la délibération tel que l'envisage Aristote en *EN* III 4.

57. *EN* VII 9, 1151a7.

comme c'est le cas du choix préférentiel et juste de l'homme prudent. C'est pourquoi on peut considérer que l'habitude vertueuse n'implique pas, pour être acquise, le choix préférentiel (προαίρεσις), intellect désirant ou désir raisonnant (ἢ ὀρεκτικὸς νοῦς ἢ ὄρεξις διανοητική)[58] au sens d'état d'excellence et de synthèse des facultés psychiques. Cependant, son acquisition concerne le choix, au sens où elle oriente durablement le désir (ὄρεξις) de celui qui agit[59]. Elle implique en ce sens une orientation globale du désir, un souhait (βούλησις) qu'accompagne une certaine représentation du bien[60], avec laquelle le choix impliqué dans une action vertueuse doit être cohérent pour être considéré comme un choix préférentiel proprement dit[61]. On peut alors interpréter cette qualification comme le fait que son existence même implique la capacité de choisir de celui qui l'a acquise. Selon cette lecture, les habitudes vertueuses seraient des dispositions qui concernent le choix parce qu'elles se constituent dans la direction droite d'un désir qui s'intensifie et se stabilise. Ainsi, l'intempérant a déjà une orientation déterminée de ses désirs, et peut faire des choix cohérents ; cependant, il peut aussi s'en détourner ou ne pas s'y tenir. Ce qui le distingue du vertueux accompli est la fermeté de son désir sous forme de bon caractère[62]. En ce sens, la disposition stable et inébranlable qui qualifie l'action vertueuse comme telle semble se distinguer non seulement d'une contrainte ou d'un conseil extérieur, mais aussi d'une velléité passagère et d'un choix seulement ponctuel. Cependant, l'action accomplie vertueusement n'est pas seulement distinguée des actions du vertueux en devenir par le dernier critère, mais aussi par la capacité à choisir l'action pour elle-même, de manière à la fois vertueuse et prudente.

58. *EN* VI 2, 1139b4-5.

59. *EN* VI, 13, 1144a20.

60. *EN* III 7, 1114b23 : les apparences (φαντασίαι) des fins accompagnent les dispositions (ἕξει) du caractère.

61. Suivant les analyses de Cagnoli Fiecconi 2018, p. 229-256 au sujet des rapports entre le choix et le caractère, notamment à propos des intempérants et des cas d'intempérance inversée. En effet, l'intempérant agit de manière incohérente en ce sens, parce qu'il ne parvient pas à engager son souhait dans un choix préférentiel, tandis que l'intempérance inversée correspond au cas de celui qui ne se résout pas à faire un mauvais choix en raison de ses habitudes vertueuses. Dans les deux cas, le conflit avec les résultats de la délibération témoigne d'une incohérence entre le désir et la règle de conduite à suivre.

62. Ainsi, comme le formule Hutchinson 2016, p. 91, ce qui distingue la vertu effective, est sa stabilisation sous forme de caractère ; c'est pourquoi on peut envisager dans le processus d'habituation une première fois, pour chacun et pour chaque catégorie de vertu, où l'action et l'agent réunissent toutes les conditions de la vertu, sauf son caractère inébranlable. En outre, la fermeté du vertueux implique une stabilité des dispositions acquises et une cohérence entre le désir et la pensée qui la distingue de celle de l'endurant, qui résiste à ses passions mais ne les maitrise pas (*EN* VII 8, 1150a33-36), et de celle l'obstiné qui demeure ferme face à la raison plutôt qu'aux appétits (*EN* VII 10, 1151b10-12).

La position d'Aristote cesse ainsi d'être paradoxale à partir du moment où l'on considère les trois conditions de l'action vertueuse d'un point de vue dynamique, c'est-à-dire comme différentes phases de l'acquisition des habitudes vertueuses. L'action accomplie vertueusement les implique toutes, mais les conditions premières sont déjà présentes dans les actions du vertueux en devenir, dans lesquelles ne s'exprime pas encore un caractère vertueux durablement acquis. Cette lecture présente l'avantage de prendre en compte à la fois le problème de l'antériorité de l'action sur la disposition vertueuse et celui de la continuité du progrès moral. En effet, ni le caractère volontaire, c'est-à-dire ni inconscient ni forcé, ni même la justesse du choix qui préside à l'action délibérée et moralement significative ne présupposent l'habitude vertueuse, puisque celle-ci est la stabilisation de cette bonne orientation dans une disposition ferme et inébranlable. Ainsi, on peut distinguer les actions préparatoires des actions accomplies vertueusement. Cependant, c'est une même puissance psychique qui se détermine et se stabilise sous la forme d'un caractère dans celui qui agit, et par laquelle se développent ses capacités à bien agir. En ce sens, il n'y a pas de discontinuité radicale entre les actions préparatoires et les actions vertueuses.

3. Les phases du progrès moral

Les problèmes herméneutiques posés par ce chapitre invitent à affiner une lecture qui réduit le progrès moral à un conditionnement passif, en prenant la mesure de l'exercice de la réflexivité intellectuelle, mais aussi de celui du désir de l'agent dans les actions répétées au moment de l'acquisition des habitudes vertueuses[63]. Ainsi il semble qu'*EN* II 3 ouvre la possibilité de distinguer différentes phases du progrès moral en développant les perspectives que donnent d'une part la comparaison avec les habitudes techniques, d'autre part les trois critères de l'action vertueuse. En effet, on peut envisager une formation affective de l'enfant sous l'effet de raisons et de règles extérieures (les lois, les principes du chef de famille et du pédagogue) d'une part, et d'autre part l'exercice des dispositions et l'acquisition des habitudes vertueuses, qui impliquent des actions et donc le désir et la pensée, et non seulement un rapport passionnel et réactif à la pratique. On peut ainsi considérer la première phase comme nécessaire, mais insuffisante au devenir vertueux, qui implique l'habitude en tant qu'elle est processus actif et réflexif.

63. Curzer 2012, p. 340-366 distingue des degrés de progrès moral, notamment à travers la capacité à éprouver des passions vertueuses ou propédeutiques à la vertu, et établit ainsi une typologie des états vertueux jusqu'à la vertu effective et complète. Monteils-Laeng 2014, p. 267 distingue trois phases relatives à l'acquisition des vertus, suivant le degré de responsabilité de l'agent dans ses actions.

De ce point de vue, la typologie des actions qu'Aristote expose en *EN* II 3 offre un cadre qui permet de saisir la dynamique du progrès moral et de reconstituer ses différentes phases, mais également de distinguer un moment de la vie morale où les actions ne témoignent pas d'une vertu durablement acquise, mais impliquent cependant l'exercice des facultés cognitives et désidératives à un état antérieur et moins déterminé.

Ainsi, une première phase de la formation des vertus pourrait consister en une orientation des états affectifs, qui comptent beaucoup pendant l'enfance, qui se caractérise par une certaine surdité de l'agent aux raisons d'agir et par une prévalence de l'état affectif, puisque le désir et les passions existent chez les individus avant la raison[64]. La vertu du caractère est une juste mesure des plaisirs et des peines : l'éducation morale implique d'abord leur droite orientation, de sorte qu'on les trouve où il convient[65]. En ce sens, la compréhension des raisons d'agir passe par une phase préparatoire, dans laquelle on s'habitue à supporter ses peurs ou à modérer les plaisirs, et dont Aristote fait aussi état dans les *Politiques*, VII 15. On peut ainsi suivre les *Politiques*, VII-VIII, où Aristote distingue les âges de la vie en groupes de sept ans. Une première phase correspondrait alors à l'enfance de l'individu, qui implique différents soins à partir de la naissance : alimentation, entraînement du corps, musique et jeux jusqu'à ses sept ans[66], puis l'éducation jusqu'à son adolescence[67]. Il s'agirait donc, durant ces deux premiers groupes de sept ans, d'une orientation préréflexive vers la vertu, parce que l'enfant est encore incapable de faire des choix rationnels. Ceci recoupe certains passages de l'*EN* et des *Politiques*, où Aristote envisage un développement séquentiel des facultés, et une première formation de l'affectivité et du désir, antérieure à celle des facultés de discrimination et de compréhension des raisons d'agir :

> Et, en général, ce n'est pas, semble-t-il, au raisonnement que cède la passion, c'est à la contrainte. Il faut donc que le caractère ait déjà une certaine disposition propre à la vertu, chérissant ce qui est noble et ne supportant pas ce qui est honteux (ὅλως τ' οὐ δοκεῖ λόγῳ ὑπείκειν τὸ πάθος ἀλλὰ βίᾳ. δεῖ δὴ τὸ ἦθος προϋπάρχειν πως οἰκεῖον τῆς ἀρετῆς, στέργον τὸ καλὸν καὶ δυσχεραῖνον τὸ αἰσχρόν, *EN* X, 10, 1179b28-31)[68].

64. *EN* III, 12, 1119b13-18. McGowan Tress 1997, p. 63-84 étudie notamment le fait que le développement de l'enfant implique différents champs de recherche (biologique, éthique, politique) qui permettent de saisir les conditions à la fois naturelles et sociales à la formation de son affectivité. Monteils-Laeng 2017, p. 659-676 analyse l'état d'incomplétude propre à l'enfance en interrogeant le rapport de ce premier stade de la vie au reste de la vie morale.

65. *EN* II 2, 1104b11-12.

66. *Pol.* VII 17, 1336a3-1337b38.

67. *Pol.* VII 17, 1336b39.

68. Voir aussi *Pol.* VII 15, 1334b15-17 : « [...] la raison et l'intellect sont la fin de notre nature, de sorte que c'est en vue de ces deux facultés qu'il faut organiser la génération et la

Dans ce passage, on ne voit pas clairement si cette première phase concerne l'enfance seule ou la jeunesse en général, et Aristote est plus explicite sur le découpage des âges de la vie dans les *Politiques.* En tout cas, cette première phase ne semble pas exclure une forme de contrainte (βίᾳ), et donc des actions involontaires car forcées. Même si elle la prépare, elle ne semble donc pas faire partie de la vie pratique. En effet, le comportement de l'enfant, en tant qu'il peut être loué ou blâmé par le pédagogue, est impliqué dans le devenir moral de l'agent. On peut à cet égard distinguer la vie morale, qui comprend ce qui compte moralement pour l'individu, et la vie pratique, comprise comme ensemble des actions moralement significatives. Ainsi, cette première phase implique aussi une éducation affective, c'est-à-dire des actions qui ne sont pas forcément voulues pour elles-mêmes, mais par crainte de la réprimande ou de la honte[69], ou qui sont dictées par le pédagogue ou par le législateur dans le but de la formation du caractère, comme la pratique de la musique[70].

C'est pourquoi on peut envisager une deuxième phase, qui implique un saut qualitatif par rapport à l'acquisition des dispositions vertueuses par des actions qui sont, comme on l'a vu, au moins volontaires, et par lesquelles le vertueux en devenir se trouve dans un rapport actif à sa formation morale. Ainsi, Aristote affirme dans certains passages l'importance d'un rapport actif à l'acquisition des dispositions vertueuses. Aussi, après avoir d'abord décrit l'importance de l'éducation pendant l'enfance, en tant qu'elle prédispose à la vertu, Aristote insiste sur l'importance de l'exercice, par lequel on se détermine soi-même :

> Mais sans doute n'est-ce pas assez que pendant leur jeunesse des hommes reçoivent une éducation et des soins également éclairés ; puisqu'ils doivent, même parvenus à l'âge d'homme, mettre en pratique les choses qu'ils ont apprises et les tourner en habitudes (διὸ νόμοις δεῖ τετάχθαι τὴν τροφὴν καὶ τὰ ἐπιτηδεύματα: οὐκ ἔσται γὰρ λυπηρὰ συνήθη γενόμενα. οὐχ ἱκανὸν δ' ἴσως νέους ὄντας τροφῆς καὶ ἐπιμελείας τυχεῖν ὀρθῆς, ἀλλ' ἐπιεδὴ καὶ ἀνδρωθέντας δεῖ ἐπιτηδεύειν αὐτὰ καὶ ἐθίζεσθαι, *EN* X, 10, 1179b34-1180a2).

Ces actions impliquent à la fois l'intelligence et le désir, et se distinguent ainsi du développement séquentiel des facultés physiques et psychiques, qui répond au programme du législateur et du pédagogue. Si, comme on l'a vu,

formation des habitudes » (ὁ δὲ λόγος ἡμῖν καὶ ὁ νοῦς τῆς φύσεως τέλος, ὥστε πρὸς τούτους τὴν γένεσιν καὶ τὴν τῶν ἐθῶν δεῖ παρασκευάζειν μελέτην).

69. Jimenez 2020, qui engage une réflexion sur le rôle des affects négatifs sur le développement moral, s'inscrivant ainsi dans la lignée de la critique du rôle central accordé au plaisir dans l'éducation morale par Burnyeat 1980, développée notamment par Curzer 2012. Ainsi, une passion telle que la honte, en tant qu'elle est une passion qui implique cependant une évaluation morale du sujet par les autres et lui-même, constitue à cet égard une « proto-vertu » (p. 12) ou une « semi-vertu » (Burnyeat 1980, p. 78).

70. *Pol.* VIII 5-6.

la première formation du caractère pendant l'enfance n'est pas involontaire, ce qui change à partir de l'adolescence est la dimension active du progrès moral, même si ces actions sont accomplies par conseil ou par l'imitation d'un modèle de vertu. Autrement dit, le fait que l'agent agisse, et agisse de manière louable ou blâmable, semble marquer le début de sa vie pratique, par distinction avec une période antérieure de formation du comportement. Dans cette perspective, les actions par lesquelles on s'exerce à la vertu font partie de la vie pratique, contrairement à la première phase de l'éducation, même si cette dernière n'est pas pour autant moralement neutre. Le caractère volontaire, voire choisi des actions préparatoires semble impliquer un exercice et un développement conjoint de la raison et du désir [71]. Le cas des intempérants et celui des endurants[72] peut ainsi offrir des modèles pour penser une phase du développement moral où les vertus du caractère et la prudence ne sont pas pleinement acquises, mais qui implique un agent responsable et en capacité de choisir. Ce stade correspond aussi un âge de la vie, l'adolescence passionnée, troisième tranche de sept ans qui va de la puberté à l'âge de vingt-et-un ans[73]. Cette intempérance en quelque sorte naturelle et passagère[74] implique une capacité d'agir de manière rationnelle, bien que prédominent les réactions passionnelles. Cette phase – si elle est dépassée et ne constitue pas un état chronique, intermédiaire entre vice et vertu – peut correspondre à la transition des actions volontaires aux actions délibérées, qui impliquent un choix préférentiel et un état accompli de vertu et de prudence. En ce sens, le développement séquentiel des facultés pendant l'enfance crée un terrain propice à l'acquisition de la vertu proprement dite. Celle-ci implique l'exercice d'actions préparatoires qui sont volontaires et moralement significatives,

71. *Contra*, Lawrence 2011, p. 276-283 envisage les stades du progrès moral à travers le passage de la vertu naturelle à la vertu habituelle, puis à la vertu proprement dite (κυρία ἀρετή), en ce qu'elle implique l'intelligence pratique. Pour une interprétation forte des vertus naturelles dans les éthiques et une conception séquentielle du développement moral, voir aussi Lennox 2015, p. 193-213. Pour un état récent de la question et une interprétation déflationniste des vertus naturelles, voir Morel 2021, p. 133-145 : les dispositions habituelles impliquent, dans leur acquisition même, l'exercice des facultés cognitives de l'agent, et en ceci elles ne peuvent être réduites à un stade antérieur – parce qu'irrationnel – de la vertu proprement dite.

72. Cité *supra* : *EN* VII 8, 1150a13-b28.

73. En effet, l'enfance est comparée au dérèglement par une « extension de sens » (*EN* III 15, 1119b115) : c'est pourquoi le gouverneur doit faire office de principe rationnel, celui-ci étant encore absent ou insuffisamment développé. On peut ainsi comprendre que ce qui est un défaut invétéré chez le déréglé est de l'ordre de l'inachèvement chez l'enfant, que pallie provisoirement la raison du pédagogue. Par distinction, l'adolescence implique déjà le rapport à un choix et à des motifs rationnels, même s'il est conflictuel ; elle semble donc plus proche de l'intempérance.

74. Tandis qu'à l'inverse, on peut rester jeune par le caractère (τὸ ἦθος νεαρός) : *EN* I 1, 1095a7.

et par lesquelles le vertueux en devenir perfectionne son caractère tout en développant son intelligence pratique. Si, comme on l'a vu, la première phase n'est pas neutre d'un point de vue moral, la deuxième semble déjà constituer une partie de la vie pratique parce qu'elle implique des actions que l'on peut louer ou blâmer, et par lesquelles, en agissant, on acquiert des dispositions habituelles dont on est responsable[75].

C'est pourquoi on peut distinguer ces premiers stades du développement moral d'une part, et d'autre part la vie pratique, en tant qu'elle est constituée par actions moralement significatives, et qu'elle implique un état plus avancé de rationalité pratique. En ce sens, le comportement des enfants que l'on éduque est louable ou blâmable, même s'il peut être partiellement contraint. Il constitue une phase de la vie moralement significative, mais durant laquelle la responsabilité de l'agent sur son caractère est relative et indirecte. En effet, il reste en grande part soumis à des influences extérieures (parentales, politiques, mais aussi somatiques et climatiques). De cette première phase se distingue une phase plus active, dans la mesure où l'action à proprement parler implique l'exercice des facultés rationnelles ; or, celles-ci sont encore imparfaites dans l'enfance[76]. Cette phase semble correspondre plus directement à la manière dont Aristote envisage la responsabilité du caractère en *EN* III 7 : l'agent moral se détermine lui-même par la manière dont il agit, et cette responsabilité semble plus directe que le conditionnement partiellement passif et multifactoriel de la première phase de l'éducation morale. Dès lors, l'existence humaine a dès son commencement une valeur morale (d'où l'importance des conditions physiologiques, climatiques, sociales et politiques pour le devenir de l'enfant en citoyen). Cependant, on peut considérer que l'on n'entre pas dans la vie pratique avant d'être capable d'actions moralement significatives, ce qui implique à la fois un état adéquat des facultés psychiques et un contexte interpersonnel et social qui donne un sens à ces actions. En ce sens, l'enfant n'est pas heureux à proprement parler, car il ne participe pas encore à la vie pratique, au bonheur en tant qu'il est constitué par les actions qu'on accomplit[77].

EN II 3 s'inscrit ainsi dans la question plus large de la vie pratique comme ensemble d'actions. La question du statut moral des actions préparatoires

75. *EN* III 7, 1114a47.

76. Je me réfère ici aux conclusions de L. Monteils-Laeng 2017 à propos du statut moral de l'enfance. Elle envisage un étagement du vouloir qui traduit le développement des facultés de l'enfance à l'âge adulte : le comportement infantile et animal est volontaire (*EN* III 3, 1111a25-26 ; 4, 1111b89), mais les enfants ne sont pas capables de choix délibéré (*ibid.* 1111b9-10), et en ce sens n'agissent pas comme le feraient des hommes adultes, en pleine possession de leurs moyens intellectuels. Ainsi, l'enfance est un état d'inachèvement psycho-physiologique, durant lequel l'individu peut exercer son désir, et en ce sens agit volontairement, mais en un sens plus faible que l'action de l'homme adulte capable de choix délibéré.

77. *EN* I 10, 1100a1-6.

conduit à se poser la question des actions qui, sans être accomplies selon une habitude vertueuse pleinement acquise, s'inscrivent cependant dans une gradation psychologique et axiologique qui englobe ce qui compte moralement dans la vie d'un individu ; ce par quoi sa progression, malgré son inachèvement essentiel, est moralement significative. Cette échelle permet d'envisager un progrès moral qui va de la formation passive de l'affectivité aux actions contraintes ou prescrites, par lesquelles on développe progressivement sa capacité de désirer et de choisir. Ce qui progresse aussi par cela est la capacité d'être pleinement responsable de ce que l'on fait, et ainsi de la manière dont on se change soi-même en agissant.

BIBLIOGRAPHIE

ANGIER, T. 2012 : *Technê in Aristotle's ethics: crafting the moral life,* London.

AUBENQUE, P. 2004 : *La prudence chez Aristote,* Paris [1963].

BODÉÜS, R. 2004 (trad.) : Aristote, *Éthique à Nicomaque. Traduction et présentation,* Paris.

BOLTON, R. 2021 : « *Technê* and *Empeiria*: Aristotle on Practical Knowledge » dans T. K. Johansen (éd.), *Productive knowledge in ancient philosophy: the concept of technê,* Cambridge University Press, p. 131-165.

BROADIE, S. 1991 : *Ethics with Aristotle,* Oxford University Press.

BROADIE, S. & C. ROWE 2002 (éd.) : *Aristotle: Nicomachean Ethics,* Oxford University Press.

BURNYEAT, M. 1980 : « Aristotle on Learning to be Good » dans A. Rorty (éd.), *Essays on Aristotle's Ethics,* University of California Press, p. 69-92.

BYWATER, I. 1894 (ÉD.) : *Aristotelis: Ethica Nicomachea,* Oxford University Press.

CAGNOLI FIECCONI, E. 2018 : « Aristote on the Structure of Akratic Action », *Phronesis,* 63/3, p. 229-256.
DOI: 10.1163/15685284-12341350

COOPE, U. 2011 : « Commentary on the six sections of the chapter, 246a10-246b3 » dans S. Maso, C. Natali et G. Steel (éd.), *Reading Aristotle's Physics VII.3: "what is alteration?", Proceedings of the European Society for Ancient Philosophy conference organized by the HYELE Institute for Comparative Studies, Vitznau, Switzerland, 12/15 April 2007,* Las Vegas – Zurich – Athens, p. 64-71.

CURZER, H. J. 2012 : *Aristotle and the virtues,* Oxford University Press.

DONINI, P. 2014 : *Abitudine e saggezza: Aristotele dall'Etica Eudemia all'Etica Nicomachea,* Alessandria.

FARINA, F. 2019 : « La natura e gli stati abituali nell'*Etica Nicomachea* » dans G. Bagnati, M. Cassan, A. Morelli (éd.), *Le varietà del naturalismo. Incontri Ca' Foscari-Paris* 1, Venezia, p. 31-45.

FREDE, D. 2020 (trad.) : *Nikomachische Ethik,* dans C. Rapp *et al., Aristoteles Werke in deutsche Übersetzung. t. VI,* Berlin.

GOTTLIEB, P. 2009 : *The virtue of Aristotle,* Cambridge University Press.

HAMPSON, M. 2019 : « Imitating Virtue », *Phronesis,* 64/3, p. 292-320.
DOI: 10.1163/15685284-12341984

HAMPSON, M. 2021 : « Aristotle on the Necessity of Habituation: Re-Reading Nicomachean Ethics 2.4 », *Phronesis,* 66/1, p. 1-26.
DOI: 10.1163/15685284-BJA10032

HUTCHINSON, D. S. 2016 : *The Virtue of Aristotle,* London ; New-York.

JIMENEZ, M. 2016 : « Aristotle on Becoming Virtuous by Doing Virtuous Actions », *Phronesis,* 61/1, p. 3-32.
DOI: 10.1163/15685284-12341297

JIMENEZ, M. 2020 : *Aristotle on shame and learning to be good,* Oxford University Press.

KRAUT, R. 2012 : « Aristotle on Becoming Good: Habituation, Reflection, and Perception » dans C. Schields (éd.), *The Oxford Handbook of Aristotle,* Oxford University Press, p. 529-557.

Lawrence, G. 2011 : « Acquiring Character: Becoming Grown-up » dans M. Pakaluk et G. Pearson (éd.), *Moral Psychology and Human Action in Aristotle*, Oxford University Press, p. 276-283.

Lennox, J. 2015 : « Aristotle on the biological roots of virtue: the natural history of natural virtue » dans D. Henry et K. M. Nielsen (éd.), *Bridging the Gap between Aristotle's Science and Ethics*, Cambridge University Press, p. 193-213.

Leunissen M. 2017 : *From Natural Caracter to Moral Virtue in Aristotle*, Oxford University Press.

McGowan Tress, D. 1997 : « Aristotle's Child: Development Through *Genesis*, *Oikos*, and *Polis* », *Ancient Philosophy*, 17/1, p. 63-84. DOI: 10.5840/ancientphil199717113

Monteils-Laeng, L. 2013 : « Aristote et l'invention du désir », *Archives de Philosophie*, 76/3, p. 441-457. DOI : 10.3917/aphi.763.0441

Monteils-Laeng, L. 2014 : *Agir sans vouloir : le problème de l'intellectualisme moral dans la philosophie ancienne*, Paris.

Monteils-Laeng, L. 2017 : « La valeur de l'enfance chez Aristote », *Archives de Philosophie*, 80/4, p. 659-676. DOI : 10.3917/aphi.804.0659

Morel, P.M. 1997 : « L'habitude : une seconde nature ? » dans P.-M. Morel (éd), *Aristote et la notion de nature*, Bordeaux, p. 131-148.

Morel, P.M. 2020 : « La mesure des plaisirs dans l'*Éthique à Nicomaque*. Remarques sur *EN* X, 5, 1176a15-29 » dans G. R. Giardina (éd.), To metron *: sur la notion de mesure dans la philosophie d'Aristote : septième rencontre aristotélicienne*, Paris ; Bruxelles, p. 183-197.

Morel, P.M. 2021 : *La nature et le bien. L'éthique d'Aristote et la question naturaliste*, Louvain-la-Neuve.

Pellegrin, P. 1990 (trad.) : *Aristote, Les Politiques, traduction et présentation*, Paris.

Petit, A. 2002 : « L'*eupraxia*, fin inconditionnelle », *Philosophie*, 73/2, p. 58-72. DOI : 10.3917/philo.073.0058

Rodier, G. 1900 : *Aristote, Traité de l'âme : commentaire*, Paris.

Sherman, N. 1989 : *The fabric of character*, Oxford.

Sorabji, R. 1980 : « Aristotle on the role of intellect in Virtue », dans A. O. Rorty (éd.), *Essays on Aristotle's Ethics*, University of California Press, p. 201-219.

Taylor, C. C. W. 2006 (trad.) : *Nicomachean Ethics: Books IIIV*, Oxford University Press.

Tricot, J. 1994 (éd.) : Aristote, *Éthique à Nicomaque*, Paris [1959].

Vasiliou, I. , 1996 : « The role of Good Upbringing in Aristotle's *Ethics* », *Philosophy and Phenomenological Research*, 56/4, p. 783-787. DOI : 10.2307/2108280

Verbeke, G. 1971 : « La doctrine aristotélicienne du changement qualitatif dans *Physique*, VII, 3 » dans J. P. Anton et G. L. Kustas (éd.), *Essays on Ancient Greek Philosophy*, New-York University Press, p. 546-665.

ARISTOTLE ON THE VOLUNTARY IN OTHER ANIMALS

Jay R. Elliott
Bard College
jelliott@bard.edu

ABSTRACT. *In his biological and ethical writings, Aristotle explicitly claims that nonhuman animals can act voluntarily. But other aspects of his treatment of the voluntary in those same writings seem to contradict this claim and to imply that the voluntary requires the distinctively human capacity for rationality. Readers of Aristotle have proposed a variety of solutions to this problem. Some hold that Aristotle can be understood as defining the voluntary solely in terms of capacities that humans and other animals share. Others argue that the voluntary properly speaking belongs only to humans, and that Aristotle attributes the voluntary to other animals only in a metaphorical sense. A third group holds that we should read Aristotle as implicitly distinguishing between the capacity for voluntary action, which we share with nonhuman animals, and the capacity for moral responsibility, which humans alone possess. In this paper, I propose an alternative to these familiar approaches. In my view, the voluntary in Aristotle is best understood as a genus which comes in rational and non-rational species.*

RÉSUMÉ. Dans ses écrits biologiques et éthiques, Aristote affirme explicitement que les animaux non humains sont capables d'action volontaire. Mais d'autres aspects de son traitement du volontaire dans ces mêmes écrits semblent contredire cette affirmation et impliquer que le volontaire nécessite une faculté rationnelle spécifiquement humaine. Les lecteurs d'Aristote ont proposé diverses solutions à ce problème. Un premier groupe dit qu'Aristote définit le volontaire uniquement en termes de capacités que nous partageons avec les autres animaux. D'autres proposent que le volontaire au sens propre soit uniquement humain, et qu'Aristote attribue le volontaire aux autres animaux seulement par métaphore. Un troisième groupe soutient qu'Aristote distingue implicitement le volontaire, que nous partageons avec les autres animaux, et la responsabilité morale, qui n'appartient qu'aux êtres rationnels. Je propose une alternative à ces approches habituelles. Je démontre que le volontaire chez Aristote fonctionne comme un genre, divisé en espèces rationnelle et non rationnelle.

Philosophie antique, n°24 (2024), 65-89

Introduction

In his biological and ethical writings, Aristotle uses *hekōn* ("voluntarily"), *hekousion* ("voluntary") and related terms to describe some of the movements of nonhuman animals.[1] Aristotle even goes so far as to say that a nonhuman animal *hekousiōs praxei*, "acts voluntarily." (*Nicomachean Ethics* (hereafter *NE*) 1111a26).[2] In both biological and ethical contexts, Aristotle's ascription of the voluntary to nonhuman animals reflects his understanding of and appreciation for their cognitive capacities. By insisting that nonhuman animals act voluntarily, Aristotle aims to reject an intellectualist outlook according to which only rational beings count as genuine agents. In these very same contexts, however, Aristotle sometimes describes voluntary actions in ways that require them to involve distinctive capacities that only human animals possess. Likewise, he sometimes describes actions that engage only the psychic capacities we share with other animals as involuntary. The result appears to be a contradiction: Aristotle seems to say both that the voluntary is something we share with other animals, and something uniquely human.

Readers of Aristotle have often discussed this problem, and they have developed three main strategies for responding to it. The first strategy I call "widening": it aims to interpret all of Aristotle's remarks about the voluntary in such a way that they can be understood as referring only to capacities we share with nonhuman animals. The second strategy I call "metaphor":

1. Charles 1984, p. 61-62 argues that *hekousion* should be translated as "intentional" rather than "voluntary." This translation captures important aspects of Aristotle's treatment of the *hekousion* in human agents, but it is not well suited to capture the full breadth of Aristotle's notion, especially its application to nonhuman animals.

2. All translations are my own unless otherwise noted. Aristotle does not use *praxis* here in the technical sense in which it applies only to the actions of human agents. For this technical sense of *praxis*, see *NE* 1139a20, *Eudemian Ethics* (hereafter *EE*) 1222b18-20, and cf. *Magna Moralia* (hereafter *MM*) 1187b8-9.

it proposes to read Aristotle's claim that nonhuman animals act voluntarily as not true in the proper sense, but only reflecting a certain resemblance between their actions and genuinely voluntary ones. The third strategy I call "ambiguity": it claims that Aristotle uses *hekōn* and related terms in two distinct senses, one that describes something we share with nonhuman animals, another that describes something uniquely human. None of these strategies offers a compelling solution to the problem. In sections 1 and 2, I survey the evidence that gives rise to the apparent contradiction. Then in sections 3-5, I consider the advantages and disadvantages of each of the three extant strategies. Finally, in section 6, I introduce a novel strategy, according to which we should think of the voluntary as a genus that comes in rational and nonrational species, and I argue that it is preferable to the other three strategies.

Section 1

Aristotle ascribes the voluntary to nonhuman animals twice in *NE*.[3] In this context, he is concerned to advance a definition of the voluntary, according to which the voluntary is "what has its principle in the agent."[4] Aristotle understands this definition in such a way that the relevant principles can be either rational or nonrational. In this way, he argues that his definition is preferable to intellectualist definitions that construe only rational actions as voluntary. He is especially concerned to argue against a specific version of intellectualism, according to which actions will be voluntary only if they are done from the rational state of *prohairesis* or "choice." As Aristotle understands it, choice is a special kind of rational state: we act from choice when we have deliberated to the conclusion that we ought to do a given action with a view to attaining the object of our rational desire.[5] Aristotle recognizes that what is done from choice is voluntary. But he insists that the voluntary should not be identified only with what is done from choice. That is to say, in his view acting from choice is sufficient, but not necessary, for voluntary action. In opposition to the intellectualist view, he emphasizes the sufficiency of the nonrational capacities of appetite and spirit for voluntary action. He writes:

3. Aristotle's position in *EE* is less clear, and some readers argue that Aristotle did not attribute the voluntary to other animals in that work: see Irwin 1980, p. 127 and Nussbaum 1985, p. 380. For an opposite view, see Müller 2015, p. 226.

4. Aristotle says that the agent has the principle of a voluntary action in him (*NE* 1110a18, 1110b7, 1111a23, 1112b28, 1113b21; *EE* 1224b15; cf. *MM* 1187b6) or is the principle of such an action (*NE* 1112b32, 1113b18, 1139b5; *EE* 1222b19, 1222b29, 1223a5, 1223a15). These formulations are equivalent for my purposes here.

5. See Aristotle's definitions of choice at *NE* 1113a9-12 and *EE* 1226b2-9.

> (A) Since what comes about by force or on account of ignorance is involuntary, the voluntary would seem to be that of which the principle is in the agent, provided that he knows the particulars with which the action is concerned. For it is probably not correct to say that what comes about through spirit or appetite is involuntary. For, first, on this view none of the other animals will act voluntarily, nor will children. (*NE* 1111a22-27)[6]

Aristotle here argues against intellectualist definitions of the voluntary by drawing out a counterintuitive implication of such definitions: "on this view none of the other animals will act voluntarily." He claims that his own definition, according to which the voluntary is "that of which the principle is in the agent" is preferable, since it avoids this counterintuitive implication. Nonhuman animals can have the principles of their actions in themselves, and thus Aristotle's definition allows that they can act voluntarily. In opposition to the intellectualist who makes the voluntary depend on the rational powers found only in the human soul, Aristotle points to the powers of spirit and appetite – which humans share with other animals – as nonrational principles that can give rise to voluntary actions.

In a second passage from *NE*, Aristotle again appeals to the intuition that nonhuman animals can act voluntarily in the service of an argument about how the voluntary should be defined. He writes:

> (B) What is done from choice seems to be voluntary, but these are not the same, and the voluntary extends more widely. For children and the other animals possess the voluntary, but not choice. (*NE* 1111b7-8)

In this passage, Aristotle explicitly argues against the proposed definition of the voluntary that identifies the voluntary with what is done from choice. He opposes this definition on the grounds that it has the counterintuitive consequence that nonhuman animals will not possess the voluntary. Other animals lack the capacity for choice, but are able to act voluntarily, and so the proposed definition should be rejected. In these passages, Aristotle assumes that other animals act voluntarily. He uses this assumption as evidence against intellectualist definitions of the voluntary that make it depend on the distinctive rational capacities of human beings, and in favor of a definition that identifies the voluntary with what has its principle in the agent. These passages show that he understands the nonrational principles present in nonhuman animals as sufficient for them to act voluntarily.

In *Movement of Animals* (hereafter *MA*), Aristotle approaches the voluntary in other animals from a rather different angle. In that work, he argues that both human and nonhuman animals are self-movers, and one of his primary aims is to provide an account of self-movement that explains the

6. I understand the requirement that the agent "knows the particulars with which the action is concerned" as clarifying rather than adding to the definition of the voluntary as "that of which the principle is in the agent."

sense in which this is true. This account applies to all animals equally, and in developing it Aristotle uses the term *zōion*, which for him designates a genus of which rational and nonrational animals are species.[7] According to this account, an animal moves itself when it is moved by an object of its desire. In Aristotle's view, being moved in this way counts as self-movement, because the animal is moved by the object only insofar as it represents that object to itself as good via some form of cognition and desire.[8] The animal is thus moved, not by the object per se, but by its cognition of and desire for the object, and so moves itself. Forms of movement in an animal body that are not mediated by cognition and desire, such as those of the nutritive soul, do not count as self-movements.[9] Aristotle applies this generic account of self-movement to both human and nonhuman animals. At the same time, he recognizes that the cognitive powers of human and nonhuman animals differ.[10] While humans can cognize their objects of desire through reason, nonrational animals do so only through perception or *phantasia* ("imagination"). That said, Aristotle insists that acting on nonrational forms of cognition and desire is sufficient for self-movement.

Aristotle's discussions of self-movement and of the voluntary are approaches to the same topic in different terms. When Aristotle defines the voluntary as what has its principle in the agent, he is inviting us to see voluntary agents as self-movers, that is, as agents who are moved by principles within themselves. Conversely, he refers to his discussion of animal self-movement in *MA* as a discussion of voluntary movement. Thus he sums up that discussion by saying "We have explained how animals move with voluntary motions." (703b3). In these ways, I understand self-movement and the voluntary to be essentially equivalent notions. From this point of view, his argument in *MA* parallels the arguments we saw above from *NE*. In the latter treatise, as we have just seen, Aristotle argues that the nonrational powers of spirit and appetite can function as internal principles and thus can explain how nonrational animals act voluntarily. Likewise, in *MA*, Aristotle argues that nonrational animals can be self-movers, insofar as they can move in accordance with their nonrational forms of cognition and desire.

In *MA* 11, Aristotle underscores the possibility of voluntary motions in nonhuman animals by contrasting them with other motions that occur in an animal body. He writes:

> (C)We have explained how animals move with voluntary motions, and on account of what causes. But some of the parts are moved with certain involuntary motions, and many of them with nonvoluntary ones. By involun-

7. See *Categories* 1a7-8.
8. See *MA* 700b14-701a5 and *De Anima* (hereafter *DA*) 433a9-433b1.
9. See *Phys.* 253a11-21 and 259b1-16.
10. On these differences, see *NE* 1147b5-6 and 1149b35, and *EE* 1224a25-27.

tary, I mean, *e.g.*, movements of the heart and the genitals. For often these are moved when something is imagined [*phanentos tinos*], but without the command of mind [*nous*]. By nonvoluntary, I mean sleep and waking and respiration, and whatever else is of this kind. For neither imagination nor desire is unqualifiedly in control of these. [703b3-11]

In the final line of this passage, Aristotle identifies the nonrational capacity of imagination, together with desire, as sufficient for voluntary movement. He brings out the voluntary character of the movements controlled by these causes by comparing them with two other classes of movements, the involuntary (*akousion*) and the nonvoluntary (*ouk hekousion*).[11] Focus for now on the third class, the nonvoluntary. (I will return to the involuntary class in section 2.) Aristotle gives as examples of nonvoluntary movements "sleep and waking and respiration." These are operations of the nutritive soul, and so are not controlled by cognition and desire in the way that voluntary movements are.[12] As Aristotle puts it, explaining why these movements are nonvoluntary, "neither imagination nor desire is unqualifiedly in control of these." Aristotle's identification of imagination as a cognitive power capable of giving rise to voluntary movement allows nonrational animals to act voluntarily. In this way, we can see Aristotle's argument in the *MA* as coinciding with that in *NE*: in both cases, he affirms that nonhuman animals perform voluntary actions and argues that the distinctively human powers of the rational soul are not necessary for the voluntary.

Section 2

Aristotle's commitment to the claim that nonhuman animals act voluntarily is clear. Yet at the same time that claim seems to be in tension with certain other commitments of his. As a result, Aristotle is apparently committed to a contradiction, in which he affirms both that nonhuman animals act voluntarily and that only humans act voluntarily. Call the set of considerations that favor ascribing to Aristotle the first claim "set 1." This is the evidence we have just reviewed in section 1. Call the body of evidence that favors ascribing to him the second claim "set 2." We will now review the evidence in set 2. The position Aristotle is advocating in each set of evidence seems clear, as long as we take each of them on its own. The difficulty lies

11. Aristotle also distinguishes between the *akousion* and the *ouk hekousion* at *NE* 1110b18-24. Nussbaum 1985, p. 379 and Morel 2020, p. 446 regard the distinction in (C) as different from that in *NE*. The context in which Aristotle frames the distinction is different, but I take the distinction to have the same fundamental grounds: the involuntary is what is contrary to the principle in the agent, while the nonvoluntary is what is neither in accordance with it nor contrary to it.

12. At *NE* 1135b2, Aristotle similarly describes "many things we undergo by nature, *e.g.*, growing old or dying" as "neither voluntary nor involuntary."

in grasping how to read the two sets of evidence together so that they are consistent with each other.[13]

By way of introducing set 2, consider first the connection he draws between the voluntary and certain reactive attitudes. In *NE* III.1, Aristotle introduces this connection as follows:

> (D) Virtue is concerned with passions and actions. Among these, praise and blame are for those that are voluntary, but forbearance, and sometimes pity, for those that are involuntary. As a result, it is perhaps necessary for those inquiring about virtue to investigate the voluntary and the involuntary. (1109b30-34)[14]

In Aristotle's view, the voluntary is subject to praise and blame. We can and should be praised when we voluntarily act well and be blamed when we voluntarily act badly. Praise and blame are not appropriate, he argues, for what is involuntary: when an agent has acted involuntarily and, *e.g.*, caused harm to someone, he should receive instead the sympathetic responses that Aristotle calls *suggnomē* ("forbearance") and pity.[15] By the same token, an agent who has done something admirable, but involuntarily, *e.g.*, because he was forced to, is not to be praised. In saying that praise and blame are for the voluntary, I take Aristotle to mean that all voluntary actions are either praise- or blameworthy.[16]

As Aristotle notes in (D), the dependence of praise on the voluntary also gives the voluntary a close connection with the topic of virtue. According to Aristotle, virtue and vice are the proper objects of praise and blame, respectively. He puts forward this claim in the context of arguing that the virtues and vices are states rather than passions. He writes:

> (E)The virtues and vices are not passions, because we are not called good or bad on account of having passions, but we are so called according to our virtues and vices. Nor are we praised or blamed on account of our passions, for a person is not praised because he is afraid or angry, nor is he blamed

13. An anonymous reviewer for *Philosophie Antique* suggested that we might avoid the contradiction by appealing to the different contexts in which different pieces of evidence appear. From this point of view, the different claims that Aristotle makes in these different contexts might be explained by the different problems and goals that govern those different contexts. This approach is often a helpful one when reading Aristotle. Unfortunately it will not work in this case, since much of the evidence in set 2 comes from the same contexts as evidence in set 1.

14. Cf. *EE* 1223a9-20.

15. Note that not all involuntary actions receive forbearance: see *NE* 1136a5-9, which I discuss below.

16. We may presume that Aristotle restricts his attention to significant actions, and is not concerned with insignificant actions such as my idly touching the tip of my nose. Alternatively, we might read (D) as saying that voluntariness is only a necessary, and not a sufficient, condition for praise or blame. I consider a view of this kind in section 5 below.

> simply because he is angry, but because he is angry in a certain way. But we are praised or blamed according to our virtues and vices. (*NE* 1105b28-1106a3)[17]

Aristotle argues that virtue and vice are the proper objects of praise and blame, because they dispose us to feel the passions in certain ways: to be angry moderately, for example, or excessively. When we are praised or blamed on account of our passions, this is because we are feeling the relevant passions in specific way, on account of our virtue or vice.

Elsewhere he explains the connection between virtue and praise in terms of how virtue disposes us to act. He writes: "we praise the just and the courageous and in general those who are good, as well as virtue itself, on account of the actions and deeds it produces" (*NE* 1101a15-16), and again, "Praise belongs to virtue, since it makes us doers of what is admirable." (1101a31-32). Aristotle is here explicitly arguing that virtue is praised because of the actions it produces. But he implies that the converse relationship also holds true: our actions are praised because they accord with virtue, since virtue "makes us doers of what is admirable." Aristotle does not explicitly say so, but he could have given a corresponding account of vice: vice is the object of blame, because it makes us doers of shameful actions. Thus Aristotle can explain the dependence of praise and blame on virtue and vice in terms of either of passions or actions. Either way, the upshot is the same: if we are praised or blamed for what is voluntary, then what is voluntary must involve either virtue or vice.[18] If all voluntary actions are praise- or blameworthy, and praise and blame depend on virtue and vice, respectively, then virtue and vice are required for the voluntary. These considerations about reactive attitudes suggest that only human agents act voluntarily, since only human agents have virtues or vices. Here we see a first way that considerations from set 2 appear to contradict those in set 1.

Let us now turn to a second key piece of evidence in set 2, Aristotle's account of involuntary movements in (C). As a reminder, Aristotle gives in that passage the following description of one kind of involuntary movement: "By involuntary, I mean, *e.g.*, movements of the heart and the genitals. For often these are moved when something is imagined [*phanentos tinos*], but without the command of mind [*nous*]." Aristotle is thinking of an agent who

17. For the dependence of praise on virtue, see also *NE* 1101b15-32, *EE* 1219b8, cf. *MM* 1183b27.

18. A full defense of these claims about praise and blame would require showing how they can accommodate apparent counterexamples, including agents who are praised without having virtue (such as enkratics) and those who are blamed without having vice (such as akratics.) I take it that these agents are praised and blamed on account of their resemblance to the virtuous and the vicious, respectively. For example, *enkrateia*, like virtue, disposes us to act well in relation to bodily pleasures. Similar remarks would apply to the praise or blame of young people who are still in the process of forming their characters.

is moved by something he imagines, in a way that is contrary to what he rationally recognizes as appropriate. In these cases, the agent moves in accord with his imagination (in conjunction with some form of desire) and not his reason.[19] By noting that these movements take place without the command of mind, Aristotle implies that he is considering only human agents, who have *nous*, but can act against it, in accordance with their imagination.[20]

Aristotle describes this movement as involuntary, and we can appreciate the ethical thought motivating this description: it makes sense to say that an agent who is, *e.g.*, sexually excited by a mere stray image in his mind is "involuntarily excited," insofar as he wishes not to be. What is essential for us to note is what this passage implies about the conditions of voluntary action. On the basis of the evidence in set 1, we are led to conclude that the nonrational powers that humans share with other animals are sufficient for voluntary action. But in passage (C)'s description of involuntary movement, Aristotle appears to contradict this claim. Here we have a movement prompted by one of the agent's nonrational powers, and yet Aristotle describes the movement as involuntary. Insofar as Aristotle's ascriptions of the voluntary to nonhuman animals in set 1 turned on treating the nonrational powers as sufficient for the voluntary, he now seems to have taken that ascription back. This is a second kind of argument in set 2.

This line of argument is also supported by Aristotle's discussion of *thēriotēs* ("beastliness") in *NE* VII. Aristotle's treatment of this topic is brief and obscure, and he appears to include rather different phenomena under this heading.[21] But we can focus on one central form of beastliness with which he is concerned, namely human beings who lack rational capacities and act solely according to the cognitive capacities that we share with other animals. Aristotle believes that there are human beings who meet this description, including entire groups of non-Greek people. As he writes, "Among those who are foolish, the ones who lack reason by nature and live only by their senses are beastly, *e.g.*, certain distant groups of barbarians." (*NE* 1149a9-12) In this description, we are of course appalled by Aristotle's casual dismissal of entire nations of human beings as nonrational. But what is relevant for our purposes is the stance he takes on the question of whether these people are capable of acting voluntarily. For reasons I set out below, I take Aristotle to deny that they act voluntarily, and this denial constitutes further evidence in set 2. As in (C), Aristotle's discussion of beastliness implies that nonra-

19. On this possibility, see also see *DA* 429a4-8. In taking this involuntary movement to be prompted by desire in addition to imagination, I follow Charles 1984, p. 104, Morel 2004, p. 172, and Nussbaum 1985, p. 382, *contra* Corcilius 2008, p. 352.

20. Here I follow the view of Corcilius 2008, p. 358, *contra* that of Morel 2020, discussed below.

21. For a helpful introduction to some of the perplexities produced by this discussion, see Thorp 2003.

tional powers are not sufficient for voluntariness after all. He thus appears to be committed to the view that those powers are not sufficient for voluntary action, contradicting his claims in set 1.[22]

Aristotle regards beastliness as a kind of ethical defect, and he describes it as one of the conditions to be avoided in the realm of character.[23] But he takes care to distinguish it sharply from vice proper, arguing that beastliness is "different in kind from vice." (*NE* 1145a28)[24] Aristotle insists that vice is a failing in human nature, but he also recognizes it as a kind of standing possibility for human beings and an exercise of specifically human capacities. As Aristotle puts it, vice is "wickedness that is in accordance with the human." (*NE* 1149a17) By contrast, beastliness is a deprivation of humanity, specifically of the rational powers that distinguish human beings from other animals. This difference in kind between beastliness and vice supports the conclusion that beastliness is not voluntary. Since beastliness is different in kind from vice, and vice is the proper object of blame, we should conclude that beastliness is not blamed. If it is not blamed (or praised), then it is not voluntary.

The idea that beastliness is not voluntary is further supported by Aristotle's description of beastly agents as lacking reason, which he identifies as "the principle" of human actions. The vicious agent possesses reason, albeit in a corrupted form, and turns it to evil ends. The beastly agent, by contrast, lacks reason altogether. In lacking reason, Aristotle claims, the beastly agent lacks the principle of action proper to human beings. As he writes:

> (F) Beastliness is less [harmful] than vice, although more frightful. For what is best is not corrupted, as it is in the human, but is altogether lacking. It is like comparing something inanimate to what is animate, and asking which is more evil. Baseness that has no principle (and reason is the principle) is always less harmful... For a bad person can do ten thousand times more evil than a beast. (*NE* 1150a2-9)

In this passage, Aristotle argues that vice is more harmful than beastliness, since vicious agents, unlike beastly agents, retain the use of reason and so can plot evil. What is crucial for our purposes is another consequence he highlights here of the fact that beastly agents lack reason. Aristotle identifies reason as "the principle" in human actions, and argues that beastly agents lack this principle. Recall that Aristotle defines the voluntary as that of which the principle is in the agent. According to (F), the principle in a human agent is reason. Since beastly agents lack this principle, we should conclude that beastly agents are not capable of acting voluntarily.

22. For other interpreters who argue that at least some kinds of beastly actions are not voluntary, see Natali 2009, p. 123 and Thorp 2003, p. 79-80.

23. See *NE* 1145a16.

24. See also *NE* 1149a17-18.

The same view is further supported by Aristotle's description of "passion that is unnatural or inhuman" in *NE* V.8. Aristotle does not here explicitly say that he has beastliness in mind, but his description of this kind of passion corresponds to descriptions he elsewhere gives of beastliness.[25] Aristotle argues that this sort of passion gives rise to involuntary action. He writes:

> (G)Among involuntary actions, some receive forbearance and some do not. Whenever someone errs not only ignorantly, but due to ignorance, he receives forbearance. But whenever someone acts ignorantly, not due to ignorance, but due to passion that is unnatural or inhuman, he does not receive forbearance. (*NE* 1136a5-9)

Aristotle's aim in this passage is to explain why some involuntary actions receive forbearance and some do not. He explains that agents receive forbearance when they act "due to ignorance," but they do not receive forbearance when they do not act "due to ignorance" but instead "due to passion that is unnatural or inhuman."[26] Aristotle says that actions motivated by this sort of passion do not receive forbearance, but he does not spell out what attitude he thinks is appropriate in response to them. He might think that these actions are appropriately blamed.[27] But this claim would be surprising, given that in (D) Aristotle presents blame as appropriate only for voluntary actions. Alternatively, he might think that the appropriate attitude toward actions due to unnatural or inhuman passion is neither forbearance nor blame, but some third attitude, such as fear or avoidance. The latter line of thought is suggested by Aristotle's saying in (F) that beastliness is less harmful and less evil than vice, but "more frightful." In any case, for our purposes what is important is that he regards actions produced by this sort of passion as involuntary.[28] Since he thinks of agents who act from this sort of passion as beastly, this claim constitutes further evidence that he takes the nonrational powers he assigns to nonhuman animals to be insufficient for voluntary action, contrary to his claims in set 1.

Section 3

In order to avoid ascribing this contradiction to Aristotle, readers have developed three main strategies. Call the first strategy "widening," since it aims to construe key terms that figure in set 2 only in a wide sense, so that

25. See *NE* 1148b20-34.

26. For Aristotle's notion of acting "due to ignorance" (*di'agnoian*), see *NE* 1110b25-27 and *EE* 1225b7-11.

27. See Cooper 2013, p. 286-87 and Taylor 2016, p. 168-69.

28. It is not clear why Aristotle describes beastliness as involuntary, as opposed to nonvoluntary. Perhaps he supposes that (at least some) beastly agents retain reason while acting against it. If so, their actions would resemble the involuntary movements described in (C).

nonhuman animals can satisfy them.[29] For example, advocates of this strategy will respond to the first piece of evidence in set 2, which shows that Aristotle thinks of the voluntary as subject to praise and blame, by arguing that we should interpret him as using "praise" and "blame" in a wide sense, such that the actions of nonhuman animals are appropriate objects of these attitudes. The key claim of the widening strategy is that, in all of his discussions of the voluntary, Aristotle only understands by the voluntary something shared among humans and other animals, so that the difference between rational and nonrational animals never enters into judgments of voluntariness.

The idea that other animals are subject to praise and blame can be philosophically motivated in the following way: the point of praising and blaming is to modify the behavior of their object. Aristotle recognizes that the behavior of nonhuman animals can be modified by training.[30] It is plausible to suppose that this process will proceed in part through verbal cues, which we can think of as praising some forms of behavior ("What a good doggie!") and blaming others ("You naughty dog!"). In this way, we can see nonhuman animals as subject to praise and blame, and on this basis conclude that Aristotle's idea that the voluntary is subject to praise and blame does not contradict his ascription of the voluntary to them.

This strategy will be no help in avoiding the contradiction unless it can show that the terms in question are used in the exact same sense for human and nonhuman agents. Thus the widening strategy is committed to arguing that when Aristotle speaks of the voluntary as, *e.g.*, subject to praise and blame, he only ever means by these terms something we share with nonhuman animals. If Aristotle uses the relevant terms in a different sense in set 2 – for instance, if he regards the voluntary as subject to a kind of praise or blame that is distinctively human – then set 2 would still suggest that only human beings are capable of the voluntary, since set 2 will then be arguing, *e.g.*, that the voluntary is subject to praise or blame in a distinctively human sense. Thus advocates of widening need to argue not simply that Aristotle thinks we praise and blame nonhuman animals in some sense, but that we praise and blame them in the exact same way we praise and blame human agents. This conclusion is defended with rigorous consistency by Jean Roberts. Roberts writes:

> Humans (and animals) are responsible for their voluntary actions in the sense that their particular desires are at least a crucial part of the explanation for what happens. Because voluntary actions thus reflect the variable and changeable aspects of souls, it is appropriate to praise and blame them.

29. See Roberts 1989, p. 25, Sorabji 1993, p. 109-112, Bostock 2000, p. 105, Nussbaum 2001, p. 284, Cooper 2013, p. 267-268, Müller 2015, p. 220-226, and Carron 2019, p. 392.

30. See *History of Animals* (hereafter *HA*) 488b26, *Politics* (hereafter *Pol.*) 1332b3.

> These are the sorts of actions that, in principle, one can be trained or become habituated or be educated to do or not do. Praise and blame, punishment and reward, are part of the training and education. (1989: 25)

Roberts gives a paradigmatic example of the widening strategy as applied to Aristotle's claim that the voluntary is subject to praise and blame. She interprets this claim so that "praise" and "blame" refer to attitudes we could appropriately take toward nonhuman animals, and only those attitudes. So understood, praise and blame function as part of a process of training that aims to alter the desires and thus the behavior of an animal. These attitudes are appropriate simply insofar as the relevant desires are capable of being altered by this sort of process. For the purposes of this argument, it is essential that Aristotle draw no distinction between a process of training that might be applied to nonhuman animals and the cultivation of the virtues in human beings. Thus Roberts quite deliberately groups together being trained, becoming habituated, and being educated. In order for the widening strategy to work, Aristotle cannot draw any distinctions among these processes.

The widening strategy is philosophically motivated by a deep sense of the similarities between humans and other animals and a reasonable suspicion of the human tendency to overestimate the differences. The difficulty for the widening strategy as a reading of Aristotle is that he does not, in set 2, only use the relevant terms in such a way that nonhuman animals can satisfy them. This is clear in the case of praise and blame. To be sure, Aristotle thinks of nonhuman animals as capable of having their behavior, and perhaps even their desires, altered by training. He never describes this process as involving praise and blame, but no doubt he could acknowledge a sense of "praise" and "blame" that would describe something that happens in this process. The trouble is that this is not how he uses the terms in set 2. As (D) makes clear, Aristotle is concerned with praise and blame as directed at our states of character, that is, our virtues and vices. These states are distinctively human, since they involve choice, and this in turn requires reason.[31] Praising and blaming can be involved in the formation of these states. But that sort of praise and blame must aim, not merely at altering the agent's behavior or even his desires, but rather at inculcating in the agent a rational grasp of the value of certain ways of acting. Thus Aristotle's claim that the voluntary is subject to praise and blame cannot be interpreted in the wide sense required by Roberts and other proponents of the widening strategy.

It is true that Aristotle sometimes uses virtue and vice terms to describe the "character" of various species of nonhuman animals. Thus in *HA* I.2, he writes:

31. On virtue and vice as involving choice, see *NE* 1105a33, 1111b6-7, 1146b22, 1150a20, and 1151a6.

> (H) Some are mild (*praa*), sluggish, and easy-going, such as the cow, others are spirited, troublesome and hard to train, such as the wild boar. Some are careful (*phronima)* and cowardly (*deila*), such as deer and hares. Others are miserly (*aneleuthera*) and calculating, such as serpents, while others are generous (*eleuthera*), courageous (*andreia*) and brave, such as the lion. Some are haughty, wild, and calculating, such as the wolf... Some are shameless and mischievous, such as the fox, while others are spirited, affectionate and fawning, such as the dog. Some are mild and easily tamed, such as the elephant. Some are bashful and wary, like the goose, while others are envious and showy, such as the peacock. (488b14-24)[32]

In this passage, Aristotle employs many of the terms he uses to describe virtues and vices in his ethical writings to describe the behavior of nonhuman animals. Thus he describes cows as mild, deer as cowardly, serpents as miserly, and lions as courageous. But in ethical contexts he is clear that this use of virtue and vice terms to describe other animals is only metaphorical. He writes: "we call beasts temperate or intemperate only by way of metaphor, insofar as one kind of animal differs from another regarding its tendency toward violence, mischief, or appetite. For beasts are capable of neither choice nor reasoning." (*NE* 1149b32-35)[33] Aristotle affirms that virtues and vices strictly so called require rationality. Since praise and blame are directed at the virtues and vices, nonhuman animals cannot be proper objects of praise and blame, and so they cannot act voluntarily.

Above we saw how advocates of the widening strategy attempt to defuse the difficulty presented by the first kind of argument in set 2 by widening the meaning of "praise" and "blame," so that nonhuman animals can be subject to them. Advocates of this strategy likewise try to address the difficulty presented by *MA* 11 by widening the meaning of *nous* so that nonhuman animals can possess it. This approach has recently been advocated by Pierre-Marie Morel. He argues that the class of involuntary actions described in *MA* 11 does not belong to humans alone, but can also be found in nonhuman animals. On this interpretation, nonhuman animals, too, can be moved by their imagination either with or against their *nous.* Nonhuman animals will then act voluntarily when they act in accordance with their *nous*, understood in this wide sense. By this argument, Morel aims to avoid the unpalatable conclusion that nonrational animals cannot act voluntarily.

Morel attempts to support his claim by appealing to a number of passages from *DA* in which Aristotle ascribes to nonhuman animals a capacity for "discrimination" that guides their movements.[34] More broadly, he points to

32. See also *NE* 1141a28, where Aristotle says that *phronēsis* can be ascribed to nonrational animals.

33. For the idea that nonhuman animals do not possess virtues or vices properly speaking, see also *NE* 1116b30-1117a1, 1144b9-10 and 1145a26.

34. See *DA* 418a14, 426b10, and 432a15-17.

passages in which Aristotle treats the cognitive capacities of other animals as analogous to those of humans, such as *DA* 433a9, where Aristotle refers to *phantasia* as "*noēsis* of a sort." According to Morel, these passages indicate that Aristotle recognizes "the presence in every animal of a principal cognitive faculty which 'judges' or 'discriminates' what is pleasant and unpleasant, good and bad, and which is therefore fitted for inciting or directing desire." (2020: 451) In this way, he aims to make room for nonhuman animals to act voluntarily by giving *nous* a wide interpretation so that it refers, not to a distinctively human rational capacity, but to a general capacity for discrimination, one that we share with nonhuman animals.

The evidence cited by Morel shows that nonhuman animals' cognitive capacities, and in particular *phantasia*, play a role analogous to the role played by reason in human agents. But the analogy need amount to no more than this: that *phantasia* is the highest cognitive faculty determining the movements of nonhuman animals, just as reason is the highest cognitive faculty determining the movements of humans. What the evidence cited by Morel does not show is that there is anything in nonhuman animals analogous to the distinction that can open up in the human soul between *phantasia* and *nous*, such that the former could operate with, or against, the latter. We saw that in the case of praise and blame, the widening strategy fails because, in the context of set 2, Aristotle clearly means something distinctively human by those terms. The same is true here. In other contexts, Aristotle might use *nous* or *noēsis* with a wide sense so that these terms can refer to capacities possessed by nonhuman animals. But in those cases, he identifies *nous* with *phantasia*. By contrast, in (C) he opposes *nous* to *phantasia*. Thus he cannot be using *nous* in that wide sense there. In (C), Aristotle claims that a human agent who acts on imagination and not *nous* fails to act voluntarily. That claim seems to imply that the nonrational powers possessed by nonhuman animals are not sufficient for the voluntary. The widening strategy attempts to avoid this conclusion by arguing that *nous* should be understood in this context to refer to a cognitive power humans share with other animals. But this strategy cannot work, because Aristotle opposes *nous*, in this context, to imagination. The widening strategy thus fails in its attempt to avoid reading (C) as implying that the movements of nonhuman animals are not voluntary.[35]

35. No advocate of the widening strategy that I am aware of has engaged with the difficulties presented by Aristotle's account of beastliness, and it is not clear how they could do so. Surely there is no analogue of beastliness in beasts!

Section 4

The widening strategy falls short because it fails to register the full weight of the evidence in set 2. The evidence in set 2 shows that Aristotle sometimes treats distinctively human capacities as necessary for the voluntary, and his references to those capacities in those contexts cannot be properly construed to bear a wide sense such that nonhuman animals can possess them. As a different approach to avoiding the contradiction, we might see whether we have better success instead by offering an alternative reading of the evidence in set 1. One strategy for doing this is to argue that, in set 1, Aristotle ascribes the voluntary to nonhuman animals only metaphorically. According to this strategy, the actions of other animals are similar in certain ways to those of human agents, and Aristotle's ascription of the voluntary to the former can be seen as warranted simply in light of those similarities. But this usage on his part should not be confused with endorsement of the claim that these animals are capable of voluntary action in a literal or proper sense. This metaphorical strategy is thus the counterpart of the widening strategy: where the widening strategy sought to expand the meaning of key terms in set 2 so that nonhuman animals could satisfy them, the metaphorical strategy insists on a narrow reading of those terms. Proponents of this strategy take the narrow reading of these terms to entail that only humans are capable of genuine voluntary action, and so they conclude that Aristotle's ascription of the voluntary to nonhuman animals must be metaphorical. We can see this approach as building on the point about character that I made above: Aristotle explicitly marks his ascription of virtues and vices to nonhuman animals as metaphorical. Observing the close connection between the voluntary and character, proponents of the metaphorical strategy argue that we should understand Aristotle's ascription of the voluntary to nonhuman animals as likewise metaphorical.

This strategy has found a modern advocate in Sarah Broadie.[36] But its most sophisticated presentation remains that in Thomas Aquinas. In *Summa Theologiae* Ia IIae q.6 a.2, Aquinas sets himself the question whether the voluntary exists in nonrational animals. He is here considering the question in his own voice, and not as a commentator on Aristotle. Strictly speaking he does not present the answer he offers as an interpretation of Aristotle. That said, Aquinas builds his account out of Aristotelian materials, and in that sense it can be understood as stating his view of what is required in order to bring coherence to Aristotle's commitments. Aquinas is moved by both kinds of arguments we set out above under set 2: that the voluntary is subject to praise and blame, and that it requires distinctively human cognitive capacities. He regards both of these arguments as offering persuasive reasons to

36. See Broadie 1991, p. 125.

say that nonhuman animals are not capable of voluntary action. At the same time, he notes that this argument appears to contradict the explicit teaching of Aristotle, according to which, as Aquinas puts it, "nonrational animals participate in the voluntary."

Aquinas resolves the apparent contradiction by arguing that nonrational animals possess the voluntary only in an imperfect sense. To do this, he turns to Aristotle's definition of the voluntary in *NE*. Aristotle there defines the voluntary, as we saw in (A), as "that of which the principle is in the agent, provided that he knows the particulars with which the action is concerned." (1111a23-24) Aquinas notes that this definition implies that some form of cognition is required for the voluntary. Aquinas's first step is to interpret this cognitive aspect of the definition as requiring what he calls "knowledge of the end." His second step is to argue that nonhuman animals possess this knowledge only in an "imperfect" sense. On this basis, he concludes that nonhuman animals possess the voluntary only in a similarly imperfect sense. He writes:

> The nature of the voluntary requires that the principle of the act be internal, with some cognition of the end. But cognition of the end comes in two degrees, perfect and imperfect. Perfect cognition of the end exists when the end is not merely apprehended, but there is also cognition of the grounds for the end, and of the fitness of the means to the end. This cognition of the end belongs only to rational nature. But imperfect cognition of an end is achieved by simple apprehension of the end, without cognition of the grounds of the end or the fitness of the means. This cognition of an end is found in nonrational animals, through their senses and imagination.

We can see Aquinas's view as motivated by Aristotle's insistence that nonrational cognition is not sufficient for the voluntary. As we saw above, taking that insistence seriously creates a difficulty for ascribing voluntary actions to nonhuman animals, since acting on nonrational cognition is all nonhuman animals are capable of. Aquinas resolves the difficulty by introducing a distinction that Aristotle does not, between the perfect and imperfect voluntary. His goal is to preserve the narrow reading of set 2, as against those who, following the widening strategy, would take Aristotle's ascription of the voluntary to nonhuman animals as a pretext to water down the distinctively rational character of human agency. He assumes that Aristotle's ascription of the voluntary to nonhuman animals, if taken literally, is a threat to this goal. Thus he is compelled to interpret that ascription as mere metaphor. Note that the imperfect voluntary that Aquinas ascribes to nonhuman animals is not a species of the voluntary. It is, rather, a mere likeness of the voluntary. As he puts it, "the voluntary is attributed to nonrational animals on account of a certain similarity" that their actions possess to voluntary actions properly so called.

The metaphorical strategy learns from the failure of the widening strategy. The widening strategy failed because Aristotle sees the cognitive capacities of human and nonhuman animals as deeply different, and he regards this difference as relevant to his treatments of the voluntary. We cannot resolve the contradiction by doing away with these differences, on pain of losing much that Aristotle wants to hold onto. The metaphorical strategy is an improvement over the widening strategy, in its insistence on those differences. Yet it falls into the opposite error, of supposing that those differences are incompatible with other animals possessing the voluntary. To avoid flatly contradicting Aristotle's clear words in set 1, the metaphorical strategy proposes to interpret those words so that they are to be taken not literally but only metaphorically. Proponents of this strategy can appeal to the model of Aristotle's metaphorical ascription of character to other animals. But they do so at their peril. For Aristotle's treatment of character shows that he is entirely capable of marking his usage as metaphorical when he means it to be. The fact that he issues no such disclaimer in set 1 is a strong reason for thinking that he did not regard his use of *hekōn* and related terms as metaphorical there. Further, note that Aristotle, in (A) and (B), uses the fact that nonhuman animals can act voluntarily as premises in an argument about how the voluntary should be defined. This is hardly what we would expect him to do, if he thought that they possessed the voluntary only metaphorically. The metaphorical strategy may be motivated by a reasonable philosophical view about other animals: their cognitive limitations mean that they only possess a likeness of voluntary agency, not the real thing. But it forces too unnatural a reading onto Aristotle's words for it to be compelling as an interpretation of Aristotle.

Section 5

The metaphorical strategy was an improvement over the widening strategy, insofar as the former appreciates the gravity of set 2 in a way that the latter does not. It recognizes the deep differences that Aristotle sees between the capacities of humans and other animals, and the relevance of those differences to his treatment of the voluntary. But it recognizes those points at the cost of giving a strained reading of set 1, which it can only construe, implausibly, as metaphorical. Is there a way to read Aristotle that takes set 1 and set 2 seriously, while avoiding the contradiction? The most prominent strategy for doing so in the literature is to suggest that Aristotle tacitly distinguishes between voluntariness and moral responsibility.[37] This view aims to bring coherence to our two sets of evidence by treating them as being about

37. See Meyer 2011, 1993, p. 52. Irwin 1980, p. 126 develops a similar view, but he is less confident that Aristotle avoids the contradiction and offers his view more as a sympathetic revision of Aristotle's approach.

different topics. Set 1 is about the voluntary, understood as something we share with nonhuman animals. Set 2 is about moral responsibility, understood as something that is distinctively human, and which requires distinctively human rational capacities. On this view, the voluntary is necessary but not sufficient for, *e.g.*, praiseworthy action: the latter requires in addition that the agent meet the conditions of moral responsibility. Proponents of this strategy identify those conditions with the capacity to form a virtuous or vicious character, which in turn depends on the rational capacity for choice. Explaining the distinction, Susan Sauvé Meyer writes:

> Voluntariness, in [Aristotle's] view, is a necessary but not a sufficient condition for moral responsibility. In addition to voluntariness, a morally responsible agent must have dispositions that satisfy the conditions for being genuinely temperate, brave, cowardly, just, etc. In his view, only agents who have a moral character are morally responsible for their voluntary actions. (1993/2011: 52)

The philosophical outlines of the distinction that Meyer wants to draw are clear. According to Meyer, voluntariness is essentially a matter of causal responsibility: our actions are voluntary when we (as opposed to someone or something else) are the cause of them. Both humans and other animals can be the cause of their actions, and so both can act voluntarily. By contrast, moral responsibility involves assessment of the agent's character. When we ask whether an agent was morally responsible for her action, we ask not merely whether she was causally responsible, but also whether her action reflects on her character, revealing her to be virtuous or vicious in some way. Because only human beings have character in the proper sense, only human beings can be morally responsible.[38]

This strategy has an intuitive philosophical appeal. But it is not clear how it is supposed to work as an interpretation of Aristotle. For Aristotle has no word that might be translated "morally responsible" other than *hekōn*, and we have already used this for "voluntary." In the places where these readers see Aristotle as speaking about moral responsibility – for instance, when he speaks about the conditions of praise and blame – he speaks about what we do *hekōn*. They do not explicitly say so, but proponents of this strategy must assume that Aristotle uses this and related terms ambiguously, so that sometimes they refer to what they call voluntariness, and at other times to what they call moral responsibility. Thus I designate this the strategy of ambiguity.

This strategy has the advantage of taking both sets of evidence seriously. It accommodates both, and avoids the appearance that they contradict each other, by treating them as concerned with different topics. Like the others, this strategy may have a reasonable philosophical view behind it: perhaps

38. In keeping with this strategy, Irwin 1980, p. 127 proposes that beastly humans cannot be morally responsible, but they can act voluntarily.

the distinction between the conditions of voluntariness and those of moral responsibility is a useful one in ethics or the philosophy of action. The problem is that it is not plausible as a reading of Aristotle. The fundamental problem with the ambiguity strategy is that it is unable to see the unity of the concept that Aristotle traces through his use of *hekōn* and related terms. When Aristotle wishes to speak about the conditions of praise and blame, for example, he uses *hekōn*, the very same term that he uses when he is describing animal self-movement, including in nonhuman animals. Aristotle sees a consistent pattern in these uses of the term: there is a single concept that he is tracking across all of these contexts. The ambiguity strategy is unable to get that concept into view, and instead takes his uses of *hekōn* to designate two different concepts. As a result, it makes for an unsatisfying reconstruction of Aristotle's thinking.

Section 6

We've now reviewed the three main strategies that Aristotle interpreters have used to reconcile set 1 and set 2 and thus avoid the contradiction. Having seen all three strategies fail, we might be tempted to conclude that Aristotle's position simply is contradictory, and leave it at that. But this conclusion is premature. There is a fourth possible strategy which has not yet been explored, but which represents our best chance to bring coherence to Aristotle's claims.[39]

According to this alternative, Aristotle understands the voluntary as a genus, which comes in rational and nonrational species. Reading Aristotle in this way captures the advantages of the ambiguity strategy, without its pitfalls. The ambiguity strategy was in a sense correct to see set 1 and set 2 as concerned with different topics. But it went wrong by supposing that Aristotle's use of *hekōn* was therefore ambiguous. If we understand *hekōn* and related terms to designate a genus, then we can regard set 1 and set 2 as concerned with different topics, while preserving the unity of Aristotle's concept. On this reading, set 1 is about the voluntary as a genus. In those contexts, Aristotle can use examples of either rational or nonrational agents to illustrate the nature of the genus. By contrast, set 2 is about the rational species of the voluntary. Aristotle's discussions of the voluntary are primarily about human agents, and they are deeply concerned with the implications of human rationality for the voluntary in human beings. Thus when

39. The closest analogue to my argument in recent Aristotle literature is Fernandez 2014. He argues that Aristotle's concept of animal movement is best understood as a determinable of which rational and nonrational animal movement are determinants. In my view, the genus-species relation better captures the logic of the concept, since we can give differentia (rational/non-rational) for the species. For a helpful account of the genus-species relation in a related context, see Caston 2008.

he speaks of the voluntary as the object of praise and blame, for example, we can assume that he has the specifically human voluntary in mind. Similarly, when he describes beastly human beings as acting involuntarily, he does this not because he means to deny that beasts act voluntarily, but because beastly humans do not exercise the specific capacities necessary for voluntary action in a human being. Taking the two sets of evidence in this way, we can avoid the appearance that they contradict each other, while preserving the unity of the topic that Aristotle treats across those texts. Aristotle always thinks of the voluntary as what has its principle in the agent. In set 2, he simply restricts his attention to the kind of principle that is appropriate for a human agent.

As a genus, the voluntary is, precisely as Aristotle defines it, "that of which the principle is in the agent." Everything *hekousion* meets this definition. But the definition is satisfied by different kinds of agents in different ways. This is because the key concept in the definition – that of a principle – applies differently across those different kinds. In human beings, the principle is rational, and so in the human case only actions that engage our rational capacities count as voluntary. These features of human agency account for the evidence in set 2, which pertains to the voluntary as it is found in specifically human actions. It is because the principle in the human is rational that human voluntary actions are subject to praise and blame and involve the virtues and vices of character. In nonhuman animals, on the other hand, the principle is nonrational, and so in their case actions that engage only nonrational capacities can be voluntary. It is because the principle in nonhuman animals is nonrational that they can act voluntarily simply by exercising the nonrational powers of spirit, appetite, perception and imagination. In this way, we can take both set 1 and set 2 seriously, without privileging either at the expense of the other, and without doing violence to the unity of Aristotle's concept.

The strongest evidence for thinking that Aristotle uses *hekōn* and related terms generically comes from his similar use of *zōion*. As I noted in section 1, Aristotle uses this term to designate a genus of which rational and nonrational animals are species. From Aristotle's point of view, *zōion* is not ambiguous, despite the fact that it is used to refer to both rational and nonrational animals. These two types of animals are fundamentally different, and they possess different basic psychological capacities. Yet Aristotle can use *zōion* to give an account of animal self-movement that operates at a level of generality prior to the distinction between rational and nonrational. At this generic level, he can say that animals move themselves when they move toward an object of their desire on the basis of their cognition of that object. Aristotle regards this account as valid, despite the fact that it does not attend to the distinction between rational and nonrational forms of movement. We can, if we wish, descend from the genus to its species and describe what self-movement looks like in a rational as opposed to a non-rational animal. When we do that, we will see that self-movement in these two cases looks rather different. Self-movement in rational animals involves rational powers, whereas self-movement in nonrational animals does not. Nonetheless there is a valid account of animal self-movement as such that can be given at the generic level.

I have argued above that for Aristotle voluntary movement is equivalent to self-movement. Given that Aristotle's account of self-movement is generic in the way I have described, we should expect that his account of voluntary movement will be similarly generic. Aristotle can give a generic account of the voluntary, akin to his generic account of self-movement. According to that generic account, the voluntary is simply "that of which the principle is in the agent." This account does not attend to the difference between rational and nonrational action, because it does not need to. It holds perfectly well at a level of generality that is higher than this difference. If we wish, we can attend to this difference, moving from the genus to its species. Then we see that voluntary action looks different in the different species: in rational agents, it involves rational powers, but in nonrational agents it does not. As a result, nonrational capacities are sufficient to make action voluntary in nonrational agents, but not in rational agents. Nevertheless there is a perfectly consistent account of the voluntary at the generic level: that of which the principle is in the agent. How we apply this account differs between rational and nonrational agents, because the internal principles in these types of agents differ. We go wrong only when we confuse these logical levels, and suppose that the conditions of voluntariness proper to one species are definitive for the voluntary in general.

Taking Aristotle to use *hekōn* and related terms generically allows us to remove the contradiction and avoid the pitfalls of the other strategies discussed above. It avoids the failing of the widening strategy, which was to lose feeling for the distinctness of the voluntary in human beings as opposed to other animals. In human beings, the voluntary does involve rationality, in ways that we should not lose sight of simply because the voluntary can also be realized in a way that does not involve rationality, as we see in nonrational animals. It avoids the failing of the metaphorical strategy, because it preserves the sense that Aristotle ascribes the voluntary to nonhuman animals literally and not metaphorically. According to the generic strategy, Aristotle thinks of the voluntary in nonhuman animals as a full and genuine instance of the voluntary. The movements of nonhuman animals are voluntary in their own right, and are not so called merely by way of a resemblance they have to the voluntary actions of humans. When nonhuman animals act in accordance with their (nonrational) internal principles, the result is voluntary action, full stop. The metaphorical strategy is right to reject the widening strategy and insist on the rational character of properly human action. But it fails to bring coherence to Aristotle's commitments, insofar as it upholds the rationality of human action at the cost of failing to see how the movements of nonhuman animals can be voluntary in their own right. Finally, the generic strategy succeeds where the ambiguity strategy fails, since it gives a unified account of the concept Aristotle is tracing through his applications of *hekōn* to both human and nonhuman agents. Proponents of the ambiguity strategy are correct in arguing that Aristotle distinguishes between the voluntary as such and the form of rational agency involved in the exercise of virtues and vices. But they misconstrue the nature of this distinction, treating the latter as if it were something added on top of the voluntary. Properly understood, Aristotle holds that rational agency is a species of the voluntary, the species proper to rational agents. It differs from the voluntary as such, not as something added to it, but rather because the voluntary as such is a genus containing all forms of animal self-movement and should not be identified with only one of its species. Reading Aristotle in this way, we can make sense of the fact that he uses *hekōn* and related terms to describe both something we share with nonhuman animals and something distinctively human.

Conclusion

In this essay, my aim has been to explain how Aristotle can consistently claim that nonhuman animals act voluntarily. Aristotle is clearly committed to this claim, and yet it seems inconsistent with other claims he makes which suggest that the voluntary requires rationality. He claims that the voluntary is subject to certain reactive attitudes that presume rationality on the part of their objects, and he denies that the exercise of nonrational powers is sufficient to make action voluntary. To remove the appearance of contradiction, we need to grasp the logic at work in Aristotle's use of *hekōn* and related terms. I considered three familiar candidates for doing this – the strategies of widening, metaphor, and ambiguity – and argued that each of them fails to fully capture the coherence of Aristotle's commitments. As an alternative to these approaches, I proposed that Aristotle treats *hekōn* and related terms as designating a genus that exists in rational and nonrational species. This generic conception of the voluntary is supported by Aristotle's generic accounts of animal self-movement. Once we read Aristotle in this way, we can see why he describes the voluntary in human beings as requiring distinctively human capacities, without reading those descriptions as excluding the possibility of voluntary action in a specifically nonrational form in nonhuman animals.

BIBLIOGRAPHY

BOSTOCK, D. 2000 : *Aristotle's Ethics*, Oxford.

BROADIE, S. 1991 : *Ethics with Aristotle*, Oxford.

CARRON, P. 2019 : « Aristotle on Blaming Animals: Taking the Hardline Approach on Voluntary Action in the *Nicomachean Ethics* III.1-5 », *Epochē*, 23/2, p. 381-97.
DOI: 10.5840/epoche2019131129

CASTON, V. 2008 : « How Hylomorphic Can You Get ? Comment on D. Charles, 'Aristotle's Psychological Theory' », dans J. Cleary et G. M. Gurtler (éd.), *Proceedings of the Boston Area Colloquium in Ancient Philosophy*, 24, p. 30-49.

CHARLES, D. 1984 : *Aristotle's Philosophy of Action*, Ithaca, NY.

COOPER, J. 2013 : « Aristotelian Responsibility », dans B. Inwood (éd.), *Oxford Studies in Ancient Philosophy*, vol. 45, p. 265-312.

CORCILIUS, K. 2008 : *Streben und Bewegen: Aristoteles' Theorie der animalischen Ortsbewegung*, Berlin.

FERNANDEZ, P. 2014 : « Reasoning and the Unity of Aristotle's Account of Animal Motion », dans B. Inwood (éd.), *Oxford Studies in Ancient Philosophy*, 47, p. 151-203.

IRWIN, T. H. 1980 : « Reason and Responsibility in Aristotle », dans A. O. Rorty (éd.), *Essays on Aristotle's Ethics*, Berkeley, p. 117-156.

MEYER, S. S. 2011 : *Aristotle on Moral Responsibility : Character and Cause*, Oxford (1e éd. 1993).

MOREL, P.-M. 2004 : « Volontaire, involontaire et non-volontaire dans le chapitre 11 du *DMA* d'Aristote », dans A. Laks et M. Rashed (éd.), *Aristote et le mouvement des animaux : dix études sur le* De motu animalium, Villeneuve d'Ascq, p. 167-184.

MOREL, P.-M. 2020 : « Voluntary or Not ? The Physiological Perspective *MA* 11 », dans C. Rapp et O. Primavesi (éd.), *Aristotle's* De Motu Animalium. *Symposium Aristotelicum*, Oxford, p. 445-471.

MÜLLER, J. 2015 : « Agency and Responsibility in Aristotle's *Eudemian Ethics* », *Phronesis*, 60/2, p. 206-251.

NATALI, C. 2009 : « *Nicomachean Ethics* VII.5-6 : Beastliness, Irascibility, *Akrasia* », dans C. Natali (éd.), *Aristotle:* Nicomachean Ethics, *Book VII. Symposium Aristotelicum*, Oxford, p. 103-129.

NUSSBAUM, M. C. 1985 : *Aristotle's* De Motu Animalium, Princeton (1st Princeton paperback printing, with corrections).

NUSSBAUM, M. C. 2001 : *The Fragility of Goodness : Luck and Ethics in Greek Tragedy and Philosophy*, Cambridge (1ère éd. 1986).

ROBERTS, J. 1989 : « Aristotle on Responsibility for Action and Character », *Ancient Philosophy*, 9/1, p. 23-36.
DOI: 10.5840/ancientphil19899123

SORABJI, R. 1993 : *Animal Minds and Human Morals: The Origins of the Western Debate*, Ithaca, N.Y.

THORP, J. 2003 : « Aristotle on Brutishness », *Dialogue*, 42, p. 673-94.
DOI: 10.1017/S0012217300005709

DIRE L'ACTION CYNIQUE

Ascèse et anecdotes chez Diogène Laërce

Julien Decker
Docteur en philosophie de l'université Bordeaux Montaigne
A.T.E.R. à l'université Rouen Normandie, laboratoire ERIAC
julien.decker@univ-rouen.fr

Résumé. Le cynisme comme philosophie des actes permet-il de penser une théorie de l'action ? Son absence de système et le foisonnement d'anecdotes contrarient a priori toute description de l'action morale. Pourtant, la théorie de l'ascèse transmise par Diogène Laërce fournit quelques réponses sur les dispositions nécessaires à l'action : développer la force du corps et de l'âme, acquérir la santé et l'autosuffisance, façonner par l'habitude une endurance contre les coups du sort et faire usage de ses représentations. Toutefois, le geste ascétique est souvent associé à une monstration de l'endurance et donc à un spectacle au point d'égarer les communautés cyniques dans la simple reproduction de l'anecdotique. Cette étude cherche donc à confronter l'action à l'anecdote et formule l'hypothèse que le texte de Diogène Laërce peut s'inspirer des mises en garde adressées aux cyniques exubérants.

Abstract. *Does Cynicism as a philosophy of action make it possible to develop a theory of action? The absence of a system and the abundance of anecdotes a priori thwart any description of moral action. Yet Diogenes Laertius's testimony about asceticism provides some answers about dispositions which are necessary for action: developing strength of body and soul, acquiring health and self-sufficiency, shaping endurance against the blows of fate through habit and making use of one's representations. However, ascetic gestures are often associated with a display of endurance and therefore with a show, so that cynical communities are astrayed into simple reproduction of anecdotes. This study therefore seeks to compare action with anecdotes, and offers the hypothesis that Diogenes Laertius's text may be inspired by warnings addressed to exuberant Cynics.*

Philosophie antique, n°24 (2024), 91-122

L'opposition entre λόγος et ἔργον, discours et acte, est un lieu commun, déjà présent dans les témoignages relatifs à Socrate[1] et déployé dans la tradition cynique[2]. Cette opposition intervient en particulier dans des procédés de dérision de théories abstruses : Diogène moque, par exemple, la théorie des Idées platonicienne quand il affirme voir la table et non la Table en soi[3], ou les sophismes mégariques quand il réfute l'argument cornu en se touchant le front et l'impossibilité du mouvement en marchant[4]. Une anecdote met ainsi en scène Diogène et son disciple Hégésias qui désire d'abord lire les livres de son maître :

1. On peut penser à ce moment des *Mémorables* de Xénophon où Socrate s'érige en exemple du juste et où tant l'acte que le discours sont objets d'une monstration : « - Eh bien, Hippias, répondit-il, ne t'es-tu pas aperçu que je n'ai de cesse de montrer ce qui me paraît juste ? – Et en quoi, demanda-t-il, consiste ton discours ? – Ce n'est pas par un discours que je le montre, répondit-il, mais par des actes. N'es-tu pas d'avis que l'acte est plus convaincant que la parole ? » (Xénophon, *Memorabilia*, IV, 4, 10, trad. L.-A. Dorion, éd. Bandini : - Τί δέ, ὦ Ἱππία ; ἔφη, οὐκ ᾔσθησαι ὅτι ἐγὼ ἃ δοκεῖ μοι δίκαια εἶναι οὐδὲν παύομαι ἀποδεικνύμενος ; - Καὶ ποῖος δή σοι, ἔφη, οὗτος ὁ λόγος ἐστίν ; - Εἰ δὲ μὴ λόγῳ, ἔφη, ἀλλ' ἔργῳ ἀποδείκνυμαι· ἢ οὐ δοκεῖ σοι ἀξιοτεκμαρτότερον τοῦ λόγου τὸ ἔργον εἶναι ;).

2. Voir Maxime de Tyr, *Orationes*, XXXVI, 5 ; Philon d'Alexandre, *Quid omnis probus liber sit*, 96. Voir également, concernant Antisthène, Diogène Laërce (= DL) VI, 11, éd. Dorandi et *Socratis et Socraticorum Reliquiae* (= *SSR*), éd. Giannantoni, V A 134 : « La vertu est dans les actes et n'a pas besoin de plus longs discours ni de connaissances » (Τήν τε ἀρετὴν τῶν ἔργων εἶναι, μήτε λόγων πλείστων δεομένην μήτε μαθημάτων). La prééminence des actes sur les discours et sur les connaissances renforce l'idée d'un héritage entre Antisthène et Diogène ; voir Fuentes González 2013, p. 226 : « *Decir que los antiguos griegos conectaron muy estrechamente la filosofía con la vida de los hombres es una afirmación que puede resultar válida como principio general y que sin duda alcanza un mayor sentido a medida que nos acercamos a la figura de Sócrates y a toda la filosofía posterior. Sin embargo, una afirmación semejante no resulta en ningún caso tan significativa y radicalmente cierta como cuando hablamos de la filosofía que protagonizaron los llamados 'cínicos'* ». Le chercheur reconnaît à Diogène un caractère plus pratique de sa philosophie (*ibid*., p. 263).

3. Voir DL VI, 53 (= *SSR* V B 62).

4. Voir DL VI, 38-39 (= *SSR* V B 479). Pour l'analyse de cette condamnation cynique, voir Bénatouïl 2011, p. 165-166.

> À Hégésias qui le priait de consulter (χρῆσαί) l'un de ses écrits, Diogène répondit : « Pauvre que tu es, Hégésias ! Quand il s'agit de figues, tu ne prends pas des figues peintes, mais des vraies ; en revanche, quand il s'agit d'ascèse, tu négliges l'ascèse véritable (ἀληθινὴν) pour te précipiter sur celle que l'on trouve dans les livres. »[5]

L'analogie entre peinture et écriture est facilitée en grec par le verbe γράφειν qui exprime les deux actions et rapproche ainsi l'écriture de l'idée d'illusion picturale[6]. L'ascèse que l'on restitue dans les livres n'est qu'une pâle copie de celle que l'on réalise par ses actes : c'est elle qui nourrit celui qui la pratique, de même que seules des figues cueillies d'un arbre contenteront les estomacs.

Les écrits que mentionne la chrie sont-ils l'œuvre de Diogène ou seulement ses possessions ? Dans le récit d'Eubule, nous apprenons que Diogène, devenu esclave et chargé de l'éducation des enfants de Xéniade, intègre, au sein d'une ascèse adaptée aux plus jeunes, l'apprentissage par cœur de ses propres écrits[7]. I. Gugliermina, après avoir remarqué que Diogène ne fait pas partie de la liste laërtienne des philosophes qui « n'ont absolument rien écrit »[8], conclut ainsi que Hégésias demande à lire l'un des ouvrages de Diogène lui-même[9]. Or, le cynisme rejetait le cursus général des études[10] et la lecture d'ouvrages[11] et ne semble pas s'être institutionnalisé dans une école[12].

Pourtant, le catalogue laërtien des œuvres d'Antisthène est très fourni[13]. En ce qui concerne Diogène, si Sosicrate et Satyros affirment qu'aucun livre n'est de lui, deux listes sont présentées[14], la deuxième étant, selon l'avis de von Fritz, d'inspiration stoïcienne[15]. De façon plus générale, les témoignages

5. DL VI, 48 (= *SSR* V B 188) : Ἡγησίου παρακαλοῦντος χρῆσαί τι αὐτῷ τῶν συγγραμμάτων, "μάταιος," ἔφη, "τυγχάνεις, ὦ Ἡγησία, ὃς ἰσχάδας μὲν γραπτὰς οὐχ αἱρῇ, ἀλλὰ τὰς ἀληθινάς· ἄσκησιν δὲ παριδὼν τὴν ἀληθινὴν ἐπὶ τὴν γεγραμμένην ὁρμᾷς."

6. À la suite du mythe de Theuth, Socrate critique l'écriture en se référant à la peinture (Platon, *Phaedrus*, 275d).

7. DL VI, 30 (= *SSR* V B 70) : τῶν αὐτοῦ Διογένους.

8. DL I, 16 : οἱ δ' ὅλως οὐ συνέγραψαν.

9. Gugliermina 2006, p. 142.

10. Voir DL VI, 27-28 (= *SSR* V B 374) ; VI, 73 (= *SSR* V B 370) ; Stobée II, 31, 118 éd. Hense (= *SSR* V B 373) ; *Gnomologium Parisinum* 17 (= *SSR* V B 437). On trouve ce rejet dans la doxographie cynique générale : « Ils repoussent également les disciplines du cursus général » (DL VI, 103 = *SSR* V A 161, trad. Goulet-Cazé : Παραιτοῦνται δὲ καὶ τὰ ἐγκύκλια μαθήματα).

11. DL VI, 103 (= *SSR* V A 161).

12. I. Gugliermina (2006, p. 96) réfute l'importance que les textes accordent au Cynosarges comme lieu de l'enseignement cynique. Voir DL VI, 13 (= *SSR* V A 22).

13. DL VI, 15-18 (= *SSR* V A 41).

14. DL VI, 80 (= *SSR* V B 117).

15. Voir von Fritz 1926, p. 54-60 ; Giannantoni 1990, vol. 4, p. 461-484.

convergent pour faire d'Antisthène, de Diogène et de Cratès des auteurs[16]. Dès lors, étudier le cynisme oblige à affronter, comme propose O. Flores-Júnior, « l'apparente dissonance entre la théorie et la pratique des cyniques, c'est-à-dire leur opinion négative sur l'écriture et leur activité littéraire assez extensive »[17].

Ce paradoxe cynique nous confronte à un problème d'histoire de la philosophie : quand bien même une école philosophique privilégierait de façon exclusive le mode de vie et l'agir, elle ne peut se passer de textes sans se vouer à disparaître ; pour devenir une tradition et préserver la cohérence de ses idées, elle doit transmettre. Ainsi convient-il de remarquer que le cynisme, qui passe pour la philosophie des actes par excellence, nous est connu à travers des narrations de gestes et les bons mots des philosophes, c'est-à-dire des discours. Diogène est d'ailleurs inséparable de son franc-parler, à savoir cet acte de discours où dire comporte un risque[18] et exprime un acte de liberté[19]. Dès lors, si les cyniques décrient les théories abstruses et privilégient les actes aux dogmes, ils ne se privent pas de tout λόγος pour autant. Bien plus, la tradition cynique est riche de différents genres littéraires et modalités d'expression.

En sermonnant son disciple Hégésias, Diogène situe le critère du vrai, exprimé par l'adjectif ἀληθινή[20], non plus dans la conformité du discours à la réalité mais dans l'acte lui-même. L'« ascèse véritable » est à la fois celle que Diogène donne à voir et celle dont Hégésias diffère la pratique, lui qui veut d'abord tirer profit (χρῆσαί) de la littérature cynique. La question de ce qui est utile (en grec χρήσιμον) pour apprendre à bien agir renvoie au terme même de chrie, χρεία, dont le sens premier est « objet utile, dont on tire profit ». La chrie, par son statut intermédiaire entre littérature et souvenir d'une action philosophique mémorable, pose la question de ce dont il est besoin pour dire les actes, sans se perdre dans ce qui rend un acte singulier et ponctuel. Dès lors, convenons que même réduit à une pâle copie, le discours cynique, qu'il soit théorique ou consigné dans des chries, exprime une exigence de transmission.

16. Voir Giannantoni 1990, vol. 4, p. 257-264 ; Dorandi 1993, p. 57-68 ; Husson 2011, p. 185-189 ; Goulet-Cazé 2016, p. 85-90 ; *ead.* 2017, p. 195-226 ; Flores-Júnior 2017, p. 117-136 ; *id.* 2021, p. 213-228 ; Chouinard 2021, p. 253-254. Nous laissons de côté l'affiliation philosophique plus précise d'Antisthène dont la pensée a été étudiée par A. Brancacci (2005), selon l'héritage de Gorgias et de Socrate ; nous retenons ici que les témoignages inscrivent sa vision rigoriste de la pratique de la vertu dans une pensée de l'action cynique.

17. Flores-Júnior 2017, p. 127.

18. Voir Foucault 2009.

19. Voir Bénatouïl 2011.

20. Pour une étude de l'adjectif appliqué à l'ascèse, au plaisir et au bonheur dans les témoignages cyniques, voir Brancacci 2019, p. 203-207.

Le cynisme nous est parvenu comme un refus de la théorie au profit d'une myriade de gestes philosophiques. Or, sous cette forme, il ne donne qu'à voir ses actions sans donner à penser la nature de l'action droite. En voulant s'ériger en philosophie des actes contre les philosophies trop bavardes, il se confronte à la difficulté de trouver la façon la plus adéquate d'exprimer ce qu'il s'évertue à mettre en œuvre.

Étant donné que nous possédons peu de textes originaux mais surtout des témoignages constitués en très grande partie d'anecdotes et de bons mots, le cynisme tient sa réputation de ces innombrables situations spectaculaires, lesquelles sont bien souvent ouvertes à l'interprétation et, en cela, sujettes à l'équivocité. Ces textes installent l'idée d'un refus de la théorie jusque dans l'embarras qu'expriment quelques lettres pseudépigraphiques[21]. Dans sa réponse à Antalcidas (lettre 17), qui a écrit un traité sur la vertu pour se concilier la faveur du maître, Diogène lui reproche de n'avoir jamais rien montré en acte : « Certes des caractères écrits [...] peuvent préserver la mémoire de ceux qui ne sont plus, mais ne sauraient démontrer la vertu de ceux qui, vivants, ne sont pas là »[22]. Par une subtile mise en abyme, les lettres interrogent leur légitimité en tant qu'écrits et le risque de contrevenir aux principes cyniques.

Le corpus des lettres développe les chries et apophtegmes qui circulaient autour de Diogène, Cratès et Hipparchia. Il témoigne d'une volonté de penser l'anecdote cynique et, comme le souligne F. Junqua, d'« expliciter les leçons et les enseignements » des chries, d'en constituer « une interprétation écrite »[23]. Les communautés cyniques semblaient en effet confrontées à de nombreuses critiques et à un besoin de penser ce qu'une littérature de l'anecdote ne permettait pas de clarifier.

Pourtant, les paragraphes 70 et 71 de Diogène Laërce proposent de penser l'action cynique à travers une courte théorie de l'ascèse. Nous proposons d'interroger ce texte : est-il suffisant pour penser l'action cynique ? Ou au contraire ne traduit-il pas la difficulté de remonter de l'anecdote à la règle ? Nous détaillerons ainsi ce que signifie une ascèse philosophique du corps pour ensuite approfondir la destination psychique de l'action. Nous tenterons enfin d'ouvrir l'interprétation du texte en demandant si le texte de Diogène Laërce ne témoigne pas avant tout d'un contexte impérial dans lequel les communautés cyniques sont accusées d'extravagances et de décadence dans leurs pratiques ascétiques. À notre sens, ce contexte constitue

21. Voir Ps.-Diogène, 3, éd. Junqua (= *SSR* V B 533) : « Car les lettres peuvent beaucoup et pas moins que le dialogue avec des personnes présentes » (δύνανται γάρ αἱ ἐπιστολαὶ πολλὰ καὶ οὐχ ἥττονα τῆς πρὸς παρόντας διαλέξεως).

22. Ps.-Diogène, 17, éd. Junqua, trad. Junqua modifiée (= *SSR* V B 547) : διὰ γραμμάτων [...], ἃ μνήμας μὲν ἂν σώζοι τῶν οὐκ ὄντων, ἀρετῆς δὲ ζώντων καὶ οὐ παρόντων.

23. Junqua 2000, p. 18.

un indice supplémentaire pour comprendre l'origine stoïcienne du texte rapporté par Diogène Laërce.

Afin de faciliter les références au texte, nous proposons de reprendre le travail de M.-O. Goulet-Cazé : la traduction[24], avec quelques légères modifications, ainsi que le découpage des propositions à l'aide de lettres[25]. Nous justifierons les choix textuels au fur et à mesure que l'interprétation de l'ascèse cynique l'exigera[26] :

(a) L'ascèse, disait-il, est double, l'ascèse psychique d'une part, et d'autre part cette ascèse corporelle,
(b) au cours de laquelle des représentations, qui se produisent dans un exercice constant, donnent de la facilité pour les œuvres de la vertu.
(c) Mais l'une est inachevée sans l'autre, car vigueur et force sont au nombre des qualités qu'il convient de rechercher tout autant pour l'âme que pour le corps.
(d) Et il avançait des preuves de ce qu'il est facile à partir de l'exercice de s'établir dans la vertu :
(e) il voyait en effet que, dans les arts manuels et les autres, les artisans possèdent, grâce à la pratique, une habileté manuelle hors du commun, combien aussi les joueurs de flûte et les athlètes, grâce au labeur approprié et constant, excellent dans leur domaine respectif, et comment, s'ils avaient reporté leur ascèse aussi sur leur âme, la peine qu'ils prennent ne serait ni inutile ni inachevée.
(f) Rien, absolument rien, disait-il, ne réussit dans la vie sans ascèse ; celle-ci est capable, en revanche, de triompher de tout.
(g) Par conséquent, alors qu'ils devraient vivre heureux en ayant choisi, au lieu des labeurs inutiles ceux qui sont conformes à la nature,
(h) les gens, à cause de leur folie, sont malheureux.
(i) Et de fait, du plaisir lui-même le mépris est des plus doux, à condition de s'y être exercé au préalable. Tout comme les gens qui se sont accoutumés à une vie de plaisir trouvent déplaisant de passer au style de vie opposé, de même ceux qui se sont exercés au style de vie opposé, éprouvent à mépriser les plaisirs un plaisir plus grand que ces plaisirs eux-mêmes.
(j) Tel était le langage que tenait Diogène et de toute évidence il y conformait ses actes, falsifiant réellement la monnaie, n'accordant

24. Goulet-Cazé 1999, p. 736-738.

25. Goulet-Cazé 2016, p. 195-198.

26. Nous laissons de côté l'interprétation de l'expression μηδὲν οὕτω τοῖς κατὰ νόμον ὡς τοῖς κατὰ φύσιν διδούς que O. Flores-Júnior (2021, p. 232-239) comprend comme un rejet double de la civilisation et de la nature. Nous avons essayé de montrer pourquoi il est important de maintenir l'opposition entre νόμος et φύσις (voir Decker 2022b, p. 107-150) contre l'idée d'un « retour à la nature » (Flores-Júnior 2021, p. 67, 93, 102, 131, 193 ; Helmer 2017, p. 110) et l'image stéréotypée du monde sauvage. Voir aussi Chouinard 2022, p. 265.

> point du tout la même valeur à ce qui relève de la loi qu'à ce qui relève de la nature, disant qu'il menait précisément le même genre de vie qu'Héraclès, en ne préférant rien à la liberté.[27]

I. L'ascèse du corps

1. La théorie se réalise dans le modèle incarné

Ce texte traitant de l'entraînement (ἄσκησις) cynique expose comment l'action répétitive est un moyen de l'endurance et de l'excellence morale du cynique. Il suit une section bio-anecdotique très longue, de quelque cinquante paragraphes, que Diogène Laërce conclut de façon brutale : « D'autres choses lui sont rapportées, mais vu qu'elles sont nombreuses, il serait long de les énumérer »[28]. Il est fort probable que le doxographe soit dépassé par la somme de chries et d'apophtegmes qu'il a recueillis : il en rajoute d'ailleurs quelques sections après la doxographie des paragraphes 70-73[29].

La proposition *j* conclut l'exposé en reprenant, selon les termes de M.-O Goulet-Cazé, les « slogans » du cynisme[30] : la conformité entre discours et actes, la falsification de la monnaie, l'opposition entre νόμος et φύσις et enfin le χαρακτήρ[31] de liberté qu'Héraclès inspire à Diogène. Ce recours final aux exemples individuels confère au concret une prééminence tout à fait remarquable : après la grande quantité d'anecdotes, le texte théorique de l'ascèse se clôt par un renvoi aux vies incarnées.

De façon générale, Diogène Laërce semble soucieux de juger la conformité des vies aux exigences morales, ainsi que le suggèrent, selon C. Veillard, ses rares interventions :

27. DL VI, 70-71 : Διττὴν δὲ ἔλεγε εἶναι τὴν ἄσκησιν, τὴν μὲν ψυχικήν, τὴν δὲ σωματικήν ταύτην καθ' ἣν ἐν γυμνασίᾳ συνεχεῖ γινόμεναι φαντασίαι εὐλυσίαν πρὸς τὰ τῆς ἀρετῆς ἔργα παρέχονται. Εἶναι δὲ ἀτελῆ τὴν ἑτέραν χωρὶς τῆς ἑτέρας, οὐδὲν ἧττον εὐεξίας καὶ ἰσχύος ἐν τοῖς προσήκουσι γενομένης, ὡς περὶ τὴν ψυχὴν καὶ περὶ τὸ σῶμα. Παρετίθετο δὲ τεκμήρια τοῦ ῥᾳδίως ἀπὸ τῆς γυμνασίας ἐν τῇ ἀρετῇ καταγίνεσθαι· ὁρᾶν τε γὰρ ἔν τε ταῖς τέχναις βαναύσοις καὶ ταῖς ἄλλαις οὐ τὴν τυχοῦσαν ὀξυχειρίαν τοὺς τεχνίτας ἀπὸ τῆς μελέτης πεποιημένους τούς τε ἀθλητὰς καὶ τοὺς αὐλητὰς ὅσον ὑπερφέρουσιν ἑκάτεροι τῇ ἰδίᾳ πονήσει τῇ συνεχεῖ, καὶ ὡς οὗτοι εἰ μετήνεγκαν τὴν ἄσκησιν καὶ ἐπὶ τὴν ψυχήν, οὐκ ἂν ἀνωφελῶς καὶ ἀτελῶς ἐμόχθουν.

Οὐδέν γε μὴν ἔλεγε τὸ παράπαν ἐν τῷ βίῳ χωρὶς ἀσκήσεως κατορθοῦσθαι, δυνατὴν δὲ ταύτην πᾶν ἐκνικῆσαι. Δέον οὖν ἀντὶ τῶν ἀχρήστων πόνων τοὺς κατὰ φύσιν ἑλομένους ζῆν εὐδαιμόνως, παρὰ τὴν ἄνοιαν κακοδαιμονοῦσι. Καὶ γὰρ αὐτῆς τῆς ἡδονῆς ἡ καταφρόνησις ἡδυτάτη προμελετηθεῖσα, καὶ ὥσπερ οἱ συνεθισθέντες ἡδέως ζῆν, ἀηδῶς ἐπὶ τοὐναντίον μετίασιν, οὕτως οἱ τοὐναντίον ἀσκηθέντες ἥδιον αὐτῶν τῶν ἡδονῶν καταφρονοῦσι. Τοιαῦτα διελέγετο καὶ ποιῶν ἐφαίνετο, ὄντως νόμισμα παραχαράττων, μηδὲν οὕτω τοῖς κατὰ νόμον ὡς τοῖς κατὰ φύσιν διδούς· τὸν αὐτὸν χαρακτῆρα τοῦ βίου λέγων διεξάγειν ὅνπερ καὶ Ἡρακλῆς, μηδὲν ἐλευθερίας προκρίνων.

28. DL VI, 69 : ἀναφέρεται δὲ καὶ ἄλλα εἰς αὐτόν, ἃ μακρὸν ἂν εἴη καταλέγειν πολλὰ ὄντα.

29. M.-O. Goulet-Cazé (2017, p. 57-60 et 127-132) estime qu'il n'a pas eu le temps de les classer.

30. Goulet-Cazé 2016, p. 207-209.

31. « signe distinctif » : χαρακτήρ signifie d'abord l'empreinte d'une monnaie dont la falsification est évoquée juste avant dans le texte.

> Au sein de la rationalité antique, l'erreur doctrinale n'importe pas, puisqu'elle n'existe pas au sens strict : il n'y a au contraire que des erreurs pratiques. Le réquisit de rationalité s'exprime donc également par la nécessité d'une conformité entre les actes et les discours[32].

Dans le cas de Diogène de Sinope à qui Diogène Laërce accorde le plus long *bios*[33], la doctrine importe moins : il importe, au contraire, de constater que l'ensemble des anecdotes suffit à valider la philosophie cynique.

Il ne s'agit donc pas de dire que la vie de Diogène corrobore la doctrine cynique mais que la doctrine cynique trouve son fondement dans la vie de Diogène qui, elle-même, se fonde dans celle d'Héraclès. La présence du demi-dieu, que l'on retrouve associé plus tard aux figures du sage dans le stoïcisme et en particulier chez Épictète[34], révèle le lien fort entre l'identité du sage et ses actions, ainsi que l'affirme P. Aubenque : « Sans ses "travaux", Héraclès ne serait pas Héraclès. Il illustre cette idée, empruntée par les Stoïciens aux Cyniques, que la vertu réside dans les seuls actes et que le héros ou le sage n'*est* que ce qu'il *fait* »[35]. Le πόνος cynique s'inspire des travaux herculéens et doit susciter la même admiration.

Toutefois, peut-on penser ensemble une vie historique comme l'est celle de Diogène et la vie légendaire d'Héraclès ? Se référer au modèle herculéen permet de décrire une vie idéale que Diogène viserait. Il est vrai que la figure d'Héraclès opère comme une autorité visant à fonder la philosophie cynique ; débattre de l'excellence morale d'Héraclès ou d'Ulysse est d'ailleurs une occasion de philosopher, ainsi qu'en témoignent les lettres pseudépigraphiques[36]. Antisthène aurait écrit trois *Héraclès*, en particulier pour parler de la force (ἰσχύς)[37] ; sa fameuse thèse selon laquelle « le πόνος est un bien » se fonde sur la vie d'Héraclès[38]. Le philosophe cynique Œnomaos du IIs. ap. J.-C. fait même d'Héraclès la seule référence du cynisme[39] : A. Brancacci suggère qu'il refusait ainsi la prédominance du *bios* de Diogène ainsi que les tentatives de légitimer le cynisme en faisant d'Antisthène son fondateur[40].

32. Veillard 2009, p. 91.
33. Voir Giannantoni 1990, vol. 4, p. 413.
34. Voir, par exemple, Arrien, *Epicteti dissertationes*, II, XVI, 35-45.
35. Aubenque 1962, p. 1345.
36. Voir les différends entre les lettres 7 et 14 de Diogène et la lettre 19 de Cratès pour qui Diogène seul est donné comme référence du cynisme. Voir Junqua 2000, p. 362.
37. DL VI, 16-18 (= *SSR* V A 41). Voir Giannantoni 1990, vol. 4, p. 309-322.
38. DL VI, 2 (= *SSR* V A 97). Sur l'importance d'Héraclès au sein du cynisme et d'autres traditions, voir Höistad 1948, p. 22-73 ; Giannantoni 1990, vol. 4, p. 317-321 y répond.
39. Julien, *Orationes* IX, 8, 187C, éd. Rochefort : « Le cynisme n'est ni l'antisthénisme ni le diogénisme » (ὁ κυνισμὸς οὔτε ἀντισθενισμός ἐστιν οὔτε διογενισμός).
40. Brancacci 2000, p. 46-50.

Mais cette précision doit nous inciter à la méfiance : les nombreuses réappropriations et idéalisations[41] dont la vie de Diogène a fait l'objet rendent illusoires les tentatives de reconstruire sa vie effective. Les historiens et archéologues ne sont pas parvenus à vérifier les détails de sa vie et en particulier à accorder les versions de la falsification de la monnaie[42], qu'évoque la proposition *(j)*. Le *bios* de Diogène est un tissu d'incohérences et de versions inconciliables. Le geste y est souvent équivoque et la chrie constitue, avant tout, un genre littéraire. En affirmant que Diogène reproduit le χαρακτήρ d'Héraclès, la proposition *(j)*, par une mise en abyme, contribue à forger, *ipso facto*, deux idéaux. Le *bios* devient l'objet d'une mystification et acquiert le statut de véritable concept philosophique : penser l'action droite c'est juger de sa conformité avec la vie de Diogène. Or, les différentes versions qui la composent ne démultiplient-elles pas les interprétations possibles ?

Se référer à un exemple et le déployer dans une grande variété d'anecdotes c'est le présenter dans la contingence inéluctable de toute action. Lorsqu'Aristote, pour décrire la φρόνησις et la possibilité d'une intelligence des choses singulières[43], se réfère d'abord à l'homme prudent (φρόνιμος), c'est-à-dire à celui qui est capable de bien délibérer alors que n'existe pas de τέχνη[44], il privilégie l'homme concret qui « affronte le monde tel qu'il est »[45]. Ainsi, bien qu'Aristote cherche à saisir quelle vertu est la φρόνησις et que la capacité de délibération ne soit pas interrogée par les cyniques, une certaine convergence peut néanmoins se faire jour : l'homme vertueux est celui par qui le possible se révèle. S'il demeure absurde d'imiter le sage puisque la contingence demeure et que les situations ne se répètent pas à l'identique, des individus d'exception, en montrant leur capacité à bien agir, ont ouvert en quelque sorte une voie que seule l'éducation et l'entraînement préalables permettront d'emprunter[46]. Même si les textes disponibles ne nous permettent pas d'affiner la question, nous pouvons affirmer que les exemples de Diogène et d'Heraclès fonctionnent comme des vérifications et des incitations : réputée difficile, l'ascèse est néanmoins réalisable[47].

41. Quelques études utilisent le terme d'idéalisation pour caractériser certaines interprétations d'époque impériale : Billerbeck 1978, p. 55 et 1993, p. 319-338 ; Goulet-Cazé 2017, p. 311.

42. Voir Seltmann 1938, p. 121 ; Giannantoni 1990, vol. 4, p. 423-433 ; Junqua 2000, p. 31-53 ; Fuentes González 2013, p. 233-239 ; Goulet-Cazé 2017, p. 51-53.

43. Voir Labarrière 2008, p. 147.

44. Aristote, *Ethica Nicomachea*, VI, 5, 1140a25-30.

45. Nicolas 2011, p. 37.

46. Voir Aubenque 2004, p. 60 ; Nicolas 2011, p. 44.

47. Voir DL VI, 35 (= *SSR* V B 266) ; Ps.-Cratès, 6, 13 et 16 ; Ps.-Diogène, 14 et 37 ; Julien, *Orationes* IX, 8, 187C. L'idée d'une émulation est suggérée en DL VI, 15 (= *SSR* V A 22). Voir également la position de Posidonius pour qui la progression (προκοπή) de Socrate, Diogène et Antisthène est un indice suffisant de l'existence de la vertu (DL VII, 91).

2. Force et habitude.

La référence à Héraclès illustre surtout l'importance de la force : acquérir de la force et de l'endurance est un préalable à la vertu. La proposition *(c)* du texte de l'ascèse mentionne, par une redondance, l'εὐεξία et l'ἰσχύς ; le champ lexical se poursuit en *(f)* et *(g)* avec ἐκνικῆσαι, πόνων.

La « vigueur » et la « force » sont donc à rechercher « autant pour l'âme que pour le corps ». L'inversion du texte est intéressante dans la mesure où il semble évident que la philosophie s'occupe d'abord de l'âme. Pourtant, nous verrons que c'est l'insistance sur la destination psychique qui peut retenir notre attention.

M.-O. Goulet-Cazé associe la théorie de la double ascèse des propositions *(a)*, *(b)* et *(c)* à un point de vue stoïcien[48] mais elle reconnaît que la référence à la force est tout à fait cynique[49]. A. Long et L.-A. Dorion y reconnaissent des préoccupations socratiques. Pour le premier, la double ascèse rappelle l'exigence d'éducation à la gymnastique et à la musique et les analogies avec les artisans, aussi bien pour le Socrate de Platon que pour celui de Xénophon[50]. L.-A. Dorion centre sa démonstration sur les textes de Xénophon : « Bien que les points de convergence entre Socrate[x] et Diogène soient nombreux, ils sont souvent méconnus, si bien que les commentateurs attribuent souvent à Diogène, comme s'il s'agissait d'éléments qui lui sont propres, des traits qui ne sont pas moins vrais de Socrate[x]. »[51]

En effet, le Socrate des *Mémorables* propose déjà des pratiques d'endurance dont il est parfois difficile de départager l'aspect corporel de l'aspect psychique. C'est pourquoi, dans un travail où nous questionnons le statut de l'ἰσχύς en tant qu'esquisse d'une volonté[52], nous avons proposé de resituer la force cynique dans un ensemble lexical qui compte la robustesse au nombre des biens et de la considérer dans un sens intensément physique : tout ce qui peut contribuer à augmenter la capacité d'agir doit être recherché par l'ascèse. L'intellectualisme n'épuise pas la compréhension de l'action mais le corps comme l'âme ont une musculature dont le renforcement accroît l'autosuffisance et la liberté. Parmi de nombreux exemples des *Mémorables*, l'apologue de Prodicos offre une ressemblance intéressante ; la prosopopée de la Vertu s'y adresse ainsi à Héraclès : « Et si tu veux avoir un corps puissant (δυνατὸς), il faut habituer (ἐθιστέον) le corps à être au service de l'intelligence

48. Goulet-Cazé 2016, p. 195-220.

49. *Ibid.* p. 34.

50. Long 1996, p. 37 qui renvoie seulement vers Platon, *Respublica*, III, 403c-412b.

51. Dorion 2018, p. 82. Par la convention « Socrate[x] », l'auteur désigne le Socrate de Xénophon.

52. Decker 2022a.

(γνώμῃ) et s'exercer (γυμναστέον) avec des peines (πόνοις) et de la sueur ».[53] Socrate convoque déjà le modèle herculéen pour mettre en garde son disciple Aristippe contre les facilités d'une liberté paresseuse et lui recommander de « fortifier le corps et l'âme »[54].

Dans le texte laërtien, la force s'acquiert au moyen d'actions hésitantes préalables, comme l'enseignent les pratiques des artisans, athlètes ou musiciens. Cette référence discute des conceptions traditionnelles de l'éducation grecque puisque la formation du corps et de l'âme s'effectuait au moyen de la discipline stricte qu'exigeaient la gymnastique et la musique[55]. L'apophtegme suivant, attribué à Diogène, reprend, somme toute, une image très traditionaliste de l'éducation :

> L'éducation des enfants ressemble aux ouvrages des potiers. Car, de même que ceux-ci façonnent et disposent comme ils veulent l'argile tendre, mais ne peuvent plus la modeler une fois qu'elle a été cuite, de même ceux qui, dans leur jeunesse, n'ont pas été éduqués par des épreuves pénibles, ne peuvent plus, devenus adultes, être remodelés.[56]

La métaphore de l'argile se retrouve chez Platon avec le fer[57] ou la cire[58]. S. Husson développe les polémiques que Diogène a pu entretenir avec les écrits de Platon autour de l'éducation[59]. Ces débats philosophiques nous permettent de remarquer comment la réflexion s'attache à déterminer quelles actions sont requises comme préalables pour acquérir une disposition vertueuse et ainsi accomplir des actions droites. Pour penser l' ἔθος et l' ἕξις, Aristote convoque aussi l'exemple musical : « c'est en jouant de la cithare que l'on devient bon ou mauvais citharède »[60] et la modération à l'égard des plaisirs[61].

Toutefois, la conception cynique de l'habitude s'en démarque : tandis que, pour Aristote, on devient juste à force de pratiquer des actes justes, pour les cyniques en revanche, notre capacité à agir avec justice dépend de notre indépendance et de notre maîtrise de soi. Le cynisme est ainsi une recherche constante de ce qui menace l'autosuffisance et serait susceptible de limiter le

53. Xénophon, *Mem.* II, 1, 28, éd. Bandini : εἰ δὲ καὶ τῷ σώματι βούλει δυνατὸς εἶναι, τῇ γνώμῃ ὑπηρετεῖν ἐθιστέον τὸ σῶμα καὶ γυμναστέον σὺν πόνοις καὶ ἱδρῶτι.

54. *Ibid.* II, 1, 19, éd. Bandini : ἵνα δυνατοὶ γενόμενοι καὶ τοῖς σώμασι καὶ ταῖς ψυχαῖς.

55. Voir Aristophane, *Nubes*, 961-1023 ; Platon, *Rsp.* II, 376e-377b ; Marrou 1948, p. 75.

56. Stobée II, 31, 87 (= *SSR* V B 382) : τὴν τῶν παίδων ἀγωγὴν ἐοικέναι τοῖς τῶν κεραμέων πλάσμασιν· ὡς γὰρ ἐκεῖνοι ἁπαλὸν μὲν τὸν πηλὸν ὄντα ὅπως θέλουσι σχηματίζουσι καὶ ῥυθμίζουσιν, ὀπτηθέντα δὲ οὐκέτι δύνανται πλάσσειν, οὕτω καὶ τοὺς ἐν νεότητι μὴ διὰ πόνων παιδαγωγηθέντας, τελείους γενομένους ἀμεταπλάστους γίνεσθαι.

57. Platon, *Leges*, II, 671b-c.

58. *Ibid.* VII, 789e.

59. Husson 2010, p. 53-57.

60. Aristote, *EN*, II, 1, 1103b8-9, éd. Bywater : ἐκ γὰρ τοῦ κιθαρίζειν καὶ οἱ ἀγαθοὶ καὶ κακοὶ γίνονται κιθαρισταί. Voir aussi *Metaphysica*, Θ, 5, 1047b31-33.

61. Aristote, *EN*, II, 2.

champ d'action. C'est pourquoi les cyniques vivent l'exil[62] et la pauvreté[63] comme une exhortation à pratiquer l'ascèse en se libérant du superflu.

En d'autres termes, l'ἔθος cynique, que la lettre 37 de Diogène associe au mode de vie philosophique[64], consiste à répéter des situations à anticiper. Si aucun besoin (la faim, le froid, le désir sexuel...) ne m'asservit, alors mon amplitude d'action reste entière : mon bonheur est assuré puisque mes besoins sont satisfaits et je demeure juste et tempérant puisque la maîtrise de soi permet de ne nuire à personne. L'habitude cynique garantit au philosophe l'αὐτάρκεια et donc la pleine et entière jouissance de sa raison : ce qu'opère l'habitude détermine les conditions de l'action morale et non le contenu[65].

3. Un anti-intellectualisme ?

Pourtant, le rejet du cursus général et l'endurance extrême à laquelle les cyniques se soumettent dessinent l'image d'un anti-intellectualisme dans lequel savoir n'implique pas bien agir[66]. Comment comprendre dès lors que le texte de Diogène Laërce insiste autant sur la finalité psychique de l'ascèse, elle qui se réalise par des exercices corporels ? L'exemple animal régulièrement convoqué pourrait amplifier l'interrogation, comme dans les créations littéraires de Dion de Pruse lorsqu'il met en scène un Diogène anti-prométhéen[67] :

> « Ne vois-tu pas comme les bêtes et les oiseaux mènent une vie beaucoup moins troublée que celle de l'homme, et beaucoup plus agréable d'ailleurs ? Ne te semble-t-il pas qu'ils jouissent d'une meilleure santé, qu'ils sont plus robustes et que chacun d'eux vit aussi longtemps qu'il lui est possible, tout en étant dépourvu de mains ou d'intelligence humaine ? »[68]

62. DL VI, 56 (= *SSR* V B 4).

63. Stobée IV, 32a, 11 (= *SSR* V B 223).

64. Pseudo-Diogène 37 (= *SSR* V B 567) : « Moi, après avoir entendu ainsi parler du bonheur, je n'ai plus mangé ni bu cela à la façon d'exercices, mais comme des plaisirs, et l'habitude aussi me renforce dans ce mode de vie » (ἐγώ, ἐπεὶ ταῦτα τῆς εὐδαιμονίας διαλεγομένης ἤκουσα, οὐκέτι ταῦτα ὡς ἀσκήματα ἤσθιον καὶ ἔπινον, ἀλλ' ὡς ἡδονάς, κρατεῖ δέ με πρὸς ταύτην τὴν δίαιταν καὶ τὸ ἔθος).

65. En cela, le cynisme est pleinement une éthique des vertus puisque l'action n'est pas morale selon une règle objectivable mais selon la qualité de l'agent.

66. Voir Meilland 1983.

67. O. Flores-Júnior (2021, p. 102-108) conteste l'attribution de ce trait aux cyniques. Nous refusons ses conclusions (Decker 2022b, p. 348-359) dans la mesure où Prométhée offre l'αἰδώς aux hommes et où les cyniques assument leur ἀναίδεια (voir aussi Giannantoni 1990, vol. 4, p. 315 et 321-322 sur le couple Héraclès-Prométhée).

68. Dion Chrysostome, *Orationes*, X, 16, trad. Paquet légèrement modifiée (= *SSR* V B 586) : οὐχ ὁρᾷς τὰ θηρία ταῦτα καὶ τὰ ὄρνεα, ὅσῳ ζῇ τῶν ἀνθρώπων ἀλυπότερον, πρὸς δὲ καὶ ἥδιον, καὶ μᾶλλον ὑγιαίνει καὶ πλέον ἰσχύει καὶ ζῇ χρόνον ἕκαστον αὐτῶν ὅσον πλεῖστον δύναται, καίτοι οὔτε χεῖρας ἔχοντα οὔτε ἀνθρώπου διάνοιαν;

L'exemple animal permet de ne pas référer ce qu'est une action droite aux seuls humains et donc à des capacités dont l'homme serait seul détenteur. Les animaux sont capables d'endurance et de renoncement, au nom de leur liberté[69].

L'image d'une double voie et d'un raccourci vers la vertu, souvent parodiée[70], s'inscrit également dans le refus cynique des savoirs : la lettre 21 de Cratès précise que la voie longue est faite de raisonnements (διὰ τῶν λόγων), tandis que le raccourci passe par l'exercice réalisé dans les actes de la vie quotidienne (ἡ δὲ διὰ τῶν καθ' ἡμέραν ἔργων μελέτη). Mais ce concept apparaît comme profondément ambivalent : d'une part, il indique que la voie courte qui promet un accès facile au bonheur est en réalité faite d'épreuves difficiles et éventuellement décourageantes[71] ; d'autre part, il laisse planer un doute quant au statut réel des connaissances dans le cynisme. En effet, ces dernières peuvent être considérées comme inutiles ou comme secondaires[72].

Tout aussi ambivalent est le modèle animal dans les usages cyniques : S. Husson, O. Flores-Júnior et D. Izzo[73] en ont montré tous les contrastes jusque dans l'impossibilité de reproduire strictement les comportements. L'exemple animal semble dès lors une occasion pour exercer son jugement : le cynique s'aperçoit à partir du bonheur immédiat de l'animal que l'intelligence humaine est utilisée contre elle-même. D'ailleurs, la proposition *(h)* précise que les souffrances inutiles et le malheur des hommes s'expliquent par leur ignorance (παρὰ τὴν ἄνοιαν).

Certes, les exercices physiques simples et difficiles dessinent un anti-intellectualisme dans lequel on se détourne de longues études pour une voie courte. Pourtant, les paragraphes laërtiens insistent bien sur la destination psychique de l'ascèse.

69. Voir DL VI, 46 (= *SSR* V B 146) ; DL VI, 22 ; Plutarque, *De profectibus in virtutem*, 77E-78A (= *SSR* V B 172) ; Dion Chrysostome, *Or.* VI, 18 (= *SSR* V B 583).

70. Lucien, *Vitarum auctio*, 11 (= *SSR* V B 80) ; Galien, *De animi cuiuslibet peccatorum dignotione et curatione*, V, 71, 9.

71. Les communautés cyniques semblent confrontées à cette difficulté puisque les lettres pseudépigraphiques reviennent régulièrement sur ce point : Ps.-Cratès 6 ; 13 ; 21 ; Ps.-Diogène 12 ; 14 ; 30, 2 ; 37, 5. Voir Junqua 2000, p. 108 : « Comme on sait que l'une des attaques qu'eurent à subir les cyniques, au moins à partir de l'époque impériale, avait trait à la "facilité" de leur philosophie, en même temps qu'au caractère "rébarbatif" de leur ascèse, qui détournait le profane de la philosophie, on peut considérer que les lettres constituent, en partie au moins, une réponse à ce reproche. »

72. Tandis que V. Emeljanow (1965, p. 182-184) juge que l'idée d'une voie courte a pu naître dans le cynisme pour dénigrer le cursus habituel des apprentissages, M.-O. Goulet-Cazé (2003, p. 109-110 et p. 158-159 ; 2016, p. 22-28) considère qu'elle provient probablement d'un compromis qui permet la cohabitation à l'intérieur du stoïcisme d'un courant ascétique fort et d'un courant tourné autant vers l'éthique que vers la physique et la logique. Voir également Chouinard 2021, p. 371-395.

73. Husson 2013 ; Flores-Júnior 2005 ; *id.* 2006 ; *id.* 2021, p. 297-298 ; Izzo 2023.

II. La finalité morale et psychique

Dès son premier mot (Διττὴν), l'exposé de l'ascèse insiste sur son caractère double. Si comme nous l'avons vu, la philosophie peut aussi s'occuper du bien du corps, c'est la destination psychique des exercices qui est davantage soulignée (καὶ ἐπὶ τὴν ψυχήν).

Cette dimension psychique, tant pour la démonstration qu'elle propose que par le lexique qu'elle convoque, a été interrogée par beaucoup de commentateurs[74]. Or, si le lexique avec lequel est développée la théorie de l'ascèse ne correspond pas seulement à un lexique cynique, il reste néanmoins possible que le fond soit cohérent avec les conceptions cyniques, comme l'affirme O. Flores-Júnior : « ce texte ne serait pas authentique si l'on considère son authenticité formelle ; en revanche, il serait authentique, si l'on considère son authenticité philosophique »[75].

D. Dudley et R. Höistad ont refusé les conclusions de K. von Fritz qui a distingué dans le lexique une liste de termes connus d'Antisthène et du cynisme et une liste spécifique au stoïcisme. K. von Fritz soumet l'hypothèse que ces paragraphes sont issus du Περὶ ἀρετῆς de Diogène, œuvre que l'on ne trouve que dans le catalogue de Sotion, d'influence stoïcienne. D. Dudley conteste que la deuxième liste soit un lexique inconnu du IVᵉ s. av. J.-C. ; R. Höistad considère l'ensemble des expressions comme typiquement cyniques et en ajoute d'autres[76].

M.-O. Goulet-Cazé partage le texte en deux : les propositions *(a)*, *(b)* et *(c)* exposeraient un point de vue stoïcien, proche de celui de Musonius Rufus ou de Sénèque, sur l'ascèse cynique. L'expression Παρετίθετο δὲ τεκμήρια *(d)* dénoterait l'intervention du doxographe et inaugurerait un développement plus conforme aux positions du philosophe de Sinope[77]. Pourtant, l'expression καὶ ἐπὶ τὴν ψυχήν en *(e)* insiste à nouveau sur la finalité psychique de l'ascèse. À notre sens, de *(f)* à *(i)*, l'exposé semble réitérer un même mouvement dans lequel l'ascèse physique est étudiée selon le risque de vanité qu'elle comporte.

Deux points restent suspects : la question de la vertu et celle des représentations.

1. La finalité de l'ascèse : vertu et santé.

À deux reprises, la vertu est désignée comme finalité de l'ascèse : πρὸς τὰ τῆς ἀρετῆς ἔργα παρέχονται *(b)*, ἀπὸ τῆς γυμνασίας ἐν τῇ ἀρετῇ *(d)*. Par ailleurs, les termes d'ἀτελῆ *(c)* et d'ἀτελῶς *(e)* reprennent l'idée d'un *télos*

74. Voir von Fritz 1926, p. 58-59 ; Dudley 1937, p. 216-220 ; Höistad 1948, p. 41-47 ; Goulet-Cazé 2016, p. 195-220 ; Dorion 2018.

75. Flores-Júnior 2021, p. 264.

76. Höistad 1948, p. 38-39.

77. Pour une critique de cette hypothèse, voir Brancacci 1987.

psychique. Pourtant, il ne semble pas si clair, au regard de l'ensemble des témoignages, que l'action ascétique modèle à la fois le corps et l'âme au profit de l'âme seule. En effet, la santé du corps intervient au nombre des biens que l'ascèse engendre, comme dans ces témoignages relatifs à Cratès :

> Il était laid à voir et l'objet de moqueries lorsqu'il s'exerçait. Il avait l'habitude de dire, en levant les mains : « Aie du courage, Cratès, pour le bien de tes yeux et du reste du corps ; car tu verras bientôt ceux-là qui se moquent être écrasés par la maladie, envier ton bonheur et se blâmer pour leur paresse »[78].

La lettre 20 de Cratès reprend cette chrie avec une conclusion différente : ceux qui se moquent finissent par imiter les exercices de Cratès et par retrouver leur santé :

> Ils me savaient gré d'être le responsable de leur santé, et ils ne me lâchaient plus mais me suivaient où j'allais, écoutant et imitant ce que je disais et faisais [...], puisqu'on apprend l'endurance plus vite par l'acte que par la parole, ce que l'on trouve seulement dans la philosophie de Diogène[79].

L'action cynique tire sa force du spectacle qu'elle donne à voir, à la fois dans les exercices pratiqués et les résultats obtenus. Mais certaines actions restent plus discrètes comme l'accouchement d'Hipparchia dont Cratès se réjouit dans la lettre 33 parce qu'il s'est déroulé sans difficultés grâce à l'ascèse cynique préalable et qu'il permet de donner naissance à un enfant en bonne santé. Le πόνος cynique est donc une anticipation de la douleur par la douleur elle-même. Fuir l'épreuve, comme le souligne la lettre 4 de Cratès[80], c'est nécessairement la subir un jour ou l'autre.

La santé concerne aussi la pédagogie et les propos de Diogène puisque Eubule, cité par Diogène Laërce, décrit comment l'éducation ascétique imposée aux enfants de Xéniade vise à leur faire acquérir de « bonnes couleurs » et de la robustesse (εὐεξία)[81]. Nous avons vu également que l'exemple animal chez Dion Chrysostome permet d'évoquer la bonne santé que procure l'ascèse[82].

78. DL VI, 91-92 (= *SSR* V H 54) : ἦν δὲ καὶ τὴν ὄψιν αἰσχρὸς καὶ γυμναζόμενος ἐγελᾶτο. εἰώθει δὲ λέγειν ἐπαίρων τὰς χεῖρας, « θάρρει, Κράτης, ὑπὲρ ὀφθαλμῶν καὶ τοῦ λοιποῦ σώματος· τούτους γὰρ ὄψει τοὺς καταγελῶντας, ἤδη {καὶ} συνεσπασμένους ὑπὸ νόσου καί σε μακαρίζοντας, αὑτοὺς δὲ καταμεμφομένους ἐπὶ τῇ ἀργίᾳ. »

79. Pseudo-Cratès 20, éd. Junqua (= *SSR* V H 107) : ἐμοί τε χάριν ἐγίνωσκον ὡς αἰτίῳ τῆς ὑγιείας καὶ οὐκ ἀπελείποντο, ἀλλ' εἵποντο ὅπου [ἂν] βαδίζοιμι ἐπακροώμενοι καὶ μιμούμενοι ἃ λέγοιμι καὶ [ταῦτα] πράττοιμι [...], ἐπεὶ διδάσκει καρτερίαν τάχιον τὸ ἔργον τοῦ λόγου, ὅπερ ἐν μόνῃ τῇ Διογένους ἐστὶ φιλοσοφίᾳ.

80. Pseudo-Cratès 4 (= *SSR* V H 91) : « en effet, en ne s'éprouvant pas, on ne fuit pas l'épreuve et, dans le cas contraire, on la chasse » (διὰ γὰρ τοῦ μὴ πονεῖν οὐ φεύγεται πόνος, τῷ δὲ ἐναντίῳ καὶ διώκεται).

81. DL VI, 30 (= *SSR* V B 70) : ἐρυθήματος χάριν καὶ εὐεξίας.

82. Dion Chrysostome, *Or.* X, 16 (= *SSR* V B 586). Voir aussi VI, 8 (= *SSR* V B 583) : « en souffrant ces choses-là, il était en meilleure santé que ceux qui sont toujours repus » (ὁ δὲ ταῦτα πάσχων μᾶλλον μὲν ὑγίαινε τῶν ἀεὶ ἐμπιμπλαμένων, μᾶλλον δὲ τῶν ἔνδον μενόντων).

L'exposé des paragraphes 70-71 mentionne seulement l'ἀρετή sans définir ni même évoquer les actes vertueux que l'ascèse facilite. Il n'est pas facile d'inférer, à partir de l'ensemble des témoignages, ce que les cyniques entendent par vertu, si tant est qu'ils aient une vision unitaire sur la question[83]. Il est en revanche clair que l'αὐτάρκεια et donc la réduction stricte des besoins constituent l'objectif cynique et l'essence de la vie vertueuse[84] : c'est le sens du « raccourci vers la vertu »[85].

La vertu est ainsi associée à l'αὐτάρκεια chez Antisthène : « La vertu est suffisante en vue du bonheur, car elle n'a besoin de rien d'autre qu'une force socratique »[86], phrase étonnante puisque si la vertu suffit, elle ne devrait avoir besoin de rien en plus. Cette apparente contradiction nous permet de constater, comme le soutient M.-O. Goulet-Cazé, que les définitions antisthéniennes de la vertu sont « stylistiquement "typée[s]" »[87] : elles subissent des simplifications qui permettaient aux doxographes de confronter les sectes philosophiques et d'établir plus facilement des héritages et des influences. En cela, la vertu fait partie des thèmes qui permettent à Diogène Laërce de construire la succession : Socrate → Antisthène → Diogène → Cratès → Zénon. Les deux doxographies d'Antisthène et la doxographie générale font souvent référence à certains *topoi* de la vertu. M.-O. Goulet-Cazé a ainsi fait la liste des formules similaires entre les livres VI et VII[88]. La vertu devient le *télos* du cynisme, selon une formule issue de l'*Héraclès* d'Antisthène[89], et le facteur d'unité de Socrate aux Stoïciens. Or, si cette définition est corroborée par d'autres témoignages[90], d'autres fins peuvent être trouvées pour qualifier la philosophie cynique, comme l'ἀτυφία ou l'ἀπαθεία[91].

Dans le stoïcisme impérial, la vertu est évidemment la finalité de l'ascèse[92], même si l'exigence de santé y est également mise en avant. Le corps apparaît comme l'instrument des vertus[93]. On constate ainsi qu'Épictète

83. Voir Long 1996, p. 38.

84. Le discours II de Télès porte sur l'αὐτάρκεια mais développe l'importance de la pauvreté volontaire. De même, un apophtegme attribué à Diogène (Stobée IV, 23, 11 ; *SSR* V B 223) fait de la vertu un discours de la philosophie et un acte de la pauvreté.

85. DL VI, 104 (= *SSR* V A 135). Voir Goulet-Cazé 2016, p. 22-28.

86. DL VI, 11 (= *SSR* V A 134) : αὐτάρκη δὲ τὴν ἀρετὴν πρὸς εὐδαιμονίαν, μηδενὸς προσδεομένην ὅτι μὴ Σωκρατικῆς ἰσχύος.

87. Goulet-Cazé 2016, p. 33. Voir aussi Long 1996, p. 33 n. 16.

88. Goulet-Cazé 2017, p. 28-30. Voir également Brancacci 1992 ; Chouinard 2021, p. 314-332 ; Decker 2022b, p. 56-59.

89. DL VI, 104 (= *SSR* V A 135).

90. Augustin, *De Ciuitate Dei*, VIII, 3.

91. Voir Goulet-Cazé 2016, p. 31-38 qui cite, entre autres, Clément d'Alexandrie, *Stromateis*, II, 21, 130, 7 et Julien, *Or.* IX, 12, 192A.

92. Sénèque, *Epistulae ad Lucilium*, XC, 46 ; Musonius, *Oratio* VI, p. 23, 1-3, p. 24, 5 -25, 4 éd. Hense. Voir Gourinat 2022, § 16.

93. Musonius, *Or.* VI, p. 24, 14-25, 4. Voir Goulet-Cazé 2016, p. 182-190.

dresse, à partir de ses conceptions stoïciennes, le portrait d'un cynique idéal (*Entretiens* III, XXII) décentré de ses pratiques ascétiques de dépouillement (§10 ; 50) et porté par sa mission divine (§23), son αἰδώς (§15), son absence de chagrin (§48) et son amour de l'humanité (§81), en somme sa vertu (§59). Le cynique y est donc dépeint comme un sage stoïcien, jusque dans le fait que l'humanité devienne sa famille (§77-82) : sa liberté, obtenue grâce à son rejet des normes et son ascèse, lui assure une facilité, comme dit la proposition *(c)* en DL VI, 70, pour les œuvres de la vertu.

L'accent mis sur la destination morale de l'ascèse et la relégation des biens du corps à une fonction instrumentale conviennent donc davantage à un contexte stoïcien puisque certains témoignages cyniques ou bien assignent d'autres finalités comme la santé, ou bien décrivent la lutte contre les besoins comme une fin en soi. On peut d'ailleurs rappeler que l'ἰσχύς et l'ὑγίεια figurent parmi les listes stoïciennes d'indifférents préférables[94]. Nous savons, à ce sujet, que Diogène Laërce comprend le cynisme à partir du stoïcisme lorsqu'il opère un rapprochement avec Ariston de Chios sur la question des indifférents[95] pour permettre une transition vers le livre VII.

2. *Une ascèse corporelle à finalité spirituelle* [96]

Pour comprendre les paragraphes de Diogène Laërce, il convient ainsi de remarquer l'insistance sur la finalité psychique de l'ascèse. Ce n'est pas tant le fait de parler d'une double ascèse qui est suspect, puisque des sources plus anciennes témoignent de telles idées, mais d'orienter nécessairement l'exercice vers l'âme.

Déterminer la place du corps et de l'âme a engendré des lectures différentes du texte de Diogène Laërce. Ainsi, pour la proposition *(i)*, O. Flores-Júnior préfère la leçon du manuscrit F μελετηθεῖσα (« s'étant entraîné »), à la leçon des manuscrits B et P προμελετηθεῖσα. Pour le chercheur, l'absence du préfixe προ- a l'avantage de supprimer l'idée de préalable, de « prévention », au profit d'un exercice « qui a sa fin en soi », d'une « ascèse quotidienne sans objet défini [...] où l'objet sur lequel porte l'entraînement est moins important que le fait même de s'entraîner »[97]. Toutefois, ce sens serait facilité par un présent exprimant la régularité, la répétition ; or, μελετηθεῖσα à l'aoriste, même sans le préfixe προ-, suggère davantage le caractère accompli et ponctuel de l'action. S'il est vrai, comme nous l'avons vu, que certains textes autorisent à ne pas faire de l'exercice un simple moyen, l'ensemble du texte impose néanmoins une telle conception.

94. Voir Plutarque, *De communibus notitiis contra Stoicos*, 1060C. Voir aussi Decker 2022a, p. 50-54.

95. DL VI, 105.

96. Nous empruntons cette expression récurrente à M.-O. Goulet-Cazé (1999, p. 130-131, n. 7 ; 2016, p. 154, 157, 187, 188, 212).

97. Flores-Júnior 2021, p. 275.

Plus fondamentale est sa proposition de traduction des propositions *(a)* et *(b)* puisqu'il considère que le pronom-adjectif ταύτην est une reprise de τὴν ἄσκησιν et non de τὴν δὲ σωματικήν[98] ; en d'autres termes, c'est dans la double ascèse et non seulement dans l'ascèse physique que l'exercice fait naître des représentations. Il s'agit d'une réelle difficulté du texte qui distingue l'ascèse psychique de l'ascèse corporelle pour affirmer ensuite que cette dernière fait naître des représentations mentales *(b)* et que l'une est incomplète sans l'autre *(c)*. La solution d'O. Flores-Júnior permet de penser ensemble les deux ascèses tandis que celle de M.-O. Goulet-Cazé est grammaticalement plus acceptable, mais aboutit à poser la même distinction qu'on lit chez Musonius Rufus : « Une partie donc de l'exercice devrait être correctement propre à l'âme seule, une autre partie devrait être commune à l'âme et au corps »[99]. Cette solution oblige à établir l'origine stoïcienne du texte laërtien.

3. *Les* φαντασίαι.

Le trouble est amplifié par la présence en *(b)* du terme de φαντασίαι, qui peut être compris soit de façon commune, soit selon son usage stoïcien.

Tandis que K. von Fritz établit son origine stoïcienne[100], D. Dudley[101] rappelle que le terme est présent chez Platon et dans le *De Anima* d'Aristote. La φαντασία est un concept que les deux philosophes approfondissent dans ses liens avec la sensation et l'opinion[102]. Pour Aristote, la φαντασία représente ainsi à l'âme une image, même en l'absence de sensation, et intervient dans le cadre moral puisque le vertueux et le vicieux sont responsables de ce qui leur apparaît comme bon[103]. Même si la φαντασία comporte le risque, clairement établi chez Platon, du faux, certains usages aristotéliciens peuvent suggérer que Diogène pouvait employer le terme dans un sens voisin.

Toutefois, Épictète associe explicitement l'enseignement d'Antisthène à l'usage des φαντασίαι et attribue les propos suivants à Diogène[104] :

98. R. Höistad (1948, p. 41-42), en dépit des usages grammaticaux, rattache ταύτην à τὴν μὲν ψυχικήν pour respecter le rejet cynique des pratiques athlétiques. Or, ce serait mal comprendre les retournements habituels des cyniques.

99. Musonius, *Or.* VI, p. 25, 4-6, trad. Goulet-Cazé (2016, p. 214) : τῆς οὖν ἀσκήσεως ἡ μέν τις ἰδία τῆς ψυχῆς μόνης γίνοιτ' ἂν ὀρθῶς, ἡ δέ τις κοινὴ ταύτης τε καὶ τοῦ σώματος.

100. Von Fritz 1926, p. 58-59.

101. Dudley 1937, p. 217.

102. Platon, *Sophista*, 264a ; *Theaetetus*, 152a-b ; *Philebus*, 39b ; Aristote, *De Anima*, 428a10-18 ; Aujoulat 1990, p. 22-23 ; Collette 2006, p. 105.

103. Aristote, *EN*, III, 7, 1114b1-5. Voir également *ibid.* VI, 13, 1144a34-35 ; Labarrière 2008, p. 156 ; Monteils-Laeng 2014, p. 277.

104. Voir Höistad 1948, p. 40 ; Goulet-Cazé 2016, p. 202-203 ; Flores-Júnior 2021, p. 269.

> « Depuis qu'Antisthène m'a délivré, je ne suis plus un esclave ». Comment l'a-t-il délivré ? Écoute ce qu'il [Diogène] dit : « Il m'a appris ce qui est à moi et ce qui n'est pas à moi ; ma fortune n'est pas à moi [...]. Qu'est-ce qui donc est à moi ? L'usage de mes représentations (χρῆσις φαντασιῶν). »[105]

Épictète ne semble pas connaître d'œuvres authentiques de Diogène, si ce n'est des lettres apocryphes[106]. Il est en revanche intéressant de remarquer que dans un fragment que l'on possède du Περὶ φιλίας, Épictète attribue à Musonius Rufus, son propre maître, l'enseignement de la χρῆσις φαντασιῶν[107]. Épictète peut ainsi projeter dans la relation entre Antisthène et Diogène ce que lui-même a reçu de son maître.

Dans l'enseignement d'Épictète, l'ascèse est, à plusieurs reprises, associée à l'usage des représentations[108] ; dans le chapitre Περὶ ἀσκήσεως, Épictète affirme que l'exercice n'a pas sa fin en lui-même mais qu'il s'applique à trois domaines : désir et aversion, impulsion et répulsion, assentiment aux représentations[109].

Pour autant, le texte de Diogène Laërce ne parle pas d'un usage des représentations mais de la naissance de représentations permise par l'ascèse. Un détail de ce texte fait débat : ἐν γυμνασίᾳ συνεχεῖ γινόμεναι φαντασίαι est en fait une correction de Kühn et Reiske puisque les manuscrits ont transmis συνεχεῖς qualifiant ainsi les φαντασίαι, et non l'exercice (γυμνασίᾳ). G. Giannantoni (*SSR* V B 291) et O. Flores-Júnior préfèrent la leçon des manuscrits. Selon ce dernier, la correction crée une redondance inutile tandis que la leçon des manuscrits est « philosophiquement plus riche »[110] : il faut comprendre les φαντασίαι comme étant « durables » ou encore « *persistantes* et, d'une certaine manière, *stables* ». Or, l'adjectif συνεχής désigne ce qui est rarement interrompu et donc ce qui est fréquent. Au paragraphe précédent, il est utilisé sous sa forme adverbiale pour évoquer les fréquentes pratiques onanistes de Diogène sur la place publique. En *(e)*, l'adjectif est employé avec πόνησις, travail ou souffrance (πονήσει τῇ συνεχεῖ), au datif. On y constate ainsi son sens concret et temporel : συνεχής désigne ce qui se répète

105. Arrien, *Epic. Diss.* III, 24, 67-69 : « ἐξ οὗ μ' Ἀντισθένης ἠλευθέρωσεν, οὐκέτι ἐδούλευσα » πῶς ἠλευθέρωσεν; ἄκουε, τί λέγει· « ἐδίδαξέν με τὰ ἐμὰ καὶ τὰ οὐκ ἐμά. κτῆσις οὐκ ἐμή· [...] σὸν οὖν τί; χρῆσις φαντασιῶν. » Voir également III, 22, 103-104 pour décrire le cynique.

106. Voir Aubenque 1962, p. 1353 n. 1 ; Decker 2022b, p. 185-187.

107. Musonius Rufus, fr. 38 Hense (= Stobée II, 8, 30) : « Parmi les choses qui existent, le dieu a établi celles qui dépendent de nous et celles qui ne dépendent pas de nous. Dépend de nous ce qu'il y a de plus beau et de plus sage, ce pour quoi lui-même est en vérité heureux : l'usage des représentations » (τῶν ὄντων τὰ μὲν ἐφ' ἡμῖν ἔθετο ὁ θεός, τὰ δ' οὐκ ἐφ' ἡμῖν. ἐφ' ἡμῖν μὲν τὸ κάλλιστον καὶ σπουδαιότατον, ᾧ δὴ καὶ αὐτὸς εὐδαίμων ἐστί, τὴν χρῆσιν τῶν φαντασιῶν). Voir Goulet-Cazé 2016, p. 215 n. 54.

108. Voir Arrien, *Epic. Diss.* I, 27 et III, III, 1.

109. Arrien, *Epic. Diss.* III, 12, 13-14. Voir Gourinat 2022, § 16 et 20.

110. Flores-Júnior 2021, p. 267.

voire qui ne s'interrompt pas[111] et, comme le proposent les corrections de Kühn et Reiske, porte sur la qualité des exercices plutôt que sur celle des représentations.

Pour M.-O. Goulet-Cazé, l'auteur « veut certainement dire que l'ascèse corporelle provoque des représentations qui favorisent l'exercice du jugement selon la raison et incitent l'homme à agir selon la vertu »[112] ; elle convoque ainsi l'exemple de la faim. Mais est-ce parce qu'elle distingue deux auteurs dans l'exposé de l'ascèse qu'elle n'ose pas se référer aux exemples du texte lui-même ?

La compréhension des φαντασίαι peut s'établir de façon interne, à notre sens. En effet, le développement sur le plaisir permet de saisir à la fois les aspects sensible et intellectuel de la φαντασία, en particulier dans la proposition *(i)* qui se caractérise par des dérivations lexicales autour du plaisir : ἡδονῆς, ἡδυτάτη, ἡδέως, ἀηδῶς, ἥδιον, ἡδονῶν. Cet ensemble répétitif caractérise bien les retournements habituels du cynisme : la fuite de l'esclave Manès enseigne la liberté[113], la seule cité c'est l'univers[114], la pudeur est dans la nudité[115], etc. Ici, la *contradictio in adjecto* est obvie : le mépris du plaisir est un plaisir. C'est pourquoi, avant de distinguer des courants hédoniste et rigoriste[116], il convient d'accepter d'abord que le cynisme fonctionne par paradoxes pour, précisément, substituer aux subtilités des raisonnements l'évidence de la vertu en acte. A. Brancacci remarque que l'emploi d'adverbes (ἡδέως, ἀηδῶς, ἥδιον) au lieu de substantifs empêche la formulation de concepts fixes, immuables et laisse ouverte la possibilité d'un passage de l'un à l'autre[117].

Dès lors, les φαντασίαι se comprennent par leur souplesse, c'est-à-dire leur capacité à passer d'un contraire à un autre (τοὐναντίον), et la nécessité d'un exercice adéquat, c'est-à-dire ininterrompu. En effet, l'entraînement atténue la douleur initiale des πόνοι au point de les rendre agréables. Les φαντασίαι se caractérisent par leur statut intermédiaire et précaire : elles sont des impressions sensibles si l'on pense aux sensations engendrées par la facilité à effectuer ce qui paraissait difficile, et des représentations intellectuelles puisqu'elles permettent de comprendre que rien n'est infaisable et que le plaisir qui nous tenait en servitude peut être dompté. Le « mépris du plaisir » (τῆς ἡδονῆς ἡ καταφρόνησις) est donc un exemple de φαντασία proposé par le texte lui-même. L'ascèse aboutit à faire naître des représentations contraires

111. Voir Foucault 1984, p. 99 : « la vie cynique peut apparaître tout entière comme une sorte d'exercice permanent. »

112. Goulet-Cazé 2016, p. 215.

113. Sénèque, *Tranq. An.* VIII, 4-8.

114. DL VI, 72.

115. Arrien, *Epic. Diss.* III, 22, 15.

116. Voir Hoïstad 1948, p. 22-73.

117. Brancacci 2019, p. 206-207.

à l'opinion et à pouvoir faire un usage de celles-ci, selon l'assentiment.

À notre sens, la référence aux représentations et l'insistance sur la destination morale des exercices indiquent une présence stoïcienne qui, toutefois, respecte l'esprit de falsification attaché au cynisme.

III. Le spectacle de l'ascèse

Dès lors, si nous acceptons que l'exposé laërtien n'est pas une citation d'une œuvre de Diogène, le resituer dans un contexte de rédaction d'époque impériale permet d'y saisir des enjeux implicites qui sont propres à cette période. Nous pouvons à partir des articles de M. Billerbeck, de M.-O. Goulet-Cazé et de M. Griffin[118]résumer quelques traits caractéristiques du mouvement et de sa popularité acquise. Les hommes et femmes les moins fortunés adoptent le style de vie et l'accoutrement cyniques dans l'espoir d'échapper à leur condition[119]. Or, manifestement, ils se contentaient de reproduire les outrances de Diogène sans en comprendre le sens philosophique. Toutefois, l'impudence de Diogène fait aussi débat. Les écoles philosophiques dissertent pour savoir si le sage peut faire le chien[120]. Ainsi, certains auteurs, comme Cicéron[121], disqualifient le cynisme ; d'autres tournent en dérision ses outrances[122].

Lucien, confronté à des hordes de cyniques, moque l'ascèse en ce qu'elle ne vise que le spectaculaire : le fouet et la torture[123] ou, pour Pérégrinus, la masturbation publique et les coups de férule sur les fesses[124]. Face à ces déviances, certains auteurs ont cru bon de rétablir un « vrai » cynisme et c'est pourquoi l'on trouve de nombreux traités intitulés Περὶ Κυνισμοῦ, aussi bien parmi les philosophes cyniques comme Œnomaos, que chez d'autres auteurs : pensons au chapitre III, XXII des *Entretiens* d'Épictète ou aux discours VI et IX de l'empereur Julien qui prétendent éduquer les cyniques sur leur propre doctrine.

Les pratiques ascétiques sont ainsi au cœur du débat parce qu'elles incitent les cyniques outranciers à se donner en spectacle et à témoigner de leur vanité.

1.L'exemple paradoxal des athlètes et des musiciens.

Les efforts vains sont pourtant ceux des athlètes et musiciens dont l'exposé de l'ascèse convoque l'exemple ambivalent. En effet, même s'ils

118. Billerbeck 1982 ; Griffin 1993 ; Goulet-Cazé 2017, p. 261-360.

119. Voir Lucien, *Fugitiui*, 12-17.

120. Voir DL VII, 121 ; X, 119 ; Stobée II, 7, 11s.

121. Cicéron, *De officiis*, I, 126-128 ; I, 148.

122. *Anthologia Palatina* XI, 154 ; Perse, I, 133 ; Martial, III, 93, 12-13 ; XI, 84, 7.

123. Lucien, *Vit. auct.* 9.

124. Lucien, *De morte Peregrini*, 17, éd. Macleod : « il s'entraînait à la remarquable ascèse » (τὴν θαυμαστὴν ἄσκησιν διησκεῖτο).

négligent l'âme, Diogène s'en inspire puisque la répétition et l'habitude sont sources de maîtrise de l'action. Un fragment présent dans l'anthologie de Jean Stobée apporte une nuance intéressante :

> Diogène remarquait quelque chose de terrible : si les athlètes et les citharèdes maîtrisent le ventre et les plaisirs, les uns dans l'intérêt de leur voix et les autres de leur corps, personne ne les méprise au nom de la modération.[125]

Dans cet apophtegme, les athlètes et les musiciens n'exercent pas seulement leur corps pour gagner en agilité mais ils entraînent leur âme également à la frustration pour maîtriser davantage leur corps. L'inanité de leurs actions réside dès lors dans le fait de diriger les actions du corps et de l'âme au profit du seul corps. Les athlètes et les musiciens ont un aspect extérieur semblable à celui du sage : maîtrise de soi, mépris du plaisir, modération ; mais ils en font le moyen de leur pratique et non la finalité de leur vie. Ce témoignage, ainsi que d'autres[126], confirme le retournement qu'opèrent les paragraphes 70 et 71 : les actions du corps et celles de l'âme sont capables de cultiver la modération.

Les figures du spectacle, l'athlète et le musicien, sont sollicitées dans ces exemples ; l'exposé de l'ascèse les associe à l'aide d'une paronomase (ἀθλητὰς, αὐλητὰς). Or, la parodie des pratiques athlétiques est récurrente dans les chries au point que Diogène fait de son ascèse leur rivale : ses propres prouesses ridiculisent les exploits inutiles d'athlètes davantage intéressés par la gloire que par le bien vivre[127]. Ce *topos* littéraire, favorisé par l'importance des gymnases dans l'éducation grecque[128], est exploité par Dion Chrysostome puisqu'il met en scène Diogène aux Jeux Isthmiques dans deux dialogues différents (VIII et IX). Le philosophe propose un contre-spectacle dans lequel il est le seul athlète admirable et parodie, à l'aide de performances et d'actes de langage, le décernement des récompenses[129] pour s'attribuer la couronne de la victoire. L'outrance n'est pas de son fait mais de celui d'athlètes dont la réussite se réduit à courir plus vite que d'autres hommes mais toujours moins vite que les alouettes[130].

125. Stobée III, 5, 39 (= *SSR* V B 451) : δεινὸν ἔλεγε ὁ Διογένης, εἰ οἱ μὲν ἀθληταὶ καὶ οἱ κιθαρῳδοὶ γαστρὸς καὶ ἡδονῶν κρατοῦσιν, οἳ μὲν τῆς φωνῆς χάριν οἳ δὲ τοῦ σώματος, σωφροσύνης δ' ἕνεκα οὐδεὶς τούτων καταφρονήσει.

126. Voir également DL VI, 27 et Stobée III, 4, 111 (= *SSR* V B 450).

127. Voir DL VI, 33 (= *SSR* V B 76) : « À qui lui avait dit : "Aux Jeux Pythiques, je l'emporte sur des hommes", il répondit : "C'est moi plutôt qui l'emporte sur des hommes ; mais toi c'est sur des esclaves." » (Πρὸς τὸν εἰπόντα, "Πύθια νικῶ ἄνδρας," " 'Εγὼ μὲν οὖν," εἶπεν, "ἄνδρας, σὺ δ' ἀνδράποδα.")

128. Voir Marrou 1948, p. 177-200 ; Hadot 2002, p. 61.

129. Dion Chrysostome, *Or.* IX, 10-13.

130. *Ibid.* 18-19.

Diogène élève ses combats à un objet digne d'admiration, en particulier sa lutte contre la Τύχη[131]. Les discours de Télès[132] font de cette dernière un dramaturge qui distribue les rôles. Le monde devient un théâtre et le sage doit jouer son rôle du mieux qu'il peut[133] : sa vie est à la fois un combat et le spectacle de ce combat. Les exemples des musiciens et surtout des athlètes agissent donc en un double sens : d'une part, ils fournissent une illustration et une preuve de l'efficacité d'une ascèse sur soi ; d'autre part, ils fonctionnent comme un rappel du caractère spectaculaire de l'ascèse diogénienne, ce que confirme la proposition *(j)*.

2. La reproduction des actions cyniques par les communautés cyniques.

Ne faut-il pas distinguer chez le cynique sa vertu et sa façon de l'enseigner ? L'action cynique est profondément ambivalente puisqu'elle doit en même temps assurer le bonheur et être exemplaire. Or, la question de l'imitation des actions a vraisemblablement posé des problèmes au sein des communautés cyniques dans la compréhension de l'ascèse[134].

L'exemple de la mendicité est assez intéressant parce qu'il fait l'objet de débats conséquents à l'époque impériale alors que les chercheurs s'accordent pour considérer la mendicité de Diogène comme un motif littéraire plutôt que comme une réalité historique[135]. Certes, deux chries montrent Diogène en train de mendier, mais il le fait ponctuellement : le bon mot et l'exercice ascétique semblent plus importants dans les anecdotes que la nécessité d'adopter la condition de mendiant[136].

Les lettres pseudépigraphiques déploient des efforts rhétoriques conséquents pour fonder philosophiquement la mendicité : sept lettres sur les

131. Voir Stobée II, 8, 21 (= *SSR* V B 148).

132. Télès, ΠΕΡΙ ΑΥΤΑΡΚΕΙΑΣ, *apud* Stobée III, 1, 98, p. 5 ; ΠΕΡΙ ΠΕΡΙΣΤΑΣΕΩΝ, *apud* Stobée IV, 44, 82, p. 52. P. P. Fuentes González (1998, p. 160) remarque que la Τύχη, dans les représentations populaires, symbolise tout ce qui peut renvoyer à l'instabilité du monde. Elle assume donc le rôle de tout adversaire possible en même temps qu'elle crée des rôles et les attribue.

133. Pour une étude de la métaphore de l'acteur, voir Brancacci 2002 ; Navaud 2010 ; Bourbon 2019.

134. M. Chapuis (2021, p. 24-32) mentionne, à partir de différentes études, l'importance de pratiques ascétiques dans la constitution de la marginalité sociale.

135. Voir Fuentes González 1998, p. 235 (« la mendicité, loin d'être un impératif absolu, n'est qu'une circonstance de plus que l'homme de bien doit affronter, si la fortune l'y contraint ») ; Helmer 2020 ; Chapuis 2021, p. 181-200.

136. DL VI, 49 (= *SSR* V B 247) : « Un jour il demandait l'aumône à une statue ; quelqu'un lui ayant demandé pourquoi il faisait cela, il répondit : "Je m'exerce à échouer". Demandant l'aumône à quelqu'un – car au début, il faisait cela à cause de son indigence – il dit : "si tu as déjà donné à quelqu'un d'autre, donne-moi aussi ; si tu n'as donné à personne, commence par moi." » (ᾔτει ποτὲ ἀνδριάντα· ἐρωτηθεὶς δὲ διὰ τί τοῦτο ποιεῖ, "μελετῶ," εἶπεν, "ἀποτυγχάνειν." αἰτῶν τινα (καὶ γὰρ τοῦτο πρῶτον ἐποίησε διὰ τὴν ἀπορίαν) ἔφη, "εἰ μὲν καὶ ἄλλῳ δέδωκας, δὸς κἀμοί· εἰ δὲ μηδενί, ἀπ' ἐμοῦ ἄρξαι.")

trente-six attribuées à Cratès abordent le sujet. À l'opposé, d'autres auteurs interdisent la mendicité dans leur école : c'est le cas d'Épicure dont la doxographie laërtienne précise : « [Le sage] ne fera pas le chien [...], ni ne mendiera »[137]. Notons également que Démétrius aux yeux de Sénèque se distingue des autres cyniques parce qu'il ne pratique pas la mendicité, tout comme Démonax aux yeux de Lucien[138].

Épictète semble confronté à la popularité du cynisme au sein même de son école et défend régulièrement à ses élèves de singer les actions cyniques : ne plus se laver, prendre les dehors du philosophe (barbe, manteau, bâton, besace), insulter, mendier[139]. Parmi les mises en garde d'Épictète, ne pas embrasser les statues peut attirer notre attention. Cette pratique fait probablement référence aux exercices de Diogène visant à supporter le froid : il embrassait des statues, nu, en plein hiver[140]. Elle s'inscrit dans la suite de l'exhibition de sa vertu dont la gymnastique offre des occasions : J.-M. Roubineau[141] rappelle que la popularité des athlètes suscitait l'exaspération des lettrés et que Diogène parodie probablement la préhension des statues pratiquée dans les gymnases pour travailler les appuis et la musculature. Le geste de Diogène comporte ainsi plusieurs niveaux de lecture.

Épictète évoque cette pratique[142], comme, par exemple, dans le chapitre III, XII des *Entretiens* :

> Nous ne devons pas nous exercer au moyen de pratiques contraires à la nature et à l'opinion, puisque nous qui disons philosopher, nous ne différerions en rien de faiseurs de tours. Il est difficile, en effet, de marcher sur une corde, et non seulement difficile, mais surtout dangereux. Pour cette raison, nous faut-il marcher sur la corde, redresser un palmier ou embrasser des statues ?
>
> Homme, exerce-toi, si tu es impétueux, à supporter d'être injurié et à ne pas souffrir d'être méprisé. Alors tu feras des progrès de sorte que, si quelqu'un te donne des coups, tu puisses te dire à toi-même : « Pense que tu embrasses une statue ».[143]

137. DL X, 119 : οὐδὲ κυνιεῖν [...] · οὐδὲ πτωχεύσειν.

138. Sénèque, *De vita beata*, XVIII, 3 ; Lucien, *Demonax*, 63.

139. Arrien, *Epict. Diss.* III, XXII, 10-11 ; 50 ; 80 ; 89 ; IV, VIII, 1-14 et 34 ; IV, XI.

140. DL VI, 23 (= *SSR* V B 174) ; Plutarque, *Apophthegmata laconica* 16, 233A (= *SSR* V B 177).

141. Roubineau 2020, p. 146.

142. Arrien, *Epict. Diss.* III, XII, 2 et 10 ; IV, V, 14 ; Arrien, *Epict. enchir.* XLVII.

143. Arrien, *Epict. Diss.* III, XII, 1-2 et 10, éd. Schenkl : τὰς ἀσκήσεις οὐ δεῖ διὰ τῶν παρὰ φύσιν καὶ παραδόξων ποιεῖσθαι, ἐπεί τοι τῶν θαυματοποιῶν οὐδὲν διοίσομεν οἱ λέγοντες φιλοσοφεῖν. δύσκολον γάρ ἐστι καὶ τὸ ἐπὶ σχοινίου περιπατεῖν καὶ οὐ μόνον δύσκολον, ἀλλὰ καὶ ἐπικίνδυνον. τούτου ἕνεκα δεῖ καὶ ἡμᾶς μελετᾶν ἐπὶ σχοινίου περιπατεῖν ἢ φοίνικα ἱστάνειν ἢ ἀνδριάντας περιλαμβάνειν ; [...] ἄνθρωπε, ἄσκησον, εἰ γοργὸς εἶ, λοιδορούμενος ἀνέχεσθαι, ἀτιμασθεὶς μὴ ἀχθεσθῆναι. εἶθ' οὕτως προβήσῃ, ἵνα, κἂν πλήξῃ σέ τις, εἴπῃς αὐτὸς πρὸς αὑτὸν ὅτι "δόξον ἀνδριάντα περιειληφέναι".

Ce chapitre « Sur l'ascèse » (Περὶ ἀσκήσεως) semble prendre ses distances avec le cynisme outrancier[144]. S'exercer ne consiste pas à chercher les prouesses des acrobates. En cela, les exercices ascétiques de Diogène sont exagérés et, à la deuxième mention, nous voyons qu'Épictète assigne un autre sens à la pratique cynique en spiritualisant l'exercice physique en une résistance symbolique aux injures. T. Bénatouïl remarque qu'Épictète réinterprète la pratique à l'aune d'une autre chrie, celle où Diogène mendie à une statue[145]. Pourquoi, dès lors, réhabiliter à moitié l'ascèse cynique ?

Il faut admettre que l'exemplarité de la vie de Diogène est source de malentendus pour de nombreux disciples intéressés par le cynisme. S'il faut imiter ses actions, nous ne saurions les reproduire telles quelles. Cette réprobation de « l'ascétisme ostentatoire », selon l'expression d'I. Chouinard[146], nous confronte au cœur du paradoxe cynique dont les actions sont à la fois une parodie, un spectacle[147] et un modèle. Comment s'inspirer de l'exemple sans reproduire l'aspect spectaculaire ? Répétée à outrance, l'action cynique, d'abord éclatante dans son surgissement, s'émousse et perd son originalité.

Épictète ne s'en prend pas au cynisme de Diogène, mais aux apprentis cyniques de son temps. Lorsqu'il complète ses avertissements de cette façon : « Mais si les exercices visent l'exhibition, c'est pour ceux qui se penchent vers le dehors, qui ne poursuivent ni ne recherchent rien d'autre que des spectateurs qui s'exclameront : “Oh ! le grand homme !” »[148], Épictète s'en prend aux mêmes fanfarons qui se réclament d'Antisthène, de Diogène et de Cratès et qui, selon Lucien, dégradent l'image de la philosophie[149]. Le *Manuel* met en garde de la même façon : « Quand tu veux t'entraîner à la peine, fais-le pour toi-même, et non pour ceux d'en dehors ; n'embrasse pas les statues »[150]. L'acte ascétique doit être dirigé vers soi, vers son âme et non vers les autres. À notre sens, l'expression « pour toi et non pour ceux d'en dehors » rappelle l'insistance du texte de Diogène Laërce sur la destination morale de l'ascèse.

144. J.-B. Gourinat (2022, § 26) s'étonne qu'Épictète critique les habitudes ascétiques de Diogène alors qu'il en fait un modèle dans le reste des *Entretiens*. Il nous semble que distinguer la figure de Diogène et les outrances du cynisme populaire permet de mieux percevoir les enjeux de l'enseignement du philosophe stoïcien : certaines pratiques de Diogène ne sont excessives que dans la mesure où elles sont reproduites machinalement par les communautés cyniques.

145. Bénatouïl 2021, p. 4.

146. Chouinard 2021, p. 228.

147. T. Bénatouïl (2021, p. 6) précise à juste titre : « La vie cynique est un spectacle spectaculaire ». Voir aussi Mansfeld 1988, p. 163 : « *If Diogenes wanted to train for total independence, then why e.g. make a habit of masturbating in the market-place [DL VI, 69] rather than in private ? He was an actor, constantly needing a public.* »

148. Arrien, *Epict. Diss.* III, XII, 16 : ἂν δὲ πρὸς ἐπίδειξιν, ἔξω νενευκότος ἐστὶ καὶ ἄλλο τι θηρωμένου καὶ θεατὰς ζητοῦντος τοὺς ἐροῦντας “ὢ μεγάλου ἀνθρώπου”.

149. Voir Lucien, *Fug.* 12-17.

150. Arrien, *Epict. enchir.* XLVII, éd. Boter : κἂν ἀσκῆσαί ποτε πρὸς πόνον θέλῃς, σαυτῷ καὶ μὴ τοῖς ἔξω. μὴ τοὺς ἀνδριάντας περιλάμβανε.

La référence aux acrobates (θαυματοποιόι) pour penser le πόνος, chez le maître d'Épictète, Musonius Rufus[151], a pu inspirer la condamnation de l'inutilité des actes spectaculaires. Mais à la différence de Musonius Rufus ou de DL 70-71, les sermons d'Épictète intègrent clairement des références aux excès cyniques dont l'ascèse s'égare dans des extravagances, qui ne peuvent être spectaculaires que tant qu'elles demeurent exceptionnelles[152].

L'ascèse cynique a donc pu engendrer des malentendus pour comprendre l'action. En effet, si l'action cynique réside dans des actes incarnés, irréductibles à une théorie abstraite, devenir cynique ne consiste pourtant pas à répéter et exhiber telle ou telle action précise. Pour comprendre le cynisme, il ne faut dès lors pas négliger la confusion qu'ont pu historiquement connaître les communautés cyniques.

Conclusion

Le livre VI de Diogène Laërce rend perceptible une tension entre la somme d'anecdotes et la théorie de l'action morale cynique. L'importance de la tradition des chries, certes, a permis d'insister sur la conformité entre la vie des philosophes et leurs discours et de questionner ce qu'est une vie de philosophe[153]. Mais elle élève ces vies à un spectacle inégalable, dans lequel l'admiration engendre une incapacité à reproduire l'intelligence des actes. Si la théorie de l'ascèse chez Diogène Laërce insiste autant sur le passage du corps à l'âme, elle témoigne de débats qui concernaient autant le siècle de Diogène que l'époque impériale. Certes, les questions de force et d'habituation émergent dès Socrate et resituent la pensée cynique au milieu de pratiques populaires auxquelles elle se confronte autant qu'elle les parodie. Toutefois, certains aspects de la doxographie de Diogène traduisent une réinterprétation stoïcienne et peuvent s'inscrire dans un projet éditorial dans lequel le cynisme permet de relier le stoïcisme à Socrate[154]. C'est pourquoi il n'est pas étonnant de remarquer une teinte stoïcienne dans la description des φαντασίαι et de la finalité morale dans la doxographie de Diogène.

151. Musonius, *Or.* VII, p. 30.

152. Voir Bénatouïl 2021, p. 6-7 : « C'est donc bien le fait d'avoir un public qui justifie l'excès de l'exercice du cynique ou du funambule [...]. Épictète [...] craint en effet que ses disciples ne se lancent dans cette voie principalement pour se donner en spectacle, en réduisant le cynique à son apparence extérieure et en oubliant les exigences et la finalité véritables de la vie cynique. »

153. F. Cossutta, P. Delormas et D. Maingueneau (2012, p. 8) proposent de distinguer « vie du philosophe », « vie de philosophe » et « vie philosophique » pour penser la congruence entre le biographique et le théorique.

154. La doxographie générale (DL VI, 103-105) établit explicitement les liens entre cynisme et stoïcisme (voir Brancacci 1992 ; Gugliermina 2006, p. 179-186 ; Goulet-Cazé 2017, p. 94-109 ; Chouinard 2021, p. 307-337 ; Decker 2022b, p. 42-59).

Or, les lettres pseudépigraphiques comme la chrie opposant Diogène et Hégésias traduisent le besoin que rencontrent les disciples de comprendre la règle cynique avant de la pratiquer. Il y a quelque chose d'ascétique dans la façon d'inviter les disciples à être toujours déjà dans la pratique avant même que de la réfléchir. Que des déviances soient survenues, reproduisant l'acte pour l'acte et non pour la vertu, était inévitable. C'est pourquoi il nous semble important de confronter le texte de Diogène Laërce à des textes visant à prévenir les outrances des cyniques, comme on le constate très régulièrement dans les enseignements d'Épictète. En effet, Diogène Laërce pouvait avoir plus facilement accès à des textes défendant un « vrai » cynisme contre ses formes déviées. Dès lors, il ne serait pas improbable que sa source intègre l'exigence spirituelle, tout en restant fidèle à l'esprit de Diogène, pour tempérer les spectacles vains de l'ascèse et favoriser une élévation morale du cynisme. Hisser son action hors de l'anecdotique a été une difficulté majeure de l'ascèse cynique et les incarnations les plus illustres de l'époque impériale ont ainsi dû s'écarter du modèle trop imposant de Diogène[155].

155. Voir par exemple le Démétrius de Sénèque (Decker 2022b, p. 433-444).

BIBLIOGRAPHIE

AUBENQUE, P. 1962 : « Notes aux *Entretiens d'Épictète* », dans P.-M. Schuhl (éd.), *Les Stoïciens*, Paris, p. 1339-1370.

AUBENQUE, P. 2004 : *La Prudence chez Aristote*, Paris [1963].

AUJOULAT, N. 1990 : « La *phantasia* dans le *De Anima* d'Aristote », *Pallas (Littérature Histoire Archéologie Cosmologie)*, 36, p. 19-51.

BÉNATOUÏL, T. 2011 : « Comment faire de la liberté avec des mots ? Critiques et usages de la parole chez Diogène le cynique », dans B. Cassin & C. Lévy (éd.), *Genèse de l'acte de parole dans le monde grec, romain et médiéval*, Turnhout, p. 161-184.

BÉNATOUÏL, T. 2021 : « Le philosophe et l'acrobate (Épictète, *Entretiens* III, 12) », *Methodos. Savoirs et textes*, 21, en ligne.
DOI : 10.4000/methodos.8427

BILLERBECK, M. 1978 : *Epiktet : Vom Kynismus*, Leiden.

BILLERBECK, M. 1982 : « La réception du cynisme à Rome », *L'Antiquité classique*, 51/1, p. 151-173.

BILLERBECK, M. 1993 : « Le Cynisme idéalisé d'Épictète à Julien », dans M.-O. Goulet-Cazé & R. Goulet (éd.), *Le Cynisme ancien et ses prolongements : actes du colloque international du CNRS (Paris, 22 - 25 juillet 1991)*, Paris, p. 319-338.

BOURBON, M. 2019 : *Penser l'individu : genèse stoïcienne de la subjectivité*, Turnhout.

BRANCACCI, A. 1987 : « *Askesis* e *logos* nella tradizione cinica », *Elenchos*, 8, p. 439-447.

BRANCACCI, A. 1992 : « I κοινῇ ἀρέσκοντα dei Cinici e la κοινωνία tra cinismo e stoicismo nel libro VI (103 – 105) delle '*Vite*' di Diogene Laerzio », dans W. Haase (éd.), *Philosophie, Wissenschaften, Technik*, Berlin-Boston, p. 4049-4075.

BRANCACCI, A. 2000 : « Libertà e fato in Enomao di Gadara », dans A. Brancacci (éd.), *La Filosofia in età imperiale : le scuole e le tradizioni filosofiche : atti del colloquio, Roma, 17-19 giugno 1999*, Napoli, p. 37-67.

BRANCACCI, A. 2002 : « L'attore e il cambiamento di ruolo nel cinismo », *Philologus*, 146/1, p. 65-86.

BRANCACCI, A. 2005 : *Antisthène : le discours propre*, trad. S. Aubert, Paris.

BRANCACCI, A. 2019 : « Eudemonismo, *askesis* e piacere in Diogene il Cinico », *Museum Helveticum*, 76/2, p. 191-207.

CHAPUIS, M. 2021 : *Figures de la marginalité dans la pensée grecque. Autour de la tradition cynique*, Paris.

CHOUINARD, I. 2021 : *Un tonneau sous le Portique : la réception du cynisme chez les stoïciens*, thèse de doctorat, Université de Montréal-Sorbonne université.
URL : https://papyrus.bib.umontreal.ca/xmlui/handle/1866/26419

CHOUINARD, I. 2022 : « Olimar Flores-Júnior, *La Vie facile. Une lecture du cynisme ancien* », *Philosophie antique*, 22, p. 263-265.
DOI : 10.4000/philosant.5638

Collette, B. 2006 : « *Phantasia* et *phantasma* chez Platon », *Les Études philosophiques*, 76/1, p. 89-106.
DOI : 10.3917/leph.061.0089

Cossutta, F., Delormas P. & Maingueneau D. 2012 : *La Vie à l'œuvre. Le biographique dans le discours philosophique,* Limoges.

Decker, J. 2022a : « L'ἰσχύς cynique entre la maîtrise de soi socratique et le *tonos* stoïcien : un volontarisme ? », dans E. Cattanei & S. Maso, *Lexis Supplements*, 5, Venezia, p. 43-71.
DOI : 10.30687/978-88-6969-583-4/002

Decker, J. 2022b : *La Normalisation du Cynisme dans ses usages philosophiques antiques*, thèse de doctorat, Université Bordeaux Montaigne.
URL : https://theses.hal.science/tel-03968931

Dorandi, T. 1993 : « La *Politeia* de Diogène de Sinope et quelques remarques sur sa pensée politique », dans M.-O. Goulet-Cazé & R. Goulet (éd.), *Le Cynisme ancien et ses prolongements : actes du colloque international du CNRS (Paris, 22 - 25 juillet 1991)*, Paris, p. 57-68.

Dorandi, T. 2013 (éd.) : Diogenes Laertius, *Lives of Eminent Philosophers,* Texts and Commentaries, New York-Cambridge.

Dorion, L.-A. 2018 : « La doctrine de la double ascèse (D.L. VI 70-71) est-elle d'inspiration socratique ? », *Philosophia,* 48, p. 71-84.

Dudley, D. 1937 : *A History of Cynicism from Diogenes to the 6th century A.D.*, London.

Emeljanow, V. 1965 : « A Note on the Cynic Short Cut to Happiness », *Mnemosyne,* 18/2, p. 182-184.

Flores-Júnior, O. 2005 : « Cratès, la fourmi et l'escarbot : les cyniques et l'exemple animal », *Philosophie antique*, 5, p. 135-171.

Flores-Júnior, O. 2006 : « *Khortos gasteri* ou le bonheur est dans le pré : éthique et politique cyniques selon un poème de Cratès de Thèbes », *Dialogue*, 45/4, p. 647-677.

Flores-Júnior, O. 2017 : « Paradoxes cyniques : l'activité littéraire d'Antisthène et de Diogène de Sinope », *Nuntius Antiquus*, 13/2, p. 117-136.
URL : https://periodicos.ufmg.br/index.php/nuntius_antiquus/article/view/17099

Flores-Júnior, O. 2021 : *La Vie facile : une lecture du cynisme ancien*, Paris.

Foucault, M. 1984 : *Histoire de la sexualité.* t. II : *L'Usage des plaisirs*, Paris.

Foucault, M. 2009 : *Le Courage de la vérité. Le Gouvernement de soi et des autres II*, Paris.

Fuentes González, P. P. 1998 (éd.) : *Les Diatribes de Télès: introduction, texte revu, traduction et commentaire des fragments,* Paris.

Fuentes González, P. P. 2013 : « En defensa del encuentro entre dos "Perros", Antístenes y Diógenes: historia de una tensa amistad », *Cuadernos de Filología Clásica. Estudios griegos e indoeuropeos*, 23, p. 225-267.

Giannantoni, G. 1990 (éd.) : *Socratis et Socraticorum reliquiae*, 4 vol., Napoli.

Goulet-Cazé, M.-O. 1999 : « Introduction, traduction et notes », dans M.-O. Goulet-Cazé (dir.), Diogène Laërce, *Vies et doctrines des philosophes illustres*, Paris, p. 657-772.

Goulet-Cazé, M.-O. 2003 : *Les* Kynica *du stoïcisme*, Stuttgart.
Goulet-Cazé, M.-O. 2016 : *L'Ascèse cynique : un commentaire de Diogène Laërce VI 70-71,* éd. revue et augmentée, Paris [1986].
Goulet-Cazé, M.-O. 2017 : *Le Cynisme, une philosophie antique*, Paris.
Gourinat, J.-B. 2022 : « Sur la philosophie comme *askêsis* (*Entretiens*, III, 2 et 12) : Épictète et la tradition stoïcienne », *Aitia*, 12, en ligne.
DOI : 10.4000/aitia.10549
Griffin, M. 1993 : « Le mouvement cynique et les Romains : attraction et répulsion », dans M.-O. Goulet-Cazé & R. B. Branham (éd.), *The Cynics: the Cynic Movement in Antiquity and its Legacy*, Berkeley, p. 241-258.
Gugliermina, I. 2006 : *Diogène Laërce et le Cynisme*, Villeneuve d'Ascq.
Hadot, P. 2002 : *Exercices spirituels et philosophie antique,* Paris.
Helmer, É. 2017 : *Diogène le Cynique*, Paris.
Helmer, É. 2020 (éd.) : *Mendiants et mendicité en Grèce ancienne*, Paris.
Höistad, R. 1948 : *Cynic Hero and Cynic King: Studies in the Cynic Conception of Man*, University of Uppsala.
Husson, S. 2011 : *La* République *de Diogène: une cité en quête de la nature,* Paris.
Husson, S. 2013 : « "Revêtir la vie des chiens", l'animal comme modèle moral », *Revista Archai*, 11, p. 69-78.
Izzo, D. 2023 : « La souris, ennemie de l'homme et modèle du cynique », *Aitia*, 13.1, en ligne.
DOI : 10.4000/aitia.10995
Junqua, F. 2000 (éd.) : *Lettres de cyniques : étude des correspondances apocryphes de Diogène de Sinope et Cratès de Thèbes*, volume 1, thèse de doctorat, Université Paris 4.
Labarrière, J.-L. 2008 : « Du *phronimos* comme critère de l'action droite chez Aristote », dans D. Lories et L. Rizzerio (éd.), *Le Jugement pratique. Autour de la notion de* phronèsis, Paris, p. 145-166.
Long, A. 1996 : « The Socratic Tradition: Diogenes, Crates and Hellenistic Ethics », dans M.-O. Goulet-Cazé & R. B. Branham (éd.), *The Cynics: the Cynic Movement in Antiquity and its Legacy*, Berkeley, p. 28-46.
Mansfled, J. 1988 : « Marie-Odile Goulet-Cazé : *L'Ascèse cynique* » [Book review], *The Classical review*, 38/1, p. 162-163.
Marrou, H.-I. 1948 : *Histoire de l'éducation dans l'Antiquité. I. Le monde grec*, Paris.
Meilland, J.-M. 1983 : « L'anti-intellectualisme de Diogène le Cynique », *Revue de théologie et de philosophie*, 115/3, p. 233-246.
Monteils-Laeng, L. 2014 : *Agir sans vouloir : le problème de l'intellectualisme moral dans la philosophie ancienne,* Paris.
Navaud, G. 2010 : Persona. *Le Théâtre comme métaphore théorique de Socrate à Shakespeare,* Genève.
Nicolas, L. 2011 : « L'exemple ambigu ou la *phronèsis* du *phronimos* », *DICE*, 8/2, p. 27-48.
Seltmann, C. 1936 : « Diogenes of Sinope, Son of Banker Hikesias », dans J. Allan, H. Mattingly et E. Robinson (éd.), *Transactions of the International Numismatic Congress Organized and Held in London by the Royal Numismatic Society,* London, p. 121.

Servais, J. 1959 : « Alexandre-Dionysos et Diogène-Sérapis : À propos de Diogène Laërce, VI, 63 ». *L'Antiquité classique*, 28/1, p. 98-106.

Veillard, C. 2009 : « Les Vies de philosophes de Diogène Laërce : une réflexion sur l'histoire de la philosophie », *Revista Dissertatio de Filosofia,* 30, p. 73-92. DOI : 10.15210/dissertatio.v30i0.8792

Von Fritz, K. 1926 : *Quellen-Untersuchungen zu Leben und Philosophie des Diogenes von Sinope,* vol. 2, Philologus Supplementband 18, Leipzig.

CHRYSIPPE, L'INÉVITABILITÉ DU DESTIN ET LA CONFATALITÉ

Olivier D'JERANIAN
Chercheur associé à l'équipe Gramata (Sphère 7219)

RÉSUMÉ. Cet article aborde la théorie des *confatalia* élaborée par Chrysippe en réponse à l'argument Paresseux. Après avoir révélé son sophisme, nous analysons la distinction qu'il utilise pour y répondre (Cicéron, *Fat.* 30). D'un côté, les *res simplices*, qui décrivent correctement l'inévitabilité du destin, d'un autre, les *res copulatae*, qui supposent une relation de dépendance entre un résultat et une action *confatals*. Rendant le fatalisme stoïcien plus robuste, les *confatalia* s'inscrivaient dans la problématique morale du deuxième livre du *Sur le destin* de Chrysippe. C'est dans cette perspective que nous examinons la nature de la relation *confatale*, pour conclure qu'elle n'est l'effet d'aucune loi du destin qui la rendrait nécessaire.

ABSTRACT. *This article discusses the theory of* confatalia *developed by Chrysippus in response to the Lazy argument. After revealing its fallacy, we analyse the distinction used to respond to it (Cicero,* Fat. *30). On the one hand,* res simplices, *which correctly describes the inevitability of fate, on the other,* res copulatae, *which assume a relationship of dependence between a result and a* confatal *action. Making Stoic fatalism more robust, the* confatalia *were part of the moral issues of the second book of Chrysippus'* On Fate. *It is from this perspective that we examine the nature of the* confatal *relationship, concluding that it is not the effect of any law of fate that would make it necessary.*

Le Paresseux

Dans son *Du destin*, Cicéron rapporte le *Paresseux* (ἀργὸς λόγος)[1], qui vise à persuader un malade qu'il est vain d'agir, si le destin existe* :

> [P1] Si ton destin est de guérir, que tu appelles le médecin ou que tu ne l'appelles pas, tu guériras.
>
> [P2] De même, si ton destin est de ne pas guérir, que tu appelles le médecin ou que tu ne l'appelles pas, tu ne guériras pas.
>
> [P3] Or, l'un des deux est ton destin.
>
> [C] Donc il ne te sert à rien d'appeler le médecin[2].

Par extrapolation, tous nos efforts dans la vie seraient vains (*nihil omnino agamus in vita*). Le *Paresseux* visant aussi bien les fatalistes que les logiciens, les stoïciens auraient été une cible idéale[3], parce qu'ils affirmaient que notre devoir est de « vivre en accord avec la nature »[4] bien que « tout arrive par le destin » (*fato omnia fiunt* ; καθ' εἱμαρμένην τὰ πάντα γίνεσθαι)[5], et parce qu'ils en voulaient pour preuve que toute proposition est vraie ou fausse[6]. En

* Je suis reconnaissant envers Jean-Baptiste Gourinat d'avoir relu la première version de cet article et de m'avoir adressé plusieurs objections décisives.

1. Parallèle grec chez Origène, *Cels.* II, 20, 62-71 (*Stoicorum Veterum Fragmenta* [désormais *SVF*] II, 957).

2. Cicéron, *Fat.* 28-29 (éd. Yon).

3. Même si, en l'absence d'autre réponse que celle de Chrysippe, rien ne prouve l'existence d'une attaque antérieure. Voir Alexandre, *Fat.* c. 11 et 16.

4. *Cf.* Diogène Laërce [désormais DL] VII, 87-89.

5. *Cf.* DL VII, 149 (*SVF* I, 175) ; Cicéron, *Fat.* 10 ; 31 ; 40 ; 43 ; *Div.* I, 55 ; 125-126 (*SVF* I, 921 = Long & Sedley 2001 [désormais LS] 55 L) ; II, 20 ; Alexandre, *Fat.* (c. 2) p. 166, 2 ; (c. 7) p. 171, 20 ; (c. 16) p. 186, 13 ; (c. 31) 202, 2 ; *de An.* (§25) p. 180, 8 ; Ps.-Plutarque, *De Fat.* 570 C ; 574 D.

6. *Cf.* DL VII, 65 ; Cicéron, *Acad. Pr.* II, 95 ; *Fat.* 20-21 (*SVF* II, 952 = LS 38 G) ; Sextus, *M.* VIII, 12 ; Ps.-Plutarque, *De Fat.* 574 F (*SVF* II, 912).

effet, dans la suite du texte, Cicéron montre qu'on peut réduire le destin à la vérité éternelle des propositions au futur :

> On peut même en changer l'expression, et, sans nommer le destin, lui conserver un sens identique, par exemple : « Si, de toute éternité, est vraie '*tu guériras de cette maladie*', que tu appelles le médecin ou que tu ne l'appelles pas, tu en guériras. Pareillement, si, de toute éternité est fausse '*tu guériras de cette maladie*', que tu appelles le médecin ou que tu ne l'appelles pas, tu n'en guériras pas », et ainsi de suite[7].

Cette réduction affilie le *Paresseux* au déterminisme logique et rappelle le raisonnement mégarique qui au moyen du principe de bivalence inférait la nécessité d'un état de choses futur *p* (LF*p*) à partir de la vérité immuable de son énoncé au futur (« F*p* »)[8], argument qu'Aristote avait justement rejeté au motif qu'il ruinerait la vie morale[9].

L'origine mégarique du *Paresseux* serait attestée par le tiers exclu en [P3], qui le rapproche d'un autre argument dilemmatique[10] attribué cette fois-ci explicitement à Diodore Cronos, le *Moissonneur* (θερίζων λόγος)[11]. Puisque « les propositions sont vraies en tant qu'elles se conforment aux choses mêmes »[12], puisque « toute vérité passée est nécessaire »[13], si le fait que « tu moissonneras » est *vraie*, celui que tu moissonneras est *nécessaire*. Ce n'est donc pas « peut-être » (τάχα) mais « certainement » (πάντως) que tu moissonneras. Et puisqu'il n'est possible ni que tu moissonnes, ni que tu ne moissonnes pas, *nécessairement* l'un des opposés est vrai et l'autre faux, celui des deux dont l'énoncé est vrai aura lieu « par nécessité » (ἐξ ἀνάγκης), le *tertium non datur* permettant de distribuer la nécessité de la disjonction vraie à l'un de ses deux membres[14]. À moins de rejeter le correspondantisme et l'inférence de la détermination sémantique des propositions à la détermination ontologique des événements sur lesquels elles portent ; à moins de nier, sinon la bivalence (comme Épicure)[15], du moins son universalité (comme Aristote)[16], il est nécessaire au *sens composé* (*de dicto*) que l'un des deux membres

7. Cicéron, *Fat.* 29.

8. Cf. *Int.* 9, 18b9-33.

9. *Int.* 9, 19a7 *sq.*

10. Bobzien 1998, p. 189-191. Voir Sextus, *M.* X, 87 (Diodore, fr. 123) et 347 (Diodore, fr. 126) : Si *p*, alors non-*q*. Si non-*p*, alors non-*q*. Or *p* ou non-*p*. Donc non-*q*. Pour ce type d'argument, voir Plutarque, *De stoic. rep.* 1034 E (*SVF* I, 78) et Gourinat 2000, p. 85.

11. *Cf.* Ammonius, *In Int.* p. 131, 24-32 (FDS 1252 = LS 38 I) ; Alexandre, *In APr.* schol. 163 et Plutarque, *De stoic. rep.* 1055 D (*SVF* II, 202) ; DL VII, 25. Voir Seel 1993.

12. *Cf.* Aristote, *Int.* 9, 19a30-35.

13. *Cf.* Arrien, *Epict.* II, 19, 1-3 ; Cicéron, *Fat.* 14 ; Aristote (cf. *Eth. Nic.* VI, 1139b8-11).

14. $L(Fp \vee F{\sim}p) \Rightarrow L(Fp) \vee L(F{\sim}p)$, ce que rejette Aristote, la bataille navale étant un futur contingent (*Int.* 9, 19a23 *sq.*).

15. *Cf.* Cicéron, *Fat.* 21-23 et 37-38 ; *Acad. Pr.* II, 97 (LS 20 I).

16. Aristote restreint la bivalence du fait de l'indétermination de *certains* futurs qui sont *en puissance* d'être ceci ou cela (*Int.* 9, 19a23 *sq.*). Voir Gaskin 1995, p. 161-166.

de la disjonction soit vrai et l'autre faux[17], de sorte que celui qui sera le cas est nécessaire au *sens divisé* (*de re*) au moment où la proposition au futur est énoncée, c'est-à-dire *avant* qu'il n'ait lieu.

La conclusion du *Moissonneur* rejoint celle du *Dominateur*[18], l'argument grâce auquel Diodore faisait prévaloir contre Aristote sa doctrine des modalités[19] en niant la réalité des possibilités contrefactuelles à partir de la conjonction de la nécessité du passé[20] et de l'impossibilité, pour un impossible, de suivre logiquement d'un possible[21]. Bien que le *Moissonneur* ne mentionne pas le destin, bien que le *Paresseux* n'évoque pas la nécessité, leur parenté serait démontrée par un argument que Cicéron rapporte comme celui qui poussa Épicure à nier la bivalence pour sauver la liberté :

> si l'un des deux [contradictoires] est vrai de toute éternité, il est aussi certain, et s'il est certain (*certum*), il est nécessaire : c'est ainsi, pense [Épicure], que la nécessité et le destin sont établis[22].

Mais à la différence du *Moissonneur*, le *Paresseux* relie un résultat à une action pour conclure que celle-ci est *toujours* vaine (*nihil attinet*, οὐ μάτην) même lorsque le résultat en dépend. Si le *Moissonneur* était considéré comme fallacieux par les stoïciens[23], on pourrait s'étonner que Diogène Laërce ne le mentionne pas dans la liste, certes non-exhaustive, des sophismes (VII, 44 et 82)[24]. Reste à savoir si et pourquoi les philosophes du Portique le regardaient comme un sophisme[25].

Selon Susanne Bobzien, pour ceux qui défendaient l'inévitabilité du destin[26] et la vérité du tiers exclu[27], le *Paresseux* devait à première vue sembler

17. En raison de la conjonction des principes de contradiction et du tiers exclu, si deux énoncés sont contradictoires, l'un d'entre eux est vrai si et seulement si l'autre est faux (Aristote, *Int.* 9, 18b28-29).

18. Pour le *Dominateur*, voir Hintikka 1964, p. 101-114 ; Blanché 1965, p. 133-149 ; Celluprica 1977, p. 55-73 ; Barreau 1978, p. 283-302 ; Vuillemin 1979, p. 225-257 et 1984, p. 15-57 ; Mc Kirahan 1979, p. 223-253 ; Muller 1984, p. 3-37 ; Seel 1982, 2005, 2018 ; D'Jeranian 2021, p. 193 *sq.*

19. Voir Bobzien 1993, p. 69-75.

20. *Cf.* Arrien, *Epict.* II, 19, 1-5 ; Cicéron, *Fat.* 14.

21. Il utilisait la doctrine des « propositions qui se détruisent », *cf.* Alexandre, *In APr.*, p. 177, 28-32 (*SVF* 202a = LS 38 F). Voir Mignucci 1978, p. 305, et Frede 1974, p. 49, n. 4 ; Papazian 2001, p. 2-3 ; Vuillemin 1984, p. 138-139 et D'Jeranian 2021.

22. *Cf.* Cicéron, *Fat.* 21 (et aussi *Fat.* 37-38). Voir Bobzien 1998, p. 78-84. Mais Épicure distinguait destin et nécessité, *cf.* DL X, 133-134.

23. *Cf.* DL VII, 44, comme les médioplatoniciens (Ps.-Plutarque, *De Fat.* 574 E).

24. Plutarque (fr. 22) extrapole le Moissonneur à partir du *Paresseux* : pas de moisson pour qui n'a pas ensemencé la terre, de même, pas de conception pour qui n'a pas ensemencé « le sillon générateur ».

25. Cicéron dit *captiosum* (*Fat.* 30), et Origène σόφισμα (*Cels.* II, 20, 27).

26. Voir Alexandre, *Mantissa*, p. 182, 11-184, 35.

27. Bobzien 1998, p. 188.

valide[28]. C'était là ce qu'on attendait d'un *bon* sophisme, c'est-à-dire d'un « discours persuasif et artificieux qui fait en sorte que l'on admet une conséquence fausse ou semblable au faux ou obscure ou inacceptable d'une autre manière »[29]. Le *Paresseux* apparaît en effet comme un raisonnement « concluant » (συνακτικός), au sens où sa conclusion suit de la conjonction de ses prémisses[30], comme le révèle son analyse comme raisonnement complexe à trois prémisses hypothétiques[31] :

> 1) S'il est éternellement vrai que *p*, il est inutile de faire *q*
> Argument : *car il est impossible de modifier la vérité éternelle de « p »*
> 2) S'il est éternellement vrai que *non-p*, il est inutile de faire *q*
> Argument : *car il est impossible de modifier la vérité éternelle de « non-p »*
> 3) Ou *p*, ou *non-p*
> 4) Donc, il est inutile de faire *q*

Dans la logique propositionnelle de Chrysippe, cela donne :

I. [A1] Si le premier, le second
[A2] Si non le premier, le second
[A3] [Donc (si le premier, le second) et (si non le premier, le second)]
[= si (le premier ou non le premier), le second]

II. [*Si (le premier ou non le premier), le second*]
[A4] Ou le premier, ou non le premier
[C] Donc le second

Si la séquence II est un premier indémontrable chrysippéen (*modus ponens*)[32] et n'a pour cette raison pas besoin d'être analysée, la séquence I doit encore être convertie en argument indémontrable grâce au premier « thème »[33] :

$$\frac{\text{A1, A2} \vdash \text{A3}}{\text{contraire de (A3), A1} \vdash \text{contraire de (A2)}}$$

28. Bobzien 1998, p. 185-189.
29. Sextus Empiricus, *P.* II, 229.
30. Sextus Empiricus, *P.* II, 137.
31. *Cf.* Plutarque, *De stoic. rep.* 1034 E (*SVF* I, 78 = LS 31 L). Voir Gourinat 2000, p. 247, 252 et 306.
32. *Cf.* Simplicius, *In Arist. Cael.* p. 224 (*SVF* II, 242) ; DL VII, 80 (*SVF* II, 241 = LS 36 A12).
33. Apulée, *Int.* p. 191, 5-10 (*SVF* II, 239a = LS 36 I) : « si de deux propositions [A1 et A2] en résulte une troisième [A3], alors de l'une des deux [A1 ou A2] et du contraire de la conclusion [ctrd A3] résulte le contraire de celle qui reste [ctrd A2 ou A1] ». Voir Bobzien 1996, p. 144 *sq.*

La séquence I est un troisième indémontrable, un argument qui « d'une combinaison négative et d'un des membres de la combinaison conclut la contradiction du membre restant »[34] :

I. [Ctrd A3] Non [(Si le premier, le second) et (si non le premier, le second)]
[A1] Si le premier, le second
[Ctrd A2] Donc non (si non le premier, le second)

Le *Paresseux* étant réductible à deux indémontrables, Chrysippe l'aurait donc qualifié de « concluant ». Bobzien soutient en outre que la question de sa validité *réelle* dépend de l'interprétation des termes utilisés dans les prémisses (*a* : « il est fatal que », *b* : « que tu consultes ou non ») et la conclusion (*c* : « il est futile de consulter »). Autrement dit, le *Paresseux* serait sophistique dans certaines interprétations et non sophistique dans d'autres[35], et ce, même si le fait de jouer sur l'ambiguïté des mots suffirait aux stoïciens pour le regarder comme un sophisme[36].

La première version valide (V^1) qu'elle identifie appartient au fatalisme logique, interprète *a* comme une proposition vraie au futur (*a1*), *b* en termes de condition suffisante (*b1*) et les deux premières prémisses comme des implications matérielles (philoniennes ou vérifonctionnelles). Ici, il serait « inutile » d'agir parce que les contraires garantiraient indifféremment le même résultat (le vrai pouvant suivre du vrai comme du faux), que détermine la *seule* vérité immuable de son énoncé au futur[37].

La seconde (V^2), qui appartient au fatalisme physique, utilise un concept métaphysique de destin (*a2*), traduit l'inévitabilité en termes d'absence de « *causally relevant necessary condition* » (*b2*) et interprète la futilité de la consultation dans un sens qui justifie l'oisiveté (*c2*). Dans les deux premières prémisses, l'inévitabilité des résultats dépend de l'omnipotence du destin. Simple effet de lecture, le sophisme apparaît lorsqu'on établit la conclusion en changeant subrepticement dans les prémisses le sens de *b*.

Mais concernant V^1, puisque la futilité de l'action ne peut justifier l'oisiveté qu'en supposant que le résultat ne dépend pas *causalement* de l'action du malade[38], reste à savoir si, bien que la médecine soit « le moyen de se relever de la maladie »[39], l'inutilité de la consultation peut *dans tous les cas* être déduite de l'inéluctabilité de l'issue. Dans les deux premières prémisses, l'insignifiance de l'action matérialisée par « *sive ..., sive non ...* » est une conséquence de l'argument fataliste : s'il est éternellement vrai que tu guériras,

34. DL VII, 80 ; Apulée *Int.*, p. 191, 5-10 (*SVF* II, 239a = LS 36 I).
35. Bobzien 1998, p. 193-198.
36. *Cf.* DL VII, 44 et 62 (LS 37 P). Voir aussi Simplicius, *In Cat.* 24, 13-20 (LS 37 S).
37. Voir Salles 2005, p. 17.
38. Voir Bobzien 1998, p. 195.
39. Origène, *Cels.* II, 20, 62-65.

tu guériras *de toute façon* (πάντως) *que* tu consultes *ou non*, parce qu'il t'est impossible de modifier la vérité *passée* de l'énoncé portant sur ton futur état. Dans V^1, cela suffit à détacher le résultat de l'action dont il est pourtant censé dépendre[40].

Or, non seulement l'argument ne prouve pas que le résultat se produirait pareillement *même si l'agent faisait autrement*, mais en vertu de l'universalité du principe de bivalence, il devrait impliquer que l'action du malade sera aussi la seule qu'il *pourra* commettre. Il est donc faux de dire qu'il est vain de consulter, tandis qu'il pourrait être éternellement vrai qu'il guérira *parce qu'*il consultera. Pas plus qu'il ne pourra éviter de guérir, il ne pourra s'empêcher de consulter, si sa guérison dépend du médecin. Et cela vaut aussi pour V^2, où la conclusion suppose que l'agent peut agir autrement mais que ses actions sont séparées de leurs résultats, qu'un destin tout-puissant réaliserait tout en éliminant pour lui la possibilité de modifier le cours des choses.

La réponse de Chrysippe

Dans la mesure où Chrysippe pensait que seule une cause peut déterminer la vérité d'une proposition[41], le fatalisme logique à l'œuvre dans V^1 n'aurait eu pour lui aucun sens. De même, puisque le destin *stoïcien* est la concaténation universelle des causes[42], un « système du monde » où tout corps est solidaire d'un autre dans la production des événements[43], il aurait aussi rejeté V^2, les actions étant incluses dans le destin au même titre que leurs résultats.

Mais Chrysippe fondait aussi l'universalité du principe de causalité sur celle du principe de bivalence[44] : parce que *toute* proposition est vraie ou fausse[45], *tout* a une cause antécédente[46], de sorte que *tout* est fatal. Or, ce qui est fatal est aussi « éternellement vrai ». En langage stoïcien, « *il est fatal que* le malade guérisse » pourrait ainsi signifier que cette proposition est *immuablement* vraie parce que la guérison est prédéterminée par un enchaî-

40. Voir Leibniz, *Essais de Théodicée*, §55.

41. Cicéron, *Fat.* 20-21 (*SVF* II, 952 = LS 38 G).

42. *Cf.* Ps.-Plutarque, *De Fat.* 574 E ; Némésius, *NH* 37 p. 299 (*SVF* II, 918). Servius rapporte (*ad. Virg. Aen.* III, 376 = Cicéron, *Fat.* fr. 2 = *SVF* II, 919) la définition du destin comme une éternelle connexion de choses bien que Cicéron dise que le destin est l'ordre et la série des causes (*Div.* I, 126) ou la liaison de toutes les causes (*Div.* I, 127). Voir Meyer 2009.

43. *Cf.* DL VII, 149 (*SVF* II, 915) ; Aétius, *Plac.* I 28, 4 = Ps.-Plutarque, 885 B6-7 (*SVF* II, 917 = LS 55 J) ; Cicéron, *Div.* I, 125-126 (*SVF* II, 921 = LS 55 L) ; Alexandre, *Mant.* p. 185, 5 (*SVF* II, 920) ; *Fat.* (c. 22) p. 191, 30. (*SVF* II, 945 = LS 55 N) ; Némésius, *NH* (c. 37) p. 108, 15-17 (*SVF* II, 918) ; Œnomaüs, dans Eusèbe, *PE* VI, 7, 1-25, 1 (*SVF* II, 978) ; Plotin, *Enn.* III, 1, 2, 31 ; III, 1, 4, 1-9 (*SVF* II, 934) ; 2, 17-38 (*SVF* II, 946) ; 7, 1-15 (*SVF* II, 986).

44. Chrysippe en conserve l'universalité (Cicéron *Fat.* 21 et 37), même pour le *Menteur*, qu'il considérait comme « inexplicable » (*Acad. Pr.* II, 97). Voir Barnes 2007, p. 1-92.

45. Voir Ps.-Plutarque, *De Fat.* 574 E.

46. Bobzien 1998, p. 61-65.

nement *inflexible* de causes[47], au risque de la rendre inévitable *pour le malade*. C'est donc pour réfuter le *Paresseux* sans nier l'universalité du destin qu'il distingua deux catégories d'événements différant par le rapport qu'ils ont avec nos actions :

> Il y a, dit-il, parmi les choses (*in rebus*), celles qui sont simples (*simplicia*) et celles qui sont couplées (*copulata*). Une chose simple c'est « Socrate mourra tel jour », parce que, quoi qu'il fasse, le jour de sa mort est déterminé (*finitus*). Mais si c'est le destin que « Œdipe naîtra de Laïos », on ne pourra pas dire « que Laïos ait été ou non avec une femme », car c'est une chose couplée et « confatale ». C'est le terme dont il use, parce que le destin est à la fois que Laïos ait des rapports avec sa femme, et que d'elle il engendre Œdipe. Mais à « Milon luttera à Olympie », si l'on rétorquait « donc il luttera, qu'il ait ou non un adversaire », on se tromperait, car « il luttera » est une chose couplée, puisque sans adversaire, pas de lutte. Tous les raisonnements captieux de ce genre se réfutent donc ainsi. « Que vous appeliez ou non le médecin, vous guérirez » est captieuse, car il est aussi fatal d'appeler le médecin que de guérir. C'est, comme je l'ai dit, ce que Chrysippe appelle des choses « confatales ».[48]

D'un côté, les « choses simples » (*res simplices*), qui décrivent *correctement* l'inévitabilité du destin, d'un autre les « choses couplées » (*res copulatae*), qui dépendent de nos actions. Cicéron utilise « res » pour désigner des propositions[49], procédant ailleurs à la même distinction à propos des mots, qui peuvent être « isolés » ou « groupés [dans des phrases] » (*genera verborum et simplicium et copulatum*)[50]. Mais parce qu'il vient de traduire le terme technique ἀξίωμα (« proposition ») par *enuntiatio*[51], *res* renverrait plutôt ici à deux types d'événements[52].

La réfutation chrysippéenne du *Paresseux* repose sur la redéfinition de l'inévitabilité fatale et sur la confatalité. Concernant un résultat *p* dont on

47. *Cf.* Plutarque, *De stoic. rep.* 1056 C1-9 (*SVF* II, 997 = LS 55 R).

48. Cicéron, *Fat.* 30 (*SVF* II, 956 = LS 55 S2-3) : « *Quaedam enim sunt, inquit, in rebus simplicia, quaedam copulata. Simplex est : 'Morietur illo die Socrates' ; huic siue quid fecerit, siue non fecerit, finitus est moriendi dies. At si ita fatum est : 'Nascetur Oedipus Laio', non poterit dici : 'siue fuerit Laius cum muliere, siue non fuerit' ; copulata enim res est et confatalis : sic enim appellat, quia ita fatum sit et concubiturum cum uxore Laium et ex ea Oedipum procreaturum, ut, si esset dictum : 'Luctabitur Olympiis Milon', et referret aliquis : 'Ergo siue habuerit aduersarium, siue non habuerit, luctabitur', erraret ; est enim copulatum 'luctabitur', quia sine aduersario nulla luctatio est. Omnes igitur istius generis captiones eodem modo refelluntur. 'Siue tu adhibueris medicum, siue non adhibueris, conualesces', captiosum : tam enim est fatale medicum adhibere quam conualescere. Haec, ut dixi, confatalia ille appellat.* » (éd. Yon).

49. Rist 1969, p. 120.

50. Cicéron, *Orat.* 115. En *Fat.* 37, le contexte de *in rebus* est sémantique, tandis qu'en *Fat.* 45 il est situationnel.

51. Cicéron, *Fat.* 20 et 37.

52. Voir White 1985, p. 122 ; Sedley 1993, p. 315 ; Bobzien 1998, p. 200 ; Long et Sedley 2001, p. 396.

ne doute pas qu'il dépend d'une action q, on conclut par *modus ponens* que q est *aussi fatal* que p si l'énoncé « Fp » est immuablement vrai, parce que q est la condition nécessaire de p : $L(p \Rightarrow q)$[53]. Et si l'on montrait l'équivalence « $p \Leftrightarrow q$ », la réciproque ($q \Rightarrow p$) et sa contraposée ($\sim p \Rightarrow \sim q$) seraient aussi vraies, un *modus tollens* concluant que, s'il est fatal pour le malade de ne pas guérir ($F{\sim}p$), il est *aussi fatal* pour lui de ne pas consulter ($F{\sim}q$).

Mais comment interpréter l'inévitabilité des *res simplices* ? S'agit-il d'événements logiquement nécessaires, comme si *simplex* équivalait à *simpliciter* (ἁπλῶς)[54], c'est-à-dire « vrai dans tous les mondes possibles » ?

C'est ce qu'indiquerait l'exemple de Socrate, cas idéal de véracité divinatoire où l'inévitabilité *connue* du résultat n'a pas conduit le sage au vice[55] mais à la croyance selon laquelle *pour chacun, son jour est établi*[56]. Insistant sur le choix des exemples, leur lien avec la divination et la référence au rêve prémonitoire du *Criton* (44a-b), David Sedley[57] juge qu'il était impossible pour Socrate de mourir un autre jour, là où Laïos aurait pu éviter d'être tué par Œdipe, s'il avait écouté l'oracle. Certains événements de nos vies seraient inévitables, même si les chemins qui y mènent ne le sont pas[58] : dans tous les mondes possibles, Socrate serait mort *le même jour* mais à chaque fois différemment.

À l'appui de cette lecture on rappellera un passage du grammairien Servius retenu par Von Arnim, où une distinction similaire est développée[59]. D'un côté, les *destins annonciateurs* (*fata quae dicuntur denuntiativa*), comme « Pompée triomphera trois fois » – car cela se produira où qu'il soit sur terre, *nec potest aliter evenire* –, d'un autre, les *destins conditionnels* (*fata condicionalia vocantur*), comme « si Pompée atteint l'Égypte après Pharsale, il sera tué par le fer ». Mais l'évocation du hasard (*si casus illum*) dans les *destins conditionnels* interdit l'identification stoïcienne, non seulement parce que ces éléments s'accordent mieux au fatalisme médioplatonicien[60], mais parce que Chrysippe rejetterait l'idée archaïque de *destin annonciateur* au motif qu'elle

53. Il est faux que « $p \wedge \sim q$ » parce qu'il est vrai que « $\sim q \Rightarrow \sim p$ ».

54. Au sens où Aristote le prend en *Int.* 9, 19a26.

55. L'attitude des sages était pour les stoïciens une preuve du destin (Ps.-Plutarque, *De Fat.* 574 E).

56. Virgile, *Aen.* X, 467. Voir Épictète, *Ench.* 17.

57. Sedley 1993, p. 315-319.

58. Long & Sedley 2001, p. 396.

59. Servius, *Commentaire sur l'*Énéide *de Virgile* IV, 696 (*SVF* II, 958).

60. Qui est « une ordonnance et une loi, parce qu'il règle les conséquences des événements à la manière de la loi civile » (Ps.-Plutarque, *De Fat.* 570 B5-6), *ce qui est fatal* et « selon le destin » ne signifiant que « les conséquences d'antécédents dans l'organisation divine du monde ». *Cf.* Ps.-Plutarque, *De Fat.* 570 A-E ; Némésius, *NH*, p. 109, 9 *sq.* (135-6 ; 101, 20 *sq.*) ; Calcidius, *In Tim.* 142-190 ; Alcinous, *Didasc.* 26, (et ch. 2 ; 31 et 32) ; Apulée, *De dog. Plat.* I, 12.

isole certains événements de la chaîne des causes[61]. Dans le monde stoïcien où tout est en sympathie et gouverné providentiellement, il ne saurait y avoir qu'*un seul* destin. Et il soutenait contre Diodore[62] que, bien qu'une proposition soit vraie parce que le futur sur lequel elle porte est *certain*, sa négation n'est pas forcément *impossible*[63]. Même si elle était inévitable *pour Socrate*, sa mort n'était pas *logiquement* nécessaire.

Pour Bobzien, la *simplicité* signifierait une liaison conceptuelle entre le résultat et l'essence de l'individu impliqué[64]. Si la mort de Socrate est *simplex*, c'est parce qu'elle ne dépend d'aucune action particulière de sa part, au contraire de la procréation d'Œdipe, qui implique copulation. Elle conclut que « *the cause for [Socrate's] death would be in that case internal* », puisque « *it is for instance part of the essence of human being that they will eventually die* »[65]. Dans le même ordre d'idées, on pourrait concevoir que les événements *simples* ne concernent *naturellement* qu'un seul agent, par opposition à la *complexité* des événements *couplés*, qui impliquent l'interaction de plusieurs : Socrate aurait pu mourir de mille manières, non engendrer Lamproclès sans s'unir à Xanthippe.

Il semble toutefois que l'on force ici l'indétermination du marqueur temporel *illo die*[66], comme si l'on disait que, parce qu'il était homme, Socrate *devait* mourir *un jour* (non *tel jour*). Or, précise Cicéron, sa mort est inévitable pour lui parce que son « jour est déterminé » (*finitus est moriendi dies*)[67]. Et ce n'est pas sans rappeler la distinction qu'il vient de faire entre « Scipion mourra » et « Scipion mourra *de telle manière* (*illo modo*) ». Bien que, dit-il, les deux propositions soient immuablement vraies, la vérité de la première est due à une cause *naturelle* qui rend l'événement *inévitable* pour Scipion, celle de la seconde dépend de causes *accidentelles* qui l'ont seulement rendue *certaine*[68]. Cette distinction ayant justement été développée par Carnéade contre Chrysippe, pour qui tous les futurs seraient déterminés par des « causes fatales », il est plus sûr de penser que la proposition « Socrate mourra tel jour » ait été pour ce dernier aussi déterminée que la proposition

61. *Cf.* Cicéron, *Div.* I, 126 (*SVF* II, 921 = LS 55 L3). Voir *Div.* II, 54. Sur l'idée archaïque du destin, voir Masi et Maso 2013.

62. Pour qui le possible est « ce qui est ou sera », *cf.* Arrien, *Epict.* II, 19, 1 (LS 38 A3) ; Boèce, *Int.* p. 234, 22-26 (LS 38 C) et Cicéron, *Fat.* 13 (LS 38 E2). Un état de choses est impossible s'il n'est ni ne sera le cas, *cf.* Cicéron, *Fat.* 13 (LS 38 E3).

63. *Cf.* Boèce, *Int.* III, 9.

64. Bobzien 1998, p. 221.

65. *Ibidem.*

66. « Une chose simple c'est 'Socrate mourra tel jour' » (*Simplex est : 'Morietur illo die Socrates'*).

67. « parce que, quoi qu'il fasse, le jour de sa mort est déterminé » (*huic siue quid fecerit, siue non fecerit, finitus est moriendi dies*).

68. *Cf.* Cicéron, *Fat.* 18-19.

datée « Épicure mourra, après avoir vécu soixante-douze ans, sous l'archontat de Pytharatos »[69]. Nous en concluons que si Chrysippe a bien soutenu que *le jour de sa mort* était inévitable pour Socrate, ce n'est pas parce que *toutes ses actions possibles lui auraient garanti de mourir le même jour*, mais parce qu'*aucune n'aurait suffi à l'en empêcher*.

On objectera que l'exemple n'aurait pas pu être plus mal choisi, puisque c'est Socrate qui fit le choix de mourir[70]. Cela impose d'admettre deux conditions supplémentaires : (1) que le choix de Socrate fut suffisant bien que non nécessaire, parce qu'il serait mort *le même jour*, bien qu'autrement, en l'absence d'initiative de sa part sous l'action d'une cause étrangère ; (2) que des circonstances l'empêchèrent de mourir chaque autre jour de sa vie, tout en lui permettant de choisir la mort *ce jour-là*.

Cette redéfinition de l'inévitabilité n'implique pas non plus que Chrysippe aurait accepté une version du *Paresseux* où le résultat serait *simplex* :

> [P1] S'il est (*simplement*) fatal pour toi de guérir, alors tu guériras, *si tu consultes et même si tu ne consultes pas* (*i.e.* tu ne consulteras pas et guériras)[71]
>
> [P2] S'il est (*simplement*) fatal pour toi de ne pas guérir, alors tu ne guériras pas, *si tu ne consultes pas et même si tu consultes* (*i.e.* tu consulteras et ne guériras pas)[72]

Car dans le *Paresseux*, ce n'est pas *n'importe quelle action* qui est liée au résultat (comme pour la mort de Socrate), mais celle dont dépend sa réalisation, dans les cas où l'on ne doute pas qu'il se réalisera parce que l'agent la commettra, ou qu'il ne se réalisera pas parce qu'il s'en empêchera. Le *Paresseux* n'ayant de sens que si le résultat est « couplé » à une action, il est clair que Chrysippe n'y voyait qu'un sophisme facilement réfutable.

Puisque la distinction *simplex/confatalis* n'est pas une disjonction exclusive[73] dans laquelle la *simplex* serait une catégorie vide définissant par défaut tout événement comme *confatal*, il ne peut s'agir que d'une division (διαίρεσις)[74]. Or, si celle-ci est présentée comme exhaustive[75], le critère des exemples de *copulatae* inclut aussi bien des événements (avoir un adversaire) que des actions (l'acte sexuel). Chrysippe répondant à un raisonnement *quod*

69. Cicéron, *Fat.* 19.

70. Platon, *Phd.* 98d-99a. Voir Koch 2014, p. 116-120. Voir aussi D'Jeranian 2018.

71. $\sim(p \Rightarrow q) \Leftrightarrow (p \wedge \sim q)$: *p* aura lieu *même sans q*, *q* n'étant pas une condition nécessaire de *p*.

72. $\sim(q \Rightarrow p) \Leftrightarrow (q \wedge \sim p)$: $\sim p$ aura lieu *même avec q*, *q* n'étant pas une condition suffisante de *p*.

73. Les stoïciens ne reconnaissaient pas la disjonction inclusive, *cf.* DL VII, 72 (*SVF* II, 207 = LS 35 A4).

74. Voir DL VII, 61.

75. Bobzien 1998, p. 201.

eadem ratione omnis et vita tolletur actio[76], seule *notre* action peut épuiser sa division[77]. Cette confusion n'est due qu'à la manière dont l'exemple du lutteur est rapporté. En choisissant l'*action* (*luctatio*) pour résultat, Cicéron fit d'un événement une condition. Chez Diogénien, l'exposition du même exemple est plus heureuse, le résultat étant un *fait* dépendant d'une *action*[78].

On objectera enfin que ce n'est qu'indirectement que la guérison est *couplée* à l'action du malade, puisque sa réalisation n'est garantie que par le médecin, qui actualise pour lui le prédicat « être guéri ». Les textes ne sont pas clairs sur la liaison des *copulatae.* Mais si l'on s'en tient à l'idée que Chrysippe avait formulé sa division contre le *Paresseux*, le fait que nous agissions ou non doit être constitutif du résultat. S'il est vrai *maintenant* que tu guériras, il doit « subsister »[79] *dans le futur* une cause qui rend vraie cette proposition *au futur*[80], et cette cause n'est autre que le médecin que *tu consulteras.* Tout cela, dit Sénèque, est inclus dans le destin, car « c'est par les mains du médecin que le bienfait du destin nous arrive »[81].

La fatalité de l'action volontaire

Cela étant, Chrysippe semble plutôt repousser le problème que le résoudre. Puisque le destin stoïcien est « un ordre naturel de la totalité des choses impliquées et entraînées de toute éternité par d'autres, ordre dont la trame ne peut être rompue »[82], puisqu'aucun futur n'est vrai qui n'a pas de cause pour le rendre tel[83], seul ce réseau causal transtemporel semble pouvoir garantir la vérité *éternelle* d'un énoncé sur un futur[84]. Mais afin que nos efforts aient un sens, il faut que nos actions dépendent de nous et non d'un enchaînement éternel de causes (*causarum seriem sempiternam*)[85]. Pourquoi la consultation n'aurait-elle pas aussi des causes antérieures qui la rendraient, par transfert de nécessité *causale*[86], aussi inévitable pour le malade que sa

76. Cicéron, *Fat.* 29.

77. Nous suivons Sorabji 1980, p. 228 ; Botros 1985, p. 288 ; Bobzien 1998, p. 202 ; Long et Sedley 2001, p. 396 ; contre Rist 1969, p. 120 et White 1985, p. 122.

78. *Cf.* Eusèbe, *PE* VI, 8, 27-30.

79. Le futur comme le passé n'existent pas, ils subsistent, voir LS 51 B4 et C5.

80. *Cf.* Cicéron, *Fat.* 26.

81. Sénèque, *QN* II, 38, 4.

82. Définition donnée par Chrysippe dans son *De la Providence*, *cf.* Aulu-Gelle, *NA* VII, 2, 4-12 (LS 55K).

83. Cicéron, *Fat.* 26.

84. Voir Bobzien 1998, p. 67 *sq.*

85. Cicéron, *Fat.* 20.

86. Cicéron, *Fat.* 14 ; 20-21 ; 27-28 ; 31-33 ; Alexandre, *Fat.* (c. 22) p. 191, 26 – 193, 2 (*SVF* II, 945 = LS 55 N). Voir Aristote, *Metaph.* E, 3, 1027a29-b13.

guérison ? Insatisfait de la réponse de Chrysippe, Carnéade objecta que, si tout arrive par une cause antécédente, la nécessité fait tout, ce qui contredit l'intuition que quelque chose est *in nostra potestate*[87].

C'était l'objection qu'on adressait aux stoïciens depuis que Zénon avait soutenu que « tout est soumis à la nécessité » (πάντα κατηναγκάσθαι). Concaténation de causes reliant toutes choses[88], le destin impose son inflexible nécessité[89], bon gré mal gré[90]. Si Zénon avait déjà esquissé l'idée de confatalité pour justifier les châtiments[91], c'est Chrysippe qui chercha dans le second livre de son *Sur le destin* à justifier la responsabilité en site fataliste[92], affirmant

> qu'il est évident que beaucoup de choses résultent de nous (τὸ μὲν ἐξ ἡμῶν)[93] mais qu'elles n'en sont pas moins aussi fatales (συγκαθειμάρθαι)[94] et soumises à l'organisation du monde[95].

Similaires, συγκαθειμάρθαι et *confatalis* ne sont pas synonymes, le second qualifiant une *relation de dépendance* entre un résultat et une action, le premier le *caractère duplice* de nos actions, *à la fois* causées par nous *et* soumises au destin. Car pour nous imputer la responsabilité de leurs résultats au sein du destin, elles doivent être *de notre fait* en étant liées à leurs conséquences. Elles sont donc « aussi fatales », *ce qui provient de nous* (παρ' ἡμᾶς) étant circonscrit par le destin[96]. Les expressions παρ' ἡμᾶς et ἐξ ἡμῶν ne sont pas non plus synonymes, comme le soutient Bobzien[97], puisque, comme le montre Gourinat[98], il y a dépendance de l'un à l'autre : « παρ' ἡμᾶς » renvoie

87. Cicéron, *Fat.* 31.

88. *Cf.* Aristoclès, dans Eusèbe, *PE* XV, 14 (*SVF* I, 98). Voir aussi Cicéron, *Div.* I, 125-126 (*SVF* II, 921 = LS 55 L) et 127 (*SVF* II, 944 = LS 55 O) ; Stobée, *Ecl.* I, p. 79, 1-12 (*SVF* II, 913 = LS 55 M) ; Alexandre, *Fat.* (c. 22) p. 191, 30 – 192, 28 (*SVF* II, 945 = LS 55 N).

89. Cf. *Commenta Lucani Lib.* II 306 p. 69 Us. (*SVF* II, 924) ; Plutarque, *De stoic. rep.* 1056 B3-C9 (*SVF* II, 997 = LS 55 R) ; *Comm. Not.* 1076 E ; Théodoret, *Graec. Aff.* VI, 14, 1-3 (*SVF* II, 916) ; Diogénien, dans Eusèbe, *PE* VI, 8, 8 ; Proclus, *Ad Hes. Op.* v. 105a p. 47, 17-19 (*SVF* II, 929) ; Stobée, *Ecl.* I, p. 79, 1, 5, 15, 21-40 (*SVF* II, 913 = LS 55 M). Zénon liait cela à la doctrine de la palingénésie, selon Aristoclès, dans Eusèbe, *PE* XV, 15 (*SVF* I, 98), et de la providence, *cf.* Aétius, I, 27, 5 et Théodoret, *Graec. Aff.* VI, 145, p. 153 Ra (*SVF* I, 176).

90. *Cf.* Hippolyte, *Haer.* I, 21 (*SVF* II, 875 = LS 62 A) ; Diogénien (fr. 1), dans Eusèbe, *PE* VI, 8, 1 (*SVF* II, 925). Même idée chez Cléanthe, *cf.* Épictète, *Ench.* 53, etc.

91. Voir l'anecdote de Zénon et de l'esclave, DL VII, 23 (LS 62 E).

92. Aulu-Gelle, *NA* VII, 2, 4 (*SVF* II, 1000) ; Cicéron, *Fat.* 39-43 (*SVF* II, 974).

93. Voir Gourinat 2014, p. 141-150.

94. *Cf.* Plutarque, *Mor. fr.* 22, 8 (Stobée, *Ecl.* II, 8, 25) ; Marc Aurèle, *P.* IV, 26, 1 ; XII, 3, 1 ; Némésius, *NH* 36, 37 ; Stobée, *Ecl.* IV, 22a, 24. La variante συνειμαρμένον apparaît chez Ps.-Plutarque, *De Fat.* 569 F.

95. Diogénien (fr. 3), dans Eusèbe, *PE* VI, 8, 25, 2 – 34, 6 (*SVF* II, 998).

96. *Cf.* Eusèbe, *PE* VI, 8, 33, 2 (*SVF* II, 998, 25-26).

97. Bobzien 1998, p. 285.

98. Gourinat 2005, p. 249, n. 7.

à une origine (ce qui est *de nous*), une action causale propre d'où *résulte* (ἐξ ἡμῶν) un événement « confatal ».

Dans la suite de son rapport, Diogénien expose des exemples en partie identiques à ceux de Cicéron :

> que le manteau ne soit pas détruit, dit-il, cela n'est pas simplement fixé par le destin (οὐχ ἁπλῶς καθείμαρτο), mais accompagné du fait qu'on en prendra soin ; et le fait pour untel d'échapper à ses ennemis, accompagné du fait qu'il les fuira ; et le fait d'engendrer des enfants, accompagné du fait qu'on voudra coucher avec une femme. En effet, dit-il, c'est comme si, en disant que le lutteur Hégésarque se sortira indemne du combat, l'on voulait étonnamment qu'il combattît les bras baissés, puisqu'il est fixé par le destin (καθείμαρτο ἀπελθεῖν) qu'il s'en sortira indemne, tandis que celui qui le dit fait cette déclaration en raison de la prodigieuse adresse de l'homme à parer les coups (...). En effet, beaucoup de choses ne peuvent advenir sans que nous le voulions et que nous y mettions beaucoup de zèle, de volonté et d'effort, puisque, dit-il, c'est avec cela que ces choses sont fatales (ἐπειδὴ μετὰ τούτο, φησίν, αὐτὰ γενέσθαι καθείμαρτο)[99].

En filigrane, le concept de confatalité : les événements imputables sont *accompagnés* (μετὰ + génitif) de nos actions, ils ne sont pas « simplement fatals » (οὐχ ἁπλῶς καθείμαρτο) au sens de « logiquement nécessaires ». Si les *res simplices* n'apparaissent pas, c'est parce qu'il ne s'agit plus de redéfinir l'inévitabilité du destin, mais de justifier notre responsabilité eu égard aux résultats *confatals* à nos actions. La relation transitive offre une réponse complète au *Paresseux* : le résultat p impliquant l'action q, qui implique à son tour l'activité α de l'agent, sans effort (σπουδή) ni volonté (προθυμία) de sa part, p ne serait pas réalisé ($\sim\alpha^{t0} \Rightarrow \sim q^{t1} \Rightarrow \sim p^{t2}$).

Chrysippe se fonde sur l'étiologie stoïcienne, selon laquelle les corps ne sont pas causes les uns *des* autres, mais les uns *pour* les autres d'effets incorporels[100], et sur le fait que le destin n'est que la chaîne des causes *antécédentes*, non des causes *et* des effets[101]. L'effet ne peut avoir lieu sans la présence de sa cause[102], puisqu'il « subsiste » aussi longtemps que celle-ci est active[103], tandis que la cause synectique ne peut entraîner seule son effet, ce qui requiert la cause antécédente. Si l'agent est « cause » pour le vêtement du prédicat

99. Eusèbe, *PE* VI, 8, 27-30 (éd. K. Mras).

100. *Cf.* Clément, *Strom.* VIII, 9, 30, 1-3 (*SVF* II, 349 = LS 55 D).

101. Voir Bobzien 1998, p. 50 et Meyer 2009.

102. La cause synectique « suffit à produire l'effet » (Clément, *Strom.* VIII 9 = *SVF* II, 346). Elle est celle dont « l'effet dure autant qu'elle est présente et disparaît quand elle disparaît elle-même » (*SVF* II, 351), car « il est impossible que la cause soit *présente* sans qu'existe ce dont elle est cause », *cf.* Stobée, *Ecl.* I, p. 138, 19-20 (*SVF* I, 89 = LS 55 A1-2). Nous suivons Frede 1980, p. 217-249.

103. *Cf.* Stobée, *Ecl.* I, p. 138-139, 23 (*SVF* I, 89 = LS 55 A3). Selon Sextus (*P.* III, 15), les causes synectiques déterminent leurs effets par leur présence, disparition, augmentation ou diminution.

incorporel « être préservé »[104], le vêtement ne pourra l'être sans son *activité*. Mais pour que le vêtement dure, il faut aussi que sa disposition soit telle qu'il puisse être conservé[105]. En tant que cause prochaine[106], voire « auxiliaire » ou « coopérante »[107] de sa conservation, l'agent jouera le rôle de cause, pour le vêtement, de sa conservation. D'un côté, l'action implique l'effort de l'agent ; d'un autre, son action n'aurait aucune efficacité sans le concours de la cause « complète » et « principale » inhérente au vêtement[108]. « Le vêtement durera » n'est vraie qu'en raison de cette interaction, qu'une cause synectique porte à elle seule la responsabilité, ou que plusieurs coopèrent.

La consultation ne peut donc être exceptée de la chaîne des causes, bien que le malade en soit la source ultime. C'est en reléguant le destin à la cause *prochaine* et en rompant la transmission de la nécessité causale que Chrysippe pensait pouvoir « retenir le destin et fuir la nécessité »[109], et garantir la légitimité des imputations morales et juridiques.

Les liaisons confatales

Mais bien qu'ils se réalisent parce que nous tentons de les obtenir, et parfois de les éviter, les résultats *confatals* à nos actions n'en sont pas moins *certains*. C'est ainsi que Laïos et Priam subirent les malheurs qu'on leur avait prédits à cause de ce qu'ils firent pour y échapper[110]. Ce paradoxe interroge la nature de la liaison *confatale* et le rôle qu'y joue le destin.

Pour un stoïcien, la confatalité doit s'exprimer dans une proposition *non simple*. Individuellement, la *copulata* est morphologiquement identique à la *simplex*, en tant que proposition « intermédiaire » (μέσον)[111] ou « catégorique »[112], décrivant ce qui arrive à untel en contenant une appellation[113]. Mais prises ensemble, les *copulatae* forment des propositions *non simples* (οὐχ ἁπλᾶ) et *non répétées*, car elles sont constituées de propositions différentes. Cicéron indique l'usage de conjonctives, comme en atteste le

104. Voir Sextus, *M.* IX, 211 (*SVF* II, 341 = LS 55 B) et Clément, *Strom.* VIII, 9, 26, 3-4 (LS 55 C).

105. Nous suivons Long et Sedley 2001, p. 172.

106. *Cf.* Cicéron, *Fat.* 34-37. Sur sa critique néoacadémicienne, voir Koch 2019, p. 354-362. *Cf.* Galien, *De causis contentivis* I 2, 4 (LS 55 F) et Plutarque, *De stoic. rep.* 47, 1055 F5 *sq.*

107. Voir Clément, *Strom.* VIII 9, 9, 33, 1-9 (*SVF* II, 351 = LS 55 I).

108. Cicéron, *Fat.* 41.

109. Cicéron, *Fat.* 39.

110. Diogénien (fr. 4), dans Eusèbe, *PE* IV, 3, 12-13 (*SVF* II, 939), en tire un argument contre l'utilité de la divination.

111. Sextus, *M.* VIII, 97 (*SVF* II, 205 = LS 34 H9).

112. DL VII, 70, si l'on accepte la correction de M. Frede, qui fait correspondre Diogène et Sextus (M. VII, 97).

113. Le nom propre étant « l'espèce la plus spécifique, qui ne contient pas d'autres espèces comme Socrate » (DL VII, 61 = *SVF* III, Diog. 25 = *FDS* 621).

double « et » dans « *fatum sit et concumbiturum cum uxore Laium et ex ea Oedipum procreaturum* ». Une conjonctive (συμπεπλεγμένον, *copulatum* ou *coniunctum*) joint deux propositions par une conjonction (« et il fait jour et il y a de la lumière »)[114]. Opérateur vérifonctionnel, elle n'est vraie que si tous ses membres le sont, de même qu'un vêtement est « sain » (ὑγιής) à moins d'une petite imperfection[115] : il est impossible que tous ses membres soient vrais sauf un, une fausse note ruinant l'harmonie du tout[116].

Mais bien que Cicéron rende ailleurs συμπεπλεγμένον par *copulatum*[117], les *copulatae* ne sont pas des conjonctives[118], de même que les *res simplices* ne sont pas des *propositions simples* (ἀξιώματα ἁπλᾶ)[119]. Chrysippe admettant qu'un résultat peut suivre une action sans lui être *couplé*, c'est l'implication qui décrit mieux le régime de confatalité. L'implication (συνημμένον, *connexum*) subordonne le conséquent à l'antécédent de sorte que le second *suit logiquement* (ἀκολουθεῖν) le premier (« s'il fait jour, il y a de la lumière »)[120]. Chrysippe jugeant insuffisant le critère diodoréen[121], il souhaitait que l'implication « saine » (ὑγιής) ne soit pas définie en termes vérifonctionnels mais par la « cohérence » (συνάρτησις) de ses deux propositions, ce dont atteste l'existence d'un « conflit » (μάχεται)[122] entre l'antécédent et la négation du conséquent. En effet, si « Œdipe naîtra de Laïos » est « une chose solidaire et confatale » (*copulata enim res est et confatalis*) de « Laïos a des rapports avec une femme », c'est parce qu'il était alors impossible qu'une naissance ait lieu sans rapport sexuel ($\sim q^{t1} \Rightarrow \sim p^{t2}$). Même si p^{t2} est fatal, il est faux que $\sim q^{t1}$ en raison de leur incompatibilité manifeste[123].

114. DL VII, 72.

115. *Cf.* Sextus, *P.* II, 138 ; *M.* VIII, 125 (*SVF* II, 211 = *FDS* 968) et 128 ; Aulu-Gelle, *NA* XVI, 8, 11. Pour le parallèle, voir Arrien, *Epict.* II, 9, 8-10.

116. Chrysippe identifiait destin et providence, *cf.* Calcidius, *In Tim.* 144 (*SVF* III, 933 = LS U1). Voir Brunschwig 1978.

117. *Et coniunctum.* Il traduisait συνημμένον par *connexum* ou *adjunctum, cf.* Aulu-Gelle, *NA* XVI, 8, 9-10 (*SVF* II, 213 = FDS 967). Cicéron, *Acad. Pr.* II, 143. Voir aussi *Fat.* 12, où Cicéron oppose la conditionnelle astrologique vraie (*conectitur verum*) à la conjonctive fausse (*coniunctio est ex repugnantibus*).

118. Nous ne suivons pas Alessandrelli 2007, p. 11.

119. DL VII, 68.

120. DL VII, 71 ; Sextus, *M.* VIII, 109-111.

121. *Cf.* Sextus, *P.* II, 110 ; *M.* VIII, 115-117 et 333 (malgré DL VII, 61). À ce sujet, voir Ebert 1993, p. 115. Pour Diodore, la vérité de l'antécédent entraîne toujours celle du conséquent.

122. « Ce qui ne peut pas être dit sous le même rapport », *cf.* Apollonios Dyscole, *Coniunct.* 218 *sq.* (*SVF* II, 176). L'incompatibilité doit être « incomplète », voir Frede 1974, p. 83. *Cf.* Sextus, *P.* II, 111 ; DL VII, 73. Cela signifie que l'un des deux faits ne coexiste pas avec l'autre, bien que cela puisse être ni l'un, ni l'autre (Galien, *Int. Log.* IV, 1-4). Voir Frede 1974, p. 83 ; Gourinat 2000, p. 222-223.

123. Nous suivons Sorabji (1980b, p. 267) contre Frede (1974, p. 85 *sq.*) ou encore Mates (1961, p. 49). Le débat sur la nature de la συνάρτησις remonte à Victor Brochard (1912 p. 220-238 ; et 1912b p. 239-251) et Octave Hamelin (1901, p. 13-26). Pour une synthèse,

L'analyse mobilise l'esquisse[124] stoïcienne du signe[125], où l'antécédent est un signe du conséquent[126] dans une implication commençant par le vrai et finissant par le vrai, comme dans « si elle a du lait, elle a enfanté » ou « s'il a craché des bronches, il a une plaie au poumon »[127]. L'antécédent « permet la découverte » (ἐκκαλυπτικόν) du conséquent, et même si la nécessité du conséquent *non valere in omnibus* de celle de l'antécédent, les exemples d'implications valides montrent que la *connexion* tient à la nature de faits dont la séparation est inconcevable[128]. Le fait manifeste qu'une femme a du lait est « connecté » au fait « occasionnellement caché » (πρὸς καιρὸν ἄδηλα) qu'elle a conçu, la lactation « remémorant » (ὑπομνηστικόν) la conception par le souvenir de leur concomitance répétée[129], comme la fumée pour le feu[130]. Et celui que la sueur transpire à travers la peau est « connecté » au fait « naturellement caché » (τὰ φύσει ἄδηλα) pour nous qu'il y a des pores[131], la transpiration étant un signe « indiquant » (ἐνδεικτικόν) leur existence par la prénotion qu'un liquide « ne peut passer à travers un corps compact »[132]. Les signes commémoratifs sont, en position d'antécédents, des signes présents de choses présentes, que l'événement découvert sur lequel porte la proposition, qui est *au présent* en position de conséquent, soit passé (« s'il a une cicatrice, *il a reçu une blessure* ») ou futur (« s'il a été blessé au cœur, *il mourra* »)[133].

Bien que les exemples de *confatalia* ne supposent pas tous une liaison causale, celui qui porte sur Laïos et Œdipe a été signifié par un oracle sans appel :

> Garde toi d'ensemencer le sillon générateur !
>
> Si tu procrées un fils, cet enfant te tuera et ta maison entière s'abîmera dans le sang ![134]

voir Gould 1967, p. 152-161 ; Verbeke 2006, p. 275 *sq.*, Bénatouïl 2017. On a pu lire cette incompatibilité en termes modaux, l'implication chrysippéenne équivalant à l'implication stricte de Lewis. Voir Vuillemin (1984, p. 131), pour qui $(p \Rightarrow q) \Leftrightarrow \sim M(p \wedge \sim q)$. Mais l'incompatibilité peut aussi être simplement liée à la nature des faits en conflit. Voir Gourinat 2000, p. 224-227.

124. Voir DL VII, 60.

125. *Cf.* Sextus, *P.* II, 97-103 ; *M.* VIII, 244-256. Chrysippe n'aurait pas écrit de traité sémiologique, et devait se fonder sur celui de Zénon (*cf.* DL VII, 7 = *SVF* I, 41). Voir Verbeke 1978, p. 418.

126. *Cf.* Sextus, *P.* II, 104 ; *M.* VIII, 245.

127. *Cf.* Sextus, *M.* VIII, 250-253.

128. *Ibid.* 252. La blessure au cœur n'entraîne pas logiquement la mort. Voir Moreau 1978, p. 418.

129. *Cf.* Sextus, *P.* II, 101.

130. *Cf.* Sextus, *P.* II, 100-1 ; *M.* VIII, 152 et 155.

131. Cf. *P.* II, 142 ; *M.* VIII, 306 et 309.

132. Cf. *P.* II, 142.

133. Cf. *M.* VIII, 153 et 254-256.

134. Euripide, *Phoen.* 19-20.

Puisqu'aucune prénotion ne fonde la *cohérence* de cette implication, faut-il que le destin rende impossible, pour Laïos, le fait d'avoir des rapports avec Jocaste sans engendrer un fils qui le tuera ? Si tel était le cas, le concept de confatalité excéderait celui de solidarité, ce qui interroge la possibilité pour l'agent de s'empêcher de commettre une action *confatale* à un résultat *certain*, d'une part, et la nécessité de leur relation, d'autre part.

Chrysippe croyant au caractère scientifique de la divination[135], gage de l'existence du destin[136], la conditionnelle doit être vraie et tirée d'un « théorème »[137] dérivé de l'observation répétée des signes[138] et de l'expérience du devin[139]. Mais si le devin a prévu que Laïos serait tué par son fils, pouvait-il encore être chaste ? Selon Chrysippe, « il n'était pas nécessaire que Cypsélos régnât à Corinthe, bien que l'oracle d'Apollon l'eût prédit mille ans auparavant »[140] : cela n'était pas certain parce que c'était *prévu*, mais parce que ce sera *causé*, cause qui ne dépendait pas d'une capacité du devin à le découvrir grâce à des signes[141]. Que la conjonctive confatale ($q^{t1} \wedge p^{t2}$) ait été infailliblement prédite n'implique pas l'impossibilité de son contraire, comme s'il avait été inutile pour Laïos de chercher à éviter le parricide (p^{t2}) en s'abstenant de visiter Jocaste ($\sim q^{t1}$).

La variante théologique de l'argument fataliste, qui infère la nécessité d'un futur de la vision du devin, se trouve dans le *Contre Celse* où Origène mobilise utilement le *Paresseux*[142]. Bien que l'issue fût certaine, la forme hypothétique de l'oracle impliquerait que « p^{t2} » n'était vraie qu'*à condition* que « q^{t1} » l'ait été (ou p^{t2} à moins que $\sim q^{t1}$). Or, dit Origène,

> il était clairement possible pour Laïos de ne pas ensemencer « le sillon générateur », l'oracle ne lui ayant pas ordonné l'impossible. Et il était possible d'ensemencer, ni l'un ni l'autre n'était soumis à la nécessité (κατηνάγκαστο).

135. *Cf.* DL VII, 149 ; Cicéron, *Div.* I, 82-83 (*SVF* II, 1192 = LS 42 D).

136. *Cf.* Cicéron, *Fat.* 11 ; Ps.-Plutarque, *De Fat.* 574 E ; Diogénien (fr. 4), dans Eusèbe, *PE* IV, 2, 14, 2 – 3, 13, 2 (*SVF* II, 939 = LS 55 P) ; Alexandre, *Fat.* (c. 30), p. 201, 32 – 202, 2. Selon Carnéade, le caractère *accidentel* de la cause rend Apollon incapable de prédire l'avenir (Cicéron, *Fat.* 32-33). Selon Alexandre, *Fat.* (c. 30), p. 201, 15 *sq.*, le devin n'est qu'un « pronostiqueur ».

137. *Cf.* Cicéron, *Fat.* 11. La mantique est « une science qui contemple et interprète les signes donnés aux humains par les dieux » (Cicéron, *Div.* II, 130 ; Sextus, *M.* IX, 132). Les régularités entre les signes et les futurs sont collectées par induction et tradition, et une fois formulées elles s'appellent « théorèmes ». Voir Hankinson 1988, p. 137 *sq.*

138. *Cf.* Cicéron, *Div.* I, 127 (*SVF* II, 944 = LS 55 O).

139. *Ibid.* 34. Voir Verbeke 1978, p. 278.

140. Cicéron, *Fat.* 13.

141. *Cf.* Cicéron, *Div.* I, 117-118 (*SVF* II, 1210 = LS 42 E).

142. *Cf.* Origène, *Cels.* II, 20, 1-2 et 82 *sq.*

> Or il s'ensuivit (Ἠκολούθησε) que, pour ne pas s'être gardé d'ensemencer « le sillon générateur », il subit les désastres tragiques d'Œdipe, de Jocaste et de leurs rejetons[143].

Autrement dit, si p^{t2} suppose q^{t1}, et si Laïos *pouvait* faire $\sim q^{t1}$, alors $\sim p^{t2}$ n'était pas impossible. On objectera que c'est une chose de dire que la chasteté de Laïos était *concevable*[144], et une autre de dire que cette possibilité contrefactuelle était *réelle*. Chrysippe répondrait en invoquant sa théorie des modalités. Afin que toute proposition vraie ne soit pas nécessaire et toute proposition fausse impossible, il ajoutait une clause de non-empêchement *physique*[145]. De deux contradictoires portant sur des événements dont l'occurrence n'est ni empêchée, ni garantie par les circonstances (τῶν ἐκτὸς), celle qui est fausse est « possible » et celle qui est vraie est « non nécessaire » (οὐκ ἀναγκαῖον), l'action du « porteur du cas » faisant la différence. Contre Diodore, il disait qu'il est *possible* qu'on brise la pierre même si cela n'est ni ne sera jamais le cas[146], car l'énoncé peut être vrai *à condition que* les circonstances ne s'y opposent pas. Et le fait que nous ne la brisions pas est « non nécessaire », car elle sera intacte *à moins que* nous le voulions (cela *peut* être faux) et *si* les circonstances ne s'opposent en rien[147]. De même que la vérité de « Dion se promène » ne dépend que de lui si sa promenade n'est ni empêchée, ni forcée[148], de même celle de « Laïos sera chaste » ne dépendait que de Laïos. Le destin ne s'y opposant pas, il n'était donc ni hypothétiquement impossible[149] qu'il fût chaste, ni hypothétiquement nécessaire qu'il ne le fût pas. Ce possible faux n'avait rien de contradictoire.

Mais si la conséquence (Ἠκολούθησε) énoncée par l'oracle est vraie, et si toute vérité passée est nécessaire, la nécessité ne devrait-elle pas se transmettre de l'antécédent au conséquent, de sorte qu'une fois la copulation accomplie, la procréation et le parricide s'ensuivraient *nécessairement*[150] ?

143. Origène, *Cels.* II, 55-61 (éd. Borret). Que tel futur se produise certainement (πάντως) n'implique pas qu'il se produira nécessairement (κατηναγκασμένως), seulement qu'il sera le cas (τοῦ ἔσται).

144. Ce qui est nécessaire *par soi* est vrai et ne peut être faux, par relation essentielle entre le sujet et son prédicat. *Cf.* DL VII, 75.

145. Le possible est « ce qui est susceptible d'être vrai » (Plutarque, *De stoic. rep.* 1055 E = *SVF* II, 202 ; Cicéron, *Fat.* 13 ; Arrien, *Epict.* II, 19, 2-3), mais si les circonstances extérieures ne s'y opposent pas, *cf.* DL VII, 75 ; Boèce, *Int.* p. 374 = V, 12, 933, 12-20 (*SVF* II, 201). Alexandre, *Fat.* (c. 10) p. 176, 14 *sq.* (*SVF* II, 959 = LS 38 H), l'interprète comme une définition épistémique du possible (Long & Sedley 2001, p. 169, n. 2).

146. Cicéron, *Fat.* 13. Voir Reesor 1965, p. 269 *sq.*

147. *Cf.* DL VII, 75.

148. Voir Arrien, *Epict.* IV, 1, 72-73.

149. *Cf.* DL VII, 75 : « ou bien celle qui est susceptible de l'être, mais que les circonstances empêchent d'être vraie » (Frede 1974, p. 110), *cf.* Sextus, *M.* IX, 203 (*SVF* II, 337). Pour des cas non intrinsèquement impossibles, voir Sextus, *M.* IX, 203 (*SVF* II, 337).

150. Voir Cicéron, *Fat.* 14.

À cela, Chrysippe aurait pu répondre en utilisant des conjonctives niées au lieu des conditionnelles[151]. Car selon lui l'incompatibilité de l'antécédent et de la négation du conséquent dans l'implication « saine » n'équivaut pas à la fausseté de leur conjonction[152]. En incluant la conjonctive niée « $\sim(q^{t1} \wedge \sim p^{t2})$ » dans un troisième indémontrable[153], le devin aurait révélé un résultat *certain* bien que *non-nécessaire* :

> Non (tu procréeras un fils et il ne te tuera pas)
> Or tu procréeras un fils
> Donc ton fils te tuera

Mais pourrait-on dire qu'à défaut d'être *logiquement* nécessaire le parricide « couplé » à la procréation l'ait été *hypothétiquement*, au sens où, une fois l'action interdite commise, ce résultat « capable d'être faux » fut empêché de l'être par les circonstances ?

C'est ainsi que Jules Vuillemin, afin de tenir ensemble la responsabilité et le sens dramatique du destin, imagina une « loi des *confatalia* »[154] enchaînant actions et conséquences dans une conjonctive niée :

> Ce qu'interdit le destin, c'est que, dans la conjonction fatale de deux événements, l'événement antérieur puisse avoir eu lieu sans être automatiquement suivi par l'événement encore futur[155].

Chrysippe aurait défini l'implication en termes modaux et nié l'équivalence $L(Pq \Rightarrow Fp) \Leftrightarrow \sim M(Pq \wedge \sim Fp)$. Dans la *loi conditionnelle*, on peut détacher LFp, et conformément au *Paresseux*, « $\sim Fp$ » serait *logiquement* impossible. Dans la *loi des confatalia*, on peut seulement dire que la conjonction de Pq et de $F\sim p$ est *hypothétiquement* impossible, le destin empêchant « $F\sim p$ » d'être vraie.

Mais puisque les actions de Laïos doivent aussi être *confatales* à des états de choses antérieurs, cette même loi les rendrait nécessaires. Sénèque ne dit-il pas que les expiations et les sacrifices permettent de conjurer les malheurs et que cela entre « dans les lois du destin » (*in lege fati sunt*)[156], l'aruspice étant

151. Cicéron, *Fat.* 15. La conjonctive niée montre l'incompatibilité des propositions par l'antéposition d'une négation. *Cf.* Galien, *Int. Log.* IV, 4 ; DL VII, 80 ; Sextus, *M.* VIII, 226. Voir Vuillemin 1984, p. 132-139. Cicéron considère cette stratégie comme un échec (*Fat.* 12).

152. Pour Chrysippe : $(p \Rightarrow q) \vee \sim(p \wedge \sim q)$. Pensant que, pour conserver le caractère scientifique de la divination Chrysippe devait donner une forme modale à la conjonctive niée, Vuillemin (1984, p. 129 *sq.*) soutient qu'il rejetait la définition croisée des modalités, c'est-à-dire $L(p) \Leftrightarrow \sim M(\sim p)$. Voir aussi Mignucci 1978, p. 312-318.

153. Non : le premier et non le second ; or le premier ; donc le second.

154. Vuillemin 1984, p. 141-142.

155. Vuillemin 1984, p. 141.

156. Sénèque, *QN* II, 38, 3.

fati minister[157] ? Car l'oracle était aussi *confatal* au parricide : si Laïos n'avait pas craint d'être tué par son fils, il ne l'aurait pas abandonné sur le Cithéron[158].

Pour réfuter efficacement le *Paresseux*, le destin stoïcien ne doit jouer qu'un rôle négatif, rendant seulement fausse la négation de la conjonctive *confatale*. Le parricide ne serait pas nécessaire à *cause* des circonstances[159] ou d'une *loi* le réglant comme conséquence des choix de Laïos[160], mais de l'action *non-nécessaire* d'Œdipe, qui seul en garantit la réalisation. De même qu'il condamnait les méchants qui se réfugient dans le destin « comme dans l'asile d'un temple »[161], Chrysippe aurait jugé Laïos et Œdipe responsables[162], car en l'absence de contraintes ils auraient pu agir autrement, *s'ils l'avaient voulu*[163]. Subjugués par leurs représentations, ils suivirent les dispositions psychologiques qu'*à ce moment* ils avaient développées[164], faisant du parricide la conséquence *certaine* de leurs actions, leur incapacité à faire le contraire *au même moment*[165] étant l'unique cause de leur malheur.

Et aucune loi du destin n'a rendu hypothétiquement nécessaire la mort de Socrate, comme si un théorème en avait prédit l'impossibilité, parce qu'il était né sous tel signe astral[166]. Pour Chrysippe, rappelons-le, la validité du

157. Voir Cicéron, *Div.* II, 20 *sq.* Si la divination permet de connaître la volonté divine et de conjurer le sort (*cf.* Cicéron, *Div.* II, 130 = *SVF* II, 1189), et si tout est fatal, alors elle est inutile, car il ne dépend pas de nous d'éviter l'issue prédite, ou notre évitement sera aussi nécessaire.

158. Sénèque inverse l'argument, comme le montre Gourinat 2005, p. 268-273, qui suit Alexandre (*Fat.* c. 31, 202, 12 *sq.* = *SVF* II, 941). Le monde est providentiellement organisé, et le bien est l'utile (*cf.* DL VII, 94 ; Sextus, *P.* III, 169-171 ; *M.* XI, 22), le parricide est *providentiel* et le devin *utile*. Pour la théodicée stoïcienne, voir Aulu-Gelle, *NA* VII, 1, 1-13 (*SVF* II, 1169-1170 = LS 54 Q).

159. C'est la critique de Diogénien, voir Eusèbe, *PE* IV, 3, 12-13 (*SVF* II, 939).

160. Pour un traitement médioplatonicien, voir Calcidius, *In Tim.* 153 et Alcinous, *Didasc.* 26.

161. *Cf.* Aulu-Gelle, *NA* VII, 2, 12-13 (*SVF* II, 1000, 23-34 ; LS 62 D5-6).

162. Nous nous opposons à Gould 1974.

163. Parce qu'on introduirait un mouvement sans cause, les stoïciens n'admettaient pas de pouvoir des contraires, selon Alexandre, *Fat.* (c. 15) p. 185, 8-10. Voir Bobzien 1998, p. 276-290 et 1998b.

164. Arrien, *Epict.* I, 28, 1-13. Épictète fonde la responsabilité sur la *prohairésis* (*e.g.* I, 16, 21-23 ; 17, 21-23), tandis qu'Alexandre juge le fatalisme stoïcien comme un retour au déterminisme (*Fat.* c. 26, 196, 24-197, 2 = *SVF* II, 984), ce qui justifie sa doctrine du « contre destin » (*Fat.* c. 6). Voir Mikeš 2016, p. 82-91.

165. Voir Alexandre, *Fat.* (c. 26) p. 196, 24 – 197, 3 (*SVF* II, 984 = LS 61 M) et (c. 38) p. 211, 30-33.

166. Voir Cicéron, *Fat.* 12 et Vuillemin 1984, p. 132-133. Frede (1980, p. 267) voit que dans la conditionnelle astrologique l'antécédent n'est pas cause du conséquent, tandis que Rashed (2010, p. 168-169) soutient que les configurations astrales à sa naissance expliquent la constitution de l'ἰδίως ποιόν de César, même si le fait qu'il franchira le Rubicon « *was not materially and presently inlayed into Caesar's substance when his* phusis, *at his birth, was tempered as a soul* ».

théorème rendait seulement faux, non impossible, que Fabius soit né à la Canicule *et* qu'il mourra en mer. L'inévitabilité de la mort de Socrate s'explique uniquement par le caractère inessentiel de toutes ses actions possibles, et par le fait qu'étant sage, il ne put s'empêcher de désirer mourir ce jour-là, plutôt que fuir. C'est ainsi que Chrysippe justifiait notre responsabilité sans s'écarter du fatalisme zénonien[167], en rejetant l'idée que l'inévitabilité du destin mène à la paresse. Car lorsque nous ignorons le futur (« ἂν ἄδηλά μοι ᾖ τὰ ἑξῆς »)[168], il recommandait de suivre ce que la « raison exige »[169] en sélectionnant ce qui suit la nature. Selon lui, la connaissance des malheurs à venir n'empêche pas le devoir[170], que nous n'accomplirons qu'en nous efforçant de « suivre les conséquences » de manière réfléchie[171]. Tant que le malade ignore l'issue, il doit s'efforcer de guérir, parce que le soin du corps est *naturel*. Mais si l'oracle était funeste, il devra accorder sa volonté au destin, pour être libre[172]. Pour en finir avec le *Paresseux*, Chrysippe aurait pu ajouter :

> « si je savais qu'il est fatal pour moi d'être maintenant malade, j'aurais une impulsion[173] vers la maladie. S'il avait de l'intelligence, le pied aurait une impulsion vers la boue. »[174]

167. *Cf.* Alexandre, *Fat.* c. 11-14 (p. 178, 8-186, 12) et Némésius, *NH* (c. 35) p. 105, 6 -106, 13. À ce sujet, voir Mikeš 2016, p. 29 *sq.*

168. Arrien, *Epict.* II, 6, 9, 2-3.

169. *Ibid.* 2, 20 ; III, 24, 44. Voir DL VII, 108 (λόγος αἱρεῖ ποιεῖν...) ; Andronicus, 5, 2, 6 (*SVF* III, 270) ; Marc Aurèle, *P.* IV, 24, 1 ; X, 32, 1.

170. Voir Épictète, *Ench.* 32, 3, 10-11 et Arrien, *Epict.* II, 7, 8.

171. Arrien, *Epict.* II, 10, 4 et III, 24, 110-112.

172. *Ibid.* IV, 1, 128-131.

173. L'impulsion est l'objet de la discipline du devoir chez Épictète, *cf.* Arrien, *Epict.* III, 2, 1-2 ; 12, 13.

174. Arrien, *Epict.* II, 6, 9-10, éd. H. Shenkl. Voir aussi II, 10, 5-6. Le sage agit ainsi même lorsque les présages sont funestes (*M.* 32 ; voir Simplicius, *In Epict.* XXXIX, 86 *sq.* ; *E.* II, 7).

BIBLIOGRAPHIE

ALESSANDRELLI, M. 2007 : « *'Ratio ignava' e causalità umana. 'De fato' 28-30* », *Lexis*, 25, p. 83-102.

BARNES, J. 2007 : *Truth, etc. Six lectures on Ancient Logic*, Oxford.

BARREAU, H. 1978 : « Cléanthe et Chrysippe face au maître argument de Diodore », dans BRUNSCHWIG (dir.) 1978, p. 283-302.

BÉNATOUÏL, T. 2017 : « Faits ou Essences ? Un débat sur la proposition conditionnelle stoïcienne, entre logique et physique », *Cahiers Philosophiques*, 151/4, p. 105-109.
DOI : 10.3917/caph1.151.0105

BLANCHÉ, R. 1965 : « Sur l'interprétation du κυριεύων λόγος », *Revue philosophique*, 155/2, p. 133-149.

BOBZIEN, S. 1993 : « Chrysippus' modal logic and its relation to Philo and Diodorus », dans K. Döring et T. Ebert (éd.), *Dialektiker und Stoiker*, Stuttgart, p. 63-84.

BOBZIEN, S. 1996 : « Stoic Syllogistic », *Oxford Studies in Ancient Philosophy*, 14, p. 133-192.

BOBZIEN, S. 1998 : *Determinism and Freedom in Stoic Philosophy*, Oxford.

BOBZIEN, S. 1998b : « The Inadvertent Conception and Late Birth of the Free-Will Problem », *Phronesis*, 43/2 , p. 133-175.

BOTROS, S. 1985 : « Freedom, Causality, Fatalism and Early Stoic Philosophy of Action », *Phronesis*, 30/3, p. 274-304.

BROCHARD, V. 1912 : « La logique des stoïciens », *Études de philosophie ancienne et moderne*, Paris, p. 220-238 (4ème éd.).

BROCHARD, V. 1912b : « Sur la logique des stoïciens (deuxième étude) », *Études de philosophie ancienne et moderne*, Paris, p. 239-251.

BRUNSCHWIG, J. 1978 : « Le modèle conjonctif », dans BRUNSCHWIG (dir.) 1978, p. 235-260.

BRUNSCHWIG, J. 1978 (dir.) : *Les stoïciens et leur logique*, Paris (2ème éd. : 2006).

BRUNSCHWIG, J. 1995 : « Sur une façon stoïcienne de ne pas être », dans J. Brunschwig (éd.), *Études sur les philosophies hellénistiques : Épicurisme, stoïcisme, scepticisme*, Paris, p. 251-268.

CELLUPRICA, V. 1977 : « L'argomento dominatore di Diodoro Crono e il concetto di possibile di Crisippo », *Scuole socratiche minori e filosofia ellenistica*, Bologna, p. 55-73.

D'JERANIAN, O. 2018 : « Les réminiscences stoïciennes du *Cratyle* : de la définition sémantique de la cause à la cosmologie », *Études platoniciennes*, 14 [En ligne].
DOI : 10.4000/etudesplatoniciennes.1291

D'JERANIAN, O. 2021 : « Chrysippe, les possibles et l'éternel retour », *Revue de métaphysique et de morale*, 110/2, p. 191-208.
DOI : 10.3917/rmm.212.0191

EBERT, T. 1993 : « Dialecticians and Stoics on the classification of propositions », dans K. Döring et T. Ebert (éd.), *Dialektiker und Stoiker*, Stuttgart, p. 83-126.

FREDE, M. 1974 : *Die Stoische Logik*, Göttingen.

FREDE, M. 1980 : « The Original Notion of Cause », dans M. Schofield, M. F. Burnyeat et J. Barnes (éd.), *Doubt and Dogmatism : Studies in Hellenistic*

Epistemology, Oxford, p. 217-249 (= « La notion de cause », trad. fr par J. Brunschwig, *Recherches sur les Stoïciens, Revue de Métaphysique et de Morale*, 1989/4, p. 483-511).

GASKIN, R. 1995 : *The Sea Battle and the Master Argument, Aristotle and Diodorus Cronus on the Metaphysics of the Future*, Berlin/New York.

GOULD, J. B. 1967 : « Chrysippus, on the Criteria for the Truth of a Conditional Proposition », *Phronesis*, 12/2, p. 152-161.

GOULD, J. B. 1974 : « The Stoic Conception of Fate », *Journal of the History of Ideas*, 35/1, p. 17-32.

GOURINAT, J.-B. 2000 : *La dialectique des stoïciens*, Paris.

GOURINAT, J.-B. 2005 : « Prédiction du futur et action humaine dans le traité de Chrysippe *Sur le destin* », dans G. Romeyer-Dherbey (dir.) et J.-B. Gourinat (éd.), *Les Stoïciens*, Paris, p. 247-292.

GOURINAT, J.-B. 2014 : « *Adsensio in nostra potestate* : 'from us' and 'up to us' in ancient Stoicism – a plea for reassessment », dans P. Destrée, R. Salles et M. Zingano (éd.), *What is up to us ? Studies on Agency and Responsibility in Ancient Philosophy*, Sankt Augustin, p. 141-150.

HAMELIN, O. 1901 : « Sur la logique des Stoïciens », *L'Année philosophique*, p. 13-26.

HANKINSON, J. 1988 : « Stoicism, Science and Divination », *Method, Medicine and Metaphysics : Studies in the Philosophy of Ancient Science*, Edmonton, p. 123-160.

HINTIKKA, J. 1964 : « Aristotle and the Master Argument of Diodorus », *American philosophical quarterly*, 1/2, p. 101-114.

KOCH, I. 2014 : « Distinctions causales stoïciennes et académiciennes dans le *De fato* de Cicéron », Chôra. *Revue d'Études Anciennes et Médiévales*, 12, p. 87-120.

KOCH, I. 2019 : *La causalité humaine. Sur le* De fato *d'Alexandre d'Aphrodise*, Paris.

LONG, A. A. & D. SEDLEY 2001 (éd.) : *The Hellenistic Philosophers*, Cambridge, CUP, 1987 (traduit de l'anglais par J. Brunschwig et P. Pellegrin sous le titre *Les philosophes hellénistiques*, Paris, GF-Flammarion, 2001).

MASI, F. & S. MASO 2013 (éd.) : *Fate, Chance and Fortune in Ancient Thought*, Amsterdam.

MATES, B. 1961 : *Stoic Logic*, Berkeley-Los Angeles (1ème éd. 1953).

MEYER, S. 2009 : « Chain of Causes. What is Stoic Fate ? », dans R. Salles (éd.), *God and Cosmos in Stoicism*, Oxford, p. 71-90.

MIKEŠ, V. 2016 : *Le paradoxe stoïcien : liberté de l'action déterminée*, Paris.

MC KIRAHAN, R. 1979 : « Diodorus and Prior and the Master Argument », *Synthese*, 42/2, p. 223-253.

MIGNUCCI, M. 1978 : « Sur la logique modale des stoïciens », dans BRUNSCHWIG (dir.) 1978, p. 303-332.

MOREAU, J. 1978 : « Immutabilité du vrai, nécessité logique et lien causal », dans BRUNSCHWIG (dir.) 1978, p. 405-420.

MULLER, R. 1984 : « Signification historique et philosophique de l'argument souverain de Diodore », *Revue de Philosophie Ancienne*, 2/1, p. 3-37.

PAPAZIAN, M. B. 2001 : « Chrysippus and the destruction of propositions: a defence of the standard interpretation », *History and Philosophy of Logic*, 22/1, p. 1-12.

RASHED, R. 2010 : « Alexander of Aphrodisias on Particulars and the Stoic Criterion of Identity », dans R. W. Sharples (dir.), *Particulars in Greek Philosophy*, Leiden/ Boston, p. 157-179.

REESOR, M. E. 1965 : « Fate and Possibility in Early Stoic Philosophy », *Phoenix*, 19, p. 285-297.

RIST, J. M. 1969 : *Stoic Philosophy*, Cambridge.

SALLES, R. 2005 : *The Stoic on Determinism and Compatibilism*, Aldershot.

SEDLEY, D. 1993 : « Chrysippus on psychophysical causality », dans J. Brunschwig et M. C. Nussbaum (éd.), *Passions and Perceptions, Studies in Hellenistic Philosophy of Mind*, Cambridge, p. 313-331.

SEEL, G. 1982 : « Diodore domine-t-il Aristote ? En hommage à J. Vuillemin », *Revue de Métaphysique et de Morale*, 87/3, p. 293-313.

SEEL, G. 1993 : « Zur Geschichte und Logik des θερίζων λόγος », dans K. Döring et Th. Elbert (éd.), *Dialektiker und Stoiker: zur Logik der Stoa und ihrer Vorläufer*, Stuttgart, p. 291-318.

SEEL, G. 2005 : « L'aporie de l'aporie de Diodore Cronos. À propos des reconstructions du dominateur par Jules Vuillemin », dans M. Rashed et P. Pellegrin (éd.), *Philosophie des mathématiques et théorie de la connaissance*, Paris, p. 81-119.

SEEL, G. 2018 : « The Puzzles of the 'Master Argument' and their Solutions », *International Philosophical Inquiry*, 41/2-3, p. 81-93.

SORABJI, R. 1980 : *Necessity, Cause and Blame*, New-York.

SORABJI, R. 1980b : « Causation, laws and necessity », dans M. Schofield, M. F. Burnyeat et J. Barnes (éd.), *Doubt and Dogmatism. Studies in Hellinistic Epistemology*, Oxford, p. 259-278.

VERBEKE, G. 1978 : « La philosophie du signe chez les stoïciens », dans BRUNSCHWIG (dir.) 1978, p. 261-282.

VUILLEMIN, J. 1979 : « L'argument dominateur », *Revue de Métaphysique et de Morale*, 84/2, p. 225-257.

VUILLEMIN, J. 1984 : *Nécessité ou Contingence. L'aporie de Diodore et les systèmes philosophiques*, Paris.

WHITE, M. J. 1985 : *Agency and Integrality*, Dordrecht.

YON, A. 1933 (éd.) : Cicéron. *Traité du destin*, Paris.

VARIA

ENTRE MÉDECINE ET PHILOSOPHIE

Le corps organique dans les psychophysiologies matérialistes antiques

Marion BOURBON
Université Bordeaux Montaigne /Sciences, Philosophie, Humanités

RÉSUMÉ. Cet article s'attache à reconstituer l'un des pans de l'histoire des échanges médico-philosophiques au sein de la tradition matérialiste en se centrant sur leur rôle décisif dans l'émergence d'une conception organique du corps. En effet, dès ses débuts, la pensée médicale se trouve en dialogue étroit avec la tradition présocratique et en particulier empédocléenne. Elles proposent toutes deux des psychophysiologies du mélange et avec elles des protoconceptions d'un modèle organique du corps. La conception stoïcienne du mélange intégral et, avec elle, le modèle d'individualité organique inédit qu'elle définit héritent incontestablement de cet apport médico-philosophique. De ce point de vue, la pensée galénique de la *krasis* qui applique ce modèle spécifiquement au corps s'inscrit aussi dans cette tradition matérialiste et corporéiste, une tradition qui ne conçoit l'individuation que dans sa puissance de variation et dans la relation à son milieu. Elle bénéficie elle-même d'un apport philosophique stoïcien indéniable, tout en lui conférant une extension médicale inédite.

ABSTRACT. *This paper attempts to trace part of the history of medical and philosophical exchanges within the materialist tradition. I focus on this decisive role that they play on the emergence of organismic conception of the body. From its very beginnings, medical thought as the thought of mixture and as psychophysiology has been in close connection with the pre-Socratic tradition, and with Empedocles in particular. Both of them propose accounts of the blending as protoconceptions of an organic model of the body. In the regard, the Stoic conception of krasis and the new model of the organismic individuality that it defines indebt to this medical and philosophical account. In this regard, the Galenic thought of mixture as an immanent and dynamic unity is also part of this materialistic and corporeist tradition. Within it, individual identity is conceived as fundamentally relational. It benefits from an undeniable Stoic account, while giving it an unprecedented medical extension.*

Philosophie antique, n°24 (2024), 151-174

Introduction

L'étude que je propose ici s'inscrit dans un questionnement sur les échanges entre la médecine grecque et les philosophies matérialistes antiques, présocratiques et stoïcienne*[1]. Mon but est de mettre en évidence le rôle de ces échanges dans l'émergence d'une conception matérialiste originale du corps organique.

J'ai déjà commencé ailleurs[2] à éclairer un aspect de cette histoire philosophique et la manière dont elle s'origine dans les pensées présocratiques de la *phusis* avant de connaître une inflexion décisive avec le stoïcisme qui lui adjoint une conception d'une prédisposition providentielle du corps et de sa nature[3]. Mais dans cette histoire « matérialiste » des pensées du mélange, le rôle des apports de la tradition médicale et de ses échanges avec les traditions matérialistes antiques non aristotéliciennes est lui aussi déterminant, dès leurs naissances respectives. C'est à lui que je vais ici m'attacher plus spécifiquement.

Dès ses débuts, la pensée médicale comme pensée du mélange et comme psychophysiologie se trouve en effet en dialogue étroit avec la tradition présocratique et en particulier empédocléenne, comme l'atteste le traité *Du régime*. Ce sont ces échanges médico-philosophiques matérialistes que le

*Je tiens ici à remercier Maria Michela Sassi, Pierre Pellegrin et Jean-Baptiste Gourinat dont les conseils et les suggestions tout au long de la rédaction m'ont été précieux.

1. Les pensées qui vont ici m'intéresser procèdent à une matérialisation ou à une corporéisation intégrale de l'être et proposent une compréhension de l'âme et des actes psychiques en termes exclusivement matériels ou corporels (c'est la raison pour laquelle j'exclus ici l'aristotélisme). Je les subsume donc sous le terme de « matérialistes », même si le corporéisme stoïcien constitue un matérialisme tout à fait spécifique puisqu'il repose sur une conception providentielle du *logos* divin.

2. Voir Bourbon 2020.

3. Sur cette conception providentielle de l'organisme, voir Bénatouïl 2006, p. 19 *sq*.

corporéisme stoïcien va poursuivre et accélérer en proposant une conception matérialiste inédite du mélange total, forgeant par là même un modèle d'individualité organique entièrement immanent alternatif au modèle aristotélicien. Or cette conception stoïcienne du mélange organique fondée sur le modèle de la sympathie doit être rapprochée de la *krasis* humorale que l'on trouve chez Galien, cette fois-ci appliquée au corps humain. Elle permet de concevoir une unité immanente et dynamique au sein de laquelle l'individualité des qualités n'est à aucun moment abolie, malgré l'unité originale que leur interaction produit. Cette conception organique du corps dans laquelle l'identité individuelle est conçue comme fondamentalement relationnelle doit ainsi être réinscrite dans l'histoire de ces transferts médico-philosophiques.

Une première psychophysiologie médicale : le traité *Du régime*

Dès les débuts de la pensée médicale, la conception du mélange est donc déjà bien attestée en particulier dans la tradition dite « hippocratique »[4]. Si l'idée que la constitution (et l'état) des êtres naturels repose de manière plus ou moins fondamentale sur un mélange d'éléments primordiaux est centrale chez les présocratiques, elle l'est aussi chez les médecins : la notion de *krasis* /*krêsis* ainsi que le verbe *kerannusthai* ont une extension spécifiquement médicale. Le traité *Nature de l'homme*, attribué à Polybe, formule explicitement l'idée que la santé est produite par le mélange équilibré des éléments de l'homme et la maladie par la rupture de cet équilibre[5]. C'est pourtant un autre texte qui s'avère décisif pour notre enquête, le traité *Du régime*[6] : on y trouve en effet une « application » de la théorie du mélange à la psychologie et à l'embryologie, soit une véritable psychophysiologie médicale.

Mélange et régime dans le traité Du régime

Le livre 1 du traité *Du Régime* se donne en effet comme une étude de la nature humaine, conçue à partir d'une analogie entre le macrocosme et le microcosme, le corps humain constituant une imitation (*apomimêsis*[7]) de l'univers en vertu de leur commune composition[8]. Comme tous les vivants,

4. Voir *VM* c. 5-7, (Littré I, 582) ; c. 20 (I, 606) ; c. 18 (I, 616) ; c. 21 (I, 618) ; *Aph*. section 4, 61, 1 (IV, 556) ; *Nat. Hom*. c. 3, 7, (VI, 38) ; c. 4, 3 (VI, 40) ; *Vict*. I 6, c. 32, 22 (VI, 506) ; *Hebd*. 40 *app*. 45 R = c. 24, 26 (VIII, 647) ; *Aer*. C. 12, 19 (II, 52). Sur cet aspect, voir Boudon-Millot 2011.

5. *Nat. Hom*. 4, CMG I.1.3, 172.13– 174.10 Jouanna. Voir aussi *VM* c14 (Littré I, 602).

6. Nous disposons de l'édition établie par Joly 1967, et de sa version amendée et complétée dans Joly & Byl 1984 puis Byl 2002. Ce traité occupe une place à part dans la Collection hippocratique (voir Jouanna 1992) et son témoignage, à ce titre, doit être envisagé avec précaution. Toutes les traductions proposées par la suite sont celles de Joly.

7. I, 6, 484, 18.23.

8. Voir par exemple Magdelaine 1997 ; Le Blay 2005.

l'homme est composé des deux éléments que sont l'eau et le feu (et on trouve ces éléments dans des proportions valables selon les individus). Ce mélange individuel détermine la nature du corps et de l'âme qui, en vertu de sa relation au tout, se trouve ainsi toujours conditionnée par des facteurs environnementaux. L'auteur du traité *Du régime* retrouve déjà par là des réflexions cosmologiques des physiologues présocratiques, à commencer par Démocrite pour lequel « l'homme est un petit monde (*anthrôpos mikros kosmos*)[9] ». Il faut dès lors connaître la nature de l'univers pour connaître celle de l'homme, préalable nécessaire à la pratique médicale[10]. Puisque c'est non seulement le corps mais aussi l'âme qui est un mélange, la pensée du mélange se trouve alors mobilisée dans la compréhension des processus psychophysiologiques mais aussi embryologiques. Le mélange et ses variations exercent leur causalité dans les phénomènes psychiques. Ces actes psychiques y apparaissent comme une *(sun)krêsis* particulière des éléments du feu et de l'eau que l'on peut modifier par des stratégies diététiques ou pharmacologiques qui visent précisément à modifier la nature de ce mélange pour restaurer son équilibre. Le traité *Du régime* tire donc toutes les conséquences du caractère relationnel de l'équilibre psychique.

La théorie du mélange comme psychophysiologie

Au chapitre 35 de la fin du livre I, l'auteur du traité *Du régime* s'intéresse à l'intelligence de l'âme et propose une compréhension à partir de sa théorie du mélange des éléments : l'état du mélange est cause de la qualité de l'intelligence. Cela justifie une diététique, un régime approprié à la nature de l'homme, c'est-à-dire capable de favoriser l'équilibre délicat qui caractérise les degrés d'intelligence les plus élevés, l'auteur présentant une typologie des degrés d'intelligence :

> Le feu le plus humide et l'eau la plus sèche se mêlant *(krêsin labonta)* dans le corps produisent la plus grande intelligence. (...) L'âme ainsi composée (*ek toutôn ...sunkrêtheisa*) est la plus intelligente et a la meilleure mémoire[11].

Les différents états de l'intelligence comme de la sensation dépendent de la qualité de l'équilibre du mélange :

9. 68 B 34 DK.

10. Tous les traités hippocratiques ne partagent cependant pas cette revendication d'une dépendance de la médecine vis-à-vis de la philosophie, puisqu'en particulier *Ancienne médecine* et *Nature de l'homme* critiquent violemment cette médecine d'inspiration philosophique. Voir par exemple : *VM* c. 20, 1-9 (Littré I, 620).

11. *Du régime* I, 35, 1 (CMG I, 2, 4, p. 150, 29-30 et p. 152, 5-6 Joly-Byl, VI 512-514 Littré).

> C'est donc ce mélange (de l'eau et du feu) qui est cause de l'intelligence de l'âme ou de son inintelligence[12].

À chaque défaut d'intelligence, c'est-à-dire à chaque déséquilibre du mélange ou domination (*krateein*) d'un des éléments sur l'autre[13], correspond un régime adapté :

> S'il a un régime correct, l'individu peut devenir plus intelligent et plus pénétrant que ne le voulait sa nature[14].

De ce point de vue, on ne peut que constater une convergence entre la théorie du mélange du chapitre 35 du traité *Du régime* et celle de la doctrine de la sensation et de la cognition d'Empédocle reconstituée par Théophraste[15] : dans les deux cas, nous avons affaire à une véritable psychophysiologie dans laquelle ce sont les états du mélange qui causent les phénomènes psychiques : le modèle harmonique. Chez Empédocle, cette théorie de la sensation et de l'intelligence repose en outre sur une conception du mélange intégral alternative au modèle de la juxtaposition et qui de ce point de vue anticipe la *krasis*.

La psychophysiologie empédocléenne : un antécédent de la *krasis* stoïcienne

Nous trouvons en effet une première version particulièrement aboutie de pensée et de physique du mélange dans la cosmogonie d'Empédocle, avec le mélange des « racines » aux propriétés contraires réalisé sous l'égide de l'Amour. Je me suis intéressée ailleurs aux caractéristiques de ce mélange[16] et ai souligné comment c'est ce mélange des « racines » qui est source de la polymorphie des formes[17]. Comme dans le traité *Du régime*, ce modèle du mélange s'applique à un double niveau, celui du monde et celui des « corps », selon une analogie entre monde et corps humain, macrocosme et microcosme.

Selon un fragment transmis par Simplicius, Empédocle concevait ainsi la « génération » cosmogonique sur le modèle de la germination[18], cette image étant elle-même rapprochée par Empédocle du mélange de poudres chromatiques (*poluchroa pharmaka*) que prépare le peintre[19] :

12. I, 36.
13. I, 35, 2 et 10 (p. 152, 8-13 et p. 154 ; 31-32 Joly-Byl, VI 514 et 520 Littré).
14. I, 35 (p. 152, 12 *sq.* Joly-Byl, VI, 514, 15 *sq.* Littré).
15. 31 A 86 DK = Théophraste, *De sensibus*, 10. Voir plus bas p. 158-159. Sur ce rapprochement entre le texte *Du régime* et la théorie de l'intelligence d'Empédocle, voir Jouanna 2007. Dans la ligne qui relie Empédocle à la doctrine de l'intelligence du *Timée* de Platon, le traité *Du régime* constitue un intermédiaire incontestable, bien que longtemps négligé.
16. Voir Bourbon 2020, p. 170-175.
17. Voir Santoro 2012.
18. B 21 DK.
19. B 23 DK.

Comme on voit les peintres, quand, sur les tableaux, ils varient la couleur,
Les maîtres savants dont l'intelligence a formé la main ;
Ils saisissent les drogues multicolores (*poluchroa pharmaka*) de leurs doigts,
Mêlent en les liant (*harmoniê meixante*) tantôt plus, tantôt moins de parts,
Et, de ces pâtes, ils composent les figures à l'image de toute chose,
Donnant forme aux arbres, aux hommes et aux femmes,
Aux bêtes, aux oiseaux et aux poissons que nourrit l'eau
Et aussi aux dieux longévifs, les premiers par le rang[20].

Ce mélange pourrait évoquer celui de la préparation alchimique et pharmaceutique, tel qu'on le trouvera chez Galien comme modèle de juxtaposition parcellaire ou alliance de couleurs qui ne se confondraient pas, fût-elle des plus subtiles[21]. Pourtant ce mélange est conçu comme une harmonie, terme qui indique une union étroite qui repose sur la proportion des parts mais qui ne menace à aucun moment l'individualité des composants du mélange. Ces poudres sont *poluchroa*, c'est-à-dire qu'elles sont chacune de couleur différente et leur mélange vient produire une nouvelle couleur. À l'image de ce mélange de poudres colorées, l'interaction qualitative des racines produit un tout homogène inédit : les mêmes produisent du différent[22]. La nouvelle couleur obtenue à la faveur du mélange porte en elle les couleurs qui ont présidé à sa formation. Bien qu'on ne puisse reconnaître dans le mélange final les couleurs qui ont présidé à la composition de la nouvelle couleur, celle-ci les porte en elle. L'image souligne ainsi le caractère intégral du mélange des « racines », sources des formes. L'harmonique du « mélange intégral » empédocléen semble de ce point de vue anticiper la *krasis di' holôn*[23] stoïcienne : il s'agit de tenir ensemble le caractère total du mélange et la conservation de l'individualité des éléments qui le constituent, une conservation qui ne menace à aucun moment l'individualité harmonique du tout. Pour mémoire, les stoïciens forgent en effet une conception originale inédite du mélange en proposant une refonte du modèle aristotélicien bipartite[24]. Là où ce dernier distinguait le mélange par juxtaposition mécanique ou par agrégation (*sunthesis*) et le mélange par fusion ou « mixture » (*mixis*)[25], ils lui substituent une tripartition entre *sunthesis*, *sunchusis* et *krasis*[26]. La juxtaposition

20. B 23 DK (= 64 Bollack, trad. Bollack).

21. Galien, *In Hipp. Nat. Hom. Comment.*XV, 32 (Kühn) = 21 A 34 DK.

22. B 21 DK.

23. Voir *De Elem. ex Hipp.* V, 15-17 (Kühn).

24. Nous laissons de côté la question de la controverse entre stoïciens et péripatéticiens sur la question de l'objet du mélange qui n'est pas décisive ici pour notre propos. Sur cette controverse, voir en particulier Collette-Ducic & Delcomminette 2007, p. 67-100.

25. Sur la théorie stoïcienne du mélange, voir Voelke 1961, p. 149-152 et Brunschwig 1995, p. 168 ; Couloubaritsis 2005, p. 187-211 ; Laurand 2005 et Collette-Ducic & Delcomminette 2007.

26. Alexandre d'Aphrodise, *Du mélange* 216, 14-218, 6 (= *SVF* II 473). Voir aussi Stobée, I, 17, p. 153, 23 - 155, 14 W (= *SVF* II 471) partiellement reproduit dans LS 48D, qui rapporte quant à lui l'existence d'une quadripartition *parathesis*/*mixis*/*krasis*/*sunchusis*. Sur

parcellaire qu'est la *sunthesis* se caractérise par un contact entre les éléments limité à un contact de surface, les éléments ne subissant aucune altération essentielle, de sorte qu'on peut les en extraire sans qu'ils ne perdent aucune de leurs qualités essentielles. La fusion (*sunchusis*) est quant à elle définie par le fait qu'elle donne naissance à un nouveau composé par perte des qualités de ses constituants, le nouveau composé différant donc de chacun de ses éléments initiaux[27]. Enfin, la *krasis* constitue ce mélange hybride : la coextensivité réciproque des éléments s'y trouve conservée comme dans la *sunchusis*, mais l'originalité et la séparabilité des composants initiaux du mélange demeurent, comme c'est le cas dans la *mixis*. En l'état de nos sources, il reste délicat de se prononcer sur la valeur ontologique de ces principes permanents de variation que sont les « racines ». Mais même si le mélange empédocléen ne présente pas ce degré de systématisation dans la théorisation de la typologie des mélanges, nous sommes avec lui déjà en présence d'une tentative de conceptualisation d'un modèle organique d'individualité au sein duquel l'individualité des parties est conservée et concourt à l'unité originale du tout : un modèle organique du corps.

La pensée empédocléenne du mélange fonde dès lors une psychophysiologie qui hérite sur ce point de la théorie parménidienne de la sensation, du moins telle qu'on en trouve trace chez Théophraste[28] : les actes psychiques (sensation et intellection) sont définis comme des variations du mélange universel des éléments[29]. La doctrine empédocléenne de la connaissance identifie ainsi cette dernière à une assimilation harmonique du pensé par le pensant[30], cette identité assurant la stabilité de la *phronêsis*. Pour percevoir et penser la vérité, le corps et ses pores doivent être adaptés à la nature de ce qu'il perçoit et pense[31].

Dès lors, selon Empédocle, l'organe où s'observe la meilleure version du mélange est celui qui dispose du plus haut degré de sensation. Les hommes possèdent des capacités intellectuelles supérieures en vertu de cet organe qu'est le sang et plus encore celui qui entoure le cœur au sein duquel on trouve

ce texte, voir Todd 1976. Voir aussi DL VII, 151 (= *SVF* II 479 = LS 48A) ; et pour la critique de Plutarque référée à celle d'Archésilas, voir *Des notions communes*, 1078 B-E (= fragment partiel de *SVF* II 465).

27. Cependant, la mixture aristotélicienne ne peut prendre place qu'entre constituants homogènes, lorsque les stoïciens lèvent cette condition.

28. B16 DK = Théophraste, *De sensibus*, 2-4 = *Doxographi Graeci*, p. 499, 18-21, 6 Diels : ὡς γὰρ ἑκάστοτε – φησίν – ἔχει κρᾶσιν μελέων πολυπλάγκτων, τὼς νόος ἀνθρώποισι παρέστηκεν· τὸ γὰρ αὐτό ἔστιν ὅπερ φρονέει μελέων φύσις ἀνθρώποισι καὶ πᾶσιν καὶ παντί· τὸ γὰρ πλέον ἐστὶ νόημα. Cette citation nous a en fait également été transmise par Aristote (*Métaphysique*, Γ, 5, 1009b22-25) mais une grande majorité des interprètes, que je suis ici, considère que la version de Théophraste est plus fidèle que celle d'Aristote. Voir Laks 2007, p. 180.

29. *Ibid.* p. 187.

30. B 106 : πρὸς παρεὸν γὰρ μῆτις ἀέξεται ἀνθρώποισιν. Voir Bourbon 2020.

31. Sur l'identification entre pore et acte intellectif, voir B3, 13-14.

la forme la plus harmonieuse du mélange[32]. Quelles que soient les différences constitutives entre les modèles empédocléen et hippocratique de mélange et les physiologies respectives qu'ils déterminent, dans les deux cas la sensation et l'intellection dépendent de la qualité du mélange[33]. C'est ce principe de la théorie empédocléenne de la sensation dont le traité hippocratique *Du régime* semble tirer toutes les conséquences diététiques et thérapeutiques[34].

Du sang à l'âme : la psychophysiologie de l'intelligence du traité *Du régime*

Dans le traité *Du régime*, le mélange est donc un mélange entre deux éléments. L'homme est ainsi un composé de feu et d'eau (*sunchrêsis echousa puros kai hudatos*[35])[36] dans des proportions variables que le régime peut venir modifier. Cette physiologie permet donc d'expliquer par la proportion d'eau et de feu du mélange la qualité de la nutrition et de la sensation ainsi que celle de l'intelligence.

L'intelligence est ainsi référée non plus spécifiquement au rôle du sang (comme chez Empédocle) mais à la vitesse des rotations de l'âme[37], elle-même fonction de l'équilibre entre le feu et l'eau, le feu ayant un effet d'accélération et l'eau un effet de ralentissement. C'est ce point qui a pu justifier qu'on établisse un lien d'antécédence avec la doctrine platonicienne du *Timée*[38].

L'auteur du traité adopte ainsi la théorie des pores : les objets perçus, sentis ou intelligés, émettent des effluves qui viennent se mêler à l'âme. Et c'est la qualité de ce mélange dont dépend la qualité de l'acte perceptif comme de l'intellection. Cette théorie des pores[39] occupait déjà une fonction centrale dans la compréhension empédocléenne des actes perceptifs et psychiques : ces derniers sont définis par l'incorporation des effluves, une incorporation qui suppose la symétrie des pores des corps en présence[40]. Cette théorie était

32. 31 B 105, 3 = Théophraste, *De Sensibus*, 10 ; voir aussi 31 A 97 [= Plutarque, *Opinions des philosophes*, IV, 5].

33. Sur les analogies entre les deux doctrines, voir le témoignage de Théophraste, *De sensibus*, 10 *sq*., 24.

34. Bartoš 2015.

35. I, 25.

36. Jouanna 2007.

37. 35, 5. Sur ce passage à la traduction difficile, voir Jouanna 2007 : 15-26.

38. Jouanna 2007.

39. 36. Sur ces aspects, voir Gemelli Marciano 2009.

40. Voir Pseudo-Plutarque, *Opinions des philosophes*, IV, 9 (éd. G. Lachenaud, Paris, Belles Lettres, 1993 = t. XII des *Œuvres morales* de Plutarque) (trad. A.-L. Therme) : « Pour Empédocle, c'est suivant la συμμετρία des pores que se font les sensations, en s'ajustant à chacun des sensibles apparentés (παρὰ τὰς συμμετρίας τῶν πόρων τὰς κατὰ μέρος αἰσθήσεις γίνεσθαι, τοῦ οἰκείου τῶν αἰσθητῶν ἑκάστῃ ἁρμόζοντος) » et Théophraste, *De sensibus*, 7 (*Doxographi Graeci*, p. 500) (trad. A.-L. Therme) : « Empédocle prétend que la sensation

cependant extrêmement partagée à l'époque, et ce bien au-delà du cercle empédocléen, ce qui ne milite donc pas en soi en faveur d'un lien entre l'auteur du traité *Du régime* et Empédocle.

On retrouve cette conception de la perception et de la cognition chez l'auteur du traité *Du régime* qui considère à ce titre que c'est cette adaptation que le régime peut favoriser[41]. La théorie des pores souligne le caractère relationnel de l'identité individuelle des corps en échange constant avec le monde. Toute distinction stricte entre le « dedans » et le « dehors » s'y trouve abolie à la faveur du *continuum* du mélange universel. L'intelligence de l'homme n'est jamais qu'une modalité de l'intelligence du monde.

Ce que montre l'auteur du trairé *Du régime* est donc que la nature de la *psuchê* comme corps n'est jamais un principe exclusivement interne : la rupture de l'équilibre entre éléments, cause des défauts de l'intelligence, peut toujours être sinon retrouvée, du moins atténuée par un régime adapté, c'est-à-dire par une interaction qualitative avec le milieu.

Les appropriations philosophiques des premières physiologies médicales

Ce premier sondage permet de rappeler l'existence de points de contact entre les physiologies philosophiques et médicales dès leur naissance, échanges qui se poursuivent aussi bien dans la pensée platonicienne[42] que dans la pensée aristotélicienne[43]. Mon propos n'est pas ici de reconstituer le détail de ces transferts qui ont déjà été étudiés. Nous savons en particulier combien la théorie aristotélicienne du mélange et son rôle décisif dans les domaines psychologiques et embryologiques peuvent à bien des égards être rapprochés de la pensée hippocratique du mélange telle qu'on la trouve dans le traité *Du régime*[44]. Pourtant, il est une différence décisive entre les deux modèles qui tient à une option ontologique : alors que les facteurs matériels constituent des causes dans le corpus médical, chez Aristote ils ne peuvent jamais jouer qu'un rôle secondaire au regard de ce principe incorporel qu'est

se produit par l'adaptation aux pores propres à chaque sens (φησι τῷ ἐναρμόττειν εἰς τοὺς πόρους τοὺς ἑκάστης αἰσθάνεσθαι) ; aussi l'un ne peut-il reconnaître ce qui appartient à l'autre, puisque les pores, selon qu'ils sont larges ou étroits, touchent d'autres choses selon l'objet à percevoir, si bien que les uns traversent sans toucher et que d'autres ne peuvent pas pénétrer du tout ». Voir aussi l'édition de Mansfeld et Runia.

41. Voir en particulier *Vict.* I, 36 (p. 156 Joly-Byl). Voir aussi I, 3, 4-5 (p. 126 Joly-Byl) et I, 5 (p. 128 Joly-Byl).

42. L. Brisson a par ailleurs montré comment la médecine hippocratique a pu influencer la conception platonicienne de la sensation dans le *Timée*, dans laquelle l'âme apparaît en relation étroite avec le corps. Voir en particulier 44b1-c4 et Brisson 2013. Voir aussi Jouanna 2007.

43. Van Der Eijk 2014 et 2020 en particulier.

44. Voir Pellegrin 1994 et 2006. Voir aussi plus récemment Mirrione 2023.

la forme[45] causalité première des processus physiques. C'est ce qui implique chez Aristote un réaménagement conséquent du modèle médical du mélange, par contraste avec le modèle stoïcien qui, en procédant à une corporéisation intégrale de l'être, conçoit les processus psychologiques dans des termes exclusivement corporéistes. Philosophie stoïcienne et pensée médicale ont ainsi en partage de reposer sur l'affirmation commune de la nature corporelle de l'âme comme souffle (*pneuma*) et mixture (*krasis*)[46].

C'est ainsi un modèle biologique et médical que reprend Cléanthe, héritier sur ce point de Zénon[47], celui de la chaleur vitale[48] en l'étendant à l'univers en son entier et à ses parties, avec la notion de tension (*tonos*)[49]. C'est ensuite Chrysippe qui l'aurait lui-même appliqué au souffle (*pneuma*) divin auquel ses prédécesseurs avaient déjà identifié l'âme[50], un souffle qui est précisément défini comme mélange (*krasis*) d'éléments. Ce mélange variable et individué combinant une proportion de feu et d'air[51] détermine donc la tension (*tonos*) et la qualité de cette portion individuelle de souffle qu'est chaque individu, distonique chez l'insensé ou eutonique chez le sage. Dès lors, si le monisme corporéiste stoïcien se définit comme une médecine de l'âme, nous ne sommes plus simplement dans l'analogie : l'âme malade est un corps pathologique dont le mélange est disharmonique, déséquilibré.

Comme j'ai pu le souligner ailleurs[52], la physique stoïcienne cherche à prendre en charge le problème de l'individuation des corps au sein du *continuum* cosmique. Car si les psychophysiologies présocratiques et médicales posent bien l'existence d'un principe de variation (les actes perceptifs et psychiques changent *tout en se maintenant*), elles laissent pour une part en suspens le problème qui est celui d'assurer l'individualité des corps, leur unité synchronique autant que diachronique, au sein de cet univers en constant devenir.

45. Il existe bien des processus qui relèvent exclusivement de la nécessité mécanique, comme la production de la bile ou la formation de la couleur des yeux. Voir *GA* V, 1, 778a32.

46. Voir Tieleman 1996. Sur les relations entre Galien et les stoïciens, voir aussi Gill 2010.

47. Ce statut principiel du feu remonterait à Zénon (Cléanthe aurait d'ailleurs en effet consacré un traité à la physique de Zénon : voir DL VII, 176), à en croire Aristoclès. Voir Aristoclès, *ap.* Eusèbe, *Préparation évangélique*, XV, 816d (= *SVF* I 98). Aristoclès précise que si le modèle peut évoquer la conception platonicienne, le caractère matériel des principes du feu, dieu et la matière, rend le rapprochement impossible.

48. Cicéron, *De la nature des dieux* II, 23-25, 28-30 = LS 47C.

49. Stobée, *Eclog.* I, 17, 3, p. 153, 13-15 (= *SVF* I 497).

50. C'est cette variation chrysippéenne qui aurait, à en croire A. A. Long et D. Sedley, provoqué une distinction entre éléments actifs et passifs, telle qu'on la trouve rapportée par Galien, *Des causes sustentatrices*, I, 1-2, 4 = LS 55F (trad. Brunschwig et Pellegrin adaptée de la version anglaise du texte arabe publiée par M. C. Lyons, l'opuscule ne nous étant parvenu qu'en traduction arabe et dans une traduction latine du XIVe siècle).

51. Alexandre d'Aphrodise, *De An.* p. 115, 6, éd. Bruns (= *SVF* II 786).

52. Bourbon 2020.

C'est précisément la fonction du mélange intégral (*krasis di' holôn*) des stoïciens que d'assurer cette individualité organique des corps au sein du *continnum* cosmique. Le mélange intégral permet en effet de penser la double modalité d'action du *pneuma* : il individue à l'échelle des corps mais il est aussi intentionnalité et providence selon un modèle intégratif et différentiel de sorte que l'unité du monde se trouve préservée. En tout point de la matière, la qualité et la tension constitutive du *tonos* sont différenciées, constituant la qualité propre d'un corps, portion différenciée de souffle divin dont ce corps tient son unicité. L'individualité de cette qualité propre qui assure l'individualité d'un corps n'est à aucun moment menacée par sa participation au mélange universel, les stoïciens cherchant par là même à se soustraire à l'objection de l'argument croissant[53]. La pensée du mélange universel permet donc de concevoir un principe d'individuation comme principe de variation, selon un modèle qu'on pourrait qualifier d'organique : l'individualité singulière des corps n'est à aucun moment abolie, sans qu'il n'y ait pour autant séparation réelle des corps : le *continuum* serait sinon menacé. Le modèle stoïcien de l'identité individuelle est de ce point de vue fondamentalement relationnel.

Avec la contribution philosophique stoïcienne, le modèle du mélange se trouve ainsi incontestablement enrichi et fonde une conception corporéiste de l'individualité organique extrêmement aboutie. À la lumière des textes de Galien, on peut se demander dans quelle mesure la reprise galénique de la pensée du mélange et la conception du corps et de son unité qu'elle fonde n'ont pas bénéficié de cet apport. C'est l'hypothèse que je souhaiterais désormais examiner.

53. Voir Plutarque, *Comm. not.* 1083B-C. Sur « l'argument croissant », voir Sedley 1982, p. 15-16. Voir aussi Bourbon 2019, p. 63-76.

La *krasis* galénique

En effet, lorsque Galien remet au premier plan en médecine la théorie du mélange, et en l'occurrence du mélange des éléments et des humeurs[54], on retrouve dans sa pensée de fortes tonalités à la fois empédocléennes et stoïcisantes parfois rétroprojetées sur Hippocrate, et ce malgré l'allégeance à Aristote revendiquée par Galien[55].

Le déni de la dette empédocléenne

Il faut d'abord remarquer que Galien refuse toute filiation empédocléenne à la pensée du mélange[56] dont il attribue en revanche la paternité à Hippocrate. Empédocle est décrit par Galien comme un atomiste et un mécaniste auquel Hippocrate ne devrait donc absolument rien :

> Hippocrate est le premier à notre connaissance qui ait prétendu que les éléments se mélangeaient, et, sur ce point, il s'écarte d'Empédocle ; car cet auteur dit bien que nous sommes nous-mêmes faits, et tous les autres corps qui vivent sur terre, des mêmes éléments dont nous sommes formés pour Hippocrate ; mais ils ne se mêlent pas (*ou kekramenôn di' hallelôn*); ils se côtoient et se touchent dans leurs parties minuscules (*kata smikra moria parakeimenôn te kai psauontôn*)[57].

À en croire Galien, le mélange empédocléen n'en serait pas un ou en tout cas ne serait jamais *in fine* qu'une forme paradoxale de juxtaposition[58] de substances de nature tellement microscopiques qu'elle en deviendrait elle-même imperceptible :

> Les corps composés étaient faits, disait Empédocle, des quatre éléments inaltérables. Les corps simples étaient mêlés comme le vert-de-gris, la calamine et le vitriol, que le chimiste, pour les allier, pile très fin et réduit en écume, au point que l'on ne peut plus tenir en main aucun des ingrédients séparés[59].

Selon Galien, le mélange empédocléen serait donc un mélange au sein duquel les individualités des substances *ne seraient plus perceptibles,* même si elles sont en réalité conservées. Il s'agirait donc d'une juxtaposition parcellaire. La version de Galien est d'ailleurs ici parfaitement conforme à

54. Jouanna 2006 p. 138-140, propose de situer l'émergence de la systématisation du lien entre les humeurs et les quatre tempéraments physiques et mentaux au Ve ou au VIe siècle de notre ère.

55. Sur les stratégies galéniques, voir Vegetti 1999.

56. Voir *supra* p. 157-159.

57. Galien, *In Hipp. Nat. Hom. Comment.* I, 13 = XV, 49 (Kühn) = CMG V 9, 1, p. 27, 22. Voir aussi Aristote, *De gen. et corr.* A 10, 328 a 12, et B 7, 334 a 29.

58. Empédocle est mis en rapport avec les atomistes par exemple aussi en *Plac. hipp. et plat.* IX, 11 (Kühn).

59. 31 A 34 DK (= Galien, *In Hipp. Nat. Hom. Comment.* I, 3 = XV, 32 (Kühn) = CMG, V, 9, 1, 19, 7–12.)

la présentation qu'Aristote fait du mélange empédocléen à partir de l'image du mur de briques rassemblées[60] : le Stagirite l'assimile à une agrégation de qualités, la conservation des éléments étant immédiatement réduite à la simple juxtaposition[61]. Nous l'avons rappelé plus haut[62], la conception empédocléenne du mélange est pourtant bien éloignée du résumé qu'en donne Galien. Le témoignage du *Peri phuseos* de Simplicius[63] nous invite plutôt à penser qu'il s'agit d'un mélange intégral, d'une *krasis*.

L'harmonique stoïcienne de la krasis *galénique*

Si l'on en croit Galien lorsqu'il mobilise la notion de *krasis*, cette dernière se trouve au cœur d'une controverse qui opposerait les stoïciens et les péripatéticiens sur la question de la nature du mélange[64]. Il s'agirait en l'occurrence de savoir ce qui est mélangé : qualités (pour les péripatéticiens) ou substances (pour les stoïciens)[65].

À cet égard, comme J. Groisard l'a montré me semble-t-il de manière convaincante, Galien produit à sa manière les conditions d'un « dépassement » d'une querelle qu'il considère comme secondaire du point de vue des préoccupations médicales qui sont les siennes[66]. Glosant Hippocrate sur sa critique des théories élémentaires des physiologues, Galien affirme ainsi qu'Hippocrate, Aristote et les stoïciens admettraient ensemble qu'il existe quatre éléments et que ces éléments sont mélangés de part en part[67] :

> Ils (*sc.* le chaud, le froid, le sec et l'humide) furent après [Hippocrate] démontrés par Aristote. Chrysippe et ses disciples ont donc hérité de concepts tout prêts et, loin de les contester, ils soutiennent que l'ensemble des choses résulte du mélange (*krasis*) de ces composants, que ceux-ci entretiennent mutuellement des relations passives et actives et que la nature est artiste[68].

60. *De la Génération et de la Corruption* (B, 7, 334a26 = A 43 DK). Sur la « crase » imparfaite qui n'est que juxtaposition, voir *De temperamentis* IX, 562-3 (Kühn). On pourra se référer à l'importante traduction commentée du *De Temperamentis* par Singer & Eijk 2019.

61. Sur cette identification, voir Groisard 2016, p. 192-193.

62. *Supra*, p. 156-159. Voir aussi Bourbon 2020.

63. B 21DK.

64. Sur ce problème, voir en particulier Collette-Ducic & Delcomminette 2007 et Groisard 2016, p. 119-153. Pour un autre point de vue sur cette controverse, voir Sextus Empiricus, *Esquisses Pyrrhoniennes*, III, 8.

65. Galien, *In Hipp. de nat. hom.* XV, 32, 8-11 Kühn = *SVF* II 463. Sur cette controverse, voir Mirrione 2023.

66. Sur les limites de cette neutralité, voir Groisard 2016, p. 182-187.

67. *De elem. ex Hipp.* V, 15-17 (Kühn).

68. Galien, *De meth. med.* I, 2 (X, 16 Kühn). Hippocrate est présenté par Galien comme « l'inventeur » de la notion de *phusis* comme nature finalisée (et également technicienne) à l'échelle du corps. Voir *De usu partium,* 16.14, 2.435,10*ff.* Helmreich = IV, 343 (Kühn) : « la nature œuvre avec providence (προνοητικῶς ἡ φύσις ἐργασαμένη) ».

C'est ce qui permet à Galien de proposer une autre histoire du problème du mélange : au sein de cette généalogie, c'est un différend cosmologique qui détermine deux conceptions opposées de la nature (*phusis*) des corps, celui qui oppose l'école hippocratique continuiste à l'école d'Asclépiade fondée sur l'hypothèse atomiste discontinuiste. La ligne de partage théorique passe donc désormais entre mécanistes et continuistes[69], ce qui justifie que péripatéticiens et stoïciens se retrouvent alignés du même côté en dignes héritiers d'Hippocrate :

> Car c'est [Hippocrate] qui, de tous les médecins ou philosophes que nous connaissons, a le premier entrepris de démontrer qu'il y a au total quatre qualités réciproquement actives sous l'effet desquelles sont engendrées et se corrompent toutes les choses susceptibles de génération et de corruption. Et tout aussi bien Hippocrate est-il le premier de tous à avoir connu qu'elles se mêlent réciproquement de part en part, et c'est bien chez lui que pour la première fois on peut trouver formulés les principes des démonstrations dont Aristote s'est emparé par la suite. Quant à savoir s'il faut penser que les substances se mêlent de part en part tout comme les qualités, ainsi que l'a affirmé par la suite Zénon de Citium, je ne crois pas qu'il soit besoin d'en traiter déjà en détail dans le présent ouvrage[70].

La divergence entre péripatéticiens et stoïciens apparaît dès lors relativement secondaire[71] au regard de ce qui fait consensus entre les deux écoles et qu'elles hériteraient d'Hippocrate, à savoir le caractère total du mélange. Ce qui importerait serait donc cet accord, même si elles ne s'entendent pas sur la question de la conservation des éléments au sein du mélange. Il s'agit ainsi de jouer les stoïciens et Aristote contre les mécanistes[72] et leur modèle

69. Voir Groisard 2016, p. 179 *sq.* Le partage rappelle celui auquel procède Alexandre d'Aphrodise au début du *De mixtione*. Voir I, 2, 4-27 (Kühn).

70. Galien, *De natur. facult.*, II, 5, 4-17 (Kühn), éd. Brock : πρῶτος γὰρ οὗτος ἁπάντων ὧν ἴσμεν ἰατρῶν τε καὶ φιλοσόφων ἀποδεικνύειν ἐπεχείρησε τέτταρας εἶναι τὰς πάσας δραστικὰς εἰς ἀλλήλας ποιότητας, ὑφ'ὧν γίγνεταί τε καὶ φθείρεται πάνθ' ὅσα γένεσίν τε καὶ φθορὰν ἐπιδέχεται. Καὶ μέντοι καὶ τὸ κεράννυσθαι δι' ἀλλήλων αὐτὰς ὅλας δι' ὅλων Ἱπποκράτης ἁπάντων [ὧν ἴσμεν] πρῶτος ἔγνω· καὶ τὰς ἀρχάς γε τῶν ἀποδείξεων, ὧν ὕστερον Ἀριστοτέλης μετεχειρίσατο, παρ' ἐκείνῳ πρώτῳ γεγραμμένας ἔστιν εὑρεῖν. Εἰ δ' ὥσπερ τὰς ποιότητας οὕτω καὶ τὰς οὐσίας δι' ὅλων κεράννυσθαι χρὴ νομίζειν, ὡς ὕστερον ἀπεφήνατο Ζήνων ὁ Κιττιεύς, οὐχ ἡγοῦμαι δεῖν ἔτι περὶ τούτου κατὰ τόνδε τὸν λόγον ἐπεξιέναι.

71. Voir aussi *De elem. ex Hipp.* 9, 32-35, CMG V 1, 2, p. 136, 13-23 De Lacy = I, 489, 6-9 Kühn = *SVF* II 464. Sur cette prétention à la neutralité, voir Groisard 2016, p. 177 *sq.*

72. *De methodo medendi*, X, 9, 12-18 (Kühn). Voir aussi l'édition de Vito Lorusso 2018. Sur cette dette supposée d'Aristote vis-à-vis d'Hippocrate, voir *ibid.* V, 15, 8-9 (Kühn) et vis-à-vis des stoïciens, voir X, 16, 8 (Kühn) = *SVF*, II, 411. Voir Groisard 2016, p. 179. Sur cette stratégie galénique de conciliation, voir aussi Fortuna 1997 dans son édition du *De constitutione artis medicae ad Patrophilum*.

combinatoire de juxtaposition, sans trancher le problème de la nature de la compénétration matérielle des corps[73].

Galien prétend ainsi adopter un point de vue anti-dogmatique, ce qui donne des formulations bivalentes qui mêlent tout à la fois des notes aristotéliciennes et des notes stoïciennes[74]: le mélange est défini dans une langue stoïcienne, celle du mélange intégral (*di' holôn*) comme mélange de qualités (*kerannusthai di' allêlôn hautas [*sc. *poiotêtas] holas di' holôn*)[75]. Or à la faveur de ce déplacement, le problème du mélange devient essentiellement celui de savoir si le mélange est total ou pas.

Doit-on pour autant conclure que Galien soit resté si indifférent que cela à la question du statut du processus d'interaction qualitative et partant de celle de la conservation de l'individualité respective des éléments qui entrent en interaction, comme le prétend Groisard ? Bien que Galien ne nous ait nullement précisé de manière explicite la manière dont il concevait le mélange des qualités primaires, cela n'est pas certain. C'est en tout cas ce que semble suggérer son usage différencié du couple notionnel *krasis* / *mixis*, absent du corpus hippocratique[76]. La distinction galénique entre les deux mélanges présente une harmonique stoïcienne, celle de la distinction entre mélange fusionnel (*sunchusis*) et mélange intégral (*krasis di' holôn*).

Il semble bien en effet que Galien fasse un usage différencié des substantifs *krasis* et *mixis* et qu'il distingue deux modalités du mélange. La pathologie galénique définit en effet les affections comme produits des interactions qualitatives du mélange. La *mixis*[77] désigne dès lors un mélange dans lequel les substances fusionnent pour produire une nouvelle substance : c'est le cas des mélanges pharmacologiques[78] qui ne relèvent donc pas de la juxtaposition, mais aussi de ce mélange spécifique qu'est la génération (*genesis*)[79] qui produit un nouvel individu. Par contraste, le substantif *krasis* caractérise la

73. Même si par ailleurs Galien semble marquer sa préférence pour la compréhension péripatéticienne du mélange ; voir *De elem. ex Hipp.* I, 489, 17-490, 15 Kühn = 136,15-138, 5 CMG V, 1,2 De Lacy et *De plac.* XV, 1, p. 116, 5-19 CMG V 3, 2 Nutton. Voir aussi *De causis contentivis*, 56, 14-19 (Lyons). Voir Groisard, 2016, p. 182-185. Galien produit par ailleurs une critique forte de la conception stoïcienne du mélange total, voir *De exp. med.* 19 et *De plac.* V, 618, 1-619, 2 (Kühn) ; *cf.* sur ce point, Collette-Ducic & Delcomminette 2007. Voir aussi Mirrione 2017, p. 86-96.

74. *De elem. ex. Hipp.*, IX, 31-34 (Kühn). Galien souligne alors qu'Hippocrate ne se prononce pas sur ce point et qu'il est suffisant de souligner qu'il s'agit d'un mélange total.

75. *De nat. facult.* I, 2 (II, 4-5 Kühn). Voir aussi *De elem ex. Hipp.*, I, 489, 19-490, 2 (Kühn).

76. Voir Boudon-Millot 2011, p. 274.

77. Sur le glissement du sens de *mixis* comme « union sexuelle » à celui, technique, de « mélange » entre deux substances, voir Boudon-Millot 2011, p. 267-275.

78. Galien, *De comp. med. sec. loc.* VIII, 3 (XIII, 156, 1-5 Kühn) et *De comp. med. per gen.* III, 3 (XIII, 617, 19- 618, 5 Kühn).

79. Galien, *In Hipp. Nat. Hom. comment.* I, 10 (CMG V 9, 1, p. 25, 25 *sq.* Mewaldt) et *De sperm.* I, 8 (CMG V 3, 1, p. 90, 21 De Lacy).

forme du mélange au sein duquel les éléments en présence conservent leur individualité propre[80] – et ne la conservent pas qu'en puissance, comme c'est le cas dans le modèle aristotélicien[81]. Incontestablement il y a là une harmonique stoïcienne : avec la *krasis* humorale nous sommes en présence d'une harmonie ou d'une disharmonie entre qualités[82]. C'est ce que suggère un passage du *De elementis* qui reprend d'ailleurs un texte hippocratique, le traité *Sur la nature de l'homme* et mobilise l'exemple du vomissement. Galien y souligne comment chacune des humeurs peut être « retrouvée », dans sa nature propre, preuve de la conservation de l'individualité de ces éléments :

> On peut se rendre compte par les faits suivants que toutes ces humeurs, bien loin d'être une substance unique, possèdent chacune leur propriété et leur nature respectives : donnez à une personne un médicament qui attire le phlegme, vous observerez un vomissement de phlegme, et si vous lui donnez un médicament qui attire la bile, vous observerez un vomissement de bile ; de même, il y aura aussi évacuation de la bile noire, si vous lui donnez un médicament qui attire la bile noire ; et si vous le blessez en un point du corps de manière à faire une plaie, son sang coulera[83].

De ce point de vue, comme l'a souligné V. Boudon-Millot, la *krasis* « mêle sans les confondre les quatre qualités primaires dans un équilibre certes changeant, mais où le froid, le chaud, le sec et l'humide conservent leur identité et leur existence propre[84] ».

Cette appropriation par Galien de la distinction stoïcienne semble confirmée par un argument emprunté au *De elementis* dans lequel une référence au *tetrapharmakos*[85], ce remède pharmacologique semble là aussi mobiliser implicitement la distinction entre mélange fusionnel et mélange total[86]. Nous ne nous arrêterons évidemment pas sur le sens de cet argument qui dépasse largement le cadre de notre étude. Rappelons simplement qu'il consiste à montrer que puisqu'il est absurde de nier que le mélange pharmacologique est composé de plusieurs éléments – même s'ils ne sont plus perceptibles entant que tels dans son résultat, il le serait tout autant de nier

80. Voir Hankinson 2014.

81. Sur ce modèle de « médiation », voir J. Groisard 2016, en particulier p. 1 à 16.

82. *De temper.* I, 1 (I, 510 Kühn).

83. *De elem. ex Hipp.*, 13, 1-5 (CMG V 1, 2, p. 150 De Lacy) = *De natura hominis*, c. 5, 1-5 (CMG I 1, 3 p. 176 Jouanna) : Γνοίης δ' ἂν τοῖσδε, ὅτι οὐχ ἓν ταῦτα πάντα ἐστὶν, ἀλλ' ἕκαστον ἔχει δύναμίν τε καὶ φύσιν τὴν ἑωυτέου· εἰ γάρ διδοίης ἀνθρώπῳ φάρμακον ὅ τι φλέγμα ἄγει, ἐμεῖταί σοι φλέγμα, καὶ ἢν διδοῖς φάρμακον ὅ τι χολὴν ἄγει, ἐμεῖταί σοι χολή. Κατὰ ταὐτὰ δὲ καὶ χολὴ μέλαινα καθαίρεται, ἢν διδοῖς φάρμακον ὅ τι χολὴν μέλαιναν ἄγει· καὶ ἢν τρώσῃς αὐτοῦ τοῦ σώματός τι ὥστε ἕλκος γενέσθαι, ῥυήσεται αὐτῷ αἷμα. (trad. Luccioni, 2020).

84. Voir Boudon-Millot 2011, p. 278.

85. *De elem. ex Hipp.* 5, 14-16 (CMG V 1, 2, p. 96 De Lacy).

86. Sur cette typologie implicite qui donne au *tetrapharmakos* un statut paradigmatique, que l'on ne retrouve d'ailleurs pas dans le *De elementis*, et sur le rôle méthodologique spécifique de cet argument, voir Giovacchini 2017.

que parce qu'on ne peut isoler les éléments purs dans le corps, on devrait critiquer les théories élémentaires des physiologues. Le point important pour notre propos réside ici dans le fait que le *tetrapharmakos* soit mobilisé comme modèle archétypal de fusion, ce mélange dans lequel les éléments sont inobservables, par contraste implicite avec le mélange des humeurs au sein duquel les éléments sont et restent observables, leur identité se trouvant conservée. Là encore, le modèle humoral apparaît bien comme un mélange au sein duquel l'individualité des éléments se trouve conservée.

Galien semble ainsi avoir trouvé dans le modèle stoïcien de quoi penser la nature du mélange humoral, ce qui lui permet en même temps de fonder un modèle explicatif de la pathologie, celui de la disharmonie : ces quatre principes sont présents en l'homme bien qu'ils ne soient pas accessibles empiriquement au médecin sinon sous la forme des mélanges pathologiques aux nuances variées des humeurs[87]. C'est ainsi que le modèle du mélange total permet d'expliquer la maladie comme déséquilibre. Comme la *krasis* stoïcienne, la *krasis* galénique permet de concevoir une unité singulière au sein de laquelle l'individualité des éléments en interaction constante ne se trouve à aucun moment abolie[88]. Elle situe ainsi la corporéité du côté d'une puissance différentielle de variation et fonde un modèle d'identité spécifiquement organique, parce que fondamentalement relationnel.

La *krasis* galénique : une rétroprojection par Galien d'un matériau stoïcien ?

La conception galénique de la *krasis* intègre ainsi à son corps défendant un apport stoïcien, hypothèse qui semble renforcée par la présence chez Galien d'une définition de la *phyuis* comme sympathie dont l'auteur attribue la paternité, une nouvelle fois, à Hippocrate. Selon ce dernier, ce serait en effet Hippocrate qui serait « l'inventeur » de la notion de *phusis*[89] définie comme une certaine qualité du mélange corporel qui assure la communauté des parties, la maladie consistant a contrario dans le dérèglement de cette *krasis*[90]. La médecine comme art (*technê*) a dès lors pour fin de rétablir cette

87. *Hygiène* (IV, 4 : 112,15 Koch ~ VI 254 K) : Ἀψευδής ἐστιν ἡ ἐκ τῆς χροιᾶς τοῦ ζῴου διάγνωσις τῶν χυμῶν. « On discerne sans se tromper les humeurs à partir du teint d'un être vivant » (trad. Luccioni qui formule au sujet de cet argument l'hypothèse convaincante d'une source médicale commune.).

88. Sur ce rapport paradoxal de Galien à la physique stoïcienne, voir Boudon-Millot 2011 et Giovacchini 2017. Voir aussi Van der Eijk 2020.

89. Galien aurait consacré un traité à la *phusis*, *Sur les termes médicaux*, mais il est perdu. Sur ce point, voir Jouanna 2003, p. 229. Voir aussi Pigeaud 1981.

90. Notion que Galien reprend à Hippocrate mais à partir de laquelle il dresse une classification de huit mélanges mauvais dont on ne trouve en revanche pas trace dans le *Corpus hippocratique*.

phusis ou, puisque c'est strictement équivalent, de « redresser » le corps[91]. Galien attribue donc ici à Hippocrate une conception finalisée de la *phusis* doublement définie comme mixture (*krasis*) et comme providentielle : « la nature œuvre avec providence (*pronoêtikôs hê phusis ergasamenê*[92]) ». Alors même qu'on ne trouve à notre connaissance aucun équivalent dans le corpus hippocratique[93], à en croire Galien, la nature hippocratique décrirait donc déjà cette unité organique d'un corps qui définit une communauté de parties, et en l'occurrence de souffle corporel, en parfaite sympathie :

> Il dit que dans nos corps il y a une communauté de flux, une communauté d'air, et que tout est en sympathie[94].

Le niveau de description se limite certes à celui du microcosme qu'est le corps (nous avons quitté le registre de l'analogie explicite avec le monde), mais nous sommes ici en présence d'une conception parfaitement stoïcienne de la sympathie universelle dont la paternité est attribuée… à Hippocrate. Certes il existe bien une proto-conception hippocratique de la sympathie à l'échelle corporelle, comme l'ont notamment montré les travaux de B. Holmes[95]. Cependant, il semble difficile de ne pas considérer que la relecture galénique de la conception hippocratique de la *phusis* n'hérite pas aussi, sinon d'abord, de la conception stoïcienne de la sympathie universelle : Galien importe le modèle du mélange intégral en l'appliquant spécifiquement à l'échelle du corps humain.

91. Cette thérapeutique requiert à ce titre une méthode de décomposition qui prête attention à tous les éléments et décompose l'unité pour identifier où se situe le dérèglement. Voir *Que l'excellent médecin est aussi philosophe* 14-19 (Mueller) (trad. J. Jouanna très légèrement modifiée dans Jouanna 2000 p. 29) : « Cette même méthode (μέθοδος) enseigne aussi ce qu'est la constitution du corps elle-même (τὴν τοῦ σώματος αὐτοῦ διδάσκει σύνθεσιν), celle qui provient des éléments premiers (τήν τ' ἐκ τῶν πρώτων στοιχείων) qui sont en totalité mêlés entre eux (ἃ δι' ἀλλήλων ὅλα κέκραται), celle des éléments seconds, les sensibles, que l'on appelle aussi les homéomères et la troisième en plus de ces deux-là, celle qui provient des parties organiques ». Sur cet opuscule, voir Jouanna 2007.

92. *De usu partium*, IV, 343, 5 (Kühn). L'adverbe est récurrent puisqu'il apparaît huit fois appliqué à la nature.

93. Sur ce constat, voir Jouanna 2003, p. 254.

94. *De naturalibus facultatibus*, II, 39, 3-4 (Kühn) : ἐν τοῖς σώμασιν ἡμῶν σύμπνοιάν τε μίαν εἶναί φησι καὶ σύρροιαν καὶ πάντα συμπαθέα. Sur la question de la sympathie chez Galien, voir Devinant 2020.

95. Voir Holmes 2014a et b.

Entre médecine et philosophie matérialiste, la *krasis* comme modèle organique d'individualité

J'ai donc cherché à éclairer quelques-uns des transferts entre la tradition matérialiste et corporéiste antique d'une part, la médecine d'autre part. J'ai voulu montrer combien ces échanges entre médecine et philosophie ont été décisifs du point de vue de l'émergence d'un modèle organique spécifiquement matérialiste de l'individualité à l'échelle du corps.

Au sein de cette tradition, lorsque les stoïciens s'emparent de la notion de *krasis* pour penser la *phusis*, autant que d'un matériau empédocléen qui esquisse déjà l'idée d'un « mélange intégral », ils héritent incontestablement aussi d'un modèle harmonique hippocratique tel qu'on peut le trouver dans le traité *Du régime*. La conception stoïcienne du mélange total doit ainsi être réinscrite dans la perspective de cette histoire philosophique et médicale, elle qui constitue un tournant de cette réflexion sur l'individuation organique. En concevant un modèle parfaitement immanent d'unité organique grâce à un principe d'individuation lui-même corporéisé, la qualité propre, qui permet donc d'assurer l'identité individuelle des corps au sein du *continuum* cosmique, les stoïciens prétendent échapper à l'argument croissant tout en dépassant à la fois le matérialisme atomiste, incapable selon eux d'assurer l'identité des corps[96], et l'hylémorphisme aristotélicien. De ce point de vue, la pensée galénique de la *krasis* qui applique ce modèle spécifiquement au corps s'inscrit aussi, sans doute à son corps défendant, dans cette tradition matérialiste et corporéiste – une tradition qui ne conçoit l'individuation que dans sa puissance de variation et dans la relation à son milieu. Elle bénéficie elle-même d'un apport philosophique stoïcien indéniable, tout en lui conférant une extension médicale inédite. Les études récentes font passer au second plan cette autre généalogie matérialiste du corps vivant, l'individualité organique, en se focalisant plus volontiers sur les échanges entre la tradition aristotélicienne et la tradition médicale. Or cette dette stoïcienne de Galien mérite d'être soulignée – autant que l'harmonique médicale de leur conception du mélange intégral et de la sympathie universelle qui permet de considérer qu'il y a bien appropriation stoïcienne d'un matériau hippocratique.

Il y a dans la richesse de tous ces échanges une contribution de premier plan à la conception de l'individualité biologique[97]. Nous sommes en effet en présence d'un modèle d'unité organique intégralement corporéisé et immanent, un modèle qui pense la variation et le caractère relationnel comme modalités constitutives de l'identité individuelle des organismes. Cela

96. Bourbon 2019, p. 49-51.

97. Sur le concept-clef d'organisme en philosophie de la biologie, voir en particulier Wolfe 2004.

témoigne de la vitalité de la réflexion matérialiste sur la nature et les limites de l'identité biologique au sein des traditions médicales et philosophiques antiques, ce que les études sur la contribution de la tradition aristotélicienne biologique tendent parfois à éclipser. De ce point de vue, lorsque la biologie et l'immunologie contemporaines cherchent à prendre en charge la plasticité des frontières de l'organisme, en particulier avec la théorie de la continuité-discontinuité[98] et la notion d'organisme « hétérogène »[99], elles s'inscrivent aussi dans cette histoire des pensées biologiques dans lesquelles l'identité est fondamentalement dynamique et relationnelle.

98. Même si l'immunologie reste encore attachée au modèle du soi, introduit par F. M. Burnet, les expérimentations des vingt dernières années sur ce qu'on nomme la tolérance immunitaire ont révélé que la partition du soi et du non-soi était en bien des cas fragilisée : il y a de l'étranger qui est intégré par l'organisme - la relation symbiotique en est un exemple paradigmatique - et, inversement, des réactions immunitaires peuvent être déclenchées par un organisme contre des constituants qu'il reconnaît par ailleurs comme sains, comme dans la phagocytose ou les réponses immunorégulatrices. La théorie de la continuité-discontinuité propose à partir de ces résultats, sur lesquels il y a aujourd'hui consensus, de renoncer à la dichotomie soi/non soi. Sur ces aspects, voir Pradeu 2008 et 2009.

99. Parce qu'elle désigne un organisme constitué d'entités différentes et ayant des origines différentes. La notion d'« organisme hétérogène » permet de dépasser la distinction entre entités endogènes – qui ont pour origine l'organisme de référence – et entités exogènes ou étrangères, ces dernières participant à la réalisation de l'harmonie de ce tout qu'est l'organisme. Sur cette conception de l'organisme et ses conséquences sur la définition de l'individualité biologique, voir Pradeu 2009.

BIBLIOGRAPHIE

Bartoš, H. 2015 : *Philosophy and Dietetics in the Hippocratic* On Regimen. *A Delicate Balance of Health*, Leyde/Boston.

Bénatouïl, T. 2006 : *Faire usage. La pratique du stoïcisme*, Paris.

Boudon-Millot, V. 2011 : « La notion de mélange dans la pensée médicale de Galien : *mixis* ou *crasis* ? », *Revue des Études Grecques*, 124/ 2, p. 261-279.

Bourbon, M. 2019 : *Penser l'individu. Genèse stoïcienne de la subjectivité*, Turnhout.

Bourbon, M. 2020 : « De la *krasis* présocratique à la *krasis* stoïcienne : l'émergence d'un modèle organique de l'individualité », *Elenchos*, 41/1, p. 165-180.

Brisson, L. 2013 : « Le *Timée* de Platon et le traité hippocratique *Du régime*, sur le mécanisme de la sensation », *Études platoniciennes*, 10 [en ligne]. DOI: 10.4000/etudesplatoniciennes.367

Brunschwig, J. 1995 : « Le modèle conjonctif », dans *Études sur les philosophies hellénistiques, Épicurisme, stoïcisme, scepticisme*, Paris, p. 161-187.

Collette-Ducic, B. & S. Delcomminette 2007 : « La théorie stoïcienne du mélange et sa postérité », *Revue de philosophie ancienne*, XXV/2, p. 67-100.

Couloubaritsis, L. 2005 : « Les pratiques hénologiques dans le stoïcisme ancien », dans G. Romeyer-Dherbey & J.-B. Gourinat (éd.), *Le stoïcisme*, Paris, p. 87-211.

Devinant, J. 2020 : « Aux limites de l'explication : le rôle de la sympathie chez Galien », *Elenchos*, 41/1, p. 117-142.

Fortuna, S. 1997 (éd.) : *Galeni de constitutione artis medicae ad Patrophilum*, CMG V 1, 3, Berlin.

Gemelli Marciano, M. L. 2009 : *Die Vorsokratiker, Bd. II. Parmenides Zenon Empedokles. Griechisch-lateinish-deutsch, Auswahl der Fragmente und Zeugnisse*, Düsseldorf.

Gill, C. 2010 : *Naturalistic Psychology in Galen and Stoicism*, Oxford University Press, 2010.

Giovacchini, J. 2017 : « *De elementis*, 5, 14-16 : la *tetrapharmakos* et l'épistémologie galénique du mélange », *Aitia*, 7/2 [en ligne]. DOI: 10.4000/aitia.1899

Groisard, J. 2016 : Mixis, *Le problème du mélange dans la philosophie grecque d'Aristote à Simplicius*, Paris.

Hankinson, R. J. 2014 : « Galen and the Ontology of Powers », *British Journal for the History of Philosophy*, 22/5, p. 951-973.

Holmes, B. 2014a : *The Symptom and the Subject : The Emergence of the Physical Body in Ancient Greece*, Princeton University Press.

Holmes, B. 2014b : « Proto-Sympathy in the Hippocratic Corpus », dans J. Jouanna et M. Zink (éd.), *Hippocrate et les hippocratismes : médecine, religion, société : Actes du XIVe Colloque International Hippocratique*, Paris, p. 123-138.

Joly, R. 1967 (éd.) : Hippocrate. *Du régime*, tome VI, 1, Paris.

Joly, R. & S. Byl 1984 [2002] (éd.) : *Hippocratis De diaeta*, éd. et trad. B. Joly complétée par S. Byl, corr. S. Byll, CMG I 2, 4, Berlin.

Jouanna, J. 1992 : *Hippocrate*, Paris.

Jouanna, J. 2000 : « La lecture du traité hippocratique *De la nature de l'homme* par Galien », dans M.-O. Goulet-Cazé (éd.), *Le commentaire entre tradition et innovation. Actes du colloque international de l'institut des traditions textuelles*, (Paris et Villejuif, 22-25 septembre 1999), Paris, p. 273-292.

Jouanna, J. 2003 : « La notion de nature chez Galien » dans J. Barnes & J. Jouanna (éd.), *Galien et la Philosophie : Huit exposés suivis de discussions, Entretiens sur l'antiquité classique de la Fondation Hardt ; XLIX*, Vendœuvres-Genève, 2003, p. 229-262.

Jouanna, J. 2006 : « La postérité du traité hippocratique de la *Nature de l'homme* : la théorie des quatre humeurs », dans C. W. Müller, C. Brockmann, C. W. Brunschön (éd.), *Ärzte und ihre Interpreten. Medizinische Fachtexte der Antike als Forschungsgegenstand der klassischen Philologie. Fachkonferenz zu Ehren von Diethard Nickel*, Munich -Leipzig, p. 117-141.

Jouanna, J. 2007 : « La théorie de la sensation, de la pensée et de l'âme dans le traité hippocratique *Du régime* : ses rapports avec Empédocle et le *Timée* de Platon », *Annali dell'Istituto Universitario Orientale di Napoli*, 29, p. 9-38.

Laks, A. 2007 : « Prépondérance et plénitude : sur la reconstruction de la doctrine parménidéenne de la sensation dans Théophraste, *Sur les sensations*, 3-4 », dans *Histoire, doxographie, vérité. Études sur Aristote, Théophraste et la philosophie présocratique*, Louvain-la-Neuve, p. 179-192.

Laurand, V. 2005 : « La sympathie universelle : union et séparation », *Revue de métaphysique et de morale*, 48/4, p. 517-535.

Le Blay, F. 2005 : « Microcosm and Macrocosm : the dual direction of analogy in Hippocratic thought and the meteorological tradition », dans Ph. J. Van Der Eijk (éd.), *Hippocrates in Context, Papers read at the XIth International Hippocrates Colloquium, University of Newcastle-upon-Tyne, 27-31 august 2002*, Leiden-Boston, p. 251-269.

Lorusso, V. 2018 (éd.) : Galeno. *Metodo Terapeutico*, Libri I-II, *Roma*.

Magdelaine, C. 1997 : « Microcosme et macrocosme dans le *Corpus hippocratique* : réflexions sur l'homme et la maladie », *Eidôlon, Cahiers du LAPRIL*, 50, Bordeaux, p. 11-39.

Mansfeld, J. et D. T. Runia 2009 (éd.) : *Aëtiana. The Method and Intellectual Context of a Doxographer, II, The Compendium*, Leiden-Boston.

Mansfeld, J. et D. T. Runia 2010 (éd.) : *Aëtiana. The Method and Intellectual Context of a Doxographer, III, Studies in the Doxographical Traditions of Ancient Philosophy*, Leiden-Boston.

Mirrione, C. 2017 : *Theory and Terminology of Mixture in Galen. The concepts of* krasis *and* mixis *in Galen's thought*, Dissertation zur Erlangung des akademischen Grades Dr. phil. eingereicht an der Philosophischen Fakultät II der Humboldt-Universität zu Berlin.

Mirrione, C. 2023 : « Galen on the Stoic-Peripatetic Controversy about Mixtures: Qualities or Bodies? », *Elenchos*, 44/2, p. 295-311.

Mueller, I. 1884-1893 (éd.) : *Claudii Galeni Scripta minora*, vol. 2, Lipsiae.

Pellegrin, P. 1994 : « Médecine hippocratique et philosophie », dans *Hippocrate, De l'Art médical*, textes présentés, commentés et annotés par D. Gourévitch, introduction par D. Gourévitch, M. Grmek et P. Pellegrin, Paris.

Pellegrin, P. 2006 : « Ancient Medicine and its Contribution to the Philosophical Tradition» dans M. L. Gill & P. Pellegrin (éd.), *A Companion to Ancient Philosophy*, Oxford, p. 664-685.

PIGEAUD, J. 1981 : *La maladie de l'âme. Étude sur la relation de l'âme et du corps dans la tradition médico-philosophique antique*, Paris.

PRADEU, T. 2008 : « Qu'est-ce qu'un individu biologique ? », dans P. Ludwig & T. Pradeu, *L'individu : perspectives contemporaines*, Paris.

PRADEU, T. 2009 : *Les limites du soi : immunologie et identité biologique*, Presses Universitaires de Montréal.

SEDLEY, D. 1982 : « The Stoic Criterion of Identity » , *Phronesis*, 27/3, p. 255-275.

SINGER, P. N. & P. J. VAN DER EIJK 2019 (trad.) : *Galen. Works on Human Nature, Volume 1 : Mixtures (De Temperamentis)*, with Piero Tassinari, Cambridge University Press, 2019

TIELEMAN, T. 1996 : *Galen and Chrysippus on the Soul. Argument and Refutation in the De Placitis Books II-III*, Leiden.

TODD, R.B. 1976 : *Alexander of Aphrodisias on Stoic physics. A study of the* De mixtione *with preliminary essays, text, translation and commentary*, Leiden.

VAN DER EIJK, Ph. 2014 : « Galen on the nature of human beings », dans P. Adamson, R. Hansberger, et J. Wilberding (éd.), *Philosophical themes in Galen*, London, p. 89-133.

VAN DER EIJK, Ph. 2020 : « Galen on Soul, Mixture and Pneuma » dans B. Inwood & J. Warren (éd.), *Body and Soul in Hellenistic Philosophy*, Cambridge University Press, p. 62-88.

VEGETTI, M. 1999 : « Historiographical Strategies in Galen's Physiology (*De usu partium*, *De naturalibus facultatibus*) » dans Ph. J. van der Eijk (dir.), *Ancient Histories of Medicine. Essays in Medical Doxography and Historiography in Classical Antiquity*, Leyde/Boston/Cologne, p. 383-395.

WOLFE, C. T. 2004 : « La catégorie d' "organisme" dans la philosophie de la biologie », *Multitudes*, 16 /2, p. 27-40.

DU CHÂTIMENT À LA HONTE

L'eschatologie du *Gorgias* comme image de la réfutation

Andreas Farina-Schroll
Université de Montréal/Université Libre de Bruxelles
andreas.farina-schroll@umontreal.ca

Résumé. L'eschatologie du *Gorgias* a laissé plus d'un lecteur de Platon perplexe, un constat que l'on peut particulièrement observer dans le traitement par les interprètes du rôle spécifique du châtiment réservé aux âmes injustes dans l'Hadès. Dans cette étude, nous souhaitons montrer que la fonction du châtiment dans l'eschatologie du *Gorgias* est d'offrir une métaphore des effets de la réfutation sur l'âme. Pour ce faire, nous montrerons que le châtiment est lui-même modelé en fonction d'une analogie médicale qui structure le dialogue dans son ensemble. Après avoir montré que Socrate introduit cette analogie au sein du mythe à l'aide du critère de la nudité, nous examinerons la description du châtiment lui-même. Enfin, si nous pouvons affirmer que le châtiment reflète la réfutation, c'est parce que la douleur qu'il provoque est analogue à la honte éprouvée lorsqu'une personne disposant des mauvaises croyances est réfutée.

Abstract. *The myth of judgment in the final pages of Plato's* Gorgias *has left more than one of its readers puzzled, a standpoint that is especially true in regards of the way that the punishment reserved to the unjust souls in Hades has been interpreted. In this paper, we shall see that the specific function of the punishment in the final myth of Plato's* Gorgias *is to offer a metaphor of the effects of refutation upon the soul. For such a claim, we intend to show that punishment itself is modelled by means of an analogy with medicine which structures the Dialogue as a whole. After we have observed how Socrates introduce this analogy inside the myth by using nudity as a criterion of the evaluation of the soul, we shall analyze how the punishment itself is characterized. In the end, if we can assert that punishment reflects the use of refutation, it is because the pain it causes is analogous to the shame that one who disposes of the wrong beliefs experiences after being refuted.*

Philosophie antique, n°24 (2024), 175-198

Le mythe final du *Gorgias*[*1] a laissé plus d'un lecteur de Platon perplexe sur sa propre signification, au point que certains y voient un constat d'échec de la démarche socratique[2]. Non seulement le recours au mythe est lui-même perçu comme un abandon de la démarche rationnelle en faveur d'une croyance en une justice divine[3], mais l'eschatologie du *Gorgias* ne serait rien de plus que la version simpliste et « optimiste » d'un mythe qui souffrirait d'un flagrant manque d'unité à travers les dialogues de Platon[4]. En bref, c'est l'intérêt et l'utilité mêmes de l'eschatologie du *Gorgias* qui sont remis en cause[5], car le mythe ruinerait à la fois la cohésion interne du dialogue et celle avec les autres récits eschatologiques présentés par Platon, un avilissement notamment illustré par le débat sur la fonction spécifique du châtiment réservé aux âmes injustes dans l'Hadès.

Dans cette étude, nous souhaitons montrer que de tels jugements manquent la portée et la signification de ce mythe. Pour ce faire, nous montrerons que le châtiment dans l'eschatologie du *Gorgias* est modelé en

* Je tiens à remercier Sylvain Delcomminette pour la bienveillance et l'acuité de ses relectures. Je tiens également à remercier les deux relecteurs anonymes de la revue *Philosophie antique* pour leurs commentaires qui ont permis d'enrichir mes réflexions et mes analyses.

1. Sauf mentions contraires, nous utiliserons la traduction de Monique Canto-Sperber (Canto-Sperber 1987).

2. Marchand & Ponchon 2015, p. 95.

3. Rowe 2012, p. 188. Cette interprétation du mythe, partagée notamment par Julia Annas, est héritée du commentaire de E.R. Dodds : *cf.* Dodds 1959, p. 377.

4. Annas 1982, p. 122-129 et 138-139. L'autrice considère que les eschatologies présentées respectivement dans le *Gorgias* d'un côté et dans le *Phédon* et la *République* de l'autre sont des versions fondamentalement différentes d'un seul et même mythe, ce qui serait un indicateur de l'évolution de la pensée platonicienne.

5. À ce sujet, Alessandra Fussi considère que cette attitude est symptomatique des interprètes de Platon, ces derniers étant plus intéressés par la prétendue relation du mythe avec l'orphisme et les pythagoriciens que par le mythe lui-même : *cf.* Fussi 2001, p. 529-552. La déconsidération du mythe par les interprètes est également soulignée par Radcliffe G. Edmonds III au début de son étude : *cf.* Edmonds 2012, p. 165-186.

fonction d'une analogie médicale, laquelle a pour ultime conséquence de penser le châtiment lui-même comme l'illustration des effets de la réfutation sur les âmes injustes. Bien que ce lien ne soit pas totalement passé inaperçu par les interprètes, il n'a jamais bénéficié d'un examen en profondeur, lequel permettrait non seulement d'améliorer notre compréhension de la réfutation socratique, mais également celle de la fonction du mythe chez Platon[6]. À cette fin, nous procéderons de la manière suivante : après avoir montré comment Socrate introduit l'analogie au sein du mythe à l'aide du critère de la nudité, nous examinerons la description du châtiment lui-même pour enfin montrer que si le châtiment reflète la réfutation, c'est parce que la douleur qu'il provoque est similaire à la honte éprouvée lorsqu'une personne disposant des mauvaises croyances est réfutée.

Le renversement des deux âges : la nudité comme condition de l'examen médical

Commençons par le déroulement du mythe lui-même, lequel débute par la transition d'un modèle de la *justice* à un autre[7]. Socrate rappelle que selon Homère, les Olympiens héritèrent de la loi de Cronos, laquelle stipule qu'une fois morts, les hommes ayant eu une vie juste et vertueuse se rendront aux Îles

6. En 523a1-3, Socrate commence son récit eschatologique en indiquant que si Calliclès prendra « le très beau discours » (μάλα καλοῦ λόγου) qu'il s'apprête à raconter pour un μῦθος, il considère à l'inverse qu'il s'agit d'un λόγος et que les choses qu'il s'apprête à lui dire doivent être comprises comme si elles étaient vraies (ὡς ἀληθῆ γὰρ ὄντα). Cette identification explicite entre λόγος et μῦθος a laissé perplexe plus d'un lecteur du *Gorgias*, précisément parce qu'une telle affirmation semble remettre en question l'opposition traditionnelle entre λόγος et μῦθος : *cf.* Brisson 1982, p. 113 et 139 ; Brickhouse & Smith 2007, p. 142-143 ; Inwood 2009, p. 48. ; Rowe 2012, p. 187-189 ; Marchand & Pochon, 2016, p. 95. Toutefois, la recherche des dernières années a permis de relativiser ce rapport d'opposition entre λόγος et μῦθος, notamment en soulignant la dimension persuasive et protreptique du mythe platonicien : *cf.* Annas 1982, p. 120-121 ; Mattéi 1996, p. 3 ; Partenie 2009, p. 1-11 ; Dixsaut 2012, p. 28 ; McCoy 2013, p. 92. En particulier, Makoto Sekimura considère que l'ambiguïté fondamentale du mythe chez Platon, lequel se rapporte à la fois à la vérité et à la fausseté, s'explique en grande partie par le fait que le mythe est une image d'une autre chose, soit d'un raisonnement : *cf.* Sekimura 2009, p. 255-264. Bien que la question de la fonction des mythes dans le *Gorgias* n'est pas sans importance, nous considérons toutefois qu'il s'agit d'un problème trop large pour en traiter convenablement dans les limites de cette étude. Ce faisant, nous nous limitons simplement à en dire que nous ne considérons pas que le mythe s'oppose radicalement au λόγος dans le *Gorgias* – qu'il serait l'autre du λόγος –, mais qu'il faut prendre Socrate au sérieux lorsqu'il identifie ces deux notions et que le mythe est tout simplement une autre forme du λόγος qui permettrait de rendre le contenu d'un raisonnement plus accessible à un interlocuteur non philosophe. L'on peut trouver un support à cette thèse en 480d4-7 où Socrate affirme à Polos que si l'on peut trouver une utilité à la rhétorique, ce n'est que dans la mesure où l'on s'en sert afin de mettre en lumière les injustices que l'on a commises et afin de s'en libérer.

7. *Gorgias*, 523a1-524a7.

des Bienheureux, alors que ceux ayant vécu une vie injuste et impie devront se rendre à la Prison du Tartare pour y recevoir leur juste paiement (τὸν δὲ ἀδίκως καὶ ἀθέως εἰς τὸ τῆς τίσεώς τε καὶ δίκης δεσμωτήριον, ὃ δὴ Τάρταρον καλοῦσιν, ἰέναι)[8]. Or lors du règne de Cronos, pour déterminer qui méritait d'être récompensé ou puni, 1) les hommes étaient jugés de leur vivant par d'autres vivants, 2) avec la connaissance du jour même de leur mort et 3) pouvaient faire appel à la fois à des témoins, à l'état de leur richesse et à la noblesse de leur origine afin de convaincre les juges de leur bonne réputation, et donc, qu'ils avaient vécu une vie en accord avec la justice.

Constatant que ce système permettait de nombreux abus, Zeus décida de remédier à la situation à l'aide de trois mesures permettant de rendre les jugements les plus justes possibles : 1) d'abord, les hommes ne seront plus jugés par des vivants qu'ils seraient susceptibles de connaître, mais par des morts qu'ils ne connaissent pas ; 2) ensuite, ils ne connaîtront plus le jour exact de leur mort et ne pourront donc plus préparer leur plaidoyer à l'avance ; 3) enfin, ils seront privés de tous leurs biens et de tout contact avec leurs proches, lesquels les enveloppent comme des vêtements, mais devront être « jugés nus, dépouillés de tout ce qu'ils ont (γυμνοὺς κριτέον ἁπάντων τούτων)[9]. »

Bien qu'à première vue, la transition de l'âge de Cronos à celui de Zeus puisse laisser penser qu'il s'agit d'un discours cosmologique, c'est plutôt comme une métaphore sur la transition d'un modèle de la justice à un autre qu'elle doit être lue. Comme le souligne à juste titre Alessandra Fussi, les règnes de Cronos et de Zeus ne nous projettent pas dans un autre monde par-delà le nôtre, mais au contraire, permettent d'illustrer comment s'opère la justice dans notre monde[10], et ce faisant, ils correspondent à deux attitudes spécifiques que les hommes entretiennent avec la justice.

Le règne de Cronos reflète ici la vision que se fait l'orateur, et tout particulièrement Calliclès, de la justice, laquelle n'est envisagée qu'en fonction d'un critère extérieur. En effet, pour l'orateur, nous ne sommes pas jugés en fonction de nos actes ou de nos motivations, mais toujours en fonction de l'impression et de l'attrait que nous suscitons chez les juges. En bref, la justice de l'orateur ne vise pas l'être d'une personne, mais toujours son apparaître.

À l'inverse, le règne de Zeus correspond à l'idéal que se fait le philosophe de la justice, laquelle ne repose pas sur la bonne réputation d'un homme, mais sur un critère interne. Pour le philosophe, la justice n'est pas la simple soumission à des lois arbitraires qui n'auraient de valeur que durant notre séjour sur terre, mais un devoir à la fois envers les hommes et les dieux que

8. *Gorgias* 523b2-4.

9. *Ibid.* 523e1-2.

10. Fussi 2001, p. 533. Fussi s'inspire fortement du commentaire d'Olympiodore sur ce point : cf. *Commentaire du Gorgias* § 47.8.

nous devons chercher à respecter tout au long de notre vie et au-delà[11]. Les trois mesures promulguées par Zeus ont ainsi une fonction purgative ; elles servent à éliminer tout élément extérieur à la justice ; à la dissocier de tout ce qu'elle n'est pas, afin de rendre transparent le seul critère sur lequel un homme doit être jugé : son âme. La nudité de l'âme correspond non seulement à l'aboutissement de ce processus de purification, mais elle s'avère également être son critère le plus important, et ce, pour deux motifs.

Premièrement, il ne suffit pas d'être nu devant les juges pour que le jugement soit juste, mais il faut que les juges soient eux-mêmes nus. Cette modalité du jugement de l'âme du défunt peut sembler curieuse, et ce, au point que Stéphane Marchand et Pierre Ponchon n'hésitent pas à dire que la nudité des juges est « [l]'une des bizarreries les plus frappantes du mythe » car si l'on peut comprendre pourquoi le prévenu est nu, on ne comprend pas pourquoi les juges doivent l'être[12]. Selon Olympiodore, Socrate introduirait le critère de la nudité des juges afin de souligner la transition d'un état imparfait à un état parfait de la justice ; de même que les jugements sous Cronos étaient mauvais et que ceux d'aujourd'hui sont bons, de même les juges étaient habillés alors qu'ils sont nus à présent[13]. De notre côté, nous considérons que l'interprétation de Marina B. McCoy est particulièrement séduisante sur ce point. Si la nudité des juges est un critère du jugement pour la compréhension du mythe, c'est parce qu'elle instaure un rapport de symétrie entre les juges et le défunt[14]. Les trois juges étant morts, ils ont eux-mêmes traversé les différentes étapes de la mise à nu qu'une âme doit subir dans l'Hadès. Non seulement ils comprennent la position d'extrême vulnérabilité dans laquelle se trouve une âme qui se présente à eux, mais ils se sont également débarrassés de tout ce qui pouvait encombrer leur jugement afin qu'il n'y ait « rien qu'une âme qui regarde une âme (αὐτῇ τῇ ψυχῇ αὐτὴν τὴν ψυχὴν θεωροῦντα)[15]. » À cet effet, Alessandra Fussi souligne que la nudité des juges peut être vue à l'intérieur de la symbolique de l'ornementation et comme une métaphore de la vérité ; un véritable jugement ne peut être offert que si les juges sont dépourvus de

11. Fussi 2001, p. 532.

12. Marchand & Ponchon 2015 p. 101. Les deux auteurs souhaitent expliquer cette « bizarrerie » en s'appuyant sur l'étude de Radcliffe G. Edmonds III, lequel défendrait l'idée que la nudité du prévenu et du juge est requise pour établir un contact direct entre les deux âmes, ce qui évoquerait la pratique socratique du dialogue. Or, il n'est jamais question de ce point dans l'article de Edmonds. S'il est vrai qu'au début de son analyse, l'auteur explique que son interprétation vise à montrer que le mythe permet de clarifier les raisons pour lesquelles le type de vie que mène Socrate est meilleur que celui de Calliclès et qu'il insiste tout au long de son étude sur la nudité de l'âme du prévenu, il évite soigneusement de faire mention de la nudité des juges eux-mêmes.

13. Olympiodore, *Commentaire du Gorgias*, § 48.1 et 50.1.

14. McCoy 2013, p. 93-94.

15. *Gorgias*, 523e3-4.

ce qui les recouvre – leurs habits, leurs liens familiaux, leurs relations sociales – bref, de tout facteur qui serait susceptible d'être exploité par le défunt afin de les corrompre[16]. Ainsi, les juges rendront leur jugement uniquement sur la base de la pensée et du raisonnement, sans aucun appel à la sensation.

Deuxièmement, si la nudité rend l'âme aussi vulnérable, c'est précisément parce qu'elle rend visibles « tous ses traits naturels ainsi que les impressions qu'elle a reçues »[17], c'est-à-dire les défauts, les cicatrices et les blessures qu'elle a subies lors de sa vie[18]. De la même manière qu'un médecin ne peut pas offrir de diagnostic précis si son patient refuse de retirer ses vêtements pour se faire examiner, il est indispensable aux juges qu'une âme se « dévête » de son corps afin d'évaluer le plus justement les maux dont elle souffre. La nudité est donc le critère qui permet à Platon d'introduire le parallèle entre la médecine et la justice au sein du mythe, et comme le souligne Sedley, cette analogie permet de présenter Socrate comme le véritable médecin de notre âme[19].

Le châtiment comme traitement de l'âme injuste

Une fois que le médecin a procédé à son examen et donné son diagnostic, il doit prescrire le traitement approprié aux maux que nous subissons. De la même manière, lorsque les juges constatent qu'une âme « est lacérée, ulcérée, pleine de tous les parjures et injustices que chaque action de sa vie a imprimés en elle »[20], ils l'envoient dans la prison du Tartare afin qu'elle y subisse le châtiment qu'elle mérite. La suite du récit de Socrate consiste presque exclusivement à retranscrire les différentes modalités du châtiment infligé à une âme injuste. Certes, le mythe se termine en spécifiant que l'âme d'un philosophe sera envoyée aux Îles des Bienheureux[21], mais il reste que Socrate passe sous silence le sort exact de l'âme juste dans l'Hadès, un élément que nous trouvons assez peu souligné dans le mythe et qui a été négligé par les interprètes[22]. Pour comprendre ce déséquilibre entre la description du sort réservé aux âmes injustes et celui réservé aux âmes justes, il faut d'abord comprendre

16. Fussi 2001, p. 545.
17. *Gorgias*, 524d5-6.
18. Ce point est par ailleurs très bien souligné dans l'étude de Radcliffe G. Edmonds III qui y voit un indicateur de la santé de l'âme : *cf.* Edmonds 2012, p. 172. L'auteur note également que la nudité du défunt peut également faire allusion à la nudité des athlètes olympiques.
19. Sedley 2009, p. 58-59.
20. *Gorgias*, 524e5-525a2.
21. *Ibid.* 526c1-5.
22. Alors que dans son livre sur les mythes, Jean-François Mattéi évacue complètement cette dimension de son analyse du *Gorgias*, Julia Annas estime que l'état des peines et des plaisirs dont fait preuve le mythe final du *Gorgias* ne correspondrait qu'à un schéma de type conséquentialiste ; si l'âme a été juste et vertueuse, elle sera récompensée, mais si elle a été injuste et criminelle, elle sera châtiée : *cf.* Mattéi 1996, p. 137-164 ; Annas 1982, p. 125. Comme nous le verrons dans la suite, nous ne pouvons pas nous accorder avec une telle lecture du mythe.

la fonction spécifique du châtiment au sein du mythe lui-même, et comme l'observe Emmanuelle Jouët-Pastré, le châtiment n'est pas ici pensé sur le modèle punitif de la torture, mais sur le modèle médical, puisqu'il a pour but de guérir l'âme injuste de son injustice, donc de la rendre juste[23].

Trevor J. Saunders remarquait que Platon ne se prive généralement pas de décrire avec un malin plaisir les « châtiments exquis » réservés aux âmes injustes dans ses récits eschatologiques[24]. S'il est vrai que les eschatologies du *Phédon* et de la *République* peuvent donner cette impression, il ne s'agit pas en revanche d'une caractéristique du *Gorgias*. Socrate y est moins préoccupé de fournir une liste exhaustive des différents châtiments spécifiques qu'à en décrire la mécanique interne. La question n'est pas de savoir quelle forme prend le châtiment, mais quel est son effet sur l'âme. Pour Socrate, la fonction principale du châtiment, c'est avant tout de donner un support afin d'améliorer l'âme de celui qui le reçoit ou de celui qui y assiste :

> Or, tout être qu'on punit et auquel on inflige le châtiment qu'il faut mérite ou bien de s'améliorer et de tirer profit de sa peine (ἢ βελτίονι γίγνεσθαι καὶ ὀνίνασθαι) ou bien de servir d'exemple aux autres hommes (ἢ παραδείγματι τοῖς ἄλλοις γίγνεσθαι), lesquels, en le voyant subir les souffrances qu'il subit, prendront peur et voudront devenir meilleurs[25].

Le châtiment n'est jamais gratuit ; il ne sert pas simplement à infliger des peines aux âmes par pur sadisme ou à leur faire subir les injustices qu'elles ont commises en retour, mais à les corriger, à les débarrasser de ce qui les enlaidit et à les rendre justes par la suite[26]. Le châtiment, c'est le remède à l'injustice, car au contraire, s'il n'avait simplement qu'une fonction dissuasive et non curative, comme l'estime Julia Annas, alors le mythe final du ***Gorgias*** tomberait dans le piège du fameux mythe de l'anneau de Gygès, lequel stipule que la justice n'a qu'une valeur relative[27] : nous serions justes non pas parce que la justice possède une valeur intrinsèque, mais seulement pour éviter les douleurs que l'on subit dans l'Hadès. Or si nous mettons en évidence la fonction curative du châtiment, alors non seulement nous comprenons que l'on ne peut pas vouloir éviter le châtiment si l'on souhaite être juste – puisqu'au contraire, il est précisément ce qui permet de rendre une âme juste –, mais cela nous permet également d'expliquer le silence relatif de Platon sur les récompenses destinées aux âmes justes. Si une âme ne présente aucun symptôme ni aucune marque caractéristique de la maladie qu'est l'injustice, alors aucun traitement n'a à être prescrit et il n'est nul besoin d'en parler davantage.

23. Jouët-Pastré 2012, p. 61.
24. Saunders 1973, p. 233.
25. *Gorgias*, 525b1-4 (trad. M. Canto-Sperber modifiée).
26. *Ibid.* 527b : « Tel est le bien qui vient en second après le fait d'être juste : c'est de le devenir et de payer sa faute en étant puni. »
27. *Resp.* II, 358e-361d.

Cela dit, l'effet curatif du châtiment ne sera pas le même en fonction de la gravité du crime commis. Deux catégories de suppliciés doivent donc être minutieusement distinguées : 1) ceux à qui l'on rend un service (οἱ ὠφελούμενοί) et 2) les âmes incurables (οἱ ἀνίατοι). La catégorie des âmes curables est celle à laquelle le mythe s'adresse le plus expressément, car ce sont les seules à pouvoir éprouver un réel bénéfice du châtiment. S'il ne spécifie pas la nature exacte de leur crime, Socrate indique toutefois que les âmes curables sont responsables de « méfaits qu'on peut guérir »[28]. Comme l'injustice n'a pas totalement corrompu ces âmes, il est encore temps de les purifier de leur crime et le seul moyen d'y parvenir, c'est de leur infliger des souffrances (ἀλγηδόνες) : « Malgré tout, les souffrances qu'ils subissent, ici et dans l'Hadès, leur sont utiles, car il n'est pas possible de les débarrasser de l'injustice autrement que par la souffrance[29]. » La douleur ressentie n'est pas une simple conséquence qui accompagne le châtiment, mais bel et bien le remède lui-même.

C'est pourquoi les souffrances provoquées par le châtiment ne doivent pas être excessives, mais proportionnées à la gravité du crime qu'il faut réparer. Si Socrate ne mentionne pas explicitement ce point, il précise néanmoins que ce sont les âmes incurables qui subissent « les souffrances les plus graves, les plus douloureuses, les plus effroyables[30]. » Le châtiment ne permet pas de guérir toutes les âmes, mais seulement celles qui peuvent l'être encore. Lorsqu'un homme commet les délits les plus graves qui soient, il entache son âme de manière irréversible, et ce faisant, celle-ci devient incurable. Le châtiment qu'une telle âme subit ne lui sera donc d'aucun profit, car elle ne peut pas être délivrée des maux qui la gangrènent. Dans ce cas, ce n'est donc pas vraiment à elle que le châtiment s'adresse, mais à tous ceux qui pourront l'observer afin de servir « un effroyable exemple, à la fois un horrible spectacle et un avertissement[31]. » De manière assez éloquente, Socrate prend comme modèle pour penser l'âme incurable la figure du tyran, trait que l'eschatologie du *Gorgias* partage avec la *République*[32]. Pour Fussi, si Socrate convoque la figure du tyran, c'est afin d'introduire un principe d'invariabilité ; personne n'est à l'abri de l'injustice, pas même le Grand Roi de Perse, car notre personnalité ne s'identifie pas à notre fonction sociale. Au mieux, tout ce que celle-ci peut faire, c'est camoufler les blessures de notre âme à la manière d'un bandage, mais sans plus[33]. De même, McCoy note que la leçon

28. *Resp.* 525b6.
29. *Ibid.* 525b6-c1.
30. *Ibid.* 525c5-6.
31. *Ibid.* 525c6-8. Sur le parallèle entre l'âme incurable et l'homme politique : *cf.* Mifsud 1961, p. 302-306.
32. *Resp.* X, 615c-e.
33. Fussi 2001, p. 547-551.

la plus importante du mythe est de rendre manifeste notre plus grande vulnérabilité : nous pouvons nous blesser nous-mêmes au travers de nos propres actions injustes[34]. La particularité du cas du tyran, c'est précisément qu'il est complètement aveugle au mal qu'il se cause lui-même, car il se croit justifié dans ses actions en raison de sa fonction sociale.

L'analogie médicale appliquée au châtiment des âmes injustes était déjà attestée par Olympiodore dans son commentaire du *Gorgias*[35] et bien qu'elle soit souvent observée, elle a laissé plus d'un interprète dubitatif[36]. Dans son étude de 2004, Anne Merker remarque bien que Socrate identifie la fonction purgative du châtiment à la douleur qu'il induit, mais l'autrice considère que la comparaison entre le châtiment et les traitements médicaux est inexacte ; si le traitement médical s'accompagne généralement de douleurs, elles ne sont ni bénéfiques au patient ni l'effet recherché, et elles peuvent être supprimées sans nuire pour autant à l'efficacité du traitement[37]. Pire encore, cette analogie aurait pour conséquence selon Merker que l'âme ne puisse être pensée autrement que par le biais du corps, et dès lors, on ne comprendrait pas en quoi les douleurs infligées par le châtiment dans l'Hadès refléteraient celles d'un traitement médical sur l'âme, car dans les deux cas, c'est le corps qui est concerné, un jugement qui recevra l'approbation de Jouët-Pastré[38]. Pareillement, les deux autrices se demandent à quoi peut bien servir de châtier le tyran pour celles et ceux qui observent son supplice s'il ne bénéficie en rien des souffrances qu'il endure dans l'Hadès. Si l'on ne peut pas soigner cette âme, alors lui administrer un traitement semble totalement superflu et lui infliger des douleurs un exercice cruel[39].

Certes, Socrate convoque l'image d'un corps nu, lacéré et enlaidi pour illustrer les dommages causés par l'injustice sur l'âme, mais justement, il s'agit d'une analogie afin de rendre visible une réalité invisible. Socrate n'indique à aucun instant de son récit que le châtiment infligé sur les âmes injustes est de nature corporelle et quand bien même ce serait le cas, Socrate caractérise la médecine comme une activité fondamentalement douloureuse tout au long du *Gorgias* ; si l'on ne veut pas suivre le traitement du médecin, c'est précisément en raison des souffrances qu'il engendre. L'exemple le plus frappant de ce constat est peut-être celui du tribunal d'enfants où le médecin serait

34. McCoy 2013, p. 104.

35. Olympiodore, *op. cit.* § 50.4

36. Si Julia Annas ne la mentionne pas une seule fois dans son article, T.J. Saunders considère pour sa part qu'il ne s'agit que d'une « *somewhat misleading analogy* », et ce faisant, qu'elle ne devrait pas être prise en compte dans l'explication du mythe : *cf.* Saunders 1973, p. 235.

37. Merker 2004, p. 11-14.

38. Jouët-Pastré 2012, p. 62.

39. *Ibid.* p. 63-64 ; Merker, 2004, p. 13. De même, Olympiodore semble également troublé par la perspective d'un châtiment éternel qui ne bénéficierait nullement à celui qui le subit : cf. *op. cit.* § 50.2.

incapable de convaincre son jury que les incisions et les cautérisations qu'il pratique sont toujours au service de leur santé et non pour les tourmenter[40]. En ce qui concerne le tourment éternel de l'âme incurable, Socrate affirme assez clairement qu'il sert d'avertissement à ceux tentés de vivre une vie remplie d'injustices, mais Martha McCoy y voit un parallèle avec la médecine hippocratique[41]. Le médecin doit s'efforcer de traiter les hommes au mieux de ses capacités, mais il doit aussi être capable de reconnaître ses propres limites. S'il ne peut pas guérir son patient, il peut néanmoins nettoyer les blessures pour retarder l'infection le plus tard possible, et s'il considère que la meilleure action est de laisser un corps déséquilibré se restaurer de lui-même, alors il sera dispensé d'intervenir ; il serait donc moins important de guérir l'âme incurable que de montrer la possibilité de la soigner s'il n'avait pas été trop tard[42].

La solution de McCoy paraît séduisante, mais elle s'accorde malheureusement mal au *Gorgias*, puisque Socrate précise que le châtiment ne sera désormais plus d'aucun bénéfice (οὐκέτι ὀνίνανται οὐδέν) pour les âmes incurables, de sorte qu'il ne peut plus agir à la manière d'un traitement. De même, au troisième livre de la *République*, Glaucon se sert de l'image du médecin en précisant que celui-ci laisse de côté ce qu'il lui est impossible de guérir[43]. À notre sens, dans les différentes tentatives d'explication de la fonction du châtiment dans l'eschatologie du *Gorgias*, l'on semble oublier un peu trop souvent que l'analogie entre la médecine et la justice est précisément une analogie. Il faut se rappeler que Socrate parle bel et bien des souffrances que les âmes injustes subissent à la fois ici et dans l'Hadès (καὶ ἐνθάδε καὶ ἐν Ἅιδου)[44]. De même que la justice est à l'âme ce que la médecine est au corps, soit l'art qui s'occupe de soigner les maux dont nous souffrons, de même le châtiment est à l'âme injuste ce que le remède est au corps malade, soit la

40. *Gorgias*, 521e3-522a6.

41. McCoy 2013, p. 109-110. Sur ce point, Cambiano rappelle qu'il est très difficile de savoir avec précision quels sont les traités du corpus hippocratique que Platon aurait pu avoir sous la main, mais les allusions à Hippocrate, notamment dans le *Phèdre*, sont assez claires pour que le parallèle entre le philosophe et le médecin soit indéniable, *cf.* Cambiano 2013, p. 1.

42. Dans la même veine, Jouët-Pastré défend en s'appuyant sur le *Protagoras* 323c-325c que si le châtiment ne répare pas le passé, il a un rôle pour l'avenir et qu'il n'est pas nécessaire d'en éprouver la douleur, car sa simple vision serait suffisante pour avoir sur nous un effet dissuasif : *cf.* Jouët-Pastré 2012, p. 63-64.

43. *Resp.* II, 360e6-361a1 : « D'abord, que l'homme injuste fasse comme les artisans de haut calibre, par exemple comme le pilote de navire, comme un grand médecin qui a conscience de ce qui est possible et de ce qui n'est pas possible dans l'exercice de son art : ce qui est possible, il l'entreprend, ce qui ne l'est pas, il le laisse de côté » (trad. G. Leroux).

44. *Gorgias,* 525b7-8. La fonction illustrative du mythe est par ailleurs anticipée à la fin de l'entretien avec Polos en 480d. En effet, Socrate déclare que si la rhétorique peut avoir une quelconque utilité, c'est uniquement « pour mettre en lumière les injustices qu'on a commises et se trouver ainsi délivré du pire des maux, l'injustice. »

douleur qui permet de purger les maux qui nous affectent. La véritable question à laquelle il faut répondre n'est pas de savoir comment un châtiment corporel pourrait avoir un effet sur notre âme, mais de quoi le châtiment corporel est l'analogue ; qu'est-ce qui agirait sur l'âme à la fois comme une douleur persistante et comme traitement de son injustice ?

De la douleur à la honte : la réfutation comme véritable châtiment de l'âme

Pour comprendre quel est le véritable analogue du châtiment, nous devons revenir à l'image du tribunal d'enfants que nous avons brièvement évoquée un peu plus haut. Socrate convoque cette analogie tout juste avant d'exposer son eschatologie ; de même qu'un médecin serait incapable de convaincre un jury composé d'enfants des bienfaits qu'il leur apporte s'il était accusé par un confiseur d'être responsable de leurs maux, de même Socrate prédit qu'il sera lui-même victime d'une telle accusation et qu'il sera impuissant à convaincre les juges qu'il a toujours œuvré dans l'intérêt des Athéniens. Il s'agit bien évidemment d'une évocation de la condamnation à mort de Socrate. Celle-ci n'est pas la seule : Calliclès prévient Socrate que sa pratique de la philosophie, totalement inadaptée aux affaires de la cité et semblable à un jeu d'enfants, risquerait de le faire condamner à mort[45]. En revanche, la spécificité de l'image du tribunal d'enfants est telle qu'elle confère à Socrate le rôle du médecin, et, ce faisant, établit un lien direct entre les traitements douloureux du médecin et la pratique de la réfutation. Cette identification entre le traitement médical et la réfutation était d'ailleurs implicitement préparée par Socrate lorsqu'il demandait à Calliclès de quelle manière il l'engage à prendre soin de la cité (τὴν θεραπείαν τῆς πόλεως) afin de supprimer l'injustice chez ses concitoyens, en faisant la guerre aux Athéniens afin qu'ils s'améliorent, comme un médecin le ferait à ses patients (τὴν τοῦ διαμάχεσθαι Ἀθηναίοις ὅπως ὡς βέλτιστοι ἔσονται, ὡς ἰατρόν) – et donc, comme le ferait Socrate en réfutant les Athéniens – ou bien en se mettant à leur service et en devenant complice de leurs désirs, comme le lui répondra Calliclès[46].

Le parallèle entre la médecine et la philosophie est sans doute l'un des

45. *Gorgias*, 485a3-486d1. Nous soulignons également qu'en 473b12-d2, Polos décrit à Socrate les supplices réservés au comploteur qui voudrait « injustement » renverser le tyran de sa cité pour le convaincre qu'il vaut mieux commettre que subir l'injustice. Si ce texte ne semble pas à première vue évoquer la condamnation à mort de Socrate, il est toutefois intéressant de noter que la liste des différents supplices qu'offre Polos sera reprise presque à l'identique par Glaucon en *République*, II, 360e-362a pour parler de la condamnation de l'homme juste, mais ayant l'apparence ou la réputation d'être injuste. Selon Glaucon, un tel homme sera « inébranlable, jusqu'à la mort » face aux accusations que l'on porte contre lui, mais les supplice qui l'attendent seront aux yeux de « ceux qui font l'éloge de l'injustice en la plaçant au-dessus de la justice » la preuve qu'il vaut mieux commettre que subir l'injustice.

46. *Ibid*. 521a2-8.

thèmes les plus récurrents du *Gorgias*, et ce, dès ses premiers instants, lorsque Chéréphon interroge Polos sur le type d'art que pratique Gorgias[47]. De même, alors que Gorgias répond que l'objet de son art, ce sont les discours, Socrate lui demande immédiatement s'ils concernent ceux « qui indiquent aux malades le traitement qu'ils doivent suivre pour être en bonne santé »[48], et le célèbre orateur reviendra à la charge un peu plus loin en affirmant qu'il aide régulièrement son frère ainsi que d'autres médecins en convaincant leurs patients de subir leurs traitements[49], ce qui n'est pas sans rappeler le §14 de l'*Éloge d'Hélène* où Gorgias affirme que la puissance du discours a le même rapport à la disposition de l'âme que les dispositions des drogues à la nature du corps[50]. Ces allusions sont loin d'être anodines. En effet, la médecine occupe une place importante et structurante au sein du *Gorgias*, et si tel est le cas, c'est parce que c'est sur son terrain qu'a lieu la bataille que se livrent la rhétorique et la philosophie : toutes deux affirment que le λόγος est leur objet de prédilection, toutes deux se présentent comme la meilleure manière de vivre qui soit et toutes deux prétendent être la seule discipline à s'occuper véritablement du bien-être d'autrui, d'où le fait qu'elles se réclament toutes deux de la médecine[51]. À cet effet, il faut se rappeler qu'en raison de sa pratique de la philosophie, Socrate considère qu'il est le seul Athénien à se soucier véritablement de l'art politique, et donc, qu'il est de ses contemporains « le seul à faire de la politique (πράττειν τὰ πολιτικὰ μόνος τῶν νῦν)[52] ». Comme le philosophe est le seul à se soucier réellement du bien-être de l'âme et comme son action vise à la débarrasser de l'injustice, il est le seul à s'intéresser à la justice au sein de la cité ; cette justice, comme espèce de la politique, est donc fondamentalement similaire à la médecine de l'âme. En effet, lors de son entretien avec Polos, Socrate nous explique que la politique, soit l'art qui s'occupe de l'âme, se divise en deux espèces : la législation et la justice. Or cette division de la politique doit être comprise en fonction d'une analogie avec la science qui s'occupe des corps ; la législation est donc à la gymnastique – soit l'art qui s'occupe du maintien de la bonne santé de l'âme/du corps –

47. *Gorgias*, 448b4-c3 : « Ch. : Bon, voici ma question. Si Gorgias connaissait le même art que son frère, Hérodicos, comment serait-il correct de l'appeler ? Comme son frère, n'est-ce pas ? Pol. : Oui, absolument. Ch. : On aurait donc raison de dire qu'il est médecin. Pol. : Oui. Ch. : Mais s'il connaissait le même art qu'Aristophon, fils d'Aglaophon, ou que, d'ailleurs, le frère d'Aristophon, comment serait-il juste de l'appeler ? Pol. : Peintre, c'est évident. Ch. : Mais alors quel est l'art que Gorgias connaît ? de quel nom faut-il l'appeler ? »

48. *Ibid.* 449e1-2.

49. *Ibid.* 456a7-c7.

50. *Éloge d'Hélène*, § 14 : τὸν αὐτὸν δὲ λόγον ἔχει ἥ τε τοῦ λόγου δύναμις πρὸς τὴν τῆς ψυχῆς τάξιν ἥ τε τῶν φαρμάκων τάξις πρὸς τὴν τῶν σωμάτων φύσιν. Je remercie Corentin Tresnie d'avoir porté à mon attention ce point.

51. Sur la manière dont Platon se sert de la médecine comme modèle de technique : *cf.* Cambiano 2013, p. 1-14.

52. *Gorgias*, 521d7-8.

ce que la justice est à la médecine – soit l'art qui s'occupe de la correction d'une âme/d'un corps déséquilibré ou malade[53]. L'enjeu de l'analogie médicale est crucial, puisqu'il s'agit pour la philosophie de restituer à la médecine ce que les rhéteurs ont indûment soustrait aux médecins ; si elle réussit dans cette tâche, c'est alors du même coup la prétention à pratiquer l'art politique qu'elle réussit à extirper des mains des rhéteurs. Ainsi, puisque la justice et la médecine ont toutes deux pour fonction de rétablir l'équilibre d'un corps ou d'une âme malades en les purgeant des maux qui les affligent, puisque Socrate affirme prendre soin de la cité au moyen de la réfutation et puisque celle-ci partage avec le traitement médical un effet douloureux, alors il devient clair que le rôle du châtiment dans l'eschatologie est entièrement analogue à celui de la réfutation.

Socrate est le médecin qui veille sur l'âme de ses patients en pratiquant sur eux l'agaçante épreuve de la réfutation, mais est-ce suffisant pour déclarer unilatéralement que la réfutation a la même fonction que le châtiment de l'eschatologie ? Il y a au moins un passage du *Gorgias* qui affirme explicitement l'identité entre le châtiment et la réfutation. De plus en plus irrité par les multiples questions de Socrate et confronté à une contradiction de son discours – celle selon laquelle être punie (τὸ κολάζεσθαι) vaut mieux pour une âme que de rester déréglée –, Calliclès invite Socrate à questionner quelqu'un d'autre que lui, ce à quoi le philosophe lui répond : « Cet homme ne supporte ni qu'on lui rende service (ὠφελούμενος) ni de subir ce dont on parle – la punition (κολαζόμενος) ! »[54] L'identification entre le châtiment et la réfutation ne saurait être plus manifeste, car c'est précisément pour éviter une réfutation publique qui heurte son amour-propre que Calliclès refuse d'avouer que son discours est contradictoire. L'*Apologie* décrivait déjà cette relation. S'adressant aux juges qui l'ont condamné à boire la cigüe, Socrate les informe que si leur intention était de se débarrasser de lui afin de « ne pas avoir à soumettre leur vie à la réfutation » (ἀπαλλάξεσθαι τοῦ διδόναι ἔλεγχον τοῦ βίου), alors leurs efforts seront en vain ; « tout de suite après ma mort, un châtiment beaucoup plus pénible vous attendra » (τιμωρίαν ὑμῖν ἥξειν εὐθὺς μετὰ τὸν ἐμὸν θάνατον πολὺ χαλεπωτέραν), car « nombreux sont ceux qui viendront vous réfuter » (πλείους ἔσονται ὑμᾶς οἱ ἐλέγχοντε)[55]. En refusant de se faire réfuter, les juges ne font que retarder l'inévitable, car non seulement la réfutation n'est pas un procédé exclusif à Socrate, mais le philosophe termine son adresse aux juges en leur annonçant qu'une fois mort, il continuera « à soumettre les gens de là-bas à l'examen et à l'enquête auxquels [il soumet] les gens d'ici-bas » (τοὺς ἐκεῖ ἐξετάζοντα καὶ ἐρευνῶντα ὥσπερ

53. *Gorgias*, 464b2-c3.
54. *Ibid.* 505c3-4.
55. *Apologie*, 39c3-d1 (trad. L. Brisson modifiée).

τοὺς ἐνταῦθα διάγειν)[56]. Socrate ne le dit peut-être pas, mais il est clair qu'il sous-entend que si personne ne vient réfuter les juges qui l'ont condamné à mort, alors il les attendra dans l'Hadès pour le faire : leur châtiment consistera ainsi à subir la réfutation.

Le parallèle entre le châtiment et la réfutation n'a pas complètement échappé aux interprètes, mais il n'a pas pour autant bénéficié d'un examen approfondi[57]. À notre connaissance, seuls deux interprètes se sont penchés sérieusement sur la question : David Sedley et Radcliffe G. Edmonds III. Nous allons surtout nous intéresser aux analyses de Sedley. En effet, celui-ci a bien observé que le châtiment et la réfutation partagent une même fonction thérapeutique – soit de nous délivrer des maux qui nous affectent au moyen d'une souffrance –, mais il refuse précisément de les identifier pour deux motifs[58]. Le premier argument de Sedley est le suivant : la bonne disposition de notre âme nécessite que l'on dispose à la fois des bonnes croyances sur la nature du bien et le contrôle de nos appétits. Quel que puisse être le rôle des appétits dans la possession de nos croyances, ceux-ci ne sont pas des états cognitifs et ne sont donc pas réductibles aux erreurs intellectuelles. Or la réfutation n'agit pas directement sur les appétits, mais seulement sur nos croyances afin de les corriger. Si l'on venait à réfuter quelqu'un qui, comme Calliclès, identifie le bien au plaisir, alors la douleur provoquée par la réfutation consisterait essentiellement dans le maintien d'appétits violents que l'on n'estimerait plus bons à satisfaire. Or, si tel est le cas, la réfutation contrasterait alors avec le châtiment conventionnel lequel permet de contrôler nos appétits en les frustrant, mais non pas de corriger nos erreurs intellectuelles. Ainsi, réfutation et châtiment ne sont pas identiques. Quant au deuxième argument, Sedley souligne que Socrate affirme trouver la réfutation plaisante, ce qui revient à dire que toute réfutation n'est pas douloureuse. Or si tel est le cas, la réfutation ne peut pas être identique au châtiment, puisque celui-ci est nécessairement douloureux. Ainsi, réfutation et châtiment doivent être distingués.

Le premier argument ne nous paraît pas convaincant. Si Sedley a raison de souligner la distinction entre les appétits et les croyances et de rappeler que les appétits ne sont pas de nature intellectuelle, il conclut trop rapidement à leur asymétrie, comme s'il n'y avait aucune communication possible entre ce qui relève de nos désirs et ce qui relève de la connaissance[59]. Cela

56. *Apologie*, 41b.

57. Delcomminette 2013, p. 145 ; Marchand & Ponchon, 2016, p. 105 ; Rowe, 2012 p. 195.

58. Sedley 2009, p. 63-65.

59. Sur ce point, il nous faut noter que l'argument de Sedley se fonde, du moins en partie, sur la supposition que l'on trouve déjà dans le *Gorgias* les premiers jalons d'une doctrine de la partition de l'âme. Selon cette thèse qui trouve son principal point d'appui en 493a1-b3, le Socrate du *Gorgias* distinguerait en l'âme une partie appétitive et une partie intellectuelle,

dit, ce n'est pas le véritable enjeu de l'identification entre la réfutation et le châtiment : la question n'est pas de savoir comment nos appétits sont liés à nos croyances, mais plutôt de savoir ce qui est la cause de la douleur lorsque l'on est réfuté, et contrairement à ce que dit Sedley, ce n'est pas parce que nous ne sommes pas débarrassés de nos appétits que la réfutation est douloureuse, mais parce qu'elle provoque de la honte (αἰσχύνη)[60].

Comme le notait déjà Louis-André Dorion dans une étude sur l'évolution sémantique du terme ἔλεγχος, le verbe « réfuter », bien qu'il soit usuel, ne peut adéquatement traduire le verbe ἐξελέγχω, « car il est à la fois trop "logique" et trop neutre du point de vue moral. L'usage d'ἐξελέγχω conserve une dimension liée à la honte, puisque la personne confondue est nécessairement humiliée, et ce par le fait même qu'elle a été démasquée »[61]. En pratiquant la réfutation, il ne s'agit pas simplement de dénicher les erreurs dans le discours de notre interlocuteur, car c'est précisément de notre manière de vivre qu'il est question et si celle-ci se révèle ignoble, alors elle le sera à la vue de tous et nous serons impuissants à la cacher. Si Calliclès ne semblait pas être choqué que Socrate compare la vie de jouissance qu'il préconise à celle d'un pluvier qui mange et fiente en même temps, il ne pourra en revanche s'empêcher de lui lancer « n'as-tu pas honte ? » (οὐκ αἰσχύνῃ ;) lorsque le philosophe lui dira sans ambages que la vie qu'il trouve la plus heureuse est celle des débauchés (ὁ τῶν κιναίδων βίος)[62]. Avec cette phrase, Calliclès projette sur Socrate la honte qu'il ressent à se faire réfuter publiquement, mais sa pointe de colère permet également de relier la honte à la réfutation, non seulement parce qu'il s'agit d'une phrase que Calliclès a lancé à Socrate

ce qui aurait pour conséquence non seulement que le *Gorgias* renonce à l'intellectualisme des dialogues de jeunesse – soit la thèse que la compréhension entraîne nécessairement la vertu et que le savoir du Bien suffit à corriger nos dispositions émotionnelles –, mais également qu'il anticipe la psychologie morale de la *République* : *cf.* Brickhouse & Smith 2015, p. 9-28 ; Dorion 2018, p. 153-213. Bien qu'importante, cette question difficile ne peut pas être traitée convenablement dans les limites de notre étude. Cela dit, nous souhaitons souligner, avec Louis-André Dorion, que le Socrate du *Gorgias* semble soutenir « deux positions incompatibles concernant les rapports entre la vertu et la connaissance », admettant la possibilité d'un conflit entre deux ordres de désir au sein de l'âme tout en continuant à soutenir que la connaissance suffit à rendre heureux : *cf.* Dorion 2018, p. 205. Si nous accordons à Sedley que l'on trouve dans le *Gorgias* des éléments indiquant une bipartition de l'âme, nous considérons en revanche que cela n'indique pas pour autant que le Socrate du *Gorgias* soit prêt à totalement rejeter l'intellectualisme ni qu'il n'y ait aucune communication possible entre ce qui relève du registre des croyances et du registre des appétits, ce que nous souhaitons montrer dans notre section sur la honte provoquée par la réfutation.

60. On peut d'ailleurs noter au passage qu'Edmonds, Merker et Jouët-Pastré ont tous les trois constaté la proximité sémantique entre la honte (αἰσχύνη) et la laideur (αἶσχος) dans leurs études respectives.

61. Dorion 1990, p. 311-344.

62. *Gorgias*, 494e7. Le terme κίναιδος sert également à désigner le partenaire passif dans une relation homosexuelle.

un peu plus tôt dans le dialogue pour railler ce qu'il nomme « faire la chasse aux mots »[63], mais aussi parce qu'il s'agit d'une référence directe à l'*Apologie* en 28b où Socrate prévoit qu'on pourrait lui reprocher la manière de vivre qui l'a conduit à mourir : « Peut-être me dira-t-on : "N'as-tu pas honte (Εἶτ' οὐκ αἰσχύνῃ), Socrate, d'avoir adopté une conduite qui aujourd'hui t'expose à la mort ?" »[64]. Les adversaires de Socrate s'accordent pour dire que la réfutation suscite de la honte – selon eux, parce qu'elle est une activité enfantine, mésadaptée à la vie politique et potentiellement dangereuse –, mais toute l'ironie consiste justement en ce que la honte n'agit pas sur celui qui pratique la réfutation, mais bien sur celui qui est réfuté. Si Socrate ne dit pas explicitement dans le *Gorgias* que c'est la honte issue de la réfutation qui permet de redresser les âmes injustes, c'est néanmoins une thèse qui sera exposé par l'Étranger d'Élée dans la sixième définition du *Sophiste*[65]. Il n'est donc pas vrai de dire avec Sedley que la réfutation agit seulement sur les croyances : elle provoque également une douleur dans l'âme, à savoir la honte. Certes, il est vrai que le *Gorgias* n'explique pas réellement comment cette action s'opère sur l'âme ni laquelle de ses parties est concernée par la réfutation, mais il ne dit pas non plus que l'effet du châtiment concerne directement les appétits ou que c'est sur cette partie de l'âme que l'on doit porter notre attention. Ainsi, lorsque Sedley nous dit que la réfutation et le châtiment ne peuvent pas être identiques, puisque l'une agit sur nos croyances tandis que l'autre agirait sur nos appétits, nous estimons que cette distinction nous induit en erreur et qu'il s'agit d'un faux problème, car l'auteur ne prend pas assez en compte le contexte de cette identification, à savoir la fonction illustrative du mythe[66]. De même que le châtiment provoque des douleurs insuppor-

63. *Gorgias*, 489b7-8 : « Dis-moi, Socrate, n'as-tu pas honte à ton âge de faire la chasse aux mots ? (οὐκ αἰσχύνῃ τηλικοῦτος ὢν ὀνόματα θηρεύων) » (trad. M. Canto-Sperber modifiée).

64. *Apologie*, 28b3-5.

65. *Sophiste*, 230b4-d4. Il n'est pas anodin non plus de remarquer que pour aborder les effets de la réfutation sur l'âme, l'Étranger d'Élée introduit lui aussi une analogie avec la médecine. Sur le redressement de l'âme au moyen de la réfutation dans le *Sophiste* : *cf.* Lott 2012, p. 36-56.

66. Sur ce point, nous devons établir une certaine précision. Sedley n'a pas entièrement tort lorsqu'il se réfère à la conception traditionnelle du châtiment, puisque Socrate y a lui-même recours en de nombreux endroits du *Gorgias*, notamment en 480c5-d3 et en 506c5-509b1. Comme exposé plus haut, le Socrate du *Gorgias* établit un lien étroit entre les traitements médicaux sur le corps et l'application de la justice sur l'âme : s'il faut que l'on soit enchaîné, que l'on paye une amende, que l'on soit exilé ou même condamné à mort pour se débarrasser de l'injustice en notre âme, alors il faut subir le châtiment que la justice recommande sans peur et avec courage. Nous ne contestons pas à Sedley que Socrate utilise également la conception traditionnelle du châtiment dans le *Gorgias*. Ce que nous contestons en revanche, c'est que la conception traditionnelle du châtiment soit la seule à être convoquée dans le *Gorgias*. Bien plus, nous considérons que la conception traditionnelle du châtiment, tout comme le mythe final, a davantage pour fonction de mettre en lumière les effets de la réfutation, laquelle agit comme le châtiment/traitement de l'âme injuste.

tables dans le corps du supplicié, la réfutation provoque une honte gênante et irritante dans l'âme injuste. Il ne s'agit pas simplement de provoquer des douleurs avec froideur, mais de soigner les âmes injustes en leur montrant la cause de leur dérèglement : leur méconnaissance de la nature exacte du bien.

Concernant le second argument de Sedley, il est vrai que Socrate affirme qu'il est quelqu'un

> qui a du plaisir à être réfuté, quand ce [qu'il dit] est faux (τῶν ἡδέως μὲν ἂν ἐλεγχθέντων εἴ τι μὴ ἀληθὲς λέγω), quelqu'un qui a aussi du plaisir à réfuter quand ce qu'on [lui] dit n'est pas vrai, mais auquel il ne déplaît pas moins d'être réfuté que de réfuter (οὐκ ἀηδέστερον μεντἂν ἐλεγχθέντων ἢ ἐλεγξάντων)[67].

Mais Socrate est également le premier à reconnaître que la réfutation est une expérience déplaisante pour la majorité de ceux qu'il interroge, ce qui est notamment illustré par l'image du tribunal d'enfants mentionné plus haut. La réfutation est à la fois source de plaisirs et de frustrations ; la question n'est pas de savoir si la réfutation s'accompagne nécessairement de douleurs, mais plutôt de savoir quand elle est plaisante et quand elle est douloureuse. Sur ce point, nous trouvons les réflexions de Sylvain Delcomminette particulièrement lumineuses[68]. Pour le dire succinctement, tout dépend de la manière dont l'interlocuteur envisage la réfutation. Si Socrate peut ressentir un véritable sentiment de plaisir lorsqu'il se fait réfuter, c'est parce que la réfutation permet de le purger de son ignorance tout en lui donnant l'opportunité de pratiquer la dialectique ; le défaut initial de l'ignorance n'est donc pas considéré comme un manque, puisqu'il est immédiatement rempli par le plaisir de la connaissance, ce qui l'incite à poursuivre davantage sa recherche au sujet de la vérité[69]. En d'autres termes, la réfutation est plaisante pour Socrate parce qu'en permettant l'acquisition de connaissances et la purgation d'opinions fausses, elle est un bien que l'on rend à soi-même et à autrui. Il s'agit précisément du sens de la remarque que Socrate adresse à Calliclès au moment où celui-ci souhaite interrompre l'entretien : « Même si tu me réfutes, je ne t'en voudrais pas comme toi tu m'en veux, mais je citerai ton nom en rappelant que tu es le plus grand bienfaiteur (μέγιστος εὐεργέτης) que j'ai eu[70]. » C'est seulement lorsque l'on identifie la connaissance au bien que la réfutation

67. *Gorgias*, 458a2-5 (trad. Canto-Sperber modifiée).

68. Delcomminette 2018, p. 29-51.

69. Sur ce point, Delcomminette estime, en s'appuyant notamment sur le *Parménide* et le *Philèbe*, que pour des philosophes accomplis tels que Socrate, Zénon ou Parménide, la réfutation ne s'accompagne jamais de souffrances, mais provoque un véritable sentiment de plaisir, puisqu'elle correspond ni plus ni moins qu'à la pratique de la dialectique, laquelle est le véritable savoir. De plus, comme les plaisirs de la connaissance sont des plaisirs purs (*Philèbe* 51e7-52b9), il s'ensuit que la pratique de la dialectique, et donc la philosophie, correspond à l'activité la plus authentiquement plaisante qui soit : *cf.* Delcomminette 2018, p. 49-50.

70. *Gorgias*, 506c1-3.

peut devenir plaisante[71]. À l'inverse, si la réfutation peut être perçue comme désagréable, c'est précisément dans la mesure où nous identifions le bien avec le plaisir immédiat. La réfutation nous confronte à notre propre ignorance là où nous croyons savoir, et du même coup, nous force à nous rendre compte de l'importance des objets que nous ignorons.

À ces remarques, l'on peut ajouter avec Radcliffe G. Edmonds III, le seul interprète à notre connaissance à avoir clairement identifié le châtiment et la réfutation, que la réfutation est à la fois dépeinte comme l'examen que les juges pratiquent sur notre âme dans l'Hadès et le remède/châtiment qu'ils prescrivent[72]. En ce sens, les différentes attitudes possibles à l'égard de la réfutation correspondent à celles que l'on peut avoir lors d'un examen médical : 1) l'attitude d'une personne comme Socrate qui sait qu'elle ignore si elle est atteinte ou non d'une maladie, mais qui se soumet de plein gré à l'examen du médecin pour les bienfaits que cela pourrait lui offrir, 2) il y aurait ensuite l'attitude d'une personne qui ignore si elle est atteinte ou non d'une maladie, mais qui accepte néanmoins de se soumettre à l'examen du médecin et de se faire prescrire des remèdes désagréables si cela est nécessaire et 3) l'attitude d'une personne comme Calliclès qui refuse en tout point de se faire examiner par le médecin et même préfère ne pas savoir du tout s'il est atteint ou non d'une maladie. Ainsi, la réfutation ne sera pas perçue comme douloureuse par tous, mais seulement par ceux qui méconnaissent la nature de leurs croyances et les tiennent pour vraies, alors qu'elles sont fausses, de même qu'une personne se croyant en bonne santé, mais étant atteinte d'une maladie, trouvera désagréable le remède qu'on lui prescrit. Si nous affirmons que la réfutation correspond à la fois à l'examen du médecin et au remède qu'il prescrit, ce n'est donc pas seulement le châtiment qui illustre la réfutation dans le mythe final du *Gorgias*, mais le mythe tout entier, car la prescription ou non d'un châtiment ainsi que la nature de celui-ci dépend de la réussite ou de l'échec de l'examen des juges.

Rien n'empêche donc de considérer que la réfutation est la clé qui permet d'interpréter la fonction du châtiment dans l'eschatologie du Gorgias. Bien plus, nous croyons également que cette interprétation du châtiment comme réfutation permet de mieux comprendre le rôle de la figure de l'âme incurable. L'eschatologie du *Gorgias*, en prenant comme fondement une analogie médicale entre le remède prescrit par un médecin et les châtiments infligés

71. Nous soulignons également que même si la réfutation n'est pas nécessairement plaisante aux yeux de tous, elle ne s'accompagne pas nécessairement d'un sentiment d'hostilité. Par exemple, en *Lachès* 188b5, Nicias affirme que pour lui, « il n'y a rien de déplacé ni même de déplaisant (ἀηδὲς) à être mis à l'épreuve par Socrate » et en *Théétète* 161a5-6, Théodore assure Socrate que Théétète n'entrera pas dans une grande colère s'il le réfute et qu'il supportera les critiques à son égard.

72. Edmonds 2012, p. 172-178.

aux âmes injustes, illustre en fin de compte les effets de la réfutation sur notre âme. Si elle permet de guérir certains des maux qui nous rongent au moyen de l'expérience douloureuse de la honte, certaines âmes sont à ce point entachées par l'injustice qu'elles ne pourront trouver aucun profit à se faire réfuter et la réfutation ne pourra servir seulement d'exemple et d'avertissement à ceux présents pour les contempler. Or il ne faut pas oublier que chacun des entretiens que Socrate mène lors du dialogue se fait devant un public, sans parler des lecteurs. Si Gorgias se laisse réfuter sans problème tout en souhaitant que Socrate poursuive sa discussion, Calliclès est réfractaire en tout point à son propre entretien ; son irritation est grandissante jusqu'à ne plus vouloir prendre la parole et il refuse d'admettre les contradictions de son propre discours. En refusant de se laisser réfuter, Calliclès refuse de recevoir le traitement au dérèglement de sa propre âme et l'entretien que Socrate conduit avec lui ressemble davantage à une longue et douloureuse série de refus d'obtempérer qu'à une guérison. Calliclès ne profite en rien de sa discussion avec Socrate, c'est bien plus à son auditoire, mais surtout au lecteur, que ce spectacle bénéficie, car il nous met en garde contre les dangers de vivre sans se soucier de la santé de notre âme.

On l'aura compris, l'eschatologie du *Gorgias* dresse un fort parallèle entre Calliclès et la figure de l'âme incurable. Sur ce point, Edmonds suggère qu'il faut voir une dimension réflexive dans la relation entre Socrate et Calliclès : tous deux se regardent mutuellement comme des cas pathologiques d'un mal nécessitant un traitement radical, soit un mode de vie qui conduirait à sa propre destruction[73]. Cependant, s'il est vrai que Socrate et Calliclès perçoivent chacun dans l'autre un cas désespéré relativement à leur idéal de vie, Calliclès n'utilise pourtant pas le vocabulaire médical que Socrate mobilise tout au long de leur échange. De plus, comme nous l'avons souligné plus haut, le châtiment de l'âme incurable ne peut être interprété à la manière d'un remède précisément du fait qu'elle est incurable. La condition de possibilité de son rétablissement, soit la disposition à se laisser réfuter, a été entièrement anéantie, et ce faisant, opérer la réfutation sur une telle âme ne pourra à chaque fois que lui infliger des douleurs. C'est en ce sens que le châtiment est pour l'âme incurable perpétuel. Encore une fois, l'image du tribunal d'enfants n'est pas anodine, puisqu'elle fait directement allusion au premier monologue de Calliclès où la philosophie est réduite à un simple bavardage, un jeu, que l'on peut admettre de la part de jeunes, mais indigne de l'homme mature. Finalement, l'eschatologie renverse totalement cette perspective. Si *pour Calliclès*, le discours de Socrate n'est rien de plus qu'un mythe, c'est précisément dans la mesure où il perçoit la philosophie comme une activité enfantine, alors que *pour nous*, lecteurs et lectrices du dialogue, le compor-

73. Edmonds 2012, p. 178-182.

tement de l'orateur est à ce point puéril que Socrate se résout à lui raconter, comme à un enfant, un discours plein de violence et d'émotions. Le fait de symboliser la réfutation dans un mythe, plutôt que de conduire à son constat d'échec, ajoute un autre niveau de représentation à la démarche socratique et intensifie la portée de l'exemple présenté par Calliclès.

Conclusion

L'eschatologie du *Gorgias* est un texte somme toute assez court. Le récit de Socrate ne dure qu'environ quatre pages et la description des châtiments, la section la plus longue, n'en occupe qu'un peu plus d'une seule. Malgré sa brièveté, il ne s'agit pas pour autant d'un simple récit qu'il faudrait négliger sous prétexte qu'il n'aurait pas de portée philosophique ou qu'il s'accorderait mal avec les autres eschatologies platoniciennes. Au contraire, nous avons cherché à retranscrire toute la complexité de cette eschatologie dans notre étude en soulignant son perspectivisme, l'analogie médicale qu'elle recèle en ses fondations ainsi que l'étroite intertextualité dont elle fait preuve. En nous narrant son eschatologie, Socrate ne nous demande pas de rester silencieux et de l'écouter comme un enfant écouterait ses grands-parents lui raconter une histoire, mais d'en interroger le sens et les images qu'il mobilise. C'est seulement de cette manière que sous les traits du châtiment, la réfutation apparaîtra à l'œil de celui qui voudra bien la voir.

BIBLIOGRAPHIE

ANNAS, J. 1982 : « Plato's Myth of Judgement », *Phronesis*, 27/2, p. 119-143.

BRICKHOUSE, T.C. & N. D. SMITH 2007 : « The Myth of the Afterlife in Plato's *Gorgias* », dans M. Erler & L. Brisson (éd.), *Gorgias-Menon. Selected Papers from the seventh Symposium Platonicum*, Sankt Augustin, p. 138-143.

BRICKHOUSE, T.C. & N. D. SMITH 2015 : « Socrates on the Emotions », *Plato Journal*, 15, p. 9-28.
DOI: 10.14195/2183-4105_15_1

BRISSON, L. 1997 (trad.) : Platon, *Apologie de Socrate/Criton*, traduction et présentation, Paris.

BRISSON, L. 1982 : *Platon, les mots et les mythes*, Paris (Textes à l'appui : Histoire classique).

BURNET, J. 1968 (éd.) : *Platonis opera*, vol. 3, Oxford, 1968.

CAMBIANO, G. 2013 : « Platon et les rapports entre théorie et *praxis* dans la médecine hippocratique », *Études platoniciennes*, 10, p. 1-14.
DOI: 10.4000/etudesplatoniciennes.351

CANTO-SPERBER, M. 1987 (trad.) : Platon, *Gorgias*, traduction et présentation, Paris.

CORDERO, N. L. 1993 (trad.) : Platon, *Sophiste*, traduction et présentation, Paris.

DELCOMMINETTE, S. 2013 : « La chaîne des vérités », dans E. Moutsopoulos & M. Protapapas-Marneli (éd.), *Plato, Poet and Philosopher. In memory of Ioannis N. Thepodracopoulos, Proceedings of the 3rd International Conference of Philosophy, Magoula-Sparta, 26-29 May 2011*, Athens, p. 135-147.

DELCOMMINETTE, S. 2018 : « Plato on Hatred of Philosophy », *Review of Metaphysics*, 72/1, p. 29-51.

DIXSAUT, M. 2012 : « Myth and Interpretation », dans C. Collobert, P. Destrée & F. J. Gonzalez (éd.), *Plato and Myth: Studies on the Use and Status of Platonic Myths*, Leiden, p. 25-46.

DODDS, E.R. 1959 (trad.) : *Plato. Gorgias*, a revisited text with introduction and commentary, Oxford.

DORION, L.-A. 1990 : « La subversion de *l'elenchos* juridique dans *l'Apologie de Socrate* », *Revue philosophique de Louvain*, 79/88, p. 311-344.
DOI: 10.2143/RPL.88.3.556101

DORION, L.-A. 2018 : « *Enkrateia* et partition de l'âme chez Platon », *Revue de philosophie ancienne*, 36/2, p. 153-213.
DOI: 10.3917/rpha.362.0153

EDMONDS, R.G. III 2012 : « Whip Scars on the Naked Soul: Myth and *Elenchos* in Plato's *Gorgias* », dans C. Collobert, P. Destrée & F. J. Gonzalez (éd), *Plato and Myth : Studies on the Use and Status of Platonic Myths*, Leiden, p. 165-186.

FUSSI, A. 2001 : « The Myth of the Last Judgement in the *Gorgias* », *The Review of Metaphysics*, 54/3 (2001), p. 529-552.

INWOOD, M. 2009 : « Plato's eschatological Myths », dans C. Partenie (éd.), *Plato's Myths*, Cambridge, p. 28-50.

JACKSON, R. & K. LYCOS & H. TARRANT 1998 (trad.) : *Olympiodorus Commentary on Plato's* Gorgia, trans. with full notes, Leiden.

JOUËT-PASTRÉ, E. 2012 : « Quelques réflexions sur le châtiment dans les dialogues platoniciens : le philosophe peut-il justifier le châtiment physique ? », *Pallas*, 88, p. 61-69.
DOI: 10.4000/pallas.2456

LEROUX, G. 2002 (trad.) : Platon, *République*, traduction et présentation, Paris.

LOTT, M. 2012 : « Ignorance, Shame and Love of Truth: Diagnosing the Sophist's Error in Plato's *Sophist* », *Phoenix*, 66/1-2, p. 36-56.
DOI: 10.7834/phoenix.66.1-2.0036

MARCHAND, S. & P. PONCHON 2016 (trad.) : Gorgias *de Platon, suivi de l'*Éloge d'Hélène *de Gorgias*, introduction et traduction, Paris.

MATTÉI, J.-F. 1996 : *Platon et le miroir du mythe : De l'âge d'or à l'Atlantide*, Paris.

MCCOY, M.B. 2013 : *Wounded Heroes: Vulnerability as a Virtue in Ancient Greek Literature and Philosophy*, Oxford, 2013.

MERKER, A. 2004 : « Corps et châtiment chez Platon », *Études Platoniciennes*, 1, p. 11-49.
DOI: 10.4000/etudesplatoniciennes.1116

MIFSUD, J. 1961 : « À propos de la notion de perversion chez Platon : les irrécupérables », *Les études philosophiques*, N.S. 16/3, *Actes du XIe Congrès des Sociétés de Philosophie de Langue Française : la nature humaine (juillet – septembre 1961)*, p. 302-306.

PARTENIE, C. 2009 : « Introduction », dans C. Partenie (éd.), *Plato's Myths*, Cambridge, p. 1-27.

ROWE, C. 2012 : « The Status of the Myth of the *Gorgias*, or: Taking Plato Seriously », dans C. Collobert, P. Destrée & F. J. Gonzalez (éd.), *Plato and Myth : Studies on the Use and Status of Platonic Myths*, Leiden, p. 187-198.

SAUNDERS, T. J. 1973 : « Penology and Eschatology in Plato's *Timaeus* and *Laws* », *The Classical Quarterly*, 23/2, p. 232-244.
DOI: 10.1017/S0009838800036715

SEDLEY, D. 2009 : « Myth, Punishment and Politics in the *Gorgias* », dans C. Partenie (éd.), *Plato's Myths*, Cambridge, p. 51-76.

SEKIMURA, M. 2009 : *Platon et la question des images*, Bruxelles.

LA MORT DE L'ÂME CHEZ PLOTIN ET LE PROBLÈME DE LA REMONTÉE VERS L'INTELLIGIBLE

Camille Guigon
Université Clermont Auvergne
guigoncamille@gmail.com

Résumé. Dans le traité 51 [I, 8] *Que sont les maux et d'où viennent-ils ?*, Plotin évoque la possibilité pour l'âme individuelle de mourir autant qu'elle peut le faire, ce qui prend à contre-pied le principe de l'immortalité de l'âme, qui existe depuis Platon et auquel Plotin souscrit. Dans cet article, nous expliquons à quoi correspond exactement la mort de l'âme et nous décrivons la manière dont cet évènement s'inscrit dans une problématique plus vaste : comment l'âme, après sa chute dans le corps et l'oubli de sa propre nature divine, peut-elle réussir à remonter vers l'intelligible et à s'extraire du sensible ?

Abstract. *In treatise 51 [I, 8], Plotinus declares that the individual soul can die, insofar it can die. This statement is completely contrary to the principle of the immortality of the soul, which has existed since Plato. In this paper, I explain what the death of the soul is. I also describe how this condition inscribes itself into a more important question: How can the soul return to the intelligible world after it has fallen in the body and forgotten its divine nature?*

Philosophie antique, n°24 (2024), 199-225

Introduction*

Dans le chapitre 13 du traité 51 [I 8], *Que sont les maux et d'où viennent-ils ?*, Plotin écrit :

> De ce fait, si l'âme est totalement dans le mal total, elle n'a plus de mal en elle, mais elle a échangé sa nature contre une autre pire : car le vice mélangé à son contraire est encore humain. Elle meurt, autant qu'elle puisse mourir[1]. (51 [I 8], 13, 18-21)

Cette possibilité de la mort de l'âme se heurte aux multiples affirmations par Plotin de son immortalité, ne serait-ce que dans le chapitre 11 du même traité où il démontre l'absurdité de l'hypothèse selon laquelle l'âme pourrait être privée de toute vie :

> Si l'âme est privée du bien, si la privation cause du mal en l'âme selon la définition de celle-ci, l'âme n'aura rien de bien. De ce fait, même si elle est une âme elle n'aura pas la vie. Ce sera donc une âme inanimée, puisqu'elle n'est pas en vie : de sorte que l'âme ne sera pas une âme [2].(51 [I 8], 11, 10-14)

* Tous nos remerciements vont à Alexandra Michalewski, à Jean-François Pradeau, ainsi qu'aux relecteurs anonymes. Leurs remarques ont grandement contribué à l'amélioration de cet article.

1. Ἐπεὶ καὶ εἰ παντελῶς εἴη ἡ ψυχὴ εἰς παντελῆ κακίαν, οὐκέτι κακίαν ἔχει, ἀλλ' ἑτέραν φύσιν τὴν χείρω ἠλλάξατο· ἔτι γὰρ ἀνθρωπικὸν ἡ κακία μεμιγμένη τινὶ ἐναντίῳ. Ἀποθνῄσκει οὖν, ὡς ψυχὴ ἂν θάνοι. Toutes les traductions de Plotin dans cet article sont les nôtres. Pour le texte en grec ancien, nous suivons l'édition de référence par P. Henry et H. R. Schwyzer.

2. Ἀλλ' εἰ ἡ στέρησις ἐπιβάλλοντός ἐστι παρεῖναι εἴδους τινός, εἰ τοῦ ἀγαθοῦ στέρησις ἐν ψυχῇ, τὴν δὲ κακίαν ἐν αὐτῇ ποιεῖ τῷ λόγῳ τῷ ἑαυτῆς, ἡ ψυχὴ οὐδὲν ἔχει ἀγαθόν· οὐ τοίνυν οὐδὲ ζωὴν οὖσα ψυχή. Ἄψυχον ἄρα ἔσται ἡ ψυχή, εἴπερ μηδὲ ζωήν· ὥστε ψυχὴ οὖσα οὐκ ἔσται ψυχή. Sur l'immortalité de l'âme, le traité le plus important est le traité 2 [IV 7]. Voir aussi O'Brien 1997, p. 39-103 et surtout Chiaradonna 2015, qui démontre comment Plotin identifie la vie et l'être à l'âme (p. 162-167).

L'hypothèse d'une mort de l'âme, même si elle ne peut pas être un anéantissement définitif de cette dernière qui est vie par nature[3], constitue donc un problème du point de vue de la cohérence de la doctrine de Plotin. Si la mort de l'âme doit donc s'entendre dans un sens nécessairement métaphorique, l'emploi d'une telle expression doit être questionné.

> Mais ce texte se double d'une autre difficulté, à savoir le lien entre mort de l'âme et nécessité de la remontée de cette même âme vers l'intelligible dont elle est issue : Sa mort, quand elle est noyée dans le corps, est de plonger dans la matière, de s'en remplir [...], jusqu'à ce qu'elle éloigne et détourne le regard de ce bourbier. (51 [I 8], 13, 22-25)

La remontée a donc un caractère irrémédiable, qui est obligatoire pour toute âme, même pour les âmes qui ont chuté aussi bas, ce qui soulève un problème supplémentaire : comment l'âme peut-elle effectuer la remontée vers l'intelligible si elle est encore pleine du vice qui l'a faite tomber[4] ?

Selon nous, ce passage sur la mort de l'âme sert avant tout un objectif éthique : toutes les âmes, quelle que soit leur situation dans le monde sensible, doivent se détourner de lui et revenir à l'intelligible[5].

Pour démontrer cette théorie, nous allons d'abord nous demander ce que cela signifie pour l'âme de mourir dans la pensée plotinienne. Puis, nous verrons pourquoi la mort de l'âme est intrinsèquement liée à la possibilité du retour dans l'intelligible. Enfin, nous expliquerons comment ce retour est possible.

3. Sur la vie (ζώη) comme nature de l'âme, voir 2 [IV 7] : 2, 5 ; 11, 8 ; 22 [VI 4] : 14, 7 ; 16, 12 ; 23 [VI 5] : 9, 12 ; 26 [III 6] : 7, 7 ; 29 [IV 5] : 6, 28 ; 38 [VI 7] : 4, 33 ; 11, 11 ; 12, 21 ; 20, 9 ; 12 ; 23, 19 ; 43 [VI 2] : 7, 2 ; 47 [III 2] : 7, 35 ; 49 [V 3] : 8, 28 ; 51 [I 8] : 2, 6 ; 53 [I 1] : 13, 6. Cette identification existe déjà chez Platon, notamment dans le *Phèdre* (Bett 2008, p. 427-432) et le *Phédon* où Platon décrit l'âme comme immortelle car elle est un mouvement qui ne cesse jamais. Le mouvement est identifié par Platon à la vie, que ce soit le mouvement spatial que manifeste l'animal vivant comme le mouvement psychologique de l'âme. L'âme ne peut donc pas mourir car elle ne cesse jamais de penser. Comme l'explique D. Bostock, le terme de grec de ψυχή désigne d'abord ce qui a la vie en général, en opposition à ce qui en est privé (Bostock 2008, p. 405-407). Pour une analyse des arguments sur l'immortalité de l'âme dans le *Phédon*, voir notamment Bostock 2008, p. 422-424. Voir aussi O'Meara 1999, p. 153.

4. Le problème existe déjà dans le *Timée* de Platon : comment les âmes qui ont chuté dans des corps animaux et surtout, dans les corps aquatiques qui sont privés de la vision de la lumière et du ciel (*cf. Timée*, 92a7-c1), peuvent-elles remonter l'échelle des réincorporations ? Sur le rôle des espèces animales dans le *Timée*, voir le commentaire de Francis Cornford à sa traduction du *Timée* (Cornford 1997, p. 292, 355), ainsi que Brisson 1998, p. 255-257.

5. Sur le détail du processus de la remontée éthique chez Plotin, voir notamment Trouillard 2011 et Ménard 2019.

I – Le sens de la mort de l'âme dans le traité 51 [I 8]

> De ce fait, si l'âme est complètement dans le mal total, elle n'a plus de mal en elle, mais elle a échangé sa nature contre une autre pire : car le vice mélangé à son contraire est encore humain. Elle meurt, autant que l'âme puisse mourir, et sa mort, quand elle est noyée dans le corps, est de plonger [καταδῦναι] dans la matière, de s'en remplir [πλησθῆναι] et, hors du corps, de se situer [κεῖσθαι] là, jusqu'à ce qu'elle éloigne et détourne le regard de ce bourbier : c'est cela la venue dans l'Hadès pour y dormir[6]. (51 [I 8], 13, 18-26)

1) La mort de l'âme durant l'incorporation

Pour traiter de la première forme de mort, nous allons nous référer à un extrait du texte que nous venons de citer : « Sa mort, quand elle est noyée [βεβαπτισμένῃ] dans le corps, est de plonger [καταδῦναι] dans la matière, de s'en remplir [πλησθῆναι] » (51 [I 8], 13, 22-23). Quand l'âme est dite être immergée dans le corps, cela signifie qu'elle incline son attention vers son corps, comme le montre l'usage de βαπτίζειν qui sert par exemple à désigner l'insertion de l'âme dans le corps[7]. Dans le cas qui nous occupe, l'âme menacée par la mort s'identifie donc profondément à son propre corps[8]. Cette situation mauvaise d'un point de vue éthique ne fera que s'aggraver, puisqu'elle plonge dans la matière, nous dit Plotin, et s'emplit d'elle[9]. Le verbe καταδύειν apparaît aussi dans le traité 1 [I 6], *Sur le beau*, pour décrire la plongée dans l'obscurité pour ceux qui n'arrivent pas à détourner leur attention du corps et du désir sexuel[10]. Quant à πλησθῆναι, Plotin ne l'emploie que rarement dans le sens psychologique. Cependant, dans le traité 6 [IV 8], *Sur la descente de l'âme dans les corps*, il évoque l'âme qui se remplit de plaisirs, de désirs et de chagrins[11]. On peut donc en déduire que Plotin, comme nous l'avons dit, décrit ici l'identification de l'âme à son corps. Il y aurait donc une première mort, durant l'incorporation, qui serait pour l'âme de considérer que son être se réduit au corps.

6. Ἐπεὶ καὶ εἰ παντελῶς εἴη ἡ ψυχὴ εἰς παντελῆ κακίαν, οὐκέτι κακίαν ἔχει, ἀλλ' ἑτέραν φύσιν τὴν χείρω ἠλλάξατο· ἔτι γὰρ ἀνθρωπικὸν ἡ κακία μεμιγμένη τινὶ ἐναντίῳ. Ἀποθνῄσκει οὖν, ὡς ψυχὴ ἂν θάνοι, καὶ ὁ θάνατος αὐτῇ καὶ ἔτι ἐν τῷ σώματι βεβαπτισμένῃ ἐν ὕλῃ ἐστὶ καταδῦναι καὶ πλησθῆναι αὐτῆς καὶ ἐξελθούσῃ ἐκεῖ κεῖσθαι, ἕως ἀναδράμῃ καὶ ἀφέλῃ πως τὴν ὄψιν ἐκ τοῦ βορβόρου· καὶ τοῦτό ἐστι τὸ ἐν Ἅιδου ἐλθόντα ἐπικαταδαρθεῖν.

7. *Cf.* 9 [VI 9], 8, 18.

8. *Cf.* 1 [I 6], 5, 36 ; 53 [I 1], 4, 3.

9. « Il s'agit d'une véritable descente aux enfers, une participation croissante de l'âme au Mal absolu, qui fait que l'âme devient le mal [...], de sorte qu'il n'y a plus de mélange de vertu et de vice en elle, mais seulement le vice total » (O'Meara 1999, p. 152-153).

10. *Cf.* 1 [I 6], 8, 14.

11. *Cf.* 6 [IV 8], 2, 44-45. On peut penser ici au *Phédon* (66c2-4), où Platon décrit la façon dont le corps nous remplit de désirs, de peurs, d'appétits, etc.

Cette idée est approfondie par Plotin dans un passage du chapitre 14 du traité 51 [I 8] :

> La chute de l'âme est de venir dans la matière et de s'y affaiblir [ἀσθενεῖν], parce que toutes ses facultés ne sont pas présentes en acte, la matière entravant leur présence car elle occupe le lieu dans lequel l'âme est descendue et elle fait comme se contracter [συσπειραθῆναι] cette dernière, car elle rend mauvais ce qu'elle prend par une sorte de vol [κλέψασα], jusqu'à ce que l'âme puisse remonter. (51 [I 8], 14, 44-49)

La matière affaiblit l'âme. La faiblesse est définie par Plotin comme l'incapacité, pour une chose, d'accomplir la fonction qui est la sienne[12]. L'âme est affaiblie par « la présence [...] d'un élément étranger » en elle, dont elle ne s'est pas purifiée[13]. Cet élément étranger ne peut être que le corps qui, en particularisant l'activité de l'âme, n'actualise qu'un nombre restreint de ses facultés[14]. En effet, on sait que le corps n'utilise de l'âme que ce qui sert ses besoins, ce qui signifie que d'autres facultés psychologiques restent en puissance car il n'a pas d'utilité à les employer[15]. Mais surtout, le corps empêche l'âme d'actualiser correctement certaines de ses facultés, à commencer par la raison et l'intellect individuel. Puisque l'âme est contrainte de s'occuper constamment du corps, qui est toujours menacé par son environnement et qui a des besoins multiples, elle doit se tourner vers le sensible la plupart du temps et elle doit, de ce fait, interrompre sans cesse sa contemplation. Le terme de rapt (κλέπτειν), quant à lui, fait écho à un passage de la *République* où Socrate dit que ceux qui sont privés de l'opinion véritable le sont par une forme de rapt (κλαπέντες), puisqu'ils ne peuvent pas accepter volontairement d'avoir des opinions fausses. Comme Glaucon ne comprend pas la métaphore, Socrate précise que certaines personnes sont persuadées par d'autres que leur connaissance de la vérité est fausse, bien qu'elles aient raison, ou qu'elles sont conduites à l'oubli du fait du passage du temps[16]. L'absence d'enseignement philosophique, l'influence des sophistes ou des gens corrompus expliquent l'apparition d'opinions fausses, à l'insu de ceux qui en sont victimes. Si l'on retourne au texte de Plotin, cela signifie que la matière détourne l'âme de la vérité, en la forçant à s'intéresser au corps.

Mais l'affaiblissement de l'âme par la matière n'a pas que des conséquences éthiques. La nature de l'âme étant la vie, sa première fonction est d'animer les corps sensibles, et plus particulièrement les corps humains[17].

12. *Cf.* 51 [I 8], 14, 10-11.

13. *Cf.* 51 [I 8], 24.

14. Les concepts d'activité et de puissance doivent s'entendre dans le sens aristotélicien. Voir sur ce point Dufour 2004, p. 193-218.

15. *Cf.* 27 [IV 3], 22, 10-11.

16. *Cf.* Platon, *République*, IV, 413a9-b7.

17. Le fait que l'âme soit faite pour donner la vie en premier lieu, et donc doive s'incorporer, est d'abord mis en avant par Platon dans le *Timée*, où les âmes immortelles sont

En effet, pour Plotin, le corps humain est le meilleur qui soit pour l'âme : « Étant pure et avant d'être corrompue, elle veut donc être homme et elle est homme, car c'est le plus beau et elle produit ce qui est le plus beau » (38 [VI 7], 6, 24-26)[18]. La corruption est liée à l'injustice (ἀδίκη) et à l'irrationalité (ἄλογον)[19]. Sachant que la justice (δικαιοσύνη) consiste en ce que chaque chose accomplisse la tâche qui lui est propre[20], on en déduit logiquement que l'injustice correspond au fait de sortir de l'ordre établi par la loi, et notamment par la loi cosmologique.

Puisque la justice comme vertu exige que notre âme soit dirigée par sa raison (λόγος) et son intellect (νοῦς)[21], l'injustice consiste donc en une soumission aux affections et à ce qui est irrationnel[22]. Mais pour que l'âme aille dans un corps humain, elle doit actualiser en premier lieu sa raison :

> L'homme étant homme quand il est en accord avec son âme rationnelle, quand nous réfléchissons, c'est le *nous* qui réfléchit, les raisonnements étant les opérations de l'âme[23]. (53 [I 1], 7, 21-24)

produites par le démiurge pour permettre au sensible d'imiter l'intelligible grâce à l'existence de toutes les espèces vivantes mortelles. Le fait que les âmes finissent d'ailleurs par commettre l'erreur de s'identifier à leur corps permet l'émergence des espèces animales inférieures à l'homme : « *Their forms are regarded as degraded types, for the sake of the mythical doctrine of punishment by transmigration, announced to the souls before their first birth at 42C. [...] The closing sentence observes that, with the formation of the three lower kinds of animal, the World has now become what the Demiurge set out to make: the unique visible image of its model, namely, 'that (intelligible) Living Creature which embraces and contains within itself all the intelligible living creatures, just as this (visible) world contains ourselves and all other creatures that have been formed as things visible' (30C)* » (Cornford 1997, p. 358-359).

18. Καθαρὰ μὲν οὖν οὖσα καὶ πρὶν κακυνθῆναι ἄνθρωπον θέλει καὶ ἄνθρωπός ἐστι· καὶ γὰρ κάλλιον τοῦτο, καὶ τὸ κάλλιον ποιεῖ.

19. *Cf.* 47 [III 2], 4, 23 ; 8, 11.

20. *Cf.* 19 [I 2], 6, 19. La définition est la même chez Platon (*cf. République*, IV, 434d7-10 ; 435b9-c2). « *Plotinus explicitly describes the justice governing the descend of souls as set in nature (en physei) or in the nature of beings (en tois ousi). In this way, justice constitutes an essential aspect of nature. It is so to speak inscribed into "the law of nature". Providence, therefore, reveals not only the benevolence of nature, but also its justice* » (Song 2009, p. 42). Voir aussi Dragona-Monachou 1994, p. 4476-4486 et Noble 2022, p. 389.

21. *Cf.* 19 [I 2], 3, 18.

22. « *This means that, conversely, the need for survival in a violent context can be treated less as a nuisance than as a first criterion to assess whether a soul properly rules its body. Of course, to fare well in the world, whether in peace or war, is by no means sufficient to achieve any kind of serenity: undue attachment to the body's affections or possessions inevitably leads to worry and unease. Nonetheless, without first a strict training, there is no point in considering any spiritual progress through care of the soul. Every war is ultimately an effect of Providence, which tends to lead every soul to improvement* » (Tresnie 2021, p. 74).

23. Συνδρόμου γὰρ ὄντος τοῦ ἀνθρώπου τῇ λογικῇ ψυχῇ, ὅταν λογιζώμεθα, ἡμεῖς λογιζόμεθα τῷ τοὺς λογισμοὺς ψυχῆς εἶναι ἐνεργήματα. Voir aussi Laurent 1999, p. 88-89 ; Girard 2023, p. 18 ; 282 ; 305-307 et Aubry 2008, p. 108-125.

L'âme plotinienne n'actualise pas toutes ses facultés de la même façon, il y en a toujours une qui domine et cette faculté dominante détermine le type d'incorporation[24]. L'incorporation humaine implique que la raison soit la faculté principale de l'âme individuelle[25].

Or, quand on lit le texte tiré du chapitre 13 du traité 51 [I 8], il est clairement fait référence à ce qui est humain : « Mais elle a échangé sa nature contre une autre pire : car le vice mélangé à son contraire est encore humain [ἀνθρωπικὸν] ». Ce que sous-entend le texte est que la nature de l'âme ici est une nature humaine, qu'elle viendrait à perdre du fait de sa corruption et de sa soumission aux affections de son corps. L'incarnation humaine n'en est qu'une parmi d'autres pour l'âme plotinienne, qui pourrait aller tout autant dans un animal que dans une plante, sachant bien sûr que l'incorporation n'est pas le meilleur état qui soit, l'âme pure (καθαρά) étant libre de tout corps[26]. Cependant, pour l'âme qui vient à s'incorporer, le corps humain est ce qui est le plus à l'image de son caractère intelligible et intellectuel. En effet, quand Plotin dit que le corps humain est ce qu'il y a de plus beau, il ne pense pas forcément à des critères esthétiques.

La beauté est d'abord une des caractéristiques de l'Intellect[27]. En effet, l'Intellect possède les formes qui vont s'imposer à la matière[28]. Là où la laideur est causée par l'absence de figure et de forme, la beauté implique l'organisation de la matière par l'imposition des λόγοι, c'est-à-dire des formules rationnelles[29]. La formule rationnelle ou λόγος est un terme technique de la

24. *Cf.* 15 [III 4], 3, 2-3. Le fait qu'une faculté soit dominante en chaque âme est important pour déterminer le type d'incorporation, ainsi que le concept de δαίμων qui est défini, dans le traité 15 [III 4], *Sur le* δαίμων *qui nous a reçus en partage*, comme la faculté qui est au-dessus de la faculté dominante en l'âme (*ibid.*, 4-5). Par exemple, si la sensation est la faculté dominante, la raison sera le δαίμων (*ibid.*, 5-6). « Dans cette perspective, la notion de δαίμων ne désigne plus une réalité spécifique, mais un rapport de subordination, elle est une notion relative, sans contenu préétabli » (Timotin 2012, p. 295). Voir aussi Vidart 2018, p. 7-10.

25. « Plotin développe cette conception dans un système de correspondances symétriques entre la faculté prédominante (rationnelle, sensitive, végétative) et les trois espèces de réincarnations (hommes, animaux, plantes » (Timotin 2012, p. 292).

26. *Cf.* 1 [I 6], 6, 14 ; 27 [IV 3], 24, 21; 51 [I 8], 4, 26 ; 54 [I 7], 4, 28.

27. *Cf.* 1 [I 6], 9, 17.

28. « *For him, the accord itself between the intelligible form and the sensible form is regarded as beauty, whereas Plato considers intelligible beauty to be a form among other intelligible forms. So Plotinus affirms that participation in intelligible forms causes beauty and that sensible things at which intelligible forms do not arrive remain ugly* » (Sekimura 2019, p. 247).

29. *Cf.* 1 [I 6], 2, 13-17. « *These lines refer to matter which for Plotinus is without any form; nor is it simply some thing without or deprived of form, but is privation itself. For this reason, it is complete ugliness. The following lines refer to bodies, that is, combinations of matter and some form—not capable of supporting complete shaping by the form; and these too are ugly insofar as they only partially share in form [...] The words "shape"* (morphe*), form (*eidos*), and "reason principle" (*logos*) have each a slightly different nuance. Shape has more the connotation of what is manifest or perceptible, "form" in the present context is the standard Platonic notion*

pensée plotinienne, qui désigne le déploiement de l'activité en puissance dans les formes intelligibles[30]. Pour le dire autrement, les λόγοι correspondent aux formes intelligibles au niveau de l'âme[31] : « Les *logoi*, ce sont les Formes au niveau de l'Âme »[32]. En effet, cette dernière est incapable de saisir intégralement les formes dans leur unité. Elle est obligée de les diviser selon les parties présentes en puissance en elles, division qui engendre donc les λόγοι[33]. Les λόγοι permettent donc à l'âme de garder un lien avec l'intelligible, notamment par sa raison. Si l'âme individuelle peut aller dans un beau corps comme celui de l'homme, c'est-à-dire ordonné et proportionné, à l'image de l'Intellect, c'est parce qu'elle est elle-même belle, car elle est capable d'accéder à l'intelligible. Mais l'âme peut être aussi laide[34]. Cette laideur consiste en l'obsession de l'âme pour le corps, ce qui va peu à peu limiter son utilisation des facultés, comme l'explique l'extrait du chapitre 14 du traité 51 [I 8]. La matière empêche l'âme de réaliser sa nature rationnelle du fait de la fascination exercée par le corps et de ce fait, l'âme s'étant enlaidie, elle devra s'incorporer dans un vivant à l'image de cette laideur.

Non seulement l'âme oublie son origine intelligible du fait de l'incorporation, mais sa raison est à son tour dominée par des facultés inférieures, comme la sensation et l'appétit. D'où l'émergence du mal total dans l'extrait du chapitre 13 du traité 51 [I 8]. Le mal n'est pas causé uniquement par la mauvaise action dans les traités plotiniens. Il est aussi une des dénominations de la matière[35]. Dire que la matière est le mal s'entend dans le sens de

of Form, whether viewed as immanent or transcendent, while logos *has a wide range of meanings, including "reason", "argument", "expression". In this context, as so often, it has a meaning* » (Smith 2016, p. 74-75).

30. « Forme formatrice, formule, force, déroulement, déploiement (= discours) de la nécessité intelligible contenu dans la Forme, telles sont les différentes notions impliquées dans l'idée plotinienne de *logoi*. Comment, pour traduire une notion si riche, trouver un mot qui puisse laisser entendre en même temps toutes ces nuances ? » (Hadot 1988 p. 215). Cette notion a par ailleurs une origine stoïcienne (Witt 1931; Fattal 1998, p. 34 ; Brisson 1999, p. 87-89).

31. « Ce *logos* est non seulement suspendu à l'Un, il est également le produit de l'intelligence (V 1 [10] 7, 42) et représente le déploiement et déroulement des formes intelligibles dans l'âme (III 5 [50] 9, 1-57). Issu à la fois de l'intelligence et de l'âme (III 2 [47], 16, 10-17), constitutif de l'âme universelle, il incarne la raison universelle dirigeant et gouvernant toutes choses (IV 3 [27] 10, 10-11 ; 16, 5-25)» (Fattal 1998, p. 20-21). Voir aussi Leroux 1992, p. 251-252 ; Fattal 2016, p. 35 ; 41.

32. Brisson 1999, p. 89. Voir aussi Fattal 2016, p. 47.

33. « Alors que, dans l'Intellect, les Formes intelligibles se trouvent *homou panta* "toutes ensemble" dans la simultanéité absolue, dans l'Âme hypostase elles se présentent sous une forme discursive, séparées les unes des autres, à la façon précisément dont elles apparaissent sur le plan de la pensée dans un raisonnement et sur le plan de la parole dans une phrase, dans un discours » (Brisson 1999, p. 93).

34. *Cf.* 1 [I 6], 2, 13-17. Voir aussi Gurtler 1997, p. 221-222.

35. « *Accordingly, primary evil consists in privation. In this special case, privation is not privation of a particular quality but total privation. However, since Plotinus speaks not just of*

privation du Bien, c'est-à-dire de l'Un et plus généralement, de l'être[36]. La matière est l'absolu non-être, elle est une privation de tout et ne retient rien de l'être qui est projeté sur elle[37]. Si l'Un est au-delà de l'être, la matière est en-deçà de l'être. Mais comme on le voit dans le texte du traité 51 [I 8], le mal de la matière n'est pas étranger au mal éthique[38]. En effet, plus l'âme est fascinée par le corps qui n'existe pas sans la matière, plus elle s'identifie à lui, plus sa raison est dominée par des facultés inférieures, c'est-à-dire par toutes les facultés qui sont en priorité tournées vers le fonctionnement du corps, comme la sensation. Pour Plotin, la nature humaine implique du vice mêlé de vertu, dans le sens où une âme incorporée a pour obligation de prendre soin de son corps. Même si cette implication peut être tout à fait minime, comme le permet le travail de détachement de l'âme qu'autorise la pratique de la vertu, le corps a toujours des besoins dont seule l'âme peut se charger. Cependant, l'âme peut aussi s'occuper de son corps tout en passant une majeure partie de son temps tournée vers l'intelligible[39]. L'âme qui a quelque chose d'humain a encore la capacité de se libérer du sensible, d'où le fait que le vice ne soit que partiel pour elle.

Mais le vice total, en revanche, implique une complète absorption de l'attention de l'âme vers le corps, le sensible et donc la matière qui les sous-tend[40]. L'activité de la raison discursive devient minimale, l'homme

absence but uses the technical term 'privation', he is envisaging the absence of something that should be there. And what should be there is form – not any particular form but form in general. In other words, primary evil consists in the rejection of form in general. It is the incapacity to accept any form and any goodness whatsoever. This is, as it were, the substance of evil » (Opsomer 2022, p. 345).

36. Rist 1963, p. 154-166 ; O'Brien 1969, p. 211-220.

37. « Plotin montre en effet que la matière est privée de tout : elle est incorporelle, sans qualité, sans grandeur ; elle ne possède ni pesanteur, ni densité, ni rareté, ni configuration, ni couleur, ni chaleur, ni froideur. Il ne faut lui ajouter aucune détermination » (Dufour 2006, p. 231). En cela, Plotin s'inspire du *Timée* de Platon : « Platon lui donne plusieurs noms : ce matériau est le porte-empreinte de toutes choses, un réceptacle, une mère, une nourrice. Ce réceptacle ne perd jamais la nature qui est la sienne. Même s'il reçoit en lui toutes choses, il ne prend jamais aucune des caractéristiques de ce qu'il reçoit et il ne ressemble à rien de ce qui entre en lui. Il permet simplement à des imitations des réalités éternelles d'apparaître en lui. Platon insiste sur le fait que le matériau ne possède aucune forme et ne retient aucune de celles qui viennent en lui. Dans le cas contraire, en effet, la nature propre du matériau l'empêcherait de bien recevoir les choses qu'il accueille » (*Ibid.*). Voir aussi Opsomer 2022, p. 341 ; 345.

38. « *The badness of the soul comes in two main types: moral failure or wickedness (ponēria), with its subspecies (1.8.5.17–18), and cognitive failures, which are either false perceptual representations or false beliefs (1.8.15.18–22). Wickedness is due to appetites, bouts of anger, fears, pains, which mostly originate in cognitive acts, thus belonging to the body–soul complex (1.8.15.14–18)* » (Opsomer 2022, p. 343).

39. Selon Porphyre, c'était l'attitude de Plotin lui-même qui ne mangeait et ne dormait que rarement (Porphyre, *Vie de Plotin* 8, 11-15).

40. La matière n'est pas accessible en elle-même. Sur les modalités de la connaissance de la matière par l'âme, voir Fauquier 2003, p. 66-71.

s'identifiant seulement à son corps et le sensible lui paraissant être la seule réalité possible. Un tableau concret du vice total nous est par exemple fourni dans le traité 50 [III 5], *Sur l'amour* :

> Ceux qui sont incapables d'engendrer selon la loi et la nature, ayant suivi d'abord une voie selon la nature, s'écartent des principes comme s'ils glissaient hors de la route, ils gisent sans savoir ni où l'amour, le désir de la génération et l'usage des belles images devaient les conduire, ni ce qu'est le beau en soi. (50 [III 5], 1, 50-55)

Ce texte nous paraît intéressant puisqu'il précède chronologiquement le traité 51 [I 8], ce qui invite à penser qu'il pourrait exister un lien argumentatif entre les deux traités. Selon nous, ce passage sur l'amour contre-nature est une illustration du mal total. En effet, Plotin considère que soit l'âme est capable de s'appuyer sur la beauté sensible pour remonter vers l'intelligible, soit elle utilise cette beauté sensible pour gagner une immortalité par l'espèce grâce à la reproduction. En revanche, l'amour contre-nature englobe les pratiques sexuelles qui ne permettent pas la reproduction[41]. Dans l'esprit de Plotin, c'est un état psychologique assez grave, car notre âme individuelle est normalement guidée par l'âme végétative lorsqu'il s'agit des besoins fondamentaux du vivant[42]. Si l'on pratique un acte sexuel contre-nature, cela signifie que l'âme végétative elle-même, qui est issue de la partie basse de l'âme du monde[43], ne peut pas effectuer sa fonction propre, du fait du désordre présent en l'âme individuelle qui finit par la gangréner également. L'homme n'est plus capable d'identifier l'intelligible qui peut être présent dans le sensible et il n'est pas non plus protégé du vice par son âme végétative

41. « *It follows that a further factor is needed if one is to be able to distinguish deviant eros not only from mixed eros but, perhaps more importantly, also from pure eros. This factor is the soul's attitude toward sensible beauty understood as an image of the archetypal Beauty of Intellect. In the case of pure eros the attitude is contemplation, while in the case of deviant eros it is an immoderate abandonment to pleasure (iii.5 [50] 1.38) resulting in the soul's inability both to recognize the desire to procreate and to use images of Beauty to recollect Beauty itself (iii.5 [50] 1.53–55)* » (Bertozzi 2021, p. 157). Ces amours contre-nature n'enveloppent pas que l'homosexualité, mais impliquent aussi l'adultère, le viol, etc. En d'autres termes, tout ce qui vise le plaisir pour lui-même, au lieu de le considérer comme un simple accompagnant de l'acte reproductif (Hadot 1990, p. 160; p. 231-232).

42. Sur les facultés et le rôle de l'âme végétative, voir par exemple Emilsson 2017, p. 229-235.

43. « C'est de la partie principale de l'âme, c'est-à-dire que c'est de l'âme universelle que l'âme végétative et génératrice reçoit son pouvoir de production. C'est parce que l'âme de l'univers a contemplé les idées, qu'elle communique à l'âme végétative et génératrice son pouvoir de production (II 3 [52] 18, 9-16). [...] L'âme de l'univers, dit Plotin, doit contempler les êtres excellents qui sont les idées. Une fois qu'elle s'en remplit, il "naît d'elle une *image* (*indalma*), qui est à sa limite inférieure ; cette image est la puissance productrice (*to poioun*) des choses, elle est la dernière des puissances productives" (II 3 [52] 18, 12-13) » (Fattal 1998, p. 25-26). Voir aussi Caluori 2015, p. 112-119 ; 185-192.

qui possède en elle les lois de la nature[44]. La conséquence en est alors la mort de l'âme durant l'incorporation.

La mort de l'âme peut donc être définie, pour ce qui est de l'incorporation, comme une identification complète de l'âme au corps et au sensible. Mais comme l'indique l'extrait du chapitre 13 du traité 51 [I 8], la mort de l'âme a aussi des répercussions sur son sort après la mort du corps.

2) La mort de l'âme après l'incorporation

D'après le chapitre 13, la mort de l'âme consiste, après la fin du corps, à « se situer [κεῖσθαι] là, jusqu'à ce qu'elle éloigne et détourne le regard de ce bourbier : c'est cela la venue dans l'Hadès pour y dormir ». Ce passage paraît assez énigmatique, notamment du fait du verbe κεῖσθαι, qui peut signifier le fait d'être quelque part, de se situer à un endroit ou dans une hiérarchie, mais aussi le fait de rester étendu et immobile. Ce deuxième sens est notamment retenu par L. Lavaud et L. P. Gerson dans leur traduction respective[45]. Dans la note 204 à sa traduction du traité 51 [I 8], L. Lavaud explique que cette seconde mort est « une mort physique où l'âme se sépare du corps et reste "étendue" là, avant de remonter »[46]. Mais comment définir cet état de l'âme ? À quoi correspond-il concrètement ? Faut-il l'entendre comme une prostration de l'âme, qui n'arrive plus à réaliser sa fonction propre, c'est-à-dire animer un corps ?

La référence que fait Plotin à la *République* de Platon peut nous aider. En effet, on lit dans le livre VII de la *République* la description suivante :

> S'il [celui qui ne sait pas reconnaître le Bien] se lie à une image [εἰδώλον], il le fera par l'opinion, non par la science, et rêvant comme s'il était

44. « *The World-Soul creates and administers the physical cosmos as a whole by communicating the logoi in its rational part to its non-rational part, nature (phusis). Finally, Plotinus takes the execution of 'laws of fate', which determine rewards and punishments for souls on the basis of their past actions, to be integral to the divine administration of the cosmos. Plotinus appears to identify fate with the lowest part of providence, that is, nature* (phusis) (3.3.5.14–20) » (Noble 2022, p. 389). Voir aussi Wildberg 2009, p. 134.

45. L. P. Gerson traduit : « *To lie there until it should turn away* ».

46. M. Aubineau commente ainsi le même passage : « Bourbier obscur, région de dissemblance, Mal en soi, autant d'expressions qui désignent la matière où l'âme tombe, se plonge, s'enfonce jusqu'à satiété si elle s'abandonne à son inclination vers en bas. Non pas la matière aristotélicienne, mais le terme ultime de la procession où l'âme irradie ses formes, sans qu'il cesse d'être indétermination absolue : bref, le non-être, l'altérité à l'état pur. Oublieuse d'elle-même, l'âme peut se matérialiser au point de s'aliéner dans une passivité, une dispersion, une différence totale : un reniement de soi, une mort ! » (Aubineau 1959, p. 194). L'idée du reniement de soi nous semble très intéressante : l'âme oublie sa nature divine et intelligible et pense qu'elle est son corps. Elle rejette donc ce qu'elle est vraiment pour se confondre avec cet être qui lui est pourtant éminemment inférieur d'un point de vue ontologique.

> endormi sa vie de maintenant, avant même de se réveiller ici-bas, il s'endort [ἐπικαταδαρθᾶνειν] ensuite définitivement dans l'Hadès après y être venu.[47]

La métaphore du rêve est ici évidente. Celui qui n'utilise que sa sensation pour connaître, croyant que seul le monde sensible est réel, n'est pas capable de se détourner du corps auquel il s'identifie. Il s'ensuit qu'il reste, durant sa vie incorporée, dans une sorte de rêve, puisqu'il vit dans un monde qui n'est que la copie de la réalité[48]. N'ayant pu se réveiller durant cette vie, il sombrera dans un sommeil définitif dans l'Hadès. Mais le rêve ne signifie pas uniquement que l'âme de celui qui ne connaît pas le bien vit dans une illusion. Toujours dans la *République*, Platon précise que, quand nous dormons, seule notre raison est inactive. En revanche, l'ἐπιθυμία reste éveillée et profite parfois de ce relâchement du λόγος pour exprimer ses désirs délirants, ce qui explique pourquoi nos rêves peuvent parfois être immoraux[49]. Dans le cas du sommeil dans l'Hadès, on peut utiliser une explication similaire : celui qui ne bénéficie pas du discours philosophique reste aussi dominé par son ἐπιθυμία et n'est pas capable d'employer son λόγος, sinon il serait conduit à reconnaître le caractère illusoire du monde dans lequel il vit.

Cette métaphore du sommeil est reprise par Plotin dans le traité 32 [V 5], *Sur l'intellect et que les intelligibles ne sont pas hors de l'intellect, et sur le Bien* :

> C'est comme si des hommes qui avaient dormi durant leur vie comprenaient les choses dans leur rêve comme fiables et évidentes, et si l'un se réveillait, après avoir ouvert les yeux, il ne croira pas ce qu'il voit et se rendormira de nouveau. (32 [V 5], 11, 19-22)[50]

On comprend bien que, comme Platon, Plotin compare le rêve à la vie sensible, et l'homme qui s'est réveillé à celui qui est confronté à l'enseignement philosophique qui porte sur l'intelligible et qui refuse de croire en sa véracité[51]. La conséquence en est qu'il se rendort, c'est-à-dire, dans le système

47. Ἀλλ' εἴ πῃ εἰδώλου τινὸς ἐφάπτεται, δόξῃ, οὐκ ἐπιστήμῃ ἐφάπτεσθαι, καὶ τὸν νῦν βίον ὀνειροπολοῦντα καὶ ὑπνώττοντα, πρὶν ἐνθάδ' ἐξεγρέσθαι, εἰς Ἅιδου πρότερον ἀφικόμενον τελέως ἐπικαταδαρθάνει (Platon, *République*, VII, 534c5-d1. Nous traduisons). Ἐπικαταδαρθᾶνειν est un hapax chez Platon.

48. « *Those familiar features of dream-consciousness which Plato seems in various passages to be drawing upon in attempting to provide a model, a conceptual analog, for some subject's epistemological condition are: its insecurity, or instability; its elements of uncertainty or doubtfulness; its unclarity; its poverty with regard to theoretical, critical, or disciplined attention to matters of language, truth, and logic; its occasionally genuine but transmogrified grasp of truth; its characteristically being deceived, systematically, with regard to its own true state; its potential for becoming aware of its own true state; and its potential receptiveness to the intrusion of waking consciousness, either suddenly, or by degrees* » (Tigner 1970, p. 211).

49. Cf. *République*, IX, 571c3-d5.

50. Οἷον εἴ τινες διὰ βίου κοιμώμενοι ταῦτα μὲν πιστὰ καὶ ἐναργῆ νομίζοιεν τὰ ἐν τοῖς ὀνείρασιν, εἰ δέ τις αὐτοὺς ἐξεγείρειεν, ἀπιστήσαντες τοῖς διὰ τῶν ὀφθαλμῶν ἀνεῳγότων ὀφθεῖσι πάλιν καταδαρθάνοιεν.

51. « Pour le philosophe, il s'agit en effet d'imiter la vie des dieux qui restent toujours éveillés ou plutôt "hors du sommeil" (*ágrupnoi*), tandis que la plupart des mortels passent une

platonicien et plotinien de la réincorporation, qu'il est de nouveau envoyé dans un corps. Le sommeil est donc intimement lié, dans les traités plotiniens, à l'idée d'incorporation et de présence dans le sensible, ce qui peut alors nous faire présupposer que la mort de l'âme, après la sortie du corps, n'est pas synonyme de la fin absolue de toute incorporation pour elle. Cette hypothèse est soutenue par la présence, toujours dans l'extrait du chapitre 13 du traité 51 [I 8], du bourbier (βόρβορος) et de l'Hadès. Le bourbier, qui est aussi un thème d'abord platonicien, est compris par Plotin comme un symbole du sensible et du corps en particulier[52]. L'âme qui ne s'est pas purifiée, c'est-à-dire qui ne s'est pas détournée du corps, est condamnée au bourbier de la réincorporation[53]. Quant à l'Hadès, il est aussi comparé au sensible. Dans le traité 22 [VI 4], *Sur la raison pour laquelle l'être, un et identique, est partout tout entier*, descendre dans l'Hadès est défini comme le fait de descendre dans un lieu inférieur[54], que l'on peut aisément interpréter comme le sensible et le corps en particulier. Un autre des thèmes liés à l'Hadès qui revient relativement souvent dans les traités plotiniens est celui de l'image d'Héraclès aux Enfers. Si l'*Odyssée* explique qu'Héraclès est à la fois auprès des dieux et dans l'Hadès, c'est parce que le poète a voulu en réalité dire que quand l'âme individuelle agit par une vertu pratique, elle est à la fois tournée vers le bien et l'intelligible, et impliquée dans le corps et le sensible, comme semble le décrire le passage suivant :

> Le poète semblait la [l'âme] diviser entre l'image d'Héraclès qu'il remet à l'Hadès et Héraclès parmi les dieux [...]. Parce qu'Héraclès avait une vertu pratique et avait donc une valeur digne de ce qui est beau et bon, il était un dieu. Mais parce qu'il était pratique, et non contemplatif [...], il est en haut et par quelque chose de lui-même, il est aussi en bas. (53 [I 1], 12, 31-38)[55]

Les vertus pratiques sont les vertus qui nous permettent de vivre en cette vie et non pas de nous libérer du corps. Elles sont similaires aux vertus dites

partie considérable de leur vie à dormir : le philosophe, qui a fait le choix de tourner toute sa vie vers l'intellect, doit l'organiser en vue de rester éveillé autant que cela lui est possible. Être en acte, comme le sont constamment les dieux, c'est être éveillé » (Flamand 2008, p. 6). Sur le sommeil et l'éveil chez Plotin, notamment le sommeil et l'éveil de l'âme, voir aussi Collette-Dučić 2011, p. 267-272.

52. *Cf.* 1 [I 6], 5, 44 ; 6, 5. Le *Phédon* met déjà en relation l'Hadès et le bourbier pour ceux qui ne sont pas purifiés (*Phédon*, 69c6). Le lien entre le bourbier et la souillure éthique serait d'origine orphique (Aubineau 1959, p. 186-187).

53. *Cf.* 38 [VI 7], 31, 26. « Tous les auteurs cités, Platon, Plutarque, les Gnostiques et Plotin, ont ceci de commun qu'ils utilisent l'image du bourbier pour désigner le corps humain dans sa matérialité » (Aubineau 1959, p. 195-196).

54. *Cf.* 22 [VI 4], 16, 37.

55. Χωρίζειν δὲ ἔοικεν ὁ ποιητὴς τοῦτο ἐπὶ τοῦ Ἡρακλέους τὸ εἴδωλον αὐτοῦ διδοὺς ἐν Ἅιδου, αὐτὸν δὲ ἐν θεοῖς [...] ὅτι δὴ πρακτικὴν ἀρετὴν ἔχων Ἡρακλῆς καὶ ἀξιωθεὶς διὰ καλοκἀγαθίαν θεὸς εἶναι, ὅτι πρακτικός, ἀλλ' οὐ θεωρητικὸς ἦν, ἵνα ἂν ὅλος ἦν ἐκεῖ, ἄνω τέ ἐστι καὶ ἔτι ἐστί τι αὐτοῦ καὶ κάτω.

aussi civiques, qui sont tournées vers la vie sensible[56]. C'est la raison pour laquelle il y a une partie de l'âme d'Héraclès qui est installée dans l'Hadès, c'est-à-dire dans le monde des corps, et une autre partie qui est dans l'intelligible. Pour comprendre ce que dit Plotin ici, il faut rappeler que, selon lui, l'âme individuelle ne descendant pas dans le corps[57], elle projette quelque chose d'elle qu'il qualifie parfois d'εἴδωλον, c'est-à-dire le reflet ou l'image de l'âme individuelle[58]. Autrement dit, Héraclès auprès des dieux est l'âme individuelle et Héraclès dans l'Hadès est donc son εἴδωλον, c'est-à-dire ce que l'âme individuelle donne au corps pour se lier à lui[59]. On peut alors déduire de toute cette analyse que la descente dans l'Hadès et l'endormissement qui en suit sont une métaphore de la venue dans le sensible et de l'incorporation. Dans ce cas, la mort de l'âme après la mort du corps peut être comprise comme la venue dans un autre corps. C'est la raison pour laquelle nous avons traduit κεῖσθαι par « se situer ». En effet, quand Plotin emploie ce mot dans d'autres traités, c'est souvent pour signifier qu'une chose est dans un endroit particulier ou dans une situation particulière[60]. En l'occurrence, dans le passage du traité 51 [I 8] qui nous intéresse, l'âme individuelle se situe dans le sensible, c'est-à-dire qu'elle reste incorporée, même si ce corps change durant toutes ses vies sensibles.

56. Sur les vertus civiques, *cf.* 19 (I, 2), 1, 17-23. Même chose chez Porphyre, *Sentences*, 32, 8-10. Voir aussi Trouillard 2011, p. 113.

57. Caluori 2022, p. 233-235.

58. Ce qui est appelé ici εἴδωλον peut aussi avoir d'autres dénominations, toutes liées au vocabulaire de l'image. Plotin évoque aussi l'illumination de l'âme (I [I 6], 1, 7). Cette image ou illumination de l'âme correspond à la puissance d'action de l'âme, qui suit de son activité interne et qui lui permet de se lier à un corps (Aubin 1953, p. 367-370 ; Schroeder 1980, p. 46-47 ; Igal 1979, p. 326 ; Santa Cruz 1979, p. 61 ; Gurtler 2008, p. 119 ; Brisson 2017, p. 623) L'εἴδωλον est parfois aussi appelée âme irrationnelle, âme inférieure ou âme passive (Militello 2010, p. 234-235 ; Noble 2013, p. 251 ; Smith 1974, p. 10-14). Sur l'ἄλογος ψυχή, voir 28 (IV, 4), 40, 24 ; 51 (I, 8), 4, 8. Sur la παθητική ψυχή, voir 26 (III, 6), 1, 14 ; 19 ; 4, 1 ; 31 ; 34 ; 44 ; 5, 3 ; 23. « *As one would expect, Plotinus distinguishes between the higher and the lower soul, corresponding to the traditional rational and irrational parts. The soul which is present as a whole everywhere in the body is the lower soul. It operates through the body and uses bodily organs. To it belong the vegetative and appetitive faculties.* » (Emilsson 1994, p. 5353-5354). Emilsson 2017 donne par ailleurs un exposé complet et clair de l'εἴδωλον (qu'il appelle « middle soul ») chez Plotin (voir notamment p. 235-241).

59. « Car l'âme ne se sépare pas d'elle-même pour descendre dans le corps, elle donne simplement à celui-ci quelque chose d'elle-même [...]. Alors elle [l'âme] est là où est son reflet (εἴδωλον). [...] De ce texte difficile, on retiendra la dualité de l'âme et de son "reflet", qui lui sert à être présente au corps sans cesser de demeurer elle-même dans l'intelligible ; considérant que l'Hadès est, par l'un de ses sens, une désignation mythique du corps, Plotin peut dire que le reflet de l'âme est dans l'Hadès, l'âme elle-même restant dans le monde supérieur. [...] Ce n'est pas par elle-même que l'âme est dans l'Hadès, mais par l'εἴδωλον dont elle est flanquée» (Pépin 1971, p. 175-177).

60. *Cf.* 1 [I 6], 6, 4 ; 4 [IV 2], 1, 9 ; 6 [IV 8], 2, 11 ; 10 [V 1], 2, 23 ; 27 [IV 3], 10, 33 ; 43 [VI 2], 16, 12 ; 47 [III 2], 17, 89 ; 50 [III 5], 1, 53.

Mais ce n'est pas la seule chose qui est sous-entendue par Plotin. Comme nous l'avons expliqué, ce n'est pas n'importe quelle âme qui peut aller dans un corps humain. Les incorporations obéissent à une loi cosmologique stricte, qui veut que le type de corps soit déterminé par la faculté dominante de l'âme. En d'autres termes, une âme qui est dans un corps humain et qui n'actualise pas sa raison n'est plus à sa place. Elle possédait une certaine qualité éthique qui a expliqué qu'elle soit venue dans un corps humain, notamment une certaine attraction pour l'intelligible, mais les aléas de son existence incorporée l'ont conduite à préférer le sensible. De ce fait, après la mort du corps, l'âme doit être conduite au lieu qui convient le mieux à son état psychologique, c'est-à-dire un corps animal. En effet, l'incorporation animale se fait pour les âmes individuelles qui ne parviennent pas à actualiser correctement leur raison et qui favorisent les facultés inférieures comme la sensation ou l'ἐπιθυμία :

> Ceux qui ont protégé l'homme deviendront de nouveau des hommes. Ceux qui ont vécu seulement par la sensation deviendront des animaux domestiques : mais s'ils ont vécu par des sensations avec l'irascible, ils deviendront des animaux sauvages, et la différence entre la sensation et l'irascible fait la différence entre les animaux sauvages. Ceux qui ont vécu avec l'appétit et les plaisirs de la faculté appétitive, ils deviendront des animaux intempérants et gloutons[61]. (15 [III 4], 2, 16-21)

Cette répartition des âmes dans les différentes espèces vivantes a une origine platonicienne puisque Platon décrit la naissance des animaux dans le *Timée* par l'évolution éthique des âmes qui sont d'abord liées à des corps humains[62]. Quand Plotin explique que ceux qui ont protégé l'homme deviendront de nouveau des hommes, il veut dire que ceux qui ont actualisé leur raison discursive pourront se réincorporer dans ce qui est le meilleur corps qui soit pour l'âme individuelle, le corps humain. Le verbe κεῖσθαι qui apparaît dans le chapitre 13 du traité 51 [I 8] pourrait alors signifier, non pas seulement l'éventuelle prostration de l'âme individuelle arrachée à son corps, mais aussi la nécessité pour une chose d'être là où elle doit être selon l'ordre cosmologique[63].

61. Ὅσοι μὲν οὖν τὸν ἄνθρωπον ἐτήρησαν, πάλιν ἄνθρωποι. Ὅσοι δὲ αἰσθήσει μόνον ἔζησαν, ζῷα· ἀλλ' εἰ μὲν αἰσθήσεις μετὰ θυμοῦ, τὰ ἄγρια, καὶ ἡ διαφορὰ ἡ ἐν τούτοις τὸ διάφορον τῶν τοιούτων ποιεῖ· ὅσοι δὲ μετ' ἐπιθυμίας καὶ τῆς ἡδονῆς τοῦ ἐπιθυμοῦντος, τὰ ἀκόλαστα τῶν ζῴων καὶ γαστρίμαργα.

62. Cf. *Timée*, 91d6-92c3.

63. « *Their forms are regarded as degraded types, for the sake of the mythical doctrine of punishment by transmigration, announced to the souls before their first birth at 42C. The three classes correspond to the three parts of the soul, which the men condemned to such degradation have respectively misused* » (Cornford 1997, p. 357-358).

Selon nous, l'interprétation de la descente et de l'endormissement dans l'Hadès permet d'interpréter la mort de l'âme après la disparition de son corps comme une référence à une nouvelle incorporation dans un corps animal. L'âme étant morte quand elle était dans un corps humain, c'est-à-dire s'étant totalement laissée fascinée par le monde sensible, elle doit aller dans la place qui lui convient à présent, c'est-à-dire un corps inférieur.

Mais le voyage de l'âme individuelle ne s'arrête pas ici car, comme indiqué en introduction, l'idée de la mort de l'âme est systématiquement liée par Plotin à la possibilité de la remontée. Mais comment cette remonté est-elle alors possible ?

II – La sortie de la mort

Comme on le voit dans les textes, la mort de l'âme implique une remontée présentée comme inévitable, même si les moyens de sortir de cet état ne sont pas explicités : « jusqu'à ce qu'elle éloigne et détourne le regard de ce bourbier » (51 [I 8], 13, 24-25) ; « jusqu'à ce que l'âme puisse remonter » (51 [I 8], 14, 49). Dans les deux cas, la mort n'est donc pas un état définitif. L'âme peut réussir à réemployer sa raison pour retourner dans un corps humain et se rapprocher de l'intelligible. Malheureusement, Plotin ne livre pas d'exposé précis sur la façon dont une âme qui est venue dans un corps animal peut en sortir pour aller vers une meilleure incorporation.

Cependant, cela ne veut pas dire que l'on ne peut pas tenter de trouver une solution à partir des indices laissés par Plotin dans les traités. Si l'on pense notamment à la référence faite à la *République* sur l'endormissement dans l'Hadès, on peut se demander si Platon lui-même ne livre pas des éléments de réponse. Or, dans le livre VII de la *République*, il explique que seule la recherche dialectique (διαλεκτικὴ μέθοδος) permet de libérer l'âme du « bourbier barbare » (βορβόρῳ βαρβαρικῷ), que l'on peut interpréter comme étant le corps[64]. Le but de la dialectique est de parvenir à l'être véritable de chaque chose[65]. Il ajoute que cette technique dialectique relève de l'exercice de la διάνοια, que l'on peut traduire ici par « pensée »[66]. Ce

64. Cf. *République*, VII, 533c8-d2. Voir aussi le commentaire de M. Dixsaut 2001, p. 92.

65. Cf. *République*, X, 596a6. « La dialectique est l'unique route, *odos* ou *methodos*, vers l'essence ; seule la puissance dialectique peut nous frayer un chemin vers l'intelligence de ce qu'une chose est en vérité » (Dixsaut 2001, p. 75).

66. Cf. *Phédon*, 65e7 ; 66a2 ; 79a3 ; *Phèdre*, 247d1 ; 249c5 ; 265e ; *Timée,* 71c4 ; *République*, V, 476d3 ; VI, 511a2.

concept étant par ailleurs difficile à interpréter[67], il ne semble pas, dans tous les cas, que la διάνοια ici soit une faculté à part entière, comme l'est la διάνοια chez Plotin[68].

Car c'est là le principal problème qui se pose si l'on veut transposer la solution platonicienne à la pensée de Plotin. Si ce dernier réutilise des concepts platoniciens, il ne leur donne pas toujours la même signification[69]. Cependant, Plotin est d'accord avec Platon sur le fait que la dialectique ne peut pas être employée par n'importe quelle âme[70]. Dans le traité 20 [I 3], *Sur la dialectique*, Plotin explique qu'elle ne peut être pratiquée que par des âmes qui sont déjà parvenues à se libérer de l'influence du corps : « Qu'est-ce que la dialectique, qu'il faut transmettre aux précédents ? » (20 [I 3], 4, 1-2)[71]. Le terme προτέροις renvoient aux trois figures centrales du traité 20 [I 3] : le philosophe, l'amant et le musicien. Tous les trois ont pour particularité d'avoir une attirance pour l'intelligible, qui est naturelle chez le philosophe et acquise pour l'amant et le musicien[72]. La dialectique est ce qui permet à ces âmes de contempler les Formes présentes dans l'Intellect et elle s'adresse donc à des individus dont la διάνοια est la faculté la plus actualisée[73]. Une âme qui a chuté dans un corps animal n'est pas capable d'employer la dialectique. La διάνοια étant ce qui permet à l'âme individuelle de se tourner vers l'intelligible[74], dans le cas des âmes qui ont chuté dans un corps animal, elle n'est plus actualisée. Or, tant qu'elle reste en puissance, l'âme ne peut revenir dans un corps humain, ce qui semble mener à une impasse. Comment l'âme qui est dans un corps animal peut-elle parvenir à actualiser sa διάνοια ?

La question est d'autant plus critique qu'au-delà du fait que l'âme est venue dans un corps animal parce qu'elle ne parvenait pas à employer sa

67. Fischer 2003 fait une revue synthétique de toutes les interprétations portant sur la διάνοια et son objet dans la *République*.

68. La διάνοια, ou raison discursive chez Plotin, correspond à la faculté la plus élevée de l'âme individuelle, qui lui permet de s'incliner vers le sensible ou vers l'intelligible. Sur la διάνοια chez Plotin, voir par exemple Caluori 2015, p. 168-171 ; 2022, p. 220-222 ; Emilsson 2017, p. 277-285 et surtout Lavaud 2006, p. 29-55 et Chiaradonna 2010, p. 41-70.

69. Sur ce sujet, voir Aubry 2004, p. 261-262.

70. *Cf. Phèdre*, 250e1-251a5 ; *Théétète*, 150d6-151b6.

71. Τίς δὲ ἡ διαλεκτική, ἣν δεῖ καὶ τοῖς προτέροις παραδιδόναι;

72. Dans le *Phèdre*, le philosophe est aussi musicien et amant (μουσικός et ἐρωτικός, *Phèdre*, 248d1). Cela s'explique par le fait qu'il est ami ou amoureux du beau (φιλόκαλος, *ibid.*), c'est-à-dire que la vue du beau corps cause en lui la réminiscence de l'Idée du beau (*ibid.* 249b6-e4). Les trois sont donc la même personne chez Platon (Hackforth 1996, p. 83), alors que Plotin les comprend comme trois types d'hommes distincts. Sur la liberté interprétative de Plotin dans ce texte, voir Gourinat 2016, p. 31-32.

73. « La dialectique permet donc de parcourir l'ensemble de l'intelligible, qui est comme un vaste tissu ou un vaste maillage de genres, de catégories et de Formes, dont les uns sont liés, les autres non, et qu'il faut apprendre à distinguer » (Gourinat 2016, p. 191).

74. *Cf.* 9 [VI 9], 5, 44 ; 7, 3 ; 34 [VI 6], 13, 58 ; 49 [V 3], 3, 9-12 ; 53 [I 1], 9, 18-22.

raison, les âmes individuelles qui sont dans les corps animaux ne peuvent pas utiliser leur διάνοια. Elles n'ont accès qu'à leurs facultés inférieures :

> Si les âmes des humains sont dans des bêtes, puisque, comme on dit, elles ont commis une faute, ce qui est séparé n'est pas parmi les bêtes, mais il est présent sans être présent en elles, car la perception n'est que celle de l'image de l'âme liée au corps[75]. (53 [I 1], 11, 8-12)

Nous avons déjà parlé de l'εἴδωλον, qui est l'image de l'âme individuelle, c'est-à-dire l'activité qu'elle projette sur le corps pour agir sur lui[76]. Or, l'âme individuelle et son εἴδωλον n'ont pas les mêmes facultés, comme l'explique cet extrait du traité 53 [I 1]. Il y a des facultés qui sont propres à l'âme individuelle, et des facultés propres à l'εἴδωλον, qui sont donc les facultés qu'utilisent l'animal. La διάνοια fait partie des facultés de l'âme individuelle qu'elle seule peut actualiser. L'εἴδωλον, si on le prend seul, ne possède pas la διάνοια, cette dernière ne fait pas partie de ses facultés. De ce fait, l'âme qui est dans un corps animal n'a accès qu'à des facultés inférieures, mais elle ne peut pas, d'après le traité 53 [I 1], actualiser sa raison, ce qui pose un problème important si l'on veut expliquer comment la remontée peut s'effectuer[77].

Si l'on se réfère aux traités, l'animal utilise la sensation, la représentation, l'impulsion, le mouvement, ainsi que les facultés végétatives comme l'ἐπιθυμία et le θυμός, qui sont toutes des facultés de l'εἴδωλον[78]. Le problème de ces facultés est qu'elles n'ont pas besoin de l'intelligible pour fonctionner. Elles suffisent à vivre dans le sensible et ne sont pas capables, seules, de se tourner vers l'intelligible. L'âme dans l'animal ne peut donc pas aller vers ce qui est supérieur au sensible. Le seul moyen pour qu'elle parvienne à se retourner vers son origine est qu'elle sorte de ce corps qui la limite tellement. Or, nous lisons la chose suivante à propos de l'âme après la mort du corps, qu'il soit humain ou animal :

75. Ἢ εἰ μὲν ψυχαὶ εἶεν ἐν αὐτοῖς ἀνθρώπειοι, ὥσπερ λέγεται, ἁμαρτοῦσαι, οὐ τῶν θηρίων γίνεται τοῦτο, ὅσον χωριστόν, ἀλλὰ παρὸν οὐ πάρεστιν αὐτοῖς, ἀλλ' ἡ συναίσθησις τὸ τῆς ψυχῆς εἴδωλον μετὰ τοῦ σώματος ἔχει. « La *sunaisthêsis* apparaît ici comme la forme que prend la conscience quand elle s'est déterminée comme sollicitude. Elle n'est rien d'autre, en effet, que ce qui accompagne la sensation (*sun-aisthêsis*), mais ne peut plus se détourner de celle-ci vers d'autres objets » (Aubry 2004, p. 306).

76. Sur la projection, voir 10 (V, 1), 3, 9 ; 27 (IV, 3), 17, 12 ; 48 (III, 3), 3, 26. Ce processus de projection est ce qu'Emilsson 2012, p. 362 appelle la doctrine de la double-activité : l'activité interne de chaque réalité entraîne toujours un effet extérieur. Voir aussi Caluori 2005, p. 90.

77. « Il faut comprendre que ces bêtes qui ont été humaines doivent bien leur vie à l'âme séparée, mais qu'elles ne sont plus capables de prendre conscience de celle-ci. C'est pourquoi l'âme séparée ne leur appartient que sur le mode d'une présence-absence : dans la mesure où elles sont incapables d'en prendre conscience, elles ne peuvent plus transformer cette présence latente en présence affective » (Aubry 2004, p. 306).

78. *Cf.* Rist 1967, p. 416 ; 418 et Caluori 2022, p. 230.

> Du temps s'étant écoulé après la mort, tous les souvenirs des vies précédentes apparaissent [...]. Si elle sort d'un corps pour aller dans un autre, d'un côté elle parlera des choses extérieures à cette vie, d'un autre côté de ce qui a lieu maintenant et de plusieurs choses d'avant. (27 [IV 3], 27, 16-22)

Ce que Plotin dit ici est que, quand l'âme se libère du corps, elle est capable d'actualiser tous les souvenirs de ses vies passées, ce qui implique la vie dans l'intelligible comme dans le sensible[79]. En effet, Plotin évoque les évènements extérieurs à cette vie, c'est-à-dire la vie sensible, et les évènements qui ont lieu maintenant. Le premier cas correspond à l'existence dans l'intelligible et le deuxième renvoie vraisemblablement à toutes les incorporations passées. Le corps a un effet restrictif, dans le sens où il empêche l'âme d'actualiser pleinement toutes ses facultés, raison pour laquelle l'incorporation nous fait oublier tant de choses[80]. En revanche, quand l'âme n'est plus incorporée, elle ne peut pas actualiser toutes les facultés inférieures qui dépendent du corps, c'est-à-dire la sensation, la représentation et toutes les autres facultés qui sont les seules que les animaux peuvent utiliser[81]. En revanche, on voit que la mémoire peut être en acte même quand l'âme n'est pas liée à un corps. La mémoire est une activité de la représentation (φαντασία)[82], qui a pour particularité d'être double : la représentation est présente à la fois dans l'âme

79. « À l'instar de Platon, Plotin croit en la métensomatose. Or c'est en fonction de la qualité de son existence antérieure qu'une âme est réincarnée en tel ou tel être vivant. Mais comment une âme peut-elle conserver la trace de son existence antérieure, si elle n'en a aucun souvenir ? Dans cette perspective, la mémoire est au fondement d'une éthique qui implique un système rétributif. À la limite, on peut dire qu'une âme est ce qu'elle est en fonction de ce qu'elle garde en mémoire de son passé. [...] Lorsqu'elle est séparée du corps, l'âme conserve donc des souvenirs de sa vie antérieure. Parvenue à l'intelligible, elle n'a plus aucune mémoire de ses vies passées, tout simplement parce qu'il ne peut y avoir de mémoire dans l'intelligible. Mais lorsque l'âme commence à se séparer de l'intelligible, alors renaissent tous les souvenirs, et notamment celui d'elle-même comme d'un être distinct de l'intelligible, le souvenir des intelligibles dont elle n'a plus la vision, le souvenir des vies terrestres ou célestes dont elle se rapproche » (Brisson 2006, p. 24).

80. « La conscience incarnée est comme saturée par ces actions et ces passions qui la déterminent et qu'elle cherche à mémoriser pour connaître son histoire et constituer son expérience. Ce n'est qu'au moment de la mort, de la déliaison du corps et de l'âme, que l'âme supérieure peut connaître, mais par ce qui en elle est voué à la procession et à l'incarnation, les évènements des autres vies. L'instant de la mort permet une sorte de surplomb où la conscience n'est plus absorbée en "une" histoire et laisse venir à elle les autres vies vécues avant » (Laurent 1999, p. 130).

81. La sensation (αἴσθησις), la représentation (φαντασία) et l'impulsion (ὁρμή) sont actualisées par le cerveau (*cf.* 27 [IV 3], 23, 9-27). Le θυμός est actualisé par le cœur et l'ἐπιθυμία par le foie (*cf.* 27 [IV 3], 19, 20-22 ; 28 [IV 4], 28, 15-26). Sur l'emploi de Galien par Plotin pour l'établissement de cette répartition, voir Tieleman 1998, p. 36-64. Sur le lien entre la sensation et l'âme inférieure ou εἴδωλον, voir Collette-Dučić 2002, p. 24 et 39.

82. R. A. H. King définit la mémoire comme « *a disposition, i.e. an acquired capacity of the representative faculty* » (King, 2009, p. 168).

individuelle et dans son εἴδωλον[83]. De la même façon, l'εἴδωλον et l'âme individuelle ont chacun leur propre mémoire[84]. La mémoire qui est présente dans l'image ne peut pas s'actualiser sans le corps, comme toutes ses facultés. À l'inverse, les facultés propres à l'âme individuelle peuvent être employées même quand l'âme n'est plus incorporée, d'autant plus que ces facultés n'ont pas besoin d'organes corporels pour être actualisées[85].

Une fois que l'âme individuelle est hors du corps, tous ses souvenirs lui reviennent car elle n'est plus limitée par le corps et l'âme individuelle peut aussi retrouver toutes les facultés qui étaient en puissance lorsqu'elle était liée au corps animal. Selon nous, cette remémoration est la clef pour comprendre comment l'âme peut remonter l'échelle des incorporations chez Plotin et s'affranchir du sensible[86]. En effet, après la mort du corps, l'âme devient en capacité de comparer la vie qu'elle vient de connaître avec les précédentes, ainsi qu'avec l'intelligible. Soit les souvenirs du sensible sont trop intenses, et elle sera conduite vers une autre incorporation encore plus proche de la matière, soit elle ressentira la nostalgie de ses vies passées et elle se détournera de ses facultés inférieures. Dans le traité 50 [III 5], *Sur l'amour*, Plotin établit

83. *Cf.* 27 [IV 3], 31, 1-16. De manière générale, le dédoublement des facultés permet de préserver l'impassibilité de l'âme individuelle supérieure : « *From this passage it appears that the function of the lower faculty is to enable Plotinus to maintain as far as possible the freedom from affection (ἀπάθεια) of the soul that his general theory requires. By means of introducing a lower imaginative faculty he is as least able to a large extent to keep the affections from the higher soul* » (Blumenthal 1971, p. 91). Voir aussi Collette-Dučić 2002, p. 27.

84. *Cf.* 27 [IV 3], 29, 3-6.

85. *Cf.* 6 [IV 8], 4, 21-31 ; 27 [IV 3], 19, 24-26. Voir Laurent 1999, p. 86.

86. Le terme de remémoration fait bien sûr penser à la réminiscence (ἀνάμνησις). De façon très large, la réminiscence comme la mémoire peuvent en effet désigner le fait, pour une âme, d'actualiser un contenu qu'elle possède en elle-même (*cf.* 2 [IV 7], 12, 9 ; 27 [IV 3], 25, 32-37 ; 49 [V 3], 2, 13). Cependant, quand on examine d'autres occurrences d'ἀνάμνησις, on comprend que Plotin l'emploie plus précisément pour qualifier la capacité de l'âme de se lier à l'intelligible et d'utiliser les données qui lui parviennent par sa partie non-descendue (*cf.* 6 [IV 8], 4, 30 ; 45 [III 7], 1, 23 ; 50 [III 5], 1, 34 ; 51 [I 8], 15, 28). Dans le cas qui nous occupe, si on peut parler de réminiscence dans un sens large, la qualification de mémoire nous semble plus pertinente pour garder la teneur individuelle et particulière de ces souvenirs. Par ailleurs, il faut noter la différence entre l'ἀνάμνησις platonicienne et l'ἀνάμνησις plotinienne : là où la réminiscence platonicienne renvoie à une contemplation passée, la réminiscence, selon Plotin, permet à l'âme d'accéder à un savoir intelligible qu'elle possède en permanence du fait de son intellect individuel. « *Il funzionamento della memoria ci consente di comprendere meglio la tesi di Plotino secondo la quale una parte o una funzione della nostra anima non si è completamente immersa nella cura del sensibile, ma rimane in perenne contatto con il mondo intelligibile. Contro-intuitiva e respinta talora con toni di incredulità dai neoplatonici posteriori, la dottrina cosidetta dell'* « *anima non-discesa* » *è in un certo senso la chiave di volta dell'epistemologia di Plotino : è infatti in virtù di questo suo permanente contatto cognitivo con il mondo intelligibile che l'anima umana non ha bisogno di effetuare un' astrazione delle forme intelligibile dalle cose sensibili* » (D'Ancona 2007, p. 98). Sur la réminiscence comme connaissance de l'intelligible, voir aussi Warren 1965, p. 256-258 ; McCumber 1978, p. 160-167 ; Chiaradonna 2010, p. 68.

d'ailleurs un lien clair entre le souvenir des λόγοι et la remontée vers l'Un : « Le manque, le désir et la mémoire des formules rationnelles [τῶν λόγων] ont généré en l'âme son activité vers le Bien » (50 [III 5], 9, 46-48)[87]. Le terme ἔλλειψις est surtout utilisé pour décrire la nature de la matière et du mal, les deux étant une privation du Bien, c'est-à-dire de l'Un[88]. Mais à la différence de la matière, pour qui ce manque est constitutif de sa nature, l'âme a toujours en elle les λόγοι, même dans la mort[89]. D'où la manifestation d'un désir (ἔφεσις), qui est par ailleurs absent de la matière. L'âme a bien en elle le contenu intelligible qu'elle recherche, car les λόγοι ont en effet une fonction conceptuelle, par laquelle chaque âme peut se tourner vers les formes intelligibles[90]. Elle a oublié cette présence du fait de sa fascination pour le sensible, mais libérée du corps, elle peut de nouveau trouver ce contenu à sa portée. Et comme l'explique Plotin, la remontée vers le Bien repose sur cette mémoire des λόγοι, qui est à la fois mémoire de l'intelligible, de la vraie nature de l'âme, et capacité à utiliser ces λόγοι pour connaître. En d'autres termes, la mémoire des λόγοι permet à l'âme de redevenir une âme, c'est-à-dire de reconquérir sa fonction et de ce fait, de sortir de cet état de mort.

Conclusion

La mort de l'âme correspond finalement à un état qui n'est pas inconnu des platoniciens : la venue dans un corps animal. Cependant, ce n'est pas une situation définitive. Pour Plotin, si les âmes venaient à être condamnées à la mort, cela les plongerait dans un état de désespoir qui les empêcherait de faire l'effort de remonter vers l'intelligible. Or, cet effort est très important du point de vue éthique. Toutes les âmes, sans exception, doivent bien agir.

87. Ἡ ἔλλειψις καὶ ἡ ἔφεσις καὶ τῶν λόγων ἡ μνήμη ὁμοῦ συνελθόντα ἐν ψυχῇ ἐγέννησε τὴν ἐνέργειαν τὴν πρὸς τὸ ἀγαθόν.

88. Sur le manque et la matière, voir 51 [I 8], 4, 24 ; 5, 12 ; 8, 23 ; 9, 14. Sur la définition du mal comme manque de bien, voir 5 [V 9], 10, 19 ; 26 [III 6], 7, 20 ; 47 [III 2], 5, 26.

89. « Ce qui est privé du bien ne peut désirer le bien que s'il a quelque chose du bien. Ce quelque chose du bien, c'est, dans l'âme, les *logoi*, qui provoquent la réminiscence. [...] La présence des *logoi* dans l'âme la fait se ressouvenir de la beauté transcendante du monde intelligible » (Hadot 1990, p. 249). Une idée similaire est défendue par G. Leroux : « L'âme possède cependant les ressources pour retrouver en elle-même, dans la mesure où elle est image, la nature véritable dont elle est l'image. Sa différence réside dans une distance, qui est à la fois dépendance et illumination ; son identité appartient néanmoins à ce qui s'est maintenu en dépit de cette distance » (Leroux 1992, p. 246).

90. « Les *logoi* sont en effet plus que des notions : ils représentent plutôt des sortes d'élans vitaux à partir desquels la vie, l'être et la pensée de l'intelligible se déploient dans le sensible. Mais si les *logoi* psychiques ne peuvent être assimilés aux notions ou aux objets de pensée (*ennoèmata*) gnostiques, ils n'en sont pas moins des pensées (*noèseis*, III 8 [30] 8, 16) génératrices et productrices de formes multiples. [...] C'est en tant qu'ils sont producteurs de formes que les *logoi* sont des pensées (*noèseis*) » (Fattal 1998, p. 57).

Cet optimisme plotinien[91], qui veut qu'aucune âme ne soit condamnée, est rendu possible par le rôle très important que joue la mémoire dans la conservation des souvenirs de toutes les vies antérieures, ainsi que des λόγοι. C'est grâce à cette conservation que l'âme peut comparer le désastre de sa situation à ce qu'elle a vécu auparavant, du moment où elle était dans l'intelligible jusqu'à sa venue dans les différents corps. C'est donc la nostalgie d'un état meilleur qui pousse ensuite l'âme à se retourner vers le haut. La mort n'est pas la fin ultime pour l'âme, mais l'opportunité de se libérer de ses fautes.

91. « En somme, l'optimisme plotinien va jusqu'à dire que les maux ne sont que des manques d'être et qu'ils ne diminuent en rien la vigueur de la relation de participation du phénomène à l'être éternel. L'optimisme plotinien suppose de mesurer en quoi l'origine des maux est une origine négative, une privation d'être, et relève donc d'une réflexion purement ontologique ou métaphysique. L'expérience du mal est en fait une expérience de la matière » (Laurent 1999, p. 24).

BIBLIOGRAPHIE

AUBINEAU, M. 1959 : « Le Thème du "Bourbier" dans la littérature grecque profane et chrétienne », *Recherches de Science Religieuse*, 47/1, p. 185.

AUBRY, G. 2004 (trad.) : Plotin, *Traité 53 : I, 1*, Paris.

AUBRY, G. 2008 : « Un moi sans identité ? Le *hémeis* plotinien », dans G. Aubry et F. Ildefonse (éd.), *Le moi et l'intériorité*, Paris, p. 108-125.

BERTOZZI, A. 2021 : *Plotinus on Love: an Introduction to his Metaphysics through the Concept of « Eros »*, Leiden.

BETT, R. 2008 : « Immortality and the Nature of the Soul in the *Phaedrus* », dans G. Fine (éd.), *Plato 2: Ethics, Politics, Religion and the Soul*, Oxford, p. 425-449.

BLUMENTHAL, H. J. 1971 : *Plotinus' Psychology: His Doctrines of the Embodied Soul*, Dordrecht.

BOSTOCK, D. 2008 : « The Soul and the Immortality in the Phaedo », dans G. Fine (éd.), *Plato 2: Ethics, Politics, Religion and the Soul*, Oxford, p. 404-423.

BRISSON, L. 1999 : « *Logos* et *logoi* chez Plotin. Leur nature et leur rôle », *Cahiers philosophiques de Strasbourg*, 8, p. 87-108.

BRISSON, L. 2006 : « La place de la mémoire dans la psychologie plotinienne », *Études platoniciennes*, 3 (octobre), p. 13-27.
DOI: 10.4000/etudesplatoniciennes.979

CALUORI, D. 2005 : « The Essential Functions of a Plotinian Soul », *Rhizai*, 2, p. 75-93.

CALUORI, D. 2015 : *Plotinus on the soul*, Cambridge.

CALUORI, D. 2022 : « The Embodied Soul », dans L. P. Gerson & J. Wilberding (éd.), *The New Cambridge Companion to Plotinus*, Cambridge, p. 219-240.

CANTO-SPERBER, M., 2017 (éd.) : *Philosophie grecque*. Paris.

CHIARADONNA, R. 2010 : « La conoscenza dell'anima discorsiva. *Enn.* V 3 (49) 2-3 », dans M. Di Pasquale Barbanti & D. Iozzia (éd.), *Anima e libertà in Plotino: atti del Convegno nazionale, Catania, 29-30 gennaio 2009*, Catania, p. 41-70.

CHIARADONNA, R. 2015 : « Plotin lecteur du *Phédon*: l'âme et la vie en IV 7 (2) 11 », dans S. Delcomminette, P. d'Hoine & M.-A. Gavray (éd.), *Ancient Reading of Plato's Phaedo*, Leyden, p. 154-172.

COLLETTE-DUČIĆ, B. 2002 : *Dialectique et hénologie chez Plotin*, Bruxelles.

COLLETTE-DUČIĆ, B. 2011 : « Sommeil, éveil et attention chez Plotin », *Chora*, 9-10, p. 259-281.

CORNFORD, F. M. 1997 (trad.) : *Plato's cosmology: the* Timaeus *of Plato*, Indianapolis.

D'ANCONA, C. 2007 : « Plotino: memoria di eventi e anamnesi di intelligibili », dans *Tracce della mente: teorie della memoria da Platone ai moderni*, Pisa, p. 67-98.

DIXSAUT, M. 2001 : *Métamorphoses de la dialectique dans les dialogues de Platon*, Paris.

DRAGONA-MONACHOU, M. 1994 : « Divine Providence in the Philosophy of the Empire », dans *Aufstieg und Niedergang der römischen Welt (ANRW). Principat. Band 36/7. Teilband Philosophie, Wissenschaften, Technik*, Berlin-Boston, p. 4417-4490.
DOI: 10.1515/9783110883732-002

DUFOUR, R. 2004 : « Actuality and Potentiality in Plotinus' View of the Intelligible Universe », *Journal of Neoplatonic Studies* 9/2, p. 193-218.
DUFOUR, R. 2006 : « Tradition et innovation : le *Timée* dans la pensée plotinienne », *Études platoniciennes,* 2, p. 207-236.
EMILSSON, E. K. 1994 : « Platonic Soul-Body Dualism in the Early Centuries of the Empire to Plotinus », dans *Aufstieg und Niedergang der römischen Welt (ANRW). Principat. Band 36/7. Teilband Philosophie, Wissenschaften, Technik,* Berlin-Boston, p. 5331-5362.
DOI: 10.1515/9783110883732-021
EMILSSON, E. K. 2012 : « Plotinus and Plato on soul and action », dans R. Barney, T. Brennan & C. Brittain (éd.), *Plato and the divided self,* Cambridge, p. 362-380.
EMILSSON, E. K. 2017 : *Plotinus,* London-New York.
FATTAL, M. 1998 : *Logos et image chez Plotin,* Paris.
FATTAL, M. 2016 : *Du* logos *de Plotin au* logos *de saint Jean : vers la solution d'un problème métaphysique ?,* Paris.
FAUQUIER, F. 2003 : « La matière comme miroir : pertinence et limites d'une image selon Plotin et Proclus », *Revue de métaphysique et de morale,* 37/1, p. 65-87.
DOI: 10.3917/rmm.031.0065
FISCHER, F. 2003 : « La nature de l'objet dianoétique en *République* VI : bilan de l'interprétation contemporaine », *Laval théologique et philosophique,* 59/2, p. 279-310.
DOI: 10.7202/007423ar
FLAMAND, J.-M. 2008 : « Plotin: le sommeil de l'âme et l'éveil à soi-même », *Camenae,* 5, p. 1-16.
GIRARD, C. 2023 : *L'homme sans dualité : la question du sujet. Le* nous *chez Plotin,* Paris.
GOURINAT, J.-B. 2016 : *Traité 20: Qu'est-ce que la dialectique ?,* Paris.
GURTLER, G. 1997 : « Plotinus and the Alienation of the Soul », dans J. J. Cleary (éd.), *The Perennial Tradition of Neoplatonism,* Leuven, p. 221-234.
GURTLER, G. 2008 : « Plotinus on the Soul's Omnipresence in Body », *International Journal of the Platonic Tradition,* 2/2, p. 113-127.
HACKFORTH, R. 1996 : *Plato's* Phaedrus, Cambridge.
HADOT, P. 1988 (trad.) : Plotin, *Traité 38,* Paris.
HADOT, P. 1990 (trad.) : Plotin, *Traité 50 : III, 5,* Paris.
HENRY, P. & H.-R. SCHWYZER 1951-1973 (éd.) : *Plotini opera,* 3 vol., Paris, Bruxelles, Leiden.
IGAL, J. 1979 : « Aristóteles y la Evolución de la Antropología de Plotino », *Pensamiento,* 35/138-139, p. 315-346.
KING, R. A. H. 2009 : *Aristotle and Plotinus on Memory,* Berlin.
LAURENT, J. 1999 : *L'homme et le monde selon Plotin,* Fontenay-aux-Roses.
LAVAUD, L. 2006 : « La diánoia médiatrice entre le sensible et l'intelligible », *Études platoniciennes,* 3, p. 29-55.
DOI: 10.4000/etudesplatoniciennes.980
LEROUX, G. 1992 : « La trace et les signes, aspects de la sémiotique de Plotin », dans M.-O. Goulet-Cazé, G. Madec & D. O'Brien (éd.), *[*Sophiēs maiētores*]* = *Chercheurs de sagesse : hommage à Jean Pépin,* Paris, p. 245-262.

McCumber, J. 1978 : « Anamnesis as Memory of Intelligibles in Plotinus », *Archiv für Geschichte der Philosophie,* 60/2, p. 160-167.
Militello, C. 2010 : « Le δυνάμεις dell'anima nelle Enneadi », dans M. Di Pasquale Barbanti & D. Iozzia (éd.), *Anima e libertà in Plotino: atti del Convegno nazionale, Catania, 29-30 gennaio 2009,* Catania, p. 227-246.
Noble, C. 2013 : « How Plotinus' Soul Animates His Body: The Argument for the Soul-Trace at Ennead 4.4.18.1-9 », *Phronesis,* 58/3, p. 249-279.
DOI: 10.1163/15685284-12341251
Noble, C. 2022 : « Plotinus on Providence and Fate », dans L. P. Gerson & J. Wilberding (éd.), *The New Cambridge Companion to Plotinus,* Cambridge, p. 386-409.
O'Brien, D. 1969 : « Plotinus on Evil: A Study of Matter and the Soul in Plotinus' Conception of Human Evil », *Downside Review,* 87, p. 68-110.
O'Brien, D. 1997 : « Immortal and Necessary Being in Plato and in Plotinus », dans J. J. Cleary (éd.), *The Perennial Tradition of Neoplatonism,* Leuven University Press, p. 39-103.
O'Meara, D. 1999 (trad.) : Plotin, *Traité 51 (I,8),* Paris.
Opsomer, J. 2022 : « Matter and Evil », dans L. Gerson & J. Wilberding (éd.), *The New Cambridge Companion to Plotinus,* Cambridge University Press, p. 341-362.
DOI: 10.1017/9781108770255.
Pépin, J. 1971 : « Héraclès et son reflet dans le Néoplatonisme », dans *Le Néoplatonisme,* Paris, p. 167-192.
Rist, J. M. 1963 : « Plotinus on matter and evil », *Phronesis,* 6, p. 154-166.
Rist, J. M. 1967 : « Integration and the Undescended Soul in Plotinus », *The American Journal of Philology,* 88/4, p. 410-422.
DOI: 10.2307/292777
Santa Cruz, M. I. 1979 : *La genèse du monde sensible dans la philosophie de Plotin,* Paris.
Schroeder, F. M. 1980 : « Representation and Reflection in Plotinus », *Dionysius,* 4, p. 37-60.
Sekimura, M. 2019 : « Purification and Forms of Beauty in Plotinus », dans H. L. Reid & T. Leyh (éd.), *Looking at Beauty to* Kalon *in Western Greece. Selected Essays from the 2018 Symposium on the Heritage of Western Greece,* Aretusa, p. 245-254.
Smith, A. 1974 : *Porphyry's Place in the Neoplatonic Tradition,* Dordrecht.
DOI: 10.1007/978-94-010-1604-9_1
Smith, A. 2016 (trad.) : *Plotinus, Ennead I.6: On Beauty,* Las Vegas, Nevada.
Song, E. 2009 : « The ethics of descent in Plotinus », *Hermathena,* 187, p. 27-48.
Tieleman, T. 1998 : « Plotinus on the Seat of the Soul: Reverberations of Galen and Alexander in *Enn.* IV, 3 [27], 23 », *Phronesis,* 43/4, p. 306-325.
Tigner, S. S. 1970 : « Plato's Philosophical Uses of the Dream Metaphor », *The American Journal of Philology,* 91/2, p. 204-212.
DOI: 10.2307/293043
Timotin, A. 2012 : *La démonologie platonicienne : histoire de la notion de* daimōn *de Platon aux derniers néoplatoniciens,* Leiden.

Tresnie, C. 2021 : « Conflict and Violence in Neoplatonism: From Cosmic Justice to Cognitive Step », *The Philosophical Journal of Conflict and Violence,* 5/2, p. 71-84.
DOI: 10.22618/TP.PJCV.20215.2.114005

Trouillard, J. 2011 : *La purification plotinienne,* Paris.

Vidart, T. 2018 : « The Daimon and the Choice of Life in Plotinus' Thought », dans L. Brisson, A. Timotin & S. O'Neill (éd.), *Neoplatonic Demons and Angels,* Leiden, p. 7-18.

Warren, E. W. 1965 : « Memory in Plotinus », *Classical Quarterly,* 15/2, p. 252-259.

Wildberg, C. 2009 : « A World of Thoughts: Plotinus On Nature and Contemplation (ENN. III.8 [30] 1-6) », dans R. Chiaradonna & F. Trabattoni (éd.), *Physics and Philosophy of Nature in Greek Neoplatonism: Proceedings of the European Science Foundation Exploratory Workshop (Il Ciocco, Castelvecchio Pascoli, June 22-24, 2006),* Leiden-Boston, p. 121-143.

COMPTES RENDUS

Jean-Claude PICOT, *Empédocle. Sur le chemin des dieux*, Paris, Les Belles Lettres, 2022 (Anagôgê), 756 pages, EAN13 : 9782251452579.

L'ouvrage de Jean-Claude Picot se présente comme un recueil d'études. Il rassemble dix articles parus entre 1998 et 2018 suivis par cinq textes inédits ; ces derniers occupent la moitié du volume. Chacun de ces quinze textes, dont la plupart se concentrent sur un seul fragment (selon la numérotation du recueil de Diels-Kranz, *Die Fragmente der Vorsokratiker*, 1951^{6}), peut se lire indépendamment des autres et dans l'ordre voulu par le lecteur. L'ouvrage n'en conserve pas moins son unité comme le démontrent, entre autres, certaines thématiques que nous avons suivies pour présenter différents chapitres rassemblés en petits groupes.

Au fil des études, qui couvrent une période de plus de vingt ans, les centres d'intérêt de l'auteur deviennent de plus en plus clairs ; leur examen, toujours minutieux, évolue et s'approfondit. On est ainsi témoin du travail du chercheur dans sa progression, de son cheminement, ainsi que de l'affirmation de sa méthode de travail marquée par l'attention au mot et aux détails, loin du recours aux généralités et aux simplifications. Car « pour lire Empédocle, il faut risquer le complexe » (p. 32).

Le fil conducteur est, comme le titre l'indique, la conception des dieux du point de vue d'Empédocle et plus précisément le rapport critique du philosophe aux dieux traditionnels, sa pensée subversive. Car, même si la remise en cause d'une certaine tradition religieuse des Grecs existait bien avant Empédocle, ce qui apparaît propre à ce dernier « c'est le fait qu'il détourne le nom de certains dieux pour en faire un usage qui lui est propre » (p. 9-10). Quand il nomme les dieux, on pourrait croire qu'il assume avec ces noms le contenu qu'ils ont traditionnellement. « Mais ce n'est précisément pas le cas ; il modifie notablement une partie du contenu et des représentations. Il décompose et recompose autrement » (p. 10).

Dans le premier article du livre « Sur un emprunt d'Empédocle au *Bouclier* hésiodique » (p. 15-32) publié en 1998, Picot explique la métaphore végétale « rameau de chair » (σάρκινος ὄζος) qui désigne l'oreille au fr. 99. La question du divin n'y est pas certes abordée directement, néanmoins la compréhension de ce fragment donne lieu à un commentaire sur cinq autres fragments très importants de ce point de vue, qu'on retrouve dans les chapitres suivants : le fr. 29 (le dieu *Sphairos*), le fr. 134 (le dieu de la *phrên hierè*), le fr. 128 (Cypris-reine), le fr. 143 (la coupure des cinq sources) et enfin le fr. 6 (les quatre dieux racines de toutes choses), fragment de référence, auquel l'auteur revient tout au long de son ouvrage.

La méthode d'interprétation appliquée au fr. 99 est très représentative : chaque fois que possible, Picot privilégie la recherche d'une matrice poétique prise dans les œuvres poétiques qu'Empédocle, poète lui-même, devait connaitre. La première étude s'ouvre ainsi d'emblée sur l'affirmation suivante : « Bien des vers d'Empédocle ne se comprennent qu'en les rapprochant de références poétiques et en particulier des paroles d'Homère et d'Hésiode » (p. 15).

L'étude qui suit met en avant le fr. 6 ; elle est intitulée « L'Empédocle magique de P. Kingsley » (p. 33-79), a été publiée en 2000 et concerne l'ouvrage de Peter Kingsley, *Ancient Philosophy, Mystery and Magic: Empedocles and Pythagorean tradition*, Oxford, 1995. Après avoir passé en revue les parties de l'ouvrage qui concernent Empédocle, Picot apporte un commentaire critique très détaillé sur les conclusions de Kingsley et démontre de manière convaincante l'insuffisance des arguments de ce dernier, notamment en ce qui concerne sa lecture du fr. 6.

Kingsley s'attache en particulier à défendre l'équation Hadès = feu que Picot refuse au profit de la thèse conventionnelle qui identifie Hadès avec la terre et Zeus avec le feu (p. 35). Il reproche notamment à Kingsley de ne pas prendre en compte l'attitude subversive d'Empédocle concernant ses allusions épiques à Zeus (fr. 149) et Héra (fr. 6) : s'ensuit une liste instructive de « contre-pieds » empédocléens (p. 47-52), à savoir de fausses allusions, le procédé affectionné par l'Agrigentin afin de créer une attente, suggérer une idée commune, pour ensuite la détourner et partir dans un autre sens.

De manière générale, toute théorie d'affectation des dieux aux quatre racines du fr. 6 doit pouvoir faire ses preuves dans la lecture des fragments. Picot parle d' « équation-clé » (p. 68) qui en s'appliquant à d'autres fragments permettra d'en éclairer le sens en confirmant ainsi à rebours l'interprétation du fr. 6. Dans cet esprit, l'article sur « La brillance de Nestis (Empédocle, fr. 96) » (p. 133-152), publié en 2008, explique l'expression Νήστιδος αἴγλη à partir de l'équation *Nestis*-Perséphone = eau et, plus précisément, grâce au mélange de l'eau avec l'air qui donne naissance à la brillance. Ou encore l'article « Un nom énigmatique de l'air chez Empédocle (fr. 21,4 DK) » (p. 267-300), publié en 2014, dans lequel Picot utilise l'équation Héra = air pour résoudre l'énigme du mot ἄμβροτα du fr. 21,4 et le comprendre comme les nuages blancs.

L'équation Héra = air revient au chapitre « Héra aux deux visages » (p. 497-533), texte inédit, dans lequel est interrogée la signification de l'épithète φερέσβιος attribuée à Héra dans le fr. 6, 2. Bien qu'il s'agisse de l'épithète traditionnelle de la terre, Picot défend de manière convaincante l'association d'Héra à l'éther (air). Il faut aussi noter que l'épithète en question est attribuée à une bonne Héra, car il y a aussi une mauvaise (p. 517 *sq.*) ; l'éther est ambivalent et Picot se penche à plusieurs reprises dans ses travaux sur cette notion de dualité.

Le fr. 6 est également l'objet de l'étude intitulée « Petite histoire d'une marginalisation (Empédocle, fr. 6 DK, les racines de toutes choses) » (p. 419-495), inédite, cette fois du point de vue de la réception du fragment. Picot met en lumière le processus de marginalisation ou même d'effacement des dieux Zeus, Héra, *Aïdoneus* et *Nestis* ; on ne parle plus que des quatre éléments (feu, eau, terre, éther). Picot réhabilite les noms divins du fr. 6 qui sont soigneusement choisis par Empédocle. Il consacre pour cela une partie de son étude (notamment p. 466 *sq.*) à la question, particulièrement intéressante, de la signification des racines divines dans la conception de la nature empédocléenne, en expliquant pourquoi il est important de penser l'attribution des éléments aux dieux et non l'inverse (p. 491).

La question de la nature des dieux chez Empédocle revient d'emblée dans deux chapitres qui se font écho dans l'ouvrage : l'article intitulé « Apollon et la φρὴν ἱερὴ καὶ ἀθέσφατος (Empédocle, fr. 134 DK) » (p. 233-265), paru en 2012, et « *Sphairos*, ou le dieu caché (sur le fr. 29 DK d'Empédocle) » (p. 337-375), inédit. Le premier se consacre à la nature de la *phrèn hierè* en liaison avec un Apollon solaire conçu par Empédocle et opposé à l'Apollon traditionnel, tandis que dans le deuxième, Empédocle met en valeur *Sphairos*, l'Éros véritable, contre un Éros anthropomorphe : les fr. 29 et 134 sont liés non seulement par leur composition mais aussi par leur contestation des conceptions anthropomorphiques du divin.

Une autre étude, inédite, est consacrée à Apollon : « Apollon chez Empédocle » (p. 377-418). Picot y démontre combien Empédocle est loin d'être « un prophète d'Apollon ». Ce chapitre aborde aussi une autre thématique qui traverse les travaux de Picot : la réflexion sur la Muse d'Empédocle, qui selon l'auteur s'identifie à la déesse *Nestis*, une des quatre racines divines de toutes choses.

Le poète et sa Muse reviennent dans l'article « Les cinq sources dont parle Empédocle » (p. 81-131), paru en 2004, qui éclaire le procédé empédocléen de la connaissance à partir d'une analyse méthodique et approfondie du fr. 143. Picot fournit un travail de philologue remarquable en tentant de retrouver la véritable parole d'Empédocle et de la comprendre. Il se base pour son interprétation sur trois mots, κρηνάων, πέντε, ταμών, et sur une idée, la purification, en ajoutant un arrière-plan hésiodique. Son analyse du fragment lui permet en outre de se positionner concernant sa place dans l'œuvre d'Empédocle, ce qu'il fait pour d'autres fragments également présentés dans cet ouvrage.

Le séjour des Bienheureux (p. 153-188), les dieux du fr. 128 et le mythe hésiodique des races (p. 189-206), une nouvelle analyse de l'édition du couple Σωπή τε καὶ Ὀμφαίη du fr. 123.3 (p. 207-232), ainsi que le Bien et le Mal du point de vue d'Empédocle (p. 301-336), font partie des sujets traités dans les autres chapitres de l'ouvrage.

Une étude inédite « Empédocle et le spectacle divin de la réincarnation » qui compte plus de 100 pages (p. 535-664) et comporte deux annexes (p. 665-694) clôt le livre en interrogeant l'origine et la nature des *daimones* qui transmigrent dans le fr. 115. Picot cherche à reconstituer une conception de la réincarnation reposant sur ce que les vers d'Empédocle dont nous disposons peuvent laisser entendre, en optant pour une approche en partie spéculative (p. 544) qui nous a paru parfois insaisissable. Un point de méthode bien clair au début du chapitre, ainsi que l'explication/systématisation des termes palingénésie, métempsychose, réincarnation (p. 541-570) sont d'une grande aide pour le lecteur.

On trouve au terme de l'ouvrage un précieux « Index du divin » (p. 737-741). Nous regrettons cependant l'absence d'un index des fragments, des témoignages et des auteurs anciens et modernes, index qui aurait été d'une grande utilité. Le livre est enfin doté d'une riche bibliographie (p. 697-735). L'auteur rappelle qu'une bibliographie étendue est consultable sur le site qu'il a créé : https://sites.google.com/site/empedoclesacragas/

Le livre de Jean-Claude Picot est d'une très grande richesse, résultat de plus de deux décennies du travail d'un véritable passionné de la pensée empédocléenne. Nous espérons avoir pu en donner un petit aperçu.

Pinelopi Skarsouli
Centre Jean Pépin – UMR 8230 CNRS-ENS-PSL

Pierrot Seban, *Le temps et l'infini. Sur les paradoxes de Zénon*, Paris, PUF, 2023 (MétaphysiqueS), postface de F. Wolff, 314 p., ISBN : 978-2-13-085227-8.

Il s'agit en somme, dans cet ouvrage, de montrer qu'un vieux problème continue de résister à ceux qui prétendent l'avoir résolu. Ce vieux problème, c'est celui qui est sous-jacent aux paradoxes zénoniens de la Dichotomie et de l'Achille, rassemblés par l'auteur en une même « aporie du passage ». Ceux qui prétendent l'avoir résolu, ce sont principalement des philosophes d'obédience analytique qui s'appuient sur certains développements contemporains des mathématiques infinitaires et sur une critique de notre conception intuitive du temps.

Non, Zénon n'est pas mort, enterré par Cantor, Russell, la théorie de la relativité, Mc Taggart et les *supertasks*. Il est toujours là, au milieu de nous, à nous contrarier et à répondre à ceux qui aimeraient le faire taire. Et il peut désormais compter, en la personne de Pierrot Seban, sur une solide recrue pour l'aider à soutenir sa résistance opiniâtre et multiséculaire.

Trois grands foyers de réflexion animent cet ouvrage. Le premier (chap. 1-9) vise à rétablir l'aporie de Zénon dans toute sa précision et sa profondeur. Son point culminant est la reformulation axiomatique donnée au chap. 7 qui, en un même geste, établit la liste des principes qui la fondent et celle des solutions qui prétendent la résoudre. Le second (chap. 11-15) développe, dans la lignée de J.-M. Salanskis, une interprétation « méta-constructiviste » des mathématiques, en vue de rétablir l'aporie zénonienne dans toute sa force, contre ceux – les « possibilistes » – qui croient que le paradis cantorien échappe à sa prise. Le troisième et dernier foyer (chap. 16-20) rejoue la même opposition sur un autre plan, celui de l'intuition que nous avons du temps qui passe et de l'analyse conceptuelle que nous pouvons en proposer.

Après une courte introduction, insistant notamment sur l'actualité de l'aporie de Zénon et la pérennité de sa matérialité textuelle, le livre s'interroge en premier lieu sur le sens du terme *apeiron* chez Zénon à la lumière de plusieurs distinctions traditionnelles (chap. 1). À partir d'une analyse du fragment LM D6 (DK B1), P. S. identifie ensuite un type de raisonnement dont Zénon serait l'introducteur, « le raisonnement par itération indéfinie » (chap. 2). Fort de ce premier point d'appui, P. S. décèle dans le fragment LM D11 (DK B3) et l'opposition *peperasmena-apeira* qui le structure une conception de l'*apeiron* comme « ce qui manque d'une égalité à soi » (p. 45). Par le jeu d'un détour cantorien hardi, l'infini zénonien se trouve ainsi interprété comme une mise en crise du support même de l'approche contemporaine des cardinalités infinies : la correspondance biunivoque (chap. 3). On passe ensuite aux deux paradoxes qui se trouvent au cœur de l'ouvrage : l'Achille et la Dichotomie. Il s'agit de montrer qu'ils ne sont pas de simples sophismes mais posent un réel défi à quiconque souhaite penser ce qu'est le mouvement (chap. 4). Une nouvelle distinction – cruciale pour la suite – entre infini « préalable » et infini « achevé » permet de rendre compte de leur force argumentative : le premier est un infini donné immédiatement ; le second désigne l'achèvement effectif d'un processus infini. Ce n'est pas l'infini préalable mais bien l'infini achevé que visent les paradoxes (chap. 5). Après avoir examiné quelques premières réponses – antiques ou non – à l'aporie (chap. 6), P. S. en propose une version axiomatisée, dont l'essentiel du poids repose sur quatre prémisses (chap. 7) :

0. « Des mouvements peuvent être accomplis. » (C'est cette prémisse qui transforme la déduction en aporie.)
1. Principe de continuité : « Le mouvement est un processus continu. » (Rejeté par les atomistes.)
2. Principe de compositionnalité : « Si un processus continu est accompli, alors sa série zénonienne se trouve avoir été achevée. » (Rejeté par les compatibilistes.)
3. Principe d'achevabilité : « Pour qu'un processus s'achève dans le temps, il faut qu'advienne, au présent, ce qui constituerait pour lui un achèvement intrinsèque. » (Rejeté par les possibilistes.)

C'est le principe d'achevabilité qui est au cœur des préoccupation de P. S. (chap. 8) car c'est lui que les possibilistes contemporains, au nom des mathématiques infinitaires nées au XIXe siècle, remettent en cause (chap. 9).

Au sein de ces neuf premiers chapitres, la pensée antique joue un rôle de premier plan. Elle laisse ensuite la place à des réflexions plus exclusivement contemporaines. Le second temps de la réflexion consiste en effet à défendre l'aporie contre les prétentions possibilistes en développant une interprétation « méta-constructiviste » des mathématiques infinitaires, soucieuse de la pratique effective des mathématiciens (chap. 11). P. S. revient ainsi à l'antique conviction impossibiliste tout en s'efforçant de rendre compte, en contemporain, de l'irruption de l'infini dans les mathématiques. Les idéalités mathématiques, imperceptibles, sont saisies ou constituées de deux manières, l'une constructive (chap. 12), l'autre postulatoire et fictionnelle (chap. 13). C'est bien sûr par ce second biais que l'infini préalable est introduit dans les mathématiques. Le tour de force méta-constructiviste est de reprendre le projet hilbertien d'une « certification » méta-mathématique (p. 159) des actes de postulation fictionnelle et d'interpréter de manière constructive ce contrôle, si bien que le constructif parvient à régir sans les fonder les ensembles infinis qui, par fiction, le transcendent. L'erreur des possibilistes consiste à croire que cette acte de postulation résout l'aporie de Zénon, alors que celle-ci vise en réalité une autre forme d'infini, « *l'infini comme inachevable* du constructif » (p. 176). Les possibilistes prennent le préalable pour l'achevé, alors même que la pratique des mathématiques est de part en part fondée sur des processus inachevables (chap. 14). Nulle postulation fictionnelle, y compris celle d'opérateurs capables de réaliser en un temps fini des tâches transfinies (les *supertasks*), ne saurait effacer cette irrémédiable inachevabilité (chap. 15). Postuler, c'est sortir du constructif, or l'idée de *processus* infini, située au cœur du raisonnement zénonien, est intrinsèquement constructive.

Le principe d'achevabilité ne doit cependant pas être défendu au seul nom de sa fécondité pour la philosophie des mathématiques. Il peut aussi être *justifié* par l'accord profond qui l'unit à notre intuition de la temporalité. En un paradoxal morceau de bravoure, l'auteur consacre ainsi les derniers chapitres de l'ouvrage à s'efforcer d'ancrer l'évidence du principe d'achevabilité dans une évidence plus profonde encore, liée à notre expérience du temps qui passe. La primauté du constructif se trouve ainsi reformulée, sur un plan plus intuitif et concret, en une primauté du « faire » sur le « fait » (chap. 16) qui, quand elle est manquée, mène à un déni du devenir et du temps (chap. 17). Pour répondre à ces dénégateurs, P. S. montre que leur approche est liée à un oubli du caractère local et situé de la vérité et de la factualité (chap. 18). À la primauté mathématique du constructif et celle, intuitive et temporelle, du faire s'ajoute désormais celle, épistémologique, du « concret » et du « local ». C'est bien un paysage philosophique entier qui, au fil des pages, se dessine. Et quel paysage ! En décrivant sa richesse et sa profondeur, P. S. critique par là-même ceux qui le fuient au profit d'un monde éternel et figé, toujours déjà là et déjà fait, décrit depuis un cadre énonciatif prétendûment global (chap. 19). C'est seulement au sein d'un tel monde que l'on peut en arriver à croire que le transfini résout l'aporie du passage. Mais à quel prix ? Celui du passage du temps, de la localité des situations et, *in fine*, de l'aporie elle-même (chap. 20). Les possibilistes n'ont pas résolu l'aporie, ils ont simplement quitté la profondeur intuitive à laquelle elle est liée comme à un sol.

On est saisi, tout au long de l'ouvrage, par la richesse et les multiples variations d'une réflexion toujours originale et personnelle (bien qu'inscrite dans une filiation « salanskienne » assumée). On est ravi par l'effort soutenu en vue d'établir un authentique dialogue entre pensée antique et pensée contemporaine. On aurait aimé que plus de pages soient consacrées à la défense de l'option que P. S. préfère au possibilisme, le compatibilisme, car cette défense demeure très « circonspecte » (p. 288) et circonscrite, et l'essentiel de l'effort porte plutôt sur la défense des problèmes que sur l'exposé de leurs solutions, – ce qui n'est certainement ni une faute ni un vice en philosophie. La personne spécialiste d'histoire de la philosophie ancienne regrettera peut-être un peu que l'analyse historique des textes ne joue pas un plus grand rôle dans la partie proprement antique. Si la matérialité textuelle compte tant dans la transmission des paradoxes zénoniens (p. 5), pourquoi ne pas lui avoir consacré davantage de temps et d'effort, ainsi qu'à son contexte historique d'énonciation ?

Il nous faut conclure en mentionnant une dernière interrogation, concernant cette fois-ci la relation que le travail de P. S. entretient avec celui mené en son temps par J. Vuillemin (cité p. 279), ce qui revient en fait à s'interroger sur le rôle dévolu à l'ontologie dans l'ouvrage. Il semble que P. S. cherche à éviter la querelle de l'ontologie des mathématiques. Il utilise de manière ingénieuse l'idéalité fictionnelle et la remontée au niveau « méta- » pour la repousser et l'isoler. Pour autant, les différentes inclinations qui animent l'ouvrage, en faveur de la *pratique*, des *procédures effectives*, des *actes* – qu'ils soient de construction ou de postulation – bref, en faveur de *tout ce qui donne accès*, semblent indiquer qu'un choix ontologique a bel et bien été fait. L'auteur s'en défend (voir par exemple p. 174 et p. 289-290) et donne alors le sentiment d'essayer de jouer *à la fois* sur les deux plans du platonisme et de l'intuitionnisme. Mais est-ce réellement possible ?

Pierre Adam
Université de Lille

Sylvain Delcomminette (trad.), *Platon. Philèbe*, introduction, traduction, commentaire et notes par S. Delcomminette, Paris, Vrin, 2022 (Les Dialogues de Platon), 472 pages, ISBN : 978-2-7116-3027-1.

Dix-huit ans après la sortie de son ouvrage consacré au *Philèbe* (*Le Philèbe de Platon. Introduction à l'agathologie platonicienne*, Leiden, Brill, 2006), S. Delcomminette revient sur ce dialogue énigmatique avec une nouvelle traduction et un commentaire suivi.

La traduction se distingue de celle plutôt récente de J.-F. Pradeau (2002) par l'effort de rendre l'atmosphère unique du *Philèbe* et ses nombreux jeux de mots. La modernité et la vivacité de la langue font émerger le ton exotérique et conversationnel de la discussion de même que son unité organique, contre la tendance assez répandue à en accentuer le caractère fragmentaire et la vocation ésotérique (sinon le lien avec les doctrines non-écrites). Le texte utilisé est celui de Burnet mais l'édition de Diès est également prise en compte.

Une brève introduction (p. 7-15) présente les lignes de force de l'interprétation développée dans le commentaire. Elle insiste sur la nécessité de lire le *Philèbe* dans la perspective la plus « unitarienne » possible (p. 15), ce qui revient non seulement à rétablir l'unité de ses différentes parties mais aussi la continuité avec les dialogues précédents, en particulier avec *République* VI. Il y a là une tentative remarquable de valoriser le caractère unitaire de la philosophie platonicienne, dont l'enjeu est cependant encore plus ambitieux : montrer que la question du bien est le véritable trait d'union entre l'éthique, l'ontologie et la gnoséologie. Delcomminette souligne à cet égard que l'idée du bien (comme toute autre idée) n'est pas à comprendre comme une entité « infiniment transcendante » (p. 12), qui serait seulement l'objet d'une « théorie » n'ayant pas de répercussions pratiques (lire : éthiques), mais plutôt comme le contenu d'une connaissance qui est en même temps une *expérience*. En ce sens, le bien est « ce dont la possession est capable de nous rendre heureux » (p. 13). Il est également la source de l'être de toute réalité intelligible (*République* VI, 509b) et en même temps une idée dont l'intelligibilité est intense au point de nous « aveugler » (voici le *megiston mathèma*). On en conclut que le bien « éthique », le bien « ontologique » et le bien « gnoséologique » sont indissociables.

Le commentaire (p. 275-455) est une version raccourcie de l'ouvrage de 2006. Il est extrêmement clair et agréable à lire. Ses points forts sont la tendance à vouloir éclaircir même les passages les plus obscurs de ce dialogue et le courage de les interpréter de manière résolue, dans un effort constant pour démontrer la cohérence interne du dialogue et l'interconnexion de ses différentes parties. Cette approche novatrice met en valeur la rigueur et la profondeur du cheminement dialectique mis en scène par Platon.

L'analyse initiale du cadre de la discussion est très convaincante, car l'accent est mis sur les jeux de mots qu'on retrouve dès le début du dialogue, qui tous s'articulent autour du couple *apeiron / peras*. Il faut surtout remarquer l'étrange défection de Philèbe, qui « s'est défilé » (*apeirèken*, 11c), et le fait qu'à la fin du dialogue Socrate aussi veut « se défiler » (le verbe employé est le même). On en déduit que le *Philèbe* émerge sur un fond d'illimitation et d'indétermination (p. 275), dans lequel il retombe dès qu'il s'arrête (p. 455). L'analyse des personnages s'inscrit dans ce même scénario : Philèbe incarne l'*apeiron* dans sa nature indéterminable (« sur laquelle la pensée n'a pas de prise ») et « son champion, le plaisir » (p. 276), alors que Socrate représente la pensée, qui seule introduit le *peras* dans l'*apeiron*. Et Protarque ? Il renvoie à l'*apeiron* (et au plaisir) en tant que *déterminable* par la pensée : c'est pourquoi il accepte de dialoguer avec Socrate, même si c'est défendre la thèse « hédoniste » de Philèbe.

Au niveau méthodologique, cette piste herméneutique est très nouvelle car elle nous suggère que le *Philèbe* est lui-même une application de la méthode dialectique décrite par Socrate dans la première partie du dialogue. À la conclusion du commentaire nous apprenons en effet, non sans étonnement, que « le *Philèbe* n'est pas seulement un dialogue *à propos* du bien : il est le bien lui-même, à la fois dans ses caractères formels et en tant que l'engagement dans son cheminement dialectique nous fait vivre la vie bonne qu'il décrit – une vie philosophique remplie de plaisirs dénués de toute douleur » (p. 454), qui s'avèrent bons exclusivement « sous le rapport de leur mélange avec la pensée » (p. 328). Voilà ce que nous pourrions considérer comme le résultat le plus emblématique, audacieux et original de l'itinéraire herméneutique inauguré par Delcomminette.

La longue discussion entre Socrate et Protarque est reconstruite de manière très claire et incisive, à commencer par son enjeu fondamental : afin de réfuter la thèse « hédoniste » défendue par Protarque, c'est-à-dire l'identité entre le bien et le plaisir, Socrate vise à démontrer qu'il existe des plaisirs bons et des plaisirs mauvais, en sorte que le plaisir puisse être divisé sous le rapport de sa bonté. Il s'interroge donc sur la possibilité que les plaisirs soient à la fois semblables (en tant que plaisirs) et dissemblables (en tant que bons et mauvais), ce qui soulève pourtant toute une série de difficultés concernant l'un et le multiple. D'abord, si le genre du plaisir est traversé par ce type de division, comment se fait-il qu'il soit un ? Aux yeux de Socrate, cette question est liée à une autre plus spécifique, dont Delcomminette souligne la proximité avec les paradoxes de la première partie du *Parménide* (128e-134e), celle de comprendre comment une espèce peut conserver son unité une fois qu'elle se trouve dans les choses qui deviennent et sont illimitées (15b). Mais Delcomminette observe aussi que la longue exploration que Socrate consacre à l'un et au multiple (14c-15c) n'a pas la fonction de résoudre ces questions. Leur solution « n'est pas à chercher dans le *Philèbe* lui-même, mais est présupposée par celui-ci » (p. 293). Toutefois elle ne résiderait pas dans le *Parménide* mais plutôt dans la trilogie *Théétète-Sophiste-Politique*, dont le *Parménide* ne serait qu'une introduction (p. 292-293).

Cette prise de position semble un peu rapide, au moins si l'on tient compte du fait que, dans le cadre du *Parménide*, la démonstration du caractère multiple de l'un lui-même est l'un des résultats les plus importants atteints par la « deuxième hypothèse » (voir 144e). Cela n'implique-t-il pas que chaque idée, si elle est à comprendre comme une unité ou une monade (*Philèbe* 15b), est à la fois une et multiple ? Il s'agit d'une question que Delcomminette n'affronte pas, ce qui explique pourquoi il distingue entre les idées et les genres. Alors qu'un genre est un « terme général », c'est-à-dire un concept universel dont la nature est inévitablement multiple, l'idée est exclusivement une et donc pas du tout universelle : elle correspond à la part d'unité impliquée par la signification du genre (p. 308). Mais cette approche ne soulève-t-elle pas les mêmes difficultés concernant la participation que celles énumérées dans la première partie du *Parménide* ? Notamment, si l'idée est une et non multiple, comment faut-il penser la participation (voir 131a-133a) ?

Cette remarque se limite à suggérer l'hypothèse d'interpréter l'identité entre l'un et le multiple, sur laquelle repose aussi bien la possibilité de diviser un genre en espèces différentes que la possibilité de poursuivre cette division jusqu'à atteindre les membres de chaque espèce, dans le sens fort indiqué par *Parménide* 144e et non seulement dans le sens plus faible indiqué par Delcomminette, qui le fait dépendre de la structure de la prédication. « Que le multiple soit dit être un et l'un multiple » (14c) n'est en effet pour lui qu'une autre manière de dire que « ce qui est à chaque fois *dit être* est fait d'un et de multiple [...] » (16c, je souligne). Ce que les anciens ont transmis comme une véritable révélation (16c-e) est donc l'identité entre l'un et le multiple telle qu'elle se produit lorsqu'on attribue plusieurs prédicats à un seul sujet (p. 304), que Socrate lui-même définit comme « une caractéristique immortelle et sans âge du langage » (15d). Delcomminette en déduit que les différents prédicats d'un sujet tel que le plaisir ou la science divisent le genre correspondant (mais non son idée !) en espèces multiples et différentes, ce qu'il fallait démontrer pour établir la possibilité que les plaisirs soient à la fois semblables et dissemblables. Il fait aussi remarquer que ce type de division, qui se fonde sur le nombre (p. 313), n'est pas seulement l'essence de la méthode dialectique mais aussi celle de l'art : lorsque Socrate se concentre sur l'art de lire et d'écrire, de même que sur la science musicale, il ne ferait qu'illustrer trois applications de la dialectique. Et une quatrième application serait justement l'art de la vie bonne, que le *Philèbe* lui-même chercherait à instituer. La lecture très novatrice que Delcomminette fait des célèbres quatre genres qui divisent « tout ce qui est maintenant dans le tout » (p. 331) s'inscrit dans le même cadre : ils ne sont que les quatre moments d'un *processus de production* inhérent à la dialectique elle-même et causé par l'intelligence productive (dont le nombre et la mesure sont les instruments), qui consiste essentiellement à limiter un illimité qui échappe initialement à la pensée, pour en faire un mélange (p. 341-343). Voilà la vie mixte, et bonne et heureuse, qui seule nous donne accès, parce qu'elle en est la *demeure*, à l'idée du bien et à ses caractères formels : la juste mesure, la proportion, la beauté et la vérité (p. 440-455). Delcomminette nous invite donc à relire le *Philèbe* pour y découvrir l'itinéraire, à la fois pratique et dialectique, esquissé par Platon en *République* VI, celui qui conduit à la connaissance du bien suprême.

Gianmarco MINESI

Nicolas ZAKS, *Apparences et dialectique. Un commentaire du* Sophiste *de Platon*, (Brill's Plato Studies Series 12), Leiden-Boston, Brill, 2023, XII + 400 p., ISBN : 978-90-04-53306-6.

Zaks' essay is a commentary of Plato's *Sophist*, offering a comprehensive discussion of the dialogue from the first page to the last. Such a feat can prove challenging due to both the inherent complexity of the text itself and the extensive body of critical literature surrounding it. Significantly, Zaks manages to both achieve great clarity and offer new interpretations of some passages of the dialogue.

Zaks' main argument is that the central focus of the dialogue is on dialectic as the form of knowledge that, through language, elucidates the way kinds are woven together.

A distinctive aspect of Zaks' interpretation is that this knowledge is true insofar as what is being said by a dialectical *logos* is internally consistent. This contrasts with *logoi* that describe appearances, whose truth consists in their correspondence to empirical state of affairs (p. 280ff.). Notably, the main quality of this book is its strong pursuit of internal consistency: just as for Zaks Plato introduces a notion of dialectic, wherein truth is grounded in the coherence of thoughts within the dialectician's mind, so also Zaks approaches his exegetical objective with marked consistency, which is also signalled by the constant cross-references between sections and chapters in his work. It remains to be determined whether, despite its internal consistency, Zaks' interpretation is also entirely convincing.

It is not possible to survey all questions addressed in the book. I will limit myself to exposing the most innovative arguments that readers of the *Sophist* may find worthwhile. I will then conclude by highlighting one key aspect of Zaks' study, which does not sound convincing.

The emphasis on the consistency requirement for any true dialectical enquiry has a Socratic origin, to which the author gives great significance throughout the commentary. In the *Sophist* the Eleatic Stranger puts forth seven different definitions of the art of sophistry. The sixth definition has also drawn particular attention insofar as it speaks of a sophistic art of noble lineage aiming to purify the souls of the interlocutors, a clear reference to Socrates. Zaks offers a very interesting reading of this passage (p. 61-84): the first six definitions of the art of the sophist are meant to dispel Theaetetus' false preconceptions on the topic culminating in the sixth definition itself, which makes the very process experienced by Theaetetus explicit.

This subtle point is part of the author's broader strategy to deal with the entirety of the dialogue, aiming to integrate the outer part (prologue, example of the angler, the first six definitions, and the final definition) with the core (paradoxes of not being, the discussion of the ontology of the predecessors, the communion of kinds, the theory of *logoi*).

The author offers an extended treatment of the core of the dialogue, proposing some new insights and readings concerning specific points. The engagement with the secondary literature is often quite detailed (the major exegetical claim Zaks seems to fully embrace is Brown's analysis of how the verb "be" is to be construed in Plato). In line with Fronterotta and Teisserenc, Zaks posits that the definition or mark of being at 247d-e (i.e. the capacity to act and to be acted upon) should be linked to the subsequent discussions on the relations between kinds. More specifically, kinds acquire this capacity by participating in the kind being (p. 162-163). Zaks then extends this view by asserting that the kind being not only connects one kind with different kinds, but also each kind with itself, thereby giving it its own nature (p. 222).

To illustrate how dialectic works, the Stranger at 253ff. employs a grammatical metaphor: some kinds are like vowels and are required for there being any connection and separation between kinds, and there are some consonant-like kinds that are being connected. Zaks argues that the vowel-like kinds are being, otherness but also sameness. This is taken to be the ontological requirement for the very existence of dialectic. Zaks then interprets what follows in the text as a description of how the method of collection and divisions operates: the entire process is designed to identify to the maximum degree of consistency the nature of an investigated kind. This implies, among other things, that this passage is the key to maintaining the cohesion between the outer part and the core of the dialogue: the method of collection and divisions *is* dialectic, and the core is meant to explain how the weave of kinds to be dialectically identified is structured. While this idea is not entirely new, the author provides a fresh perspective on the issue.

The connection between outer part and core is also signalled, according to Zaks, through the reference to the dialectician being characterised by freedom. Building on a paper published in *Elenchos* in 2017, Zaks assigns methodological significance to the freedom of the dialectician. During the initial selection of jointly exhaustive kinds with which to weave the kind one is starting with (e.g., acquisitive/productive woven with the kind craft or skill), the dialectician is considered free, constrained only by the requirement of consistency in exploring how kinds are to be distinguished. An interesting claim by Zaks (p. 199) is that the definitional process, far from disrupting the unity of each kind or form, is precisely what makes it unique: it is only by retrieving its unique set of relations that a given kind is what it is and thus only for this reason it is properly *one*.

A very interesting point made by the author regarding the communion of kinds, including the greatest ones, is that their relations are always to be conceived as characterising the *nature* of each kind. For instance (*cf.* p. 211), the sameness and otherness of the kind change (*changement*) "ne désignent pas des attributs possédés par le changement conçu comme forme ou genre, mais bien des caractéristiques indissociables de sa nature". This view, which would be worth further development, entails that there is no room for the distinction between ordinary and essential predication, or between identity and predication in the Stranger's treatment of the communion of kinds. Consequently, the commonplace notion that the kind change, as a kind, should possess the character of stability derived from the relative kind, is to be rejected.

To briefly touch on a couple more exegetical propositions, Zaks presents a new reading of the notorious distinction between *ta kath' hauta* and *ta pros alla* at 255c (p. 213-223). The argument is intricate, but the key idea is that the two expressions correspond to kinds or forms and to sensibles, respectively. This is brough to bear on the Stranger's argument that the kind being and the kind otherness are distinct in a way that, I am afraid, may leave some readers quite unconvinced. Then, the author analyses the remaining passage 256-259 concerning being, otherness and not-being. His view is summarised at p. 266: "le non-être n'est pas seulement concevable comme partie de l'autre analogue aux parties de l'autre, mais également comme une généralisation de toutes ces parties". In other words, there is only a shift of perspective: not-being is other than being and is a part of the other just as the part not-beautiful is other than the kind beautiful, but at the same time, Zaks claims, being is always being determined and therefore, since all being is "being *y*" and the parts of the kind other are "not-being *y*", not-being (*y*) ultimately coincides with the *entirety* of the kind other.

I wish now to conclude by addressing the part I find most problematic. Zaks makes a sharp distinction between speaking of kinds and speaking of sensibles. He argues that the former is always true, with each different association of terms identifying different kinds. By contrast, ordinary talk of empirical state of affairs can be either true or false, depending on its correspondence with the empirical world. Accordingly, Zaks claims that the famous statement at 259e that "the *logos* has come to be for us from the reciprocal interweaving of forms" only applies to dialectic, while the description of how *logoi* work only applies to ordinary statements.

Zaks correctly recognises (p. 277) that one can use predicates without being a dialectician – for example, stating that Theaetetus is sitting without having a full grasp of the nature of the kind sitting. However, from this, he draws the uncompelling conclusion that there is no relation at all between kinds and ordinary predicates.

Ultimately, Zaks' overarching reading hinges on the notion that the dialectical *logos* does not state something but *names* a kind (p. 281). Such a *logos* makes the conditions of individuation of a kind explicit, and this holds for both the method of collection and division and the description of the communion of kinds. Dialectical *logoi* always convey something true, representing what the dialectician is thinking. The most unfavourable scenario occurs when this type of *logos* speaks of kinds that do not mix, indicating, for Zaks, that the dialectician is contemplating nothing at all (for that mix or weave does not exist). This conclusion sounds quite paradoxical in the context at hand, which is devoted to reshaping the notion of not-being. Similarly, the idea of "naming *logoi*" being true could also sound rather paradoxical. More generally, the important distinction drawn by the author, namely that speaking of forms can significantly differ from speaking of sensibles, can be explored without accepting his interpretation (as suggested, perhaps, by a more natural reading of *Soph.* 262d2-3 and *Tim.* 37e3-38b3).

In conclusion, despite some unconvincing claims, Zaks' work provides a comprehensive, undoubtedly clever interpretation of the dialogue, and offers a nuanced discussion of the scholarly literature. In doing so, he tackles vexed questions, presenting new insights that are likely to foster the ongoing debate on the *Sophist*.

Lorenzo GIOVANETTI
CNR
Istituto Per Il Lessico Intellettuale Europeo E Storia Delle Idee

Vladimír MIKEŠ (éd.), *Plato's* Cratylus *: Proceedings of the Eleventh Symposium Platonicum Pragense*, Leiden, 2022 (Brill's Plato Studies, n°8), xii-210 p., ISBN : 978-90-04-47301-0.

L'ouvrage est un recueil des actes du onzième symposium platonicien à Prague, tenu les 9 et 10 novembre 2017. Vladimír Mikeš, dans l'avant-propos (p. VII), rappelle que le *Cratyle* est un dialogue qui, en général, n'a pas réussi à occuper une position de prééminence, ou à être reconnu pour son importance dans l'interprétation de la philosophie de Platon. La cause, possiblement, se trouverait dans le fait que les différents sujets abordés tout au long de la discussion – tels que les parties du discours, la nature des actions, la théorie du flux de toutes choses – aucun d'entre eux n'a une interprétation consensuelle. Autrement dit, sur bon nombre de ces questions, on peut difficilement être sûr de la position que Platon entendait défendre. En effet, même le thème central du dialogue, la controverse sur « la rectitude des noms », fait l'objet d'intenses débats et de désaccords de la part des commentateurs. C'est précisément ce contexte d'apparente incompréhension qui donne naissance à cet ouvrage et qui est résumé dans le titre de l'avant-propos : « Making Sense of the *Cratylus* ».

La première contribution, due à Steffen Lund Jørgensen, est une tentative de réhabiliter Hermogène en tant que disciple de Socrate et d'en tirer quelques conclusions. L'auteur constate que le début du dialogue est souvent négligé, comme s'il s'agissait d'une simple introduction de peu d'importance, alors qu'il renferme en réalité un contenu philosophique substantiel (p. 3), par exemple toute la discussion sur la forme des noms, qui n'a de sens que si l'on suppose qu'Hermogène a déjà une certaine connaissance des théories socratiques (p. 21). Jørgensen défend la thèse selon laquelle le *Cratyle* dans son ensemble doit être lu comme un dialogue socratique, ce qui permettrait d'attendre, selon lui, une participation des interlocuteurs à un mouvement de construction dialectique et, peut-être, de mieux comprendre la raison de l'échec de la discussion à la fin du dialogue.

Dans son article intitulé « Why the *Cratylus* Matters », Ademollo propose une lecture du *Cratyle* visant à souligner que bon nombre de ses problématiques sont en réalité très proches des enjeux philosophiques contemporains. Étant donné le caractère audacieux de cette interprétation, l'auteur a cherché, dans le cadre limité d'un article, à présenter à nouveau certains des points centraux du *Cratyle*, comme la possibilité de dire un nom vrai ou faux (p. 29 ; *Crat.* 385c), et à les interpréter à la lumière de la distinction entre sens et référence dans la philosophie de Frege et la contre-argumentation de Kripke. Cette proposition, même si elle n'a été que partiellement réalisée, vise à illustrer les possibles contributions que ce dialogue pourrait encore apporter aux débats philosophiques modernes.

Francesco Aronadio explore la relation entre l'intentionnalité et la référentialité dans le *Cratyle*, mettant en évidence les complexités du langage en tant qu'outil de communication et de représentation de la réalité. L'auteur examine le cadre conceptuel de Platon, en se concentrant particulièrement sur le verbe *dianoeisthai* en tant qu'élément clé pour comprendre l'intentionnalité. En effet, selon Aronadio, ce verbe signifie la direction structurelle des éléments linguistiques vers autre chose qu'eux-mêmes, illustrant la vision de Platon selon laquelle le langage est intrinsèquement orienté vers des référents externes (p. 49). De plus, l'article présente quelques implications de cette lecture pour une interprétation épistémologique de la doctrine du *Cratyle* et du *Sophiste*.

Dans sa brillante étude, Vladimír Mikeš met en évidence les limites de la thèse conventionnaliste que Socrate semble soutenir à la fin du dialogue, en argumentant que quelque chose du naturalisme doit demeurer pour que la relation entre les noms et les *nominata* soit compréhensible. Le point principal de l'article réside dans la discussion sur la forme des noms, car cette forme peut manifester une structure rationnelle derrière les noms. Selon l'auteur, c'est précisément cette structure qui sert de base à la compréhension de la sémantique platonicienne (p. 81). En ce sens, Mikeš soutient que la proposition d'une forme pour les noms n'est pas rejetée dans la discussion finale avec Cratyle, mais qu'elle a été réinterprétée, abandonnant tout lien avec la matérialité phonétique pour être totalement intériorisée dans l'acte même de penser les noms.

Poursuivant la discussion sur la forme des noms, Anna Pavani présente une lecture perspicace qui distingue cette forme des autres « formes platoniciennes », tout en rejetant son interprétation comme sens des mots. En analysant l'analogie entre la production de la *kerkis* et la production du nom, l'auteur soutient que l'aspect naturel des noms, le *pephykos onoma*, doit être compris comme un concept (p. 103). La différence entre *meaning* et « concept » est mise en évidence, car *meaning* est nécessairement lié au langage, alors que, selon Pavani, le « concept » peut être compris de manière non-linguistique (p. 103).

Jakub Jinek propose une interprétation audacieuse des noms des dieux discutés dans les étymologies, exposant comment ces noms peuvent être lus à travers une lumière métaphysique. Bien que tout le monde ne soit pas nécessairement convaincu par ce type d'entreprise spéculative, Jinek avance néanmoins quelques points intéressants, notamment en ce qui concerne les implications cosmologiques de certaines des étymologies qui peuvent être lues en parallèle avec d'autres dialogues. Dans le même esprit, la contribution d'Olof Pettersson propose une interprétation du *Cratyle* à partir de l'étymologie du dieu Hermès. L'auteur soutient que les trois termes utilisés pour décrire le langage par rapport à Hermès – commercial, voleur et trompeur (*Crat.* 408a) – sont une clé pour comprendre la fin du dialogue et sa structure comique. La vision de Pettersson est, à cet égard, assez différente de « l'optimisme linguistique » que nous pouvons trouver dans certaines des autres contributions.

Mariapaola Bergomi cherche à expliciter, dans son article, la relation entre le dialogue *Cratyle* et le sophiste Gorgias, en particulier en ce qui concerne son traité *Peri tou me ontos*. L'auteur soutient que le conventionnalisme de Gorgias a eu une influence déterminante sur la discussion contre le naturalisme présente à la fin du dialogue. En fait, elle souligne que tant Platon que Aristote semblent faire usage du traité de Gorgias sans le mentionner directement, peut-être comme une stratégie d' « interprétation et d'appropriation » (p. 149). Les éléments textuels que Bergomi apporte pour corroborer sa vision sont assez convaincants et méritent d'être notés, contribuant à éclairer l'argumentation en faveur du conventionnalisme.

Dans « Quelques Différences entre le *Cratyle* et le *Sophiste* », Frédérique Ildefonse se penche sur la relation entre ces deux dialogues, spécialement en ce qui concerne la question de la vérité dans le discours et de la distinction entre *logos* et *legein*. En effet, l'auteur met en évidence que, dans le *Sophiste*, la vérité est toujours un attribut de l'énoncé, mais, dans le *Cratyle*, Socrate semble admettre que la vérité puisse résider dans le nom en tant que plus petite partie du discours (*Crat.* 385c). Ildefonse enrichit beaucoup cette discussion en montrant comment ces deux compréhensions de la relation entre *logos* et vérité se sont développées dans l'Antiquité, préparant certaines des doctrines stoïciennes en ce qui concerne le langage et la logique, et notamment en ce qui concerne le concept de *lekton* (p. 164).

La dernière contribution, due à Filip Karfík, remplit très bien son rôle qui est de clôturer ce recueil d'actes, car elle se concentre sur le point culminant du *Cratyle* : la possibilité de connaissance au-delà des noms. En effet, l'auteur montre comment la présupposition de cette question réside dans la discussion sur le flux de toutes choses, et le postulat de la possibilité d'une nature fixe. Cette discussion réapparaît dans le *Théétète* et le *Sophiste*, nous permettant de voir encore plus clairement la relation entre la théorie du langage et l'ontologie chez Platon. En ce sens, Karfík soutient que c'est précisément parce que le *Sophiste* établit de nouvelles bases pour une ontologie qui rompt avec l'opposition entre la fluidité totale et les réalités fixes, qu'est rendue possible une nouvelle vision du langage (p. 183). L'accent que l'auteur met sur les différences entre le *Cratyle* et le *Sophiste* est très significatif dans le sens où il montre à quel point les problèmes du *Cratyle* n'ont pas encore été pleinement expliqués et compris et, en ce sens, combien il est encore nécessaire *to make sense of the* Cratylus.

Cássio Mercier RAMOS
Pontifícia Universidade Católica de São Paulo

Lorenzo GIOVANNETTI, *Eidos and Dynamis: The Intertwinement of Being and Logos in Plato's Thought*, Napoli, Istituto Italiano per gli Studi Filosofici Press, 2022, 344 p., ISBN : 9788897820628.

L'ouvrage de L. Giovannetti (G.) est composé de trois parties : la première porte sur la notion d'εἶδος dans les dialogues de maturité, et les deux suivantes proposent une analyse détaillée de trois sections du *Théétète* (151-157, 181-183, 184-187) et de deux sections du *Sophiste* (251-254, 259-263) — analyse qui montre de quelle manière les caractéristiques de l'εἶδος déployées dans la première partie continuent de jouer un rôle central au sein de ces dialogues. L'auteur cherche à montrer, comme l'indique le titre, le caractère inextricable de l'εἶδος et du λόγος dans la pensée de Platon, et insiste tout au long de l'ouvrage sur la coexistence des thématiques de l'être et du langage dans les passages centraux du *Théétète* et du *Sophiste*. Il argumente toutefois en faveur de la préséance de la dimension ontologique sur la dimension épistémique (p. 42, 63, 73), et soutient une conception réaliste de l'être et de la vérité (p. 121, 140, 213), cette dernière nécessitant un ancrage extra-linguistique fourni par l'existence indépendante des Formes.

La première partie de l'ouvrage consiste en un exposé transversal, sur la base d'extraits des dialogues de maturité (*Phédon, République, Phèdre, Banquet*), des caractéristiques principales de l'εἶδος platonicien. Les deux premiers chapitres sont consacrés à la présentation de ce que G. nomme métaphoriquement la physiologie (approche fonctionnelle) et l'anatomie (approche structurelle) de l'εἶδος. Le chap. 1 distingue quatre fonctions exercées par les Formes au fil des dialogues : une fonction purement ontologique, d'abord, de détermination eidétique du sensible (DE) (p. 42) ; trois fonctions cognitivo-linguistiques, ensuite — les Formes sont les objets du savoir et lui assurent un ancrage ontologique (p. 51-52), fournissent son contenu objectif à l'activité définitionnelle (p. 65), et donnent sens à tout énoncé du langage ordinaire (p. 67). Ces quatre fonctions sont indissociables des cinq traits « anatomiques » repris dans le chap. 2 : les Formes sont αὐτὸ καθ'αὑτὸ, ce qui leur permet d'exercer DE (p. 78) ; elles sont unes, inaltérables et éternelles, ce qui assure l'infaillibilité du savoir qui les prend pour objet (p. 87) ; elles sont intelligibles donc dépourvues de tout aspect sensible, notamment de toute existence spatio-temporelle (p. 79). Cette intelligibilité signalerait aussi bien l'entrelacement des plans ontologiques et épistémiques que leur distinction : si l'εἶδος ne peut être séparé de ses fonctions cognitives et linguistiques (p. 56, 64, 73, 120), les Formes sont toutefois, pour G., des réalités existantes extra-cognitives (p. 89), dont l'indépendance à l'égard de la pensée s'avère indispensable. Le chap. 3 propose pour sa part une riche synthèse du débat qui polarise la littérature secondaire entre une compréhension des Formes comme universelles (permettant de rendre compte de DE et de la prédication) ou comme particulières (mettant l'accent sur leur perfection et leur autonomie ontologique) (p. 95-111). Selon G., c'est l'alternative même entre ces termes non platoniciens qui fait difficulté. Envisager plutôt une séparation entre fonctions et structure de l'εἶδος, comme effectué dans les deux premiers chapitres, permettrait *a contrario* de préserver la distinction entre ces différents aspects tout en insistant sur leur liaison inextricable en une seule et même réalité (p. 119).

Dans la deuxième partie, G. procède à une analyse approfondie de trois sections du *Théétète* : l'exposé de la doctrine secrète de Protagoras (chap. 4), l'argument de l'effondrement du langage contre le mobilisme héraclitéen (chap. 5), et la réfutation finale de la première définition de Théétète (chap. 6). La doctrine secrète aurait moins pour objectif de fournir une théorie de la perception qu'une assise ontologique à la première définition de Théétète, qui identifie savoir et sensation (p. 132). G. retient surtout du déploiement de la position héraclito-protagoréenne la stricte dépendance de la nature des choses à l'égard de la perception subjective (p. 142), perception qui précède la constitution même de l'objet perçu et du sujet percevant, ce qui implique qu'elle se fonde elle-même sans référentiel externe (p. 167). Cette auto-fondation, couplée à la thèse du mobilisme universel, transformerait le langage en *flatus vocis* (p. 192) : à partir de 182c, Socrate montre que, si tout est en mouvement, aussi bien les qualités perçues que les sensations ne sont jamais suffisamment stables pour constituer la référence d'un acte de langage quelconque, y compris l'activité définitionnelle. La première proposition de Théétète s'effondre sur elle-même puisque le savoir ne sera pas plus perception que non-perception, rien de tangible ne pouvant être désigné par ces mots (p. 188). G. interprète alors la section 184-187, à savoir l'introduction par Socrate des κοινά, qui échappent à la perception et témoignent d'une activité indépendante de l'âme, non pas uniquement comme l'affirmation par Platon du caractère nécessairement propositionnel du savoir, mais également, dans la stricte continuité de l'argument précédent, comme celle de l'existence d'une réalité non subjective indépendante, dont les traits sont découverts - et non pas produits - par l'âme, notamment à l'occasion de la perception (p. 198-200). Autrement dit, l'être ne serait pas restreint à la copule de la prédication, mais signifierait aussi l'existence d'une réalité autonome qui fonde la vérité du savoir et la possibilité du langage, contrairement à ce que soutenait la thèse protagoréenne qui avait été examinée jusque-là (p. 212).

Les chapitres 7 et 8 sont consacrés, respectivement, à l'analyse des sections 251-254 et 259-263 du *Sophiste*. G. y expose son interprétation de la communauté des genres (chap. 7) et du fonctionnement de la prédication (chap. 8). Il présente d'abord sa lecture du genre de l'être (p. 222-223) avant de restituer l'argumentation en faveur d'une communication sélective des genres entre eux à partir de l'exemple du mouvement et du repos (p. 224-235), ainsi que la métaphore des voyelles et des consonnes employée par l'Étranger pour expliciter les règles qui régissent cette communauté sélective (p. 236-251). Au fil de son interprétation, G. opère à nouveau une synthèse entre l'être compris comme détermination et son sens existentiel : tous les genres seraient précisément déterminés en tant qu'ils existent tous, en vertu de leur communication avec le genre de l'être, et ce dans un réseau spécifique de relations, donné une fois pour toutes, qui dépend de *ce que* chaque genre est en lui-même (p. 248-249). La dialectique serait alors la science qui divise selon les genres, c'est-à-dire qui reconnaît le rôle structurel des genres-voyelles que sont l'être, le même et l'autre, et qui étudie ensuite les relations ainsi déterminées entre les genres-consonnes, en recourant notamment à la méthode de rassemblement et de division (p. 242). Identifiant les genres aux Formes, l'auteur se tourne ensuite, au chap. 8, vers le problème de la prédication, et distingue *condition* et *valeur* de vérité pour rendre compte de la possibilité de formuler des énoncés signifiants, mais faux, au sujet des sensibles particuliers. L'entrelacement des Formes se produit au niveau ontologique et fournit la condition de vérité du discours : pour qu'un λόγος soit signifiant, même s'il parle d'un sensible particulier, il doit tisser des termes qui désignent des genres communiquant réellement entre eux (p. 290-292). Sa valeur de vérité, toujours contingente, dépendra pour sa part de l'état de fait dans lequel se trouve le sensible en question au moment de l'énonciation (p. 284). Condition et valeur de vérité convergent par ailleurs dans la dialectique, car c'est l'entrelacement des Formes lui-même qui y est pris pour objet et constitue ainsi aussi bien le fondement que le contenu du λόγος (p. 295-296). Se trouve alors répétée la thèse centrale de l'ouvrage : c'est en vertu de l'existence indépendante des Formes, caractérisée dans le chap. 2 et réaffirmée dans le chap. 6, que ces dernières peuvent exercer leurs fonctions essentielles d'objets d'un savoir infaillible et de références conférant son sens au langage ordinaire.

Cet ouvrage privilégie la clarté et la cohérence à l'exhaustivité : si l'auteur reconnaît à plusieurs reprises ne pas pouvoir développer certains points qui mériteraient un examen plus approfondi et auraient pu intéresser lecteur et lectrice, il parvient de cette manière à concentrer son propos et à énoncer ses thèses principales de manière très didactique, aspect bienvenu étant donné l'ampleur de la thématique traitée et la complexité des textes étudiés. Cela ne l'empêche pas de dialoguer avec une littérature secondaire abondante et de situer précisément son approche au sein des multiples débats qui animent les études platoniciennes contemporaines. Son souci de cohérence s'étend également à sa lecture des dialogues eux-mêmes : l'interprétation qu'il propose de *Théét.* 184-187 a le mérite d'articuler la réfutation finale de la première définition aux critiques de l'héraclitéisme, point qui fait notoirement difficulté. De même, sa lecture ciblée du *Sophiste* insiste sur la continuité entre la description des genres suprêmes et la possibilité de la prédication ordinaire. On peut néanmoins s'interroger sur le sens précis que l'auteur confère à la notion d'existence des Formes, qui côtoie tout au long de l'ouvrage le sens d'εἶδος compris comme détermination, mais qui n'est définie que négativement comme non matérielle, non spatio-temporelle (à la « perpendiculaire » de celle du sensible (p. 92)), et non psychologique. L'insistance sur le sens existentiel de l'εἶδος semble par moments devenir synonyme de l'affirmation de l'indépendance des Formes à l'égard de toute subjectivité, mais envisager l'être autrement que dans ce sens existentiel condamne-t-il nécessairement aux travers du protagoréisme dénoncés dans le *Théétète* ?

Suzanne POLGER
Université Libre de Bruxelles – Aspirante au FNRS

Timothy CLARKE, *Aristotle and the Eleatic One*, Oxford University Press, 2019 (Oxford Aristotle studies), 227 p., ISBN : 9780198719700.

La présence des Éléates, plus précisément de Mélissos et surtout de Parménide, au début de la *Physique* d'Aristote est un sujet d'une difficulté que Clarke (C. dorénavant) met en lumière dans cet ouvrage. Le livre ne se contente pourtant pas de faire une étude purement aristotélicienne, mais il vise également à contribuer aux études parménidiennes. C. propose en effet d'éclaircir les arguments fournis contre l'éléatisme en *Physique* I.2-3, lesquels lui permettent de dégager les thèses qu'Aristote vise à critiquer et de pouvoir, faute d'une citation *verbatim* en *Phys.* I.2-3, repérer les lignes du poème parménidien qui motivent ses critiques.

Le livre de C. est structuré en huit chapitres qui suivent le développement de *Phys.* I.2-3. Les sept premiers chapitres sont presque tous (à l'exception du chapitre cinq) un commentaire suivi du texte aristotélicien et le dernier chapitre soutient que la lecture dégagée peut s'appliquer à l'ensemble du corpus d'Aristote.

C. effectue deux tâches différentes et ce de façon asymétrique, car il commence par passer au crible le texte de *Phys.* I.2-3, pour ensuite fournir une explication moins détaillée d'un corpus plus hétérogène qui inclut quelques passages de *Phys.* I.8, de *Métaphysique*, de *Du Ciel*, de *Sur la Génération et la Corruption* et un rapport doxographique de Sextus Empiricus. Il va de soi que, puisque l'étude est organisée ainsi, les résultats et les conclusions sont plus ou moins convaincants.

Le livre contient deux thèses différentes que C. vise à articuler étroitement. Afin d'expliquer pourquoi le texte de *Phys.* I.2-3 s'intéresse à Parménide et à Mélissos, C. soutient que le monisme éléatique oscille, selon Aristote, entre deux interprétations, à savoir le monisme d'entité et le monisme d'essence (p. 4) : il existerait, d'une part, une seule entité et, d'autre part, une essence qui rend compte de toute la réalité. Ce sont ces deux interprétations qui permettent à C. d'analyser les chapitres de *Phys.* I.2-3. En outre, la deuxième thèse forte de l'étude de C. est que cette interprétation double du monisme parménidien fait système chez Aristote. Autrement dit, C. propose une lecture unitariste de l'interprétation qu'Aristote fait du monisme de Parménide et soutient que tous les *loci* parménidiens du corpus aristotélicien sont cohérents avec la lecture moniste exposée au début de la *Physique*.

Afin de défendre l'idée d'une double lecture du monisme, C. propose dans son introduction (p. 1-9) un état de l'art sur l'interprétation de Parménide et aussi sur la place que Parménide et Mélissos jouent dans la *Physique* d'Aristote. C. est d'avis que depuis l'Antiquité Parménide est interprété comme soutenant que l'univers est un et immobile. De cette thèse éléatique, il s'ensuit que la pluralité et la différentiation sont illusoires. C. clarifie ensuite sa méthode de travail : en reconstruisant les remarques qu'Aristote fait au sujet de l'éléatisme, il reconstitue les arguments de Parménide qui affirmeraient ce monisme qui décrie la pluralité.

Héritier d'une doxographie probablement platonicienne (cf. *Soph.* 242c-243a et *Theaet.* 180c-d), Aristote offre un état de l'art où les Éléates soutiennent qu'il existe un seul principe et que ce principe est immobile. C'est en examinant le passage de *Phys.* 184b25-185a17 où Aristote renvoie dos à dos les notions de principe et de l'un que C. explique de façon convaincante que les critiques d'Aristote supposent une version précise du monisme. Si l'enquête sur le principe présuppose la pluralité, en ce sens qu'un principe est mobilisé pour expliquer quelque chose de différent du principe même, alors Aristote considère que le monisme éléatique a une portée de monisme d'entité, car s'il n'existe qu'une seule chose alors cette chose-là ne pourrait point expliquer autre chose (p. 14-15).

Même si cette lecture du monisme d'entité est derechef utilisée par Aristote, ceci n'empêche pas que nombre de passages de *Phys.* I.2-3 témoignent du fait qu'Aristote soutient que le monisme chez Parménide est aussi d'essence. Un exemple notable de cette interprétation est l'examen du passage 180a20-b5 au chapitre deux, où C. montre (p. 24-27) que l'examen par Aristote du dicton « tout est un » s'interroge sur la portée précise de l'un, dans la mesure où l'être se dit de plusieurs manières. Du côté du monisme d'entité, Aristote se demande si le tout est un être unique qui correspond à la catégorie de la substance, ou bien si cet être unique correspond plutôt à une des catégories accidentelles. Du côté du monisme d'essence, il analyse si le tout contient seulement des substances, ou bien si le tout contient des catégories accidentelles. Cette compréhension essentialiste du monisme, qui inclut la pluralité, expliquerait (p. 23) pourquoi Aristote emploie le pluriel (« ou des quantités, ou des qualités », ἢ ποσὰ ἢ ποιά). C. évoque enfin le fait que ces deux aspects du monisme parménidien peuvent être critiqués en ayant recours à ce qu'il dénomme « la thèse de l'interdépendance » (p. 21) : toute substance sollicite une non-substance et de façon réciproque, toute non-substance sollicite une substance. Avec ces outils en main, C. démontre qu'Aristote peut critiquer les deux sortes de monisme, car si un être unique est qualifié de substance alors il suppose aussi une non-substance et de même, si le tout contient seulement l'essence des substance alors ce tout requiert aussi l'essence des non-substances.

Cette lecture, convaincante, est appliquée ensuite à chaque argument mobilisé dans la suite de *Phys.* I.2-3 où Aristote s'appuierait sur l'une ou l'autre de ces deux interprétations du monisme. C'est le cas dans l'étude du texte 185b5-9, où Aristote propose l'idée que le monisme éléate signifie soit la continuité, soit l'indivisibilité, soit l'énoncé. Premièrement, la critique du monisme selon la continuité et l'indivisibilité aide le lecteur à saisir qu'Aristote cible la version du monisme d'entité. Puisque la continuité est définie comme divisible à l'infini, il s'ensuit que le continu est forcément divisible et, de ce fait, la notion de partie émerge : un seul être unique se morcelle et devient multiple, ce qui contrevient à la thèse du monisme d'entité. Deuxièmement, la critique contre l'indivisibilité montre que le monisme d'entité présuppose, selon Aristote, l'étendue voire le corporel (Aristote évoquerait alors la sphéricité de l'être parménidien, voir p. 38). Si le monisme est en effet indivisible, alors on ne saurait concevoir la moindre qualité et le monisme devrait envisager l'existence d'une sorte d'atome qui élimine l'extension. Troisièmement, l'examen du monisme selon l'énoncé montrerait son aspect essentialiste. C. pense (p. 40) qu'Aristote a en tête la thèse parménidienne sur l'impossibilité de penser le non-être, ce qui impliquerait que toute qualité soit redondante, de sorte qu'on aurait toujours affaire au même énoncé ou encore, que l'essence de cheval ou d'homme décrirait en réalité la même essence.

Si Parménide a mobilisé ces deux types de monisme, les analyses du chapitre quatre sur Mélissos (p. 58-75) montrent que celui-ci semble, aux yeux d'Aristote, s'être borné au monisme d'entité au sens d'une entité étendue spatialement à l'infini. Que Mélissos soutienne une seule version de monisme expliquerait pourquoi Aristote semble le mésestimer par rapport à Parménide.

La deuxième thématique importante du livre est la figure de Parménide chez Aristote de façon générale. C. propose au chapitre cinq (p. 76-102) de reconstruire la pensée parménidienne et de repérer les *loci* parménidiens qui motiveraient les critiques d'Aristote contre Parménide. La suggestion est que le groupe des vers DK B 8.22-25 est un candidat adéquat pour combler ce vide en ce qui concerne les critiques sur le continu et l'énoncé. En outre, C. cite *Phys.* III.6 207a17 où Aristote mentionne la sphéricité de l'être, passage qui permet à C. de renforcer sa lecture d'un monisme multiforme chez Parménide. Aristote se serait inspiré de ces vers pour ses critiques de *Phys.* I.2-3. L'originalité de C. est de proposer qu'Aristote comprenait Parménide comme niant explicitement le vide, puisque le monisme d'entité suggère une entité équidistante qui englobe tout.

Le chapitre huit du livre (p. 167-188) est aussi consacré à la thématique de Parménide chez Aristote. Plusieurs textes du corpus aristotélicien signalent que Parménide aurait été non seulement un moniste (p. 168-169), mais aussi un dualiste de telle sorte que deux principes auraient été véhiculés au sein de sa pensée comme par exemple, le froid et le chaud, le féminin et le masculin ou encore l'être et le non-être (p. 171, 183-186). La lecture de C. suppose que ces dualités se trouvent bel et bien dans la pensée de Parménide, mais que ceci n'est pas déterminant pour affirmer que Parménide a soutenu la pertinence de ces dualités. Selon les termes du débat des études parménidiennes (p. 186), C. est d'avis que la *Doxa* du poème parménidien est un exercice dialectique en ce sens qu'on est capable de façonner une théorie sans être pourtant engagé à la défendre. Selon les termes de C. (p. 177-178), il faut distinguer entre décrire une théorie et accepter que cette théorie soit pertinente. De ce fait, toutes les dualités évoquées devraient être lues en tenant compte du fait que Parménide ne les défend pas et que de ce fait, Aristote est cohérent au sujet de sa lecture moniste.

Je voudrais pour terminer faire trois brèves remarques.

D'abord, en ce qui concerne l'intérêt de retrouver les passages du poème parménidien dont Aristote se serait inspiré pour ses critiques, il serait utile de penser au milieu doxographique dont Aristote se servirait. En ce sens et malgré les références au *Théétète* et au *Sophiste* de Platon dans l'étude de C. (p. 52-54 et 75), il est tout de même étonnant que les similitudes presque systématiques entre ces deux dialogues et *Phys.* I.2-3 n'aient pas été explorées. Cette mise en perspective aurait été utile pour saisir non seulement que Platon citait des vers parménidiens –et cela aurait suffi à fournir les éléments de travail recherchés par C. au chapitre cinq–, mais aussi pour observer que les arguments mobilisés dans le *Sophiste* sont repris, sinon presque calqués, par Aristote et, enfin, pour considérer que la stratégie dialectique repérée dans les deux œuvres est assez similaire, car on y voit comment Parménide est poussé (voire, pour reprendre une image platonicienne, chassé) à affirmer que le monisme amène au multiple.

Deuxièmement, l'analyse détaillée de *Phys.* I.2-3 contraste avec la lecture parfois expéditive d'un corpus plus vaste. Pour ne mentionner qu'un cas, il serait intéressant de mettre dos à dos les deux occurrences de la notion de perception attribuées à Parménide dans *Du Ciel* (298b11-24) et dans *Métaphysique* (986b10-17). Dans le premier cas, C. défend qu'Aristote avance une thèse sur la portée ontologique de la sensation (p. 82) et dans le deuxième cas, qu'Aristote considère la sensation comme étant une faculté psychologique sans rapport ontologique (p. 179).

Troisièmement, la thèse selon laquelle Parménide est le créateur des dualités sans pour autant s'être engagé à affirmer leur pertinence explicative semble ne pas répondre suffisamment à des remarques textuelles. Le texte de *Métaphysique* mobilisé par C. contient une description selon laquelle Parménide « pose » (τίθησι) ou « place » (τάττει) l'ordre des dualités par rapport à l'être et au non-être. Ces verbes sembleraient avoir une force supérieure à celle proposée par C. en les limitant à des notions où il n'y a point d'engagement épistémologique.

Le livre de C. s'achève sur une traduction accompagnée du texte grec, une bibliographie, un *index locorum* et un index général. L'étude est bien menée et les arguments exposés sont à la fois pédagogiques, rigoureux et souvent brillants, notamment en ce qui concerne l'étude de Parménide et Mélissos dans la *Physique*. Malgré les questionnements que nous avons soulevés, la lecture proposée par ce livre conserve sa valeur et l'on salue l'effort pour inviter à une interaction étroite entre les études sur Aristote et sur Parménide. C. a suffisamment montré aux spécialistes de Parménide qu'Aristote a un mot à dire sur le sens précis du monisme éléate.

José Manuel DURÓN-GARCÍA
Académie de Lille

Selene BRUMANA, *La scienza del divino nel* Περὶ κόσμου *Ps.-Aristotelico,* Milano, Vita e Pensiero, 2023 (Temi metafisici e problemi del pensiero antico, n°150), 396 pages, ISBN : 9788834352823.

The Περὶ κόσμου was considered a central text in the study of Aristotle's corpus in both the ancient and medieval worlds. However, despite a small revival of interest in the text in the 20th century, scholarship has somewhat set the Περὶ κόσμου aside, considering it merely to be a work of poetical and theological rather than philosophical import. Selene Brumana's *La scienza del divino nel* Περὶ κόσμου *Ps.-Aristotelico* aims to address this lacuna in the literature, and to show how the author of the Περὶ κόσμου makes a substantial contribution to our understanding of ancient debates regarding not only the notion of the divine, but also the methodological aspects of approaching and discussing theology as a philosophical discipline.

The book is laid out in the following manner. Brumana begins with an extensive introduction which does an excellent job not only of summarizing the literature and laying out the central debates, but also establishing the goals and general approach of the book. Although Brumana gives extensive treatment of the views of Giovanni Reale and Abraham Bos about the text's authorship by Aristotle himself, Brumana considers the Περὶ κόσμου a work of the peripatetic school, without singling out any name in particular. However, this does not mean that Brumana's work is not for scholars of Aristotle as well. Brumana's analogy to the Capella degli Scrovegni, a composite work of Giotto and his workshop, is apt: one who wishes to study the work of Giotto is still interested in those faces which were painted not by Giotto himself, but by his students. This is a useful illustration because it allows Brumana to open up questions about what is or is not an idea of Aristotle (particularly with respect to his lost works) regardless of the fact that the text may not be by Aristotle himself.

The author's interpretation of θεολογῶμεν is discussed briefly in the introduction but is fully outlined in the first chapter of the book. This establishes a key theme in the monograph which makes the reader question the divisions between what is literary, theological, scientific and properly "philosophical" – insofar as these divisions were not set in stone in the ancient world.

The book proceeds with two further short chapters, first of all to discuss (chapter 2) the many meanings of the term "cosmos," and (chapter 3) the substance (οὐσία) and power (δύναμις) of the divine principle. The book then systematically continues to address the nature of the divine in itself (chapter 4), the meaning of the names which are assigned to God, and the mythological/allegorical themes utilized in the text (chapter 5). A final chapter (chapter 6) then addresses the causal efficacy of the divine. The monograph finishes with concluding remarks, followed by an extensive bibliography, indices of ancient and modern names, as well an *index locorum*.

This monograph does an excellent job not only of systematizing the philosophical content of a difficult text, including analysing the influences on it and the philosophical and theological context in which it was composed, but – as we mentioned above – it offers a particularly nuanced study of the text insofar as it applies a method of deconstructing modern notions of what is and is not "philosophy" in order to show the relevance and importance of this work so long overlooked – considered to possess only "beaucoup d'enthousiasme, de piété et de littérature, mais bien peu de philosophie" (to quote Brumana, p. 285, quoting Duhot 1990, p. 223). Thus, the present work is an invaluable tool in approaching a study of the Περὶ κόσμου, but perhaps even more importantly it also invites us to reconsider our own biases when approaching and attempting to categorise ancient texts.

Franziska VAN BUREN
FWO Research Fellow De Wulf - Mansion Centre
for Ancient, Medieval and Renaissance Philosophy

Francesco VERDE (ed.), *Epicuro, Epistola a Pitocle.* In collaborazione con Mauro Tulli, Dino De Sanctis, Francesca G. Masi, Baden-Baden, Academia, 2022 (Diotima. Studies in Greek Philology, volume 7), 329 p., ISBN 978-3-98572-022-4.

Four complete philosophical works have been transmitted by Diogenes Laertius under Epicurus' name: three doctrinal letters, addressed to Herodotus, to Pythocles and to Menoeceus respectively, and a collection of maxims known as the Κύριαι δόξαι (variously translated as 'Principal Doctrines' or 'Sovran Maxims'). While the *Maxims* and the Letters *to Menoeceus* and *to Herodotus* each enjoy a certain fame, the *Letter to Pythocles* has long suffered neglect. Symptomatic of this neglect is, for instance, the fact that in the beautifully concise and affordable Reclam-edition of Epicurus' works (*Epikur: Briefe, Sprüche, Werkfragmente.* Griechisch/Deutsch. Übers. und hrsg. von Hans-Wolfgang Krautz, Leipzig: Reclam, 1980), the *Letter to Pythocles* is not included, nor even mentioned. The reasons for this general neglect seem to be twofold: on the one hand the persistent doubts about the *Letter*'s authenticity, and on the other hand a certain prejudice against its content: its subject matter – the explanation of astronomical and meteorological phenomena – being perceived as intrinsically uninteresting and unimportant, and its philosophical method – the so-called method of multiple explanations – as 'unscientific'. In recent decades much work has been done to correct this view of Epicurus' *Letter to Pythocles* and the methods employed therein, and no small part of this work is due to the authors of the volume here discussed. The present volume can be seen as the culmination of this work, providing a complete guide to Epicurus' *Letter to Pythocles*, including a new edition, translation and commentary, and offering a new and very sophisticated interpretation of Epicurus' method of multiple explanations.

The volume consists of five contributions: (1) an essay on the form and the style of the *Letter to Pythocles*, by Mauro Tulli, (2) a treatise on Epicurean meteorology and the method of multiple explanations, by Francesco Verde, (3) a critical edition with translation of the *Letter to Pythocles*, by Dino De Sanctis, (4) a detailed commentary on the *Letter*, again by Francesco Verde, and (5) an epilogue about the ontological status of multiple explanations, by Francesca Masi.

In the first essay, Tulli undertakes to explain how the *Letter*'s form and style contribute to its function. Whereas for Plato the ideal form for transmitting philosophy is the (written) dialogue, whose function is not so much to convey knowledge but to actively engage the reader in the act of thinking, the goal of Epicurus' doctrinal letters is to help the reader remember the main points of Epicurus' philosophy, and so acquire a complete grasp of the system, which will enable one to live one's life with serenity. Tulli argues that the style and structure of the *Letter* is tailored precisely to promote this step-by-step memorization. He points out that throughout the *Letter* nearly every new subject is clearly identified by the first word or words of the corresponding section (almost as a chapter title), and he suggests that this structure may originally have been enhanced typographically (p. 21-22) by indenting or outdenting the first line of each section, or by marking it with a παράγραφος. Although Tulli's essay is certainly enlightening and generally convincing, it is no easy read. Its style is alternately elliptical and repetitive; it abounds in long Greek quotations which are generally left untranslated and unexplained. Nor is the information always correct or up to date. On p. 15, for instance, Tulli speaks about "the decline of the [philosophical] schools in the IVth century [BC]", as if this were an evident fact. However, as far as I know, the two major philosophical schools of the fourth century BC, Plato's Academy and Aristotle's Lyceum, continued to flourish under Plato's and Aristotle's successors well into the third century BC. Twice, moreover, on p. 15 and 17, Tulli claims incorrectly that the subject matter of the *Letter to Pythocles* would have corresponded to that of books XII and XIII of Epicurus' *On nature*. However, on p. 82 of the volume, Verde states that the corresponding part of *On nature* would have been books XI-XIII of *On nature*.

The second contribution to the volume (p. 27-107) is a long and erudite treatise by Francesco Verde on Epicurus' *Letter to Pythocles* and Epicurean meteorology in general, in which he sketches the historical and intellectual background of the *Letter*, its intended readership, its ethical aim, its scientific method, its relation to the subsequent Epicurean tradition, and its relation to earlier Peripatetic views. The treatise is divided into six chapters. In the introductory chapter, Verde defends the *Letter to Pythocles* against the charges of being irrelevant and unscientific. In chapter 1, Verde rehearses and enforces the arguments in favour of Epicurus' authorship. Chapter 2 paints a portrait of Pythocles, the addressee of the *Letter*. According to the sources, Pythocles was a bright young student of Epicureanism, in whose formation Epicurus took a special interest. With this *Letter*, Epicurus intends to provide Pythocles, who must already have made some progress in philosophy, with a summary of his meteorology that can be easily memorized.

The next four chapters of Verde's treatise provide, in my view, some of the most interesting and exciting pages of the whole book, on which I will dwell at some greater length. Chapters 3 and 4 form a slightly updated and expanded version of Verde's seminal 2013 article, 'Cause epicuree' (*Antiquorum Philosophia* 7 (2013), p. 127-142). In chapter 3, Verde argues for an interpretation of Epicurus' multiple explanations in which each explanation is not merely possible or probable, but actually true, in the sense that it represents a real and objective possibility. With this position Epicurus would have stricken a middle ground between the dogmatism of those who claim to have found the one true cause, and the scepticism of those who believe that truth is unattainable. Throughout the treatise as well as in the commentary, this interpretation is rigorously and consistently applied to several key passages (not just in the *Letter to Pythocles* but also in the relevant portion of the *Letter to Herodotus*), which have often eluded earlier scholars. Significant, according to Verde (p. 55), is the fact that Epicurus in *Letter to Herodotus* 79, referring to the explanation of celestial phenomena, speaks of πλείους αἰτίας, i.e., 'multiple *causes*', not 'multiple *explanations*'. The difference is explained clearly by Francesca Masi (p. 264): "while an explanation operates on a linguistic-epistemological level and essentially consists in the description of a cause that is at the origin of a phenomenon under investigation, the cause operates on an ontological level and refers to a factor that produces an effect in the world." Although Masi is less confident than Verde that αἰτία can always and unambiguously be translated as 'cause' rather than 'explanation', still they both arrive at a similar conclusion: αἰτία is a *possible cause* (Verde) or a *causal possibility* (Masi), which is real in the sense that it is really and objectively capable of producing the phenomenon under investigation. Nevertheless, although Verde's and Masi's interpretation is very attractive and stimulating, I feel that its validity is too readily assumed. The claim that every one of a number of alternative explanations is individually true – which is at the core of their interpretation – is not based on any explicit statement by Epicurus, nor is it self-evident, and therefore requires a strong supporting argument. Most other scholars who have argued for the individual truth of multiple explanations refer to Epicurus' claim in *Letter to Herodotus* 51 (see also Diog. Laërt. 10.34; and Sext. Emp. *Math.* 7.211) that an opinion is *true* when it is *not counter-witnessed* (μὴ ἀντιμαρτυρηθῇ) by something evident. Given that in the *Letter to Pythocles no-counter-witnessing* is sometimes used to support several alternative explanations, it could be inferred that all these explanations are true. Curiously, neither Verde nor Masi makes any mention of this argument. Nor do they waste many words on competing interpretations of Epicurus' method of multiple explanations. Many scholars reject the individual truth of multiple explanations, and not without compelling arguments of their own (see *e.g.* Gisela Striker, 'Κριτήριον τῆς ἀληθείας', in G. Striker, *Essays on Hellenistic epistemology and ethics*, Cambridge 1996, p. 22-76, esp. 42-49). Another problematic aspect of Verde's interpretation is that it requires a – sometimes quite radical – redefinition of certain terms. As we saw above, αἰτία ('cause') would have to be redefined as 'possible cause' or 'causal possibility'. Elsewhere (p. 63-64, 150-151), ἐνδέχομαι ('to be possible') becomes 'to be effectively realisable' or 'to be objectively possible', meaning incapable of *not* being the case. Another word that must be redefined is πιθανός ('probable' or 'plausible'), which occurs as part of the compound τὸ πιθανολογούμενον ('that which can be plausibly concluded'), in *Letter to Pythocles* 87. According to Verde (p. 66-67), this does not refer to any epistemological deficit, but to the absolute plausibility (read: 'certainty') that derives from an explanation's conformity to the phenomena here with us. One wonders whether such redefinitions do not go against Epicurus' injunction in *Letter to Herodotus* 37-38 that "we must grasp *the concepts that underly the words*" and that "it is necessary to regard *the first concept that is associated with each word* and to have no need at all for demonstration, if we are to have a standard to which we may refer the content of our searches, our doubts and our opinions."

In chapter 4, Verde goes on to discuss the method of multiple explanations in later Epicurean tradition as represented by Lucretius and Diogenes of Oinoanda. With respect to the latter, Verde argues that Diogenes' claim (fr. 13.III.9-13 Smith) that "it is okay to say that, while all explanations are possible, this one is more plausible than that," deviates from Epicurus', who in the *Letter to Pythocles* never distinguishes between alternative explanations in terms of greater or smaller plausibility. Regarding Lucretius, Verde focuses on two passages (V 526-533 and VI 703-711) in which Lucretius reflects on the method of multiple explanations. In these passages Lucretius puts forward a view of causation that is more conventional than the one Verde ascribes to Epicurus. According to Lucretius, in our world only one explanation is true, but we don't know which. It is only with respect to the infinity of the universe that all explanations are true, since everything that is possible must be realised somewhere, though not necessarily in the same world. Many scholars who favour a 'realist' interpretation of multiple explanations, have used these Lucretian passages as additional information about Epicurus' own views on the subject, providing a plausible account of how several, sometimes incompatible explanations about the same thing can be true at the same time without infringing on the law of non-contradiction. In contrast, Verde points out (p. 77-78) that in the *Letter to Pythocles* there is no trace of a distinction between causes operating in our world and those operating in others, nor any indication that, according to Epicurus, only one cause would be actually productive of a certain phenomenon. Verde concludes therefore that the accounts of multiple explanations given by Lucretius and Diogenes of Oinoanda must represent later theoretical developments in Epicurean philosophy that cannot be used to reconstruct Epicurus' original views.

In chapter 5, Verde explores the similarities and differences between, on the one hand, Epicurus' method of multiple explanations, and, on the other hand, the scientific methods that are described and applied by Aristotle and especially Theophrastus. He concludes that, although there are clear parallels, and although Epicurus may well have been influenced by Aristotle and Theophrastus, Epicurus' method as a whole is a highly original contribution to scientific theory that cannot be reduced to something that came before. Finally, in chapter 6, Verde briefly discusses a text he refers to as 'the Syriac-Arabic Meteorology' that is traditionally attributed to Theophrastus. Pointing out the remarkable similarities with Epicurus' meteorology, Verde suggests that it may have been falsely ascribed to Theophrastus in order to dissociate it from Epicurus, whose name had become a byword for materialism and atheism.

Verde's treatise is followed by Dino De Sanctis' contribution (p. 109-144), which consists of four parts: (1) a 'critical note' explaining and justifying his editorial choices, (2) a synoptic table, specifying the contents of the *Letter*, (3) an edition of the text, and (4) an Italian translation. At the beginning of his Critical note De Sanctis explains that the note is intended "to offer a preliminary, albeit cursory, overview of the *Letter to Pythocles* in the light of which it will be possible to understand some of the adopted solutions with respect to, or in accordance with, the edition of Peter Von der Mühll, *Epicuri Epistulae tres et Ratae Sententiae a Laertio Diogene servatae*, published in Leipzig in 1922." I am not exactly sure what this means, but since the number of editorial choices discussed in the Critical note is relatively small, I suppose that for minor editorial choices we are silently referred to Von der Mühll's edition. Anyway, those editorial choices that are discussed offer interesting insights into De Sanctis' editorial practice. In general, De Sanctis prefers to explain rather than emend the transmitted text, but he does not shy away from emendation when the grammar or the general sense seem to require it. His edition of the text is also clearly coordinated with Verde's commentary: whenever an editorial decision affects the general sense, Verde will remark on it as well. In this way, De Sanctis has produced a text that, one feels, may be close – as close as one could possibly get – to Epicurus' actual words. The text itself is printed without a critical apparatus, and although this makes the text more attractive to read, there is a certain risk to this: without a critical apparatus at the bottom of each page, one may easily forget that this text, for all its merits, is still only one editor's approximation. The translation is readable and accurate, but I would have preferred to have the translation directly facing the text. I sense one missed opportunity: following Tulli's suggestion in the introductory essay of the volume (p. 21-22) that every new subject in the *Letter to Pythocles* may have been marked typographically by indenting or outdenting the first line of the text or by placing a παράγραφος in front of the first line, the modern text could also have been enhanced typographically so as to highlight the individual subjects and make their sequence more visible. I also found one typo: in the Critical note (p. 112-113) ἐμπεπλεγμένοις (§85) is written ἐμπεπληγμένοις (with η) three times, but in the text edition it is written correctly.

The text and translation of the *Letter to Pythocles* are followed by the longest contribution to the volume: Francesco Verde's commentary (p. 145-257). This commentary seems to serve a double purpose: on the one hand it helps to deepen the argument that was developed in Verde's essay, by further analysing passages that inform us about the method of multiple explanations (hence the title of the commentary, 'La realtà del possibile', which sums up the core of Verde's interpretation of the method), on the other hand it does what any commentary needs to do: provide detailed exegesis of individual passages. In this respect Verde's commentary does not disappoint. With great care and erudition, Verde explains every section of the *Letter*, summarizing the doxographical parallels, sketching the intellectual background, identifying the textual problems, and clarifying the philosophical argument. His commentary is supported by references to almost every relevant publication that I knew, and many more that I didn't know.

The last contribution (p. 259-275) is a paper by Francesca Masi. The paper, titled 'L'indeterminatezza ontologica dei *meteora*', is a constructive engagement with the interpretation developed by Verde in the treatise and the commentary. Mostly in agreement with Verde, Masi summarizes, corrects and expands the interpretation. While praising Verde for bringing out the ontological potential of the *pleonachos tropos*, Masi is remarkably modest about her own contribution to this sophisticated interpretation: Masi's first publication on Epicurus' method ('The Method of Multiple Explanations: Epicurus and the Notion of Causal Possibility', in C. Natali & C. Viano (eds.), *AITIA II, Avec ou sans Aristote: Le débat sur les causes à l'âge hellénistique et imperial*, Leuven: Peeters, 2014, p. 37-63) was developed at the same time and appeared almost simultaneously with Verde's first publication on the subject ('Cause epicuree', *Antiquorum Philosophia* 7 (2013), p. 127-142).

The contributions are followed by a general bibliography, an *Index Locorum* and two indices of ancient and modern names respectively. The book is beautifully designed and carefully edited: I found only one typo.

Francesco Verde and his colleagues have produced a remarkable and admirable book. With extreme erudition and philosophical grasp, it not only offers a broad and encompassing view of the matter, but also pays meticulous attention to details, both textual and philosophical. There may be some omissions, some arguments may not be conclusive; yet, this commentary will no doubt remain the principal work of reference for the *Letter to Pythocles* and its method of multiple explanations for many years to come.

Frederik BAKKER
Center for the History of Philosophy and Science
Radboud University, The Netherlands

Wim Nijs, *The Epicurean Sage in the Ethics of Philodemus*, Leiden-Boston, Brill, 2023 (Philosophia Antiqua, 168), viii+307 p., ISBN : 978-90-04-68480-5.

En 2007, Voula Tsouna offrait avec *The Ethics of Philodemus* une présentation ambitieuse de l'éthique du philosophe épicurien, rendue possible par l'accroissement de nos connaissances sur son œuvre depuis les années 1970. L'exploration du vaste ensemble papyrologique figé dans les cendres de la villa d'Herculanum qui abritait sa bibliothèque n'a pas cessé : elle a donné lieu à l'étude, l'édition ou la traduction de fragments significatifs de ses œuvres éthiques. Wim Nijs (W. N.) perpétue ce mouvement dans *The Epicurean Sage in the Ethics of Philodemus*, où il reconnaît bien volontiers une dette importante à l'égard des travaux pionniers de Voula Tsouna (p. 3). Cet ouvrage issu de sa thèse de doctorat interroge l'éthique épicurienne sous un angle à la fois familier et peu étudié pour lui-même : celui du sage. Philodème est pour cela un lieu idéal, car les textes conservés comprennent de véritables portraits du sage. Ceux-ci ont déjà reçu une certaine attention critique (ils ont donné lieu à plusieurs travaux de Daniel Delattre), mais la reconstruction de W. N. en permet une compréhension beaucoup plus large. Elle prend d'ailleurs en compte non seulement les fragments dans lesquels le sage est décrit positivement, mais aussi ceux qui le dessinent négativement à travers l'évocation du fou, et encore ceux dans lesquels Philodème discute de conduites ou d'émotions correctes (p. 16-17). Le rassemblement de ces sources de description résulte dans la construction d'une « figure multiface » (p. 260), flexible et plurielle, ancrée dans la vie réelle, et par là susceptible de faire concurrence à la rigidité générique, à la dimension fictive ainsi qu'à l'abstraction présumées du sage stoïcien (p. 7-9, 262).

W. N. fait porter son examen sur la faisabilité de la sagesse ainsi incarnée. Il explore différentes dimensions des savoirs du sage, de ses activités et de ses dispositions affectives au cours d'un développement thématique. Le bref propos introductif est poursuivi par un deuxième chapitre qui s'efforce de contextualiser l'approche épicurienne de la figure du sage en montrant qu'elle combine deux pratiques textuelles. L'une relève de la tradition biographique consistant à rapporter les qualités et la vie d'un sage historiquement attesté, l'autre, d'une tradition « plus abstraite » (p. 7) qui débattait sur les caractéristiques d'un sage anonyme, dont la description avait une valeur impérative. Dans l'épicurisme ces deux approches se complètent et se mêlent, s'il est vrai qu'Épicure revendiquait pour lui-même le titre de sage, comme s'en indigne Cicéron (*De finibus* II, 7).

Le troisième chapitre examine les différents aspects de la vie sociale du sage, dont l'ouverture à autrui est motivée à la fois par une inclination naturelle et par l'espoir raisonnable de tirer avantage des amitiés nouées. L'analyse du traitement des actes de générosité et de la notion gratitude (χάρις), dont l'importance pour Philodème est suggérée par l'existence d'un *De gratia* malheureusement très mutilé, contribue à reconstruire une réponse possible du philosophe à une question classique pour l'épicurisme : celle de savoir comment accorder les principes de l'hédonisme avec la possibilité pour le sage d'agir contre ce qui semble être son utilité et sa tranquillité. Ce problème, qui se voit reconduit sous diverses déclinaisons par W. N. à chaque fois que le sage semble risquer de se mettre dans une situation désagréable (p. 67-68, 128-132, 174-184), se pose par excellence à propos de l'amitié s'il est vrai que le sage ressent des émotions déplaisantes quand, par exemple, ses amis sont en danger (p. 44). Pour le résoudre, Philodème pourrait avoir souligné que l'utilité d'une amitié n'est ni toujours ni exclusivement d'ordre matériel et que sa dimension contractuelle se double d'une réalité affective que l'on ne peut négliger.

Les deux chapitres suivants sont consacrés aux relations, activités et attitudes du sage à l'égard de ceux qui ne sont pas sages, qu'ils soient amicaux ou hostiles. Il s'agit d'abord (chap. 4) de questionner les ressorts et les fins de son rôle d'enseignant-thérapeute, puisque cet art (τέκνη) se présente à lui comme une source d'avantages, voire de revenus. Il s'agit ensuite (chap. 5) de s'intéresser à d'autres dispositions affectives et actions du sage envers les non-sages. Il y est discuté de la possibilité pour lui d'éprouver du mépris, de la pitié et de la colère envers autrui, ou de l'empêcher de nuire en l'évitant, en le punissant et même en se vengeant de lui. Au nombre des résultats de ces enquêtes, on peut mentionner la manière convaincante avec laquelle W. N. montre que Philodème semble retravailler avec une grande subtilité les caractérisations aristotéliciennes du mépris (καταφρόνησις) propre au magnanime (désormais compris comme l'évaluation correcte d'autrui à la mesure de ses opinions) et de la pitié (désormais due au fou au titre de sa faiblesse morale) qui vient le compléter (p. 128).

Le sixième chapitre approfondit la question de la colère en évoquant plus généralement le niveau de contrôle qu'un sage peut avoir sur lui-même et sur ses émotions car, tout comme pour la peine, voire même pour la jalousie, il existe un niveau affectif spontané que Philodème appelle « morsure » (δηγμός) ou « pincement » (νυγμός) survenant aussi dans le cas du sage (p. 164-171). W. N. argumente ensuite en défaveur de l'hypothèse tentante d'attribuer au sage des colères feintes et examine les traces d'une contribution Philodème au débat antique sur la nature et la possibilité d'une ivresse du sage.

Le septième chapitre propose une lecture originale de textes apologétiques sur le sage dont W. N. montre qu'ils ont des structures en partie similaires et un même arrière-plan épistémologique : s'il importe de défendre le sage contre l'apparence qu'il peut avoir d'être flatteur, arrogant ou irascible, c'est en effet parce que l'épicurisme tient toutes les impressions sensibles pour vraies.

Le huitième chapitre aborde enfin deux sujets : la question de l'administration par le sage d'un domaine agricole puis celle de son rapport à ses esclaves, invitant W. N. à se demander s'ils peuvent ou non prétendre à la sagesse épicurienne. Une inspection minutieuse du *De oeconomia* de Philodème révèle que ce traité, loin de dialoguer uniquement, comme il le fait de manière explicite, avec une tradition grecque issue de l'*Économique* de Xénophon, est en réalité sous-tendu par des débats romains demeurant toujours implicites. W. N. replace certaines affirmations de Philodème dans le contexte de prises de position sur le rapport entre la vie agricole, le travail et le plaisir que l'on trouve chez Varron dans le *De rustica* ou Cicéron dans le *De senectute* (p. 237, 239). Il montre ainsi que le sage du *De oeconomia* s'oppose à la fois au modèle traditionnel du *bonus agricola* laborieux (Caton, *De agri cultura* 2) et au mode de vie luxueux de la nouvelle aristocratie romaine (p. 242-244).

Le problème de la faisabilité de la sagesse épicurienne trouve finalement une réponse « nuancée » (p. 260) qui ne parvient pas complètement à déconstruire les tensions découvertes. Il est vrai que les sages de Philodème se voient offrir de multiples ressources pour leur assurer une existence tranquille : les échanges de biens entre amis (chap. 3 et 7), l'enseignement de la philosophie (chap. 4), la bonne administration, sans effort et par le travail d'autrui, d'une propriété qu'on possède (chap. 3 et 8). Les textes de Philodème, adressés comme le *De oeconomia* à des publics délimités avec précision, sont attentifs à faire correspondre le sage qu'ils décrivent avec les situations de leurs lecteurs. Leur commentaire par W. N. montre de manière convaincante qu'on peut penser le sage sous des figures plurielles, pratiquant des arts différents à des niveaux d'expertise variables et ayant des dispositions affectives diverses. Mais un tel soin ne confirme pas sans quelques limites la thèse épicurienne de la facilité du bien (*Lettre à Ménécée* : DL X, 133). W. N. reconnaît qu'il existe des conditions très défavorables à la sagesse, comme celle des esclaves travaillant dans les champs (p. 254-259).

L'étude de W. N., très rigoureuse, complète et richement documentée, offre une contribution utile à la connaissance de l'épicurisme antique et en général à l'histoire de l'éthique ancienne, qui n'a pas assez étudié le rôle attribué à la figure du sage dans les différentes traditions de pensée. On pourrait regretter le choix d'un développement thématique qui ne s'efforce pas toujours de donner au propos une unité de questionnement très nette, même s'il est certainement justifié par le caractère fragmentaire des textes sur le sage et leur diffraction dans des contextes hétérogènes. Notre compréhension du sage épicurien gagnerait peut-être aussi à évaluer précisément le rapport entre les deux usages de cette figure identifiés par W. N. dans l'Antiquité, comme « modèle descriptif » et « impératif moral implicite » (p. 8). En questionnant directement les ressorts prescriptifs de la description du sage, on situerait sans doute mieux la fonction philosophique que Philodème lui confère. Enfin, une meilleure prise en compte des positions concurrentes à l'épicurisme pourrait enrichir cette enquête. Par exemple, le sage stoïcien se présente le plus souvent sous l'hypothèse d'une figure désincarnée, sans épaisseur humaine ni nuance et utilisée comme un repoussoir (p. 215, 262-263). Or, des comparaisons circonstanciées pourraient suggérer que le sage de Philodème dialogue autant avec les épicuriens qu'avec leurs adversaires. Ainsi, les interventions sur le travail (πόνος) du sage trouvent un écho dans les fragments stoïciens le décrivant comme φιλόπονος (*SVF* III, 683). De même, il serait intéressant de confronter les textes commentés par W. N. et ceux dans lesquels les stoïciens décrivaient quelles sources de revenu conviennent le mieux à un sage (*SVF* III, 623, 685, 686, 693, 701 etc.) ou quel type d'expertise on peut lui attribuer. Mais ces quelques remarques, loin de diminuer les mérites de l'ouvrage, soulignent au contraire la fécondité des perspectives qu'il ouvre.

Florent GIRANDIER
Université de Lille, UMR 8163 STL

Stéphane MARCHAND (coord.), *Épistémologie épicurienne*, Dossier thématique des *Cahiers philosophiques* 173(2), 2e trimestre 2023, 182 p., ISBN : 978-2-7116-6026-1.

Il faut commencer par saluer le choix qu'a fait la rédaction des *Cahiers philosophiques* de consacrer un numéro entier de la revue à la théorie épicurienne de la connaissance, la canonique. Celle-ci en effet est restée longtemps le parent pauvre des études épicuriennes, en dépit de l'intérêt manifesté dès le XIXe siècle par des savants prestigieux comme Pierce, dont nous aurons à reparler, et de travaux plus récents qui ont fait date, dont ceux d'E. Asmis ou de G. Striker. Certes, comme le signale pertinemment N. Chouchan la directrice de la rédaction dans son éditorial, la recherche en la matière s'est aujourd'hui enrichie de sources nouvelles, souvent d'un grand intérêt, grâce surtout aux progrès spectaculaires accomplis ces dernières années dans le déchiffrement et/ou la relecture de nombreux papyrus d'Herculanum (voir à ce sujet le très instructif entretien avec Daniel Delattre, « Autour de l'édition des papyrus d'Herculanum », p. 159-166). Il n'en reste pas moins que l'intérêt proprement philosophique de cette épistémologie semble être demeuré presque inaperçu, en tout cas tout à fait mésestimé durant des siècles, à l'exception notable d'un Gassendi ou d'un Diderot. Dédain, voire condamnation, que résume le jugement négatif de Hegel dans ses *Leçons sur l'histoire de la philosophie*. Sans doute la teneur sensualiste de cette épistémologie, le statut dérivé qu'elle accorde aux notions générales et aux concepts, son parti-pris global de naturalisation des processus cognitifs s'opposent-ils trop frontalement aux tendances idéalistes des courants dominants de notre histoire philosophique pour trouver grâce auprès de celle-ci.

Les cinq études qui constituent le dossier consacré à la canonique épicurienne offrent une circulation entre synthèses permettant d'évaluer l'intention et la cohérence de cette discipline, et analyses plus spécialisées.

Le titre de la contribution de Pierre-Marie Morel, « L'épistémologie d'Épicure : le bonheur et la science », sonne comme un nécessaire rappel du principe architectonique qui subordonne physique et canonique aux fins de l'éthique. Pour la canonique, cela impose de garantir les vérités de la physique.

Pour cela, il faut commencer par exhiber un critère qui ne peut être pris en défaut, et qu'Épicure désigne comme étant la sensation. Directement ou indirectement, les autres critères (affection, prolepse) s'enracinent dans l'évidence première du sentir. Le sens que l'on attribue à la canonique dépend par conséquent de la manière dont on interprète ce privilège : revient-il à minimiser le rôle du *logos* dans le processus de connaissance ? Nullement. L'épicurisme, sur ce terrain, s'affronte à un défi en forme de paradoxe : si la sensation garantit toute vérité, les objets fondamentaux de la physique, atomes et vide, s'y dérobent par nature. Ce sera par conséquent à la raison de construire un dispositif, l'inférence sémiotique, qui, s'appuyant sur une observation méthodique des phénomènes, établira par l'analogie l'existence et les propriétés des éléments premiers de la nature. Comme le résume l'auteur : « (...) l'épicurisme apparaît bien plutôt comme un empirisme rationnel, qui légitime pleinement l'usage des notions, étant entendu que celui-ci doit être en accord avec l'expérience, à tout instant et à chaque étape ».

C'est dans cet éclairage qu'est examinée la genèse des préconceptions (*prolepseis*), qui garantit précisément à celles-ci une certitude directement dérivée de celle des sensations qu'elles concatènent. Leur rôle non seulement critériologique, mais heuristique est justement souligné. Il en va de même pour l'économie de la démonstration, qui rejette les procédures simplement formelles et circonscrit le domaine du démontrable ; ainsi que pour la méthode des attestations directes et indirectes du jugement, toujours arrimée en dernier ressort au critère sensible. Au total, l'auteur souligne la subtile circulation que cette épistémologie instaure entre les critères et l'élaboration rationnelle, et il insiste à raison sur la manière dont elle trace les limites du connaissable en respectant l'impératif éthique de garantir les connaissances indispensables au bonheur.

Le texte de José Kany-Turpin vient épauler et compléter le précédent en rassemblant les éléments d'épistémologie épicurienne épars dans le *De rerum natura* de Lucrèce. L'auteure montre de manière convaincante la fidélité de l'exposé lucrétien aux grands principes de la canonique, qui cependant n'en explicite que très peu les attendus, à l'exception notable du critère de la sensation. L'analyse aborde ensuite l'usage par le poète de l'analogie. Celle-ci, on l'a vu, constitue un élément clé de la *semêiôsis*, l'inférence par signes qui permet de se prononcer sur le non-visible à partir d'une observation réglée du sensible. JKT montre l'intérêt de cette procédure pour Lucrèce, en ce qu'elle lui permet de mettre la puissance d'invention du langage poétique au service de l'exposition philosophique.

Une autre dimension de la canonique épicurienne est abordée par Francesca Masi, avec « La physiologie épicurienne de la représentation mentale ». Sensation et pensée renvoient en effet à une physique. Notons qu'on ne saurait chercher dans celle-ci un fondement de la véracité de la sensation, sauf à tomber dans un cercle logique, car l'établissement des thèses physiques repose sur cette évidence première. La physiologie ne peut fournir ici qu'une confirmation et une explicitation après-coup du principe canonique fondateur. L'étude de FM se situe à un point délicat de la théorie épicurienne de la perception : l'articulation entre sensation visuelle, et perception mentale. La *Lettre à Hérodote* et le chant IV de Lucrèce attestent que l'une comme l'autre reposent sur les flux permanents de simulacres issus des objets extérieurs pénétrant aussi bien l'âme sentante que l'esprit, ce qui autorise Lucrèce à nommer la pensée une « sensation de l'esprit ». La spécificité de cette dernière tient au caractère plus subtil des simulacres mentaux, mais les causes d'une telle différence sont en débat. À l'inverse de la plupart des interprètes, FM propose d'établir une continuité directe entre les processus sensoriel et mental, en considérant que les mêmes simulacres qui pénètrent l'œil cheminent ensuite jusqu'à l'esprit en étant affinés par leur passage dans les minuscules canaux, les pores qui les y conduisent. Elle en conclut à la présence, chez Épicure, d'une théorie de la « *phantasia* mentale » inspirée d'Aristote, qui, à la différence de la représentation sensible, ne retiendrait que les caractères essentiels des objets, leurs « propriétés permanentes et typologiques ».

La construction est méticuleuse, mais attribuer aux épicuriens une dérivation directe des représentations intelligibles à partir des contenus sensibles, à la manière des empiristes de l'âge classique qui feront de l'idée une impression affaiblie, paraît solliciter les sources de manière excessive. On se demandera, partant, si une telle hypothèse n'engendre pas plus de difficultés qu'elle ne permet d'en résoudre.

Un témoignage rare d'Aétius dans les *Placita* résume la conception épicurienne des végétaux et de la place qui leur est attribuée dans la doctrine du Jardin. À partir de ce texte, Giulia Scalas , sous l'intitulé « Plantes sans âme dans le Jardin. La conception des végétaux dans la physiologie épicurienne », pose le problème peu discuté à ce jour des raisons pour lesquelles les épicuriens excluent les plantes de la catégorie des vivants. L'âme définit le vivant, et Épicure associe sa présence à des activités comme la sensation ou la pensée, dont sont dépourvues les plantes. Pour ce qui touche à la nutrition et au mouvement, la question est de savoir si l'on doit en inférer l'existence d'une âme. L'auteure montre que les schémas principaux qui, dans la physique épicurienne, régissent le mouvement et les échanges de la matière, permettent de faire l'économie d'une telle inférence.

Enfin, l'étude d'Aurélien Robert « Tout ce qui apparaît est vrai. Nicolas d'Autrécourt, l'épicurien malgré lui » fournit l'occasion, à travers la figure de cet atomiste médiéval, de reconsidérer une des thèses les plus controversées de l'épistémologie d'Épicure. En affirmant la vérité de toutes les perceptions, Épicure entendait réfuter à la fois le relativisme démocritéen et les arguments sceptiques, s'exposant évidemment à d'épineuses objections. Nicolas d'Autrécourt a repris la défense de cette position, en imputant comme Épicure la responsabilité de l'erreur au jugement de la raison, qui outrepasse l'évidence. Il entreprit ainsi de défaire les arguments sceptiques à partir d'attendus très proches de ceux d'Épicure, mais en complétant ces derniers par une théorie originale de l'image.

Ce détour médiéval ouvre une perspective originale sur la réception de la canonique épicurienne. La rubrique des « Introuvables » poursuit dans cette voie avec la publication du texte d'un élève de Peirce, Allan Marquand, « La Logique des épicuriens » (1883), qui projette sur la canonique un éclairage empiriste moderne. S'appuyant sur une analyse précise du traité *De Signis* de Philodème, Marquand montre comment les arguments défendant et précisant la procédure des inférences sémiotiques inaugurent une théorie générale de l'induction sans équivalent dans la pensée antique. Dans une riche Introduction, les traducteurs de ce texte en reconstruisent le contexte, et soulignent son importance pour mieux comprendre l'élaboration de l'ensemble de la pensée de Peirce lui-même.

À ce précieux « Introuvable » s'ajoute une importante étude de Bernard Besnier sur le refus épicurien de la définition, initialement parue en 1994. Ce refus participe du rejet plus général du syllogisme et de la dialectique. L'auteur montre comment la canonique épicurienne, en dépit des objections sceptiques, peut répudier les procédures logiques formelles sans compromettre la recherche et l'établissement des vérités.

La qualité d'ensemble de ces contributions fait que ce numéro des *Cahiers philosophiques* atteint pleinement ses objectifs : réhabiliter une partie injustement méconnue de la doctrine épicurienne, éclairer un moment singulier de l'héritage antique en matière d'épistémologie.

Alain GIGANDET
Université Paris-Est Créteil

Scott AIKIN & William O. STEPHENS, *Epictetus's* Encheiridion. *A New Translation and Guide to Stoic Ethics*, London, New York (NY), Oxford, New Delhi, Sidney, Bloomsbury Academic, 2023, 304 p., ISBN : 978-1-3500-0951-6.

The topic of this volume is the meaning, for a 21st century reader, of Epictetus' *Handbook* (henceforth *Ench.*). Aikin and Stephens' (henceforth A. & S.) goal is to explain each chapter of *Ench.* by showing, on the one hand, what role it plays in the overall structure of the work and how it enacts one or more concerns proper to Epictetus and to the Stoics; on the other hand, the content of *Ench.* is unfolded into a message relevant to a present-day reader. This project, to which *Ench.* lends itself easily, is in line with the ongoing popularization of ancient Stoicism which has been taking place in the last decades.

This enterprise demands a preliminary «introduction to ancient Stoicism» (p. 1-48), which the authors carry out by firstly identifying Socrates and Diogenes the Cynic as the main inspirers for the core ideas of the Stoics. Afterward, A. & S. briefly present some of the main figures of the Stoic tradition, starting with the founder of the school, Zeno, and ending with key representatives of Roman Stoicism. We may regret the absence from this catalog of the representatives of the so-called *intermediate Stoicism* and of the *Stoic opposition*; evoking some of these figures would have enriched the reconstruction of Epictetus' philosophical background, as, on the one side, some intermediate Stoics like Panetius seem to have influenced Epictetus' doctrine (on this see T. Bénatouïl, «Épictète et la doctrine des indifférents et du *telos* d'Ariston à Panétius», *Elenchos*, 40 (2019), p. 99-121); on the other side, Epictetus praises as role models numerous individuals who defied Emperors Nero and Vespasian, such as Thrasea Paetus (*Disc.* 1.1.26), Paconius Agrippinus (1.1.28-30), and Helvidius Priscus (1.2.19-24).

A. & S. follow this historical review with a succinct description of the Stoic «system», articulated in the three branches of logic, physics, and ethics, the most extensively deployed, given A. & S.'s practical aim with their book. This interest in ethics is carried on in the next two segments. The first one explains what the authors recognize as six «themes» constituting «the core of Stoicism» (p. 22) which, though not labeled by A. & S. as specifically pertaining to ethics, clearly do: they comprise (1) the encouragement to master one's own desires; (2) «the Fundamental Divide» (p. 23), i.e., the dichotomy between what is up to us and what is not. In this regard, it would have been appropriate to point out, for the sake of historical accuracy and to enhance Epictetus' philosophical contribution, that, although the Fundamental Divide is in tune with the orthodox Stoic doctrine, in the extant sources it is outlined only by Epictetus; (3) the identification of happiness with life in accordance with nature; (4) the idea that every individual has social 'roles', determining what they ought to do; (5) the Stoics' commitment to an intellectual ethics, in which the moral quality of an action depends on the knowledge of the agent; (6) the 'aspirationalist' character of the Stoic message, that spurs people to strive for a moral status extremely hard to attain. This list of topics is well-selected, as they effectively make up the theoretical foundation of *Ench.* The first part of the book is rounded out with a discussion of the paradoxical *tenets*, concerning the virtue, the sage, and their counterparts, presented in Cicero's *Paradoxa Stoicorum*, to which A. & S. add the one according to which « all non-sages are ugly; only the sage is beautiful ».

Part 2 of the book offers a biographical sketch for Epictetus that expands the one already traced at p. 14-15, and shortly delves into the structure of *Disc.* and *Ench.* This part is closed by an account of « the historical influence of the *Encheiridion* » (p. 54-59), which cannot but be a partial overview of what the authors regard as highlights of the history of the reception of *Ench.*, since, as they write, it is « fair to say that no other text its size has exercised as wide, deep and lasting an impact in the history of Stoicism, or indeed arguably the history of Western philosophy, as the *Encheiridion* » (p. 59).

A new translation of *Ench.* is offered in the next part of the book, after a short « note » (p. 61) in which the authors inform that their « twin goals » in this respect « are to present Epictetus's ideas in a fresh, contemporary idiom that reflects his brisk, direct style while also keeping close to the sense of the Greek » (*ibid.*); when a « tension » arises between these objectives « fidelity to the Greek has been relaxed to accommodate his [*scil.* Epictetus'] message to contemporary life » (*ibid.*). This choice is debatable, as among its consequences we discover that the absence of affections (ἀπάθεια) discussed in *Ench.* 12.2 becomes – without any explanation in the commentary – « mental health », and the single combats between gladiators (μονομαχία) and horse-races (ἱπποδρομία) evoked in *Ench.* 33.2 are 'updated' into kickboxing fights and NASCAR races. These cases exemplify different issues related to the 'accomodation' of *Ench.* accomplished by A. & S.

The Stoic concept of ἀπάθεια has a narrower meaning than mental health: by lack of « disturbing passions » (p. 21) the Stoics mean being devoid of false judgments about the value of things and, therefore, of their consequences in terms of mental and physical distress; mental health, as defined e.g. by the World Health Organization has the broader denotation of « state of mental well-being that enables people to cope with the stresses of life, realize their abilities, learn well and work well, and contribute to their community ». Stoic ἀπάθεια enables a person to realize themselves on the individual and social level, but these ideas are implied by the concept of 'absence of affections' rather than being at its core. A & S. ought probably to be more precise on this point – and the same comment may be made about the very heart of Epictetus' psychology, i.e., προαίρεσις –, as they duly do for the occurrence of εὐροέω in *Ench.* 8 (p. 102) or for that of ἡγεμονικόν in *Ench.* 38 (p. 200).

Regarding gladiators and horse-racers turning into kickboxers and NASCAR drivers, the problem of these translations concerns, in the first place, them being superfluous and arbitrary: on the one hand, anyone with an average historical consciousness is familiar with the gladiator games and knows that they had almost nothing to do with kickboxing matches. On the other hand, horse-racing is still a popular sport in most countries, and it is thus unclear why A. & S. felt appropriate to transpose a sport still in vogue pretty much everywhere to a much more specific one such as NASCAR racing. These translation choices can entail however a more serious difficulty: like any other writing, *Ench.* bears the signs of the milieu where it was produced; it is the reviewer's opinion that this inevitable anchoring ought to be preserved in a commented translation, even if the translator primarily aims at maximizing the practical effectiveness of *Ench.* Neglecting this component of *Ench.* impoverishes its depiction provided to the reader and, therefore, risks precisely decreasing the power of its message. This is, however, a personal judgment given by a scholar who, on the other hand, finds A. & S.' s translation of *Ench.* overall convincing.

In Part 4 the authors offer an in-depth analysis of each chapter of *Ench.* in order to bring forth the core lesson condensed in it. A. & S. do this by explaining the content of *Ench.* with a diffuse use of examples and sometimes by lingering on issues they acknowledge as implicit in Epictetus' reasoning, like (1) the tension they envision, in *Ench.* 13, between the «social impulse of Stoicism», spurring «to be an active part of a community» and the «hard Stoic perspective», according to which only virtue is valuable (p. 115-116), or (2) their reflection, starting from *Ench.* 31, on how the Stoic attitude towards the divine might «present in a contemporary context» (p. 175-176). On the critical side regarding this section, we have a minor observation and a major perplexity, which in this context we can only briefly expose: on the one hand, we think that the presentation of *Ench.* 43 (p. 212-214) would have benefited from explaining that with σχέσις Epictetus seems to denote not the social relationships, but rather the «social configurations» (S. Alexandre, Évaluation et contre-pouvoir. *Portée éthique et politique du jugement de valeur dans le stoïcisme romain*, Grenoble, Million, 2014, p. 84) of a person, that are completely up to them. On the other hand, A. & S.'s pondering on *Ench.* 40 (p. 202-207) inflates Epictetus' words with a feminist message, addressed to the «oppressed» women as well as to their male «oppressors» and aiming at the former' emancipation, that does not evidently reflect the content of the chapter.

In line with the authors' delving, in Part 4, into issues implicitly raised by *Ench.*, in the final part of the book they examine six «problems» (p. 247) to which Stoic philosophy lends its flank with its fatalism, its devaluation of external things, its allegedly systematic structure, its apparent compliance with the *status quo*, and the practical difficulty of respecting its *tenets*. In considering these issues, the authors evoke different strategies the Stoics resorted to or might have resorted to in order to shelter their philosophy from their critics; but, in this regard, A. & S. can also test the urgency for the Stoic thought to be «revised» and the «proper limits» (p. 247) of this revision, which, after all, is *the* question underlying the operation they tried to accomplish with their book.

All in all, except for the specific issues we raised in the course of our review, this book presents itself as an accomplished attempt to vulgarize *Ench.* and to show its enduring relevance. Hopefully, the considerable length of this useful «guide» will not discourage people to whom Stoicism and the teaching of Epictetus are little known from reading it through.

Gabriele FLAMIGNI
Sorbonne Université

Christopher GILL, *Learning to Live Naturally. Stoic Ethics and its Modern Significance,* Oxford University Press, 2022, ISBN : 978-0-19-886616-9.

L'ouvrage de Christopher Gill a une double ambition : traiter de près les questions fondamentales de l'éthique stoïcienne, et les penser dans le débat éthique moderne. Le livre est constitué de trois grandes parties.

La première partie, comportant trois chapitres, traite de l'idée stoïcienne du bonheur comme « vie en accord avec la nature » qui, d'après Gill fait la force et la cohérence de l'éthique de l'école du Portique. L'auteur aborde ici les thématiques centrales de l'éthique stoïcienne : la relation entre la vertu et les indifférents et le rôle de la nature dans le développement éthique.

Le premier chapitre traite de la vertu comme seul élément nécessaire à la vie heureuse, ce qui distingue l'éthique stoïcienne de l'éthique aristotélicienne. Gill aborde la définition stoïcienne du bonheur comme « vie en accord avec la nature », soulignant ainsi l'originalité de son propos. Que veut dire vivre selon nature ? À la différence de Sénèque dans les *Lettres à Lucillius* mais aussi de Inwood (« Ethics and Human Action in Early Stoicism », 1985), l'auteur souligne non seulement le caractère rationnel de la nature humaine mais aussi son caractère social. La sociabilité et la rationalité font écho à la structure et au caractère providentiel de la nature, ce qui explique le lien entre nature humaine et nature universelle. Les êtres humains peuvent se conformer à la nature universelle via l'appropriation (*oikeiosis*) de leur propre nature. L'énoncé de départ (la vertu comme seul élément nécessaire pour parvenir au bonheur) est ainsi éclairci par la conception de la vertu comme capacité à vivre en accord avec la nature.

Dans le deuxième chapitre Gill étudie l'importance de la relation entre la vertu et les indifférents afin de délibérer sur les actions appropriées (*kathekon*). Dans ce cadre la vertu est présentée comme la capacité à trier parmi les indifférents. Pour l'auteur la notion d'indifférent, ainsi que l'idée de vertu comme seule nécessaire au bonheur, constituent la plus grande contribution des stoïciens à l'éthique moderne. Gill présente la distinction entre les préférables (les indifférents qui peuvent concourir à une vie heureuse) et les non-préférables (les indifférents qui ne concourent pas à une vie heureuse). Néanmoins il souligne bien le propos stoïcien d'après lequel les indifférents ne peuvent en aucun cas faire obstacle au bonheur. Gill insiste ainsi sur l'originalité de la pensée stoïcienne qui théorise une catégorie intermédiaire n'appartenant ni au Bien ni au mal.

Dans le troisième chapitre l'auteur aborde les implications de la conception d'une nature universelle dans le domaine éthique. Ce qui est débattu parmi les stoïciens est la capacité de la nature universelle à fonder l'éthique. Gill, en accord avec Brüllmann (« Grounding Ethics in Nature : A Study of Stoic Naturalism », 2015), soutient qu'il ne s'agit pas de penser que la bonté de l'univers permet à toute chose une participation au Bien, mais plutôt de reconnaître que l'univers, du fait de ses qualités (rationalité et ordre), possède les caractéristiques qui le rendent bon. À la différence de l'éthique kantienne, qui fonde sa normativité sous l'impératif catégorique, et du christianisme, qui fonde son éthique sur la bonté extérieure de Dieu, l'éthique stoïcienne n'est pas dérivée d'un critère fondateur externe. Elle présente plutôt un caractère d'immanence qui exclut toute détermination autoritaire de ses préceptes. La nature n'est donc pas une source de normativité pour les actions. Gill apporte ainsi une démonstration claire de l'impossibilité de la subordination de l'éthique à la physique ou à la théologie.

Dans la deuxième partie, qui comporte deux chapitres, Gill s'occupe du processus de développement éthique qui permet de « vivre en accord avec la nature ». Pourquoi faut-il apprendre un processus qui devrait être naturel ? Gill répond à ce paradoxe en s'appuyant sur les théories stoïciennes de l'appropriation et des émotions. Il souligne, de manière originale, le rôle central des bonnes émotions (*eupatheiai*) pour mener une vie selon la vertu et le bonheur, alors que la théorie des émotions est le plus souvent analysée du point de vue de la maîtrise des passions.

Au chapitre 4 Gill revient sur la théorie de l'appropriation entendue comme progressive réalisation de la nature humaine (rationnelle et sociable) qui conduit l'être humain à prendre soin de soi-même et des autres. L'appropriation, en tant que représentation naturelle, permet de comprendre le développement éthique comme un processus naturel. Ainsi l'instinct de préservation de soi-même et l'amour parental sont les marques de la nature humaine. Gill répond de ce fait à une critique souvent adressée à l'idéal de sagesse stoïcien considéré comme inatteignable, en soutenant que le chemin vers la sagesse ne se distingue que quantitativement de la sagesse même ; ce qui laisse sa plénitude et sa raison d'être au parcours de développement éthique qui exprime à la fois une adéquation croissante à sa propre nature et un écart toujours mineur vis-à-vis de la vertu.

Dans le chapitre 5 l'auteur critique deux interprétations de la thérapeutique stoïcienne de l'âme : celle qui la décrit comme un acte intellectuel d'hyper rationalisme et celle qui l'interprète comme un parcours voué à l'autosuffisance et au détachement vis-à-vis des autres (R. Sorabji, « Emotion and Peace of Mind », 2000 et M. C. Nussbaum, « The Therapy of Desire : Theory and Practice in Hellenistic Ethics », 1994). L'auteur traite aussi de la différence entre les stoïciens d'une part, Platon et Aristote de l'autre. Les stoïciens croient que le développement éthique est accessible à tous les êtres humains en raison de leur nature et que ce processus, qui concerne uniquement l'âge adulte, est possible en dépit du contexte social et de l'éducation philosophique. Cela s'explique par le monisme rationnel qui conduit les stoïciens à concevoir le processus psychologique humain comme uniforme et rationnel au-delà du conflit binaire entre les parties rationnelle et irrationnelle de l'âme que l'on retrouve chez Platon et Aristote.

La troisième partie, se composant de trois chapitres, répond à la deuxième ambition de cet ouvrage, celle de penser l'éthique stoïcienne dans le débat éthique contemporain.

Premièrement Gill souligne qu'Aristote est une référence majeure pour l'éthique de la vertu (Anscombe, MacIntyre et Williams), qui est l'une des approches contemporaines de l'éthique. Cette approche se caractérise par le refus de l'utilitarisme et du kantisme qui négligent le rôle de la vertu et qui légitiment le désir de l'agent moral de vivre une vie heureuse à tout prix. Gill soutient que, sur ce point, les stoïciens plutôt qu'Aristote pourraient venir au secours de l'éthique de la vertu. En effet, l'éthique stoïcienne se présente comme plus cohérente, systématique et rigoureuse que l'éthique aristotélicienne au sujet de la relation exclusive entre vertu et bonheur. De plus, la théorisation stoïcienne d'une nature sociable de l'être humain semble offrir un appui nécessaire à la critique contemporaine de toute éthique qui produit des idéaux égoïstes. Sur ce point la position d'Aristote est beaucoup plus ambiguë car, même quand elle traite de la relation d'amitié, elle semble renvoyer à un intérêt personnel.

Au chapitre 7, il s'agit de penser ce que la conception de la nature humaine du stoïcisme apporte à l'éthique environnementale. La théorie naturaliste stoïcienne envisage un lien entre l'être humain, les autres formes de vie et la nature, ce qui se manifeste par un caractère de rationalité commun à tous. Cette manière de penser la nature est partagée par les éthiques de l'environnement qui conçoivent une valeur intrinsèque de la nature, indépendamment de celle que les êtres humains lui attribuent. En ce sens la théorie de l'appropriation stoïcienne offre une base et un appui aux éthiques de l'environnement. En effet, à la différence d'Aristote, pour les stoïciens le bonheur ne consiste pas seulement dans le fait de vivre la meilleure vie humaine possible, mais de le faire de manière que la nature humaine soit en cohérence avec la nature universelle. Établir ce lien et promouvoir une structure naturelle de l'homme et du monde pourrait offrir un fondement aux discours environnementalistes.

Dans le chapitre 8, Gill analyse le rapport entre le stoïcisme, le développement éthique et la conduite à maintenir pour bien vivre dans la pensée moderne. Comme pour l'éthique de la vertu contemporaine, Aristote a été un modèle central dans les théories modernes du développement éthique. Toutefois, les stoïciens peuvent représenter, encore une fois, une référence plus pertinente, car ils ne conditionnent pas la possibilité de la vertu à un contexte social spécifique, comme c'est le cas pour Aristote. De plus, le stoïcisme peut se faire guide de vie et Gill soutient l'hypothèse d'une présence importante du stoïcisme dans le discours contemporain, y compris dans le domaine de la psychothérapie cognitive. Sur ce sujet Aristote n'est pas pertinent. Le stoïcisme en effet s'adresse aux adultes, contribue au développement éthique et il conçoit les émotions comme le reflet d'une croyance ou d'un raisonnement. Ce dernier point, qui différencie la psychologie stoïcienne de celle aristotélico-platonicienne, est notamment pris comme point théorique fondamental pour les thérapies cognitivo-comportementales.

Gill conclut son ouvrage en soutenant non seulement que le stoïcisme offre un discours éthique puissant et cohérent (parties 1 et 2), mais également que l'approche stoïcienne peut informer la pensée moderne dans différents domaines (partie 3) en raison de son caractère universel et naturaliste.

Chiara CICCHETTI
Centre Léon Robin UMR 8061

Phillip MITSIS, Natura aut Voluntas *: recherches sur la pensée politique et éthique hellénistique et romaine et son influence*, trad. Vincent Jolivet et Charlotte Walbecq. Tournhout : Brepols, 2020 (Philosophie hellénistique et romaine, XI), 394 pages, ISBN : 978-2-503-58945-9.

L'ouvrage de Phillip Mitsis est un recueil constitué par une série d'articles déjà publiés, entre 1992 et 2022, auquel s'ajoute un article inédit (l'Appendice 1, « La vie nue du sage stoïcien »). Il se propose d'y étudier deux concepts fondamentaux, *Natura* et *Voluntas*. À travers le premier, c'est la théorie stoïcienne de la loi naturelle qui est d'abord présentée dans l'ouvrage, comme source des théories déontologiques qui culminent avec Kant. Mitsis prend ainsi résolument ses distances avec les rapprochements aristotélicien et platonicien qui ont pu être effectués jusqu'alors dans le travail des différents spécialistes, notamment Vander Waert (« The original theory of natural law », 2003), longuement discuté au chapitre 2. Le concept de *voluntas* quant à lui renvoie à la conception épicurienne de la volonté, du plaisir et de la mort, qui aurait donné naissance dans la philosophie moderne à la notion de libre-arbitre. C'est donc une entreprise de généalogie que Mitsis se propose d'effectuer, en présentant les philosophies stoïcienne et épicurienne comme l'origine de certains concepts qui imprègnent toute notre philosophie politique et éthique moderne – droits naturels et politiques, propriété privée, cosmopolitisme, libre arbitre.

La première partie, des chapitres 1 à 6 – auxquels s'ajoute l'appendice 1 concernant le sage stoïcien – regroupe les articles consacrés aux Stoïciens et à leur théorie de la loi naturelle. Cette étude approfondie de la notion de *natura* met en lumière le lien entre les théories déontologiques modernes et la conception de la loi naturelle comme loi morale et divine développée dès l'Antiquité. Mitsis entend montrer l'apport propre des Stoïciens en termes de philosophie morale, lorsqu'ils pensent que l'action morale est le fait de l'application d'une règle. Mitsis s'intéresse tout d'abord au jugement moral. Faut-il adopter une position intentionnaliste considérant que le raisonnement moral est un choix absolu qui procède d'une disposition vertueuse singulière de l'individu, ou bien une vision externaliste, considérant le raisonnement moral comme influencé par des déterminations extérieures, qui doivent être intégrées au choix mais sont perçues comme des contraintes ? Mitsis discute ici en particulier les thèses que Vander Waert a développées dans ses articles depuis 1989, selon lesquelles l'éthique stoïcienne ne fonctionne pas de manière prescriptive, parce que le jugement moral repose sur le raisonnement moral de l'individu, ce qui ouvre la voie à une théorie intentionnaliste de la moralité. Mitsis veut montrer contre Vander Waert et Inwood, que la position stoïcienne est à la fois intentionnaliste et externaliste, et qu'il n'y a pas d'évolution de l'Ancienne à la nouvelle *Stoa*. Notons toutefois qu'Inwood comprend la loi morale de façon procédurale, précisément parce qu'elle vient de la raison de l'individu. C'est la raison humaine, les vertus et les dispositions intérieures de l'agent qui donnent une valeur prescriptive à l'action morale. La réponse d'Inwood au problème philosophique posé entre intentionnalisme et externalisme est ainsi peut être plus proche de celle de Mitsis que ce dernier ne laisse entendre.

Les chapitres suivants s'intéressent au rôle des règles et des lois dans le développement moral et l'éducation, étudiant deux notions fondamentales, les *praecepta* et les *decreta* (chap. 3). Il s'agit de comprendre l'articulation entre les lois morales et la possibilité d'une expérience morale spécifique, c'est-à-dire la possibilité de prendre en compte la particularité de l'action morale et les exceptions à la règle. Tout ce développement travaille donc le passage de principes théoriques issus de la loi naturelle à leur application pratique dans le domaine de l'action morale.

Les chapitres 4 à 6 analysent, à partir de l'exposition de la théorie stoïcienne des lois naturelles, les notions de droit naturel, propriété privée et cosmopolitisme. Doit-on considérer les stoïciens comme les fondateurs de ces différents concepts, ou faut-il tracer une ligne nette qui sépare les conceptions antiques et modernes ? Sur la question des droits naturels, Mitsis s'oppose à MacIntyre (*After virtue: a study in moral theory,* 1981) et Brown (« The Emergence of natural law and the cosmopolis », 2009) en montrant qu'on peut considérer les stoïciens comme l'origine de la question des droits naturels, si l'on prend en compte le fait que leur théorie diffère de la conception actuelle des droits humains et de la vision politique contemporaine. Concernant le concept de propriété privée, Mitsis prétend s'éloigner des thèses de Long (« Stoic philosophers on persons, property, ownership and community », 1997) qui selon lui considère que les stoïciens sont au fondement d'une théorie moderne de la propriété privée, telle qu'on la trouve chez Locke ou Hegel. Mitsis s'appuie sur les textes de Cicéron mentionnés par Long pour montrer qu'on ne peut pas, en lisant ces textes, tracer un parallèle entre Locke et les stoïciens : cela ne prend pas en compte les thèses générales de Cicéron sur la justice, la société et le bien commun, ni les époques respectives des premiers Stoïciens et de Cicéron. Néanmoins, Long montre qu'il s'agit plus précisément d'affinité et non pas d'influence au sens strict du terme, ce qui permet de comprendre le lien établi par les stoïciens entre les concepts de conscience, de propriété privée, et de personne. Les stoïciens avancent que tout être humain possède au moins une chose, lui-même, comme être capable de jugement moral. À partir des écrits de Cicéron, eux-mêmes enracinés dans ceux de Panétius et de Chrysippe, Long montre que la tradition stoïcienne inclut l'idée de propriété qui dériverait des lois naturelles et de la nature humaine, et que même les stoïciens qui semblent opposés à cette idée maintiennent que la propriété est un indifférent préférable. S'il existe donc bien une affinité entre les idées de Locke, Hegel et les stoïciens, leur conception de la propriété privée reste différente. Pour Mitsis comme pour Long, il n'y a donc pas de droit à la propriété privée chez les stoïciens : elle reste un indifférent et en ce sens, ne coïncide pas parfaitement avec les thèses de Locke ou Hegel. Quant à la question du cosmopolitisme, Mitsis entend réviser certaines thèses soutenues par Berlin (« The Birth of Greek Individualism », 2002) selon lesquelles le recentrage stoïcien sur la vie intérieure va de paire avec la déconstruction de la cité grecque et la perte d'autonomie politique. Mitsis établit qu'au contraire les stoïciens ont eu un grand impact sur la pensée politique moderne, notamment dans la possibilité de critiquer un certain nombre de positions cosmopolites.

L'appendice 1, « La vie nue du sage stoïcien », présente une nouvelle interprétation de DL, VII. 33, texte dans lequel Zénon « demande (*keleuô*) que les femmes et les hommes portent le même vêtement et que leurs parties génitales ne soient pas couvertes ». Traduisant *morion* par « parties génitales » et non comme on le fait habituellement par « partie du corps », Mitsis propose de voir dans la recommandation de Zénon une prescription morale plus qu'une prescription juridique. Ce texte pose une question troublante : pourquoi un stoïcien, qui considère tout ce qui a trait au corps comme un indifférent, demanderait-il à ses concitoyens de porter des vêtements qui laissent dénudées les parties génitales ? Mitsis conclut que les stoïciens contribueraient ici à désexualiser les organes génitaux, ce qui corrobore la vision du corps comme un indifférent.

La deuxième partie (chapitres 7 à 10, et les deux derniers appendices) analyse la notion de *voluntas* et la manière dont la théorie épicurienne du plaisir, de l'amitié et de la mort a contribué à la développer. Cette notion a été influente dans la pensée moderne, particulièrement dans la philosophie de Locke et sa conception du libre-arbitre. Contrairement à ce que nombre de chercheurs ont avancé, Mitsis montre qu'on peut trouver une certaine forme d'héritage épicurien dans la philosophie de Locke. Cela contrevient à l'idée longtemps défendue selon laquelle les conceptions modernes et antiques du libre-arbitre s'opposent. En effet, certains spécialistes comme Bobzien (« Did Epicurus discover the Free-Will Problem? », 2000) considèrent que pour les Anciens, le libre arbitre ne consisterait pas à pouvoir choisir entre différentes possibilités, ce que Mitsis refuse en montrant qu'on trouve déjà cette conception d'un choix multiple chez Aristote lorsqu'il associe libre choix et possibilités alternatives (*Éthique à Nicomaque*, 1110a14-18). Selon Mitsis, l'influence des Épicuriens sur Locke est indéniable, même si cela peut paraître étonnant. C'est en effet Épicure qui met en place les termes dans lesquels la volonté comme libre choix sera pensée par les Modernes, même s'il use d'éléments déjà présents chez Homère ou Aristote. Cette deuxième partie s'ouvre par deux chapitres consacrés à des notions essentielles de l'épicurisme – plaisir, mort, hédonisme, amitié – qu'il convient de définir et d'analyser pour comprendre en quoi elles ont pu forger la notion moderne de volonté. Tout l'enjeu est de comprendre comment les Épicuriens ont pu concilier cette forme nouvelle de libre choix avec la nécessité qui découle des lois des atomes. Les conclusions de Mitsis ici conduisent surtout à réfuter certaines positions, notamment soutenues par Bobzien ou O'Keefe (« Is Epicurean Friendship Altruistic ? », 2001) visant à désarticuler le matérialisme et l'hédonisme des épicuriens. Les chapitres 9 et 10 se consacrent respectivement à la question de la mort chez Montaigne et à celle de la volonté chez Locke, pour montrer la permanence et la fécondité des idées épicuriennes dans la philosophie moderne. Les appendices 2 et 3 viennent préciser ces idées en analysant les notions de libre arbitre et de devoirs chez Locke, toujours dans cet héritage épicurien.

L'ouvrage est donc traversé par une volonté de retracer la généalogie de certaines de nos idées modernes, tout en reconnaissant que si les écoles antiques peuvent être à leur fondement, ces idées modernes gardent une spécificité irréductible. Tout lecteur intéressé par les concepts de jugement moral, de responsabilité ou encore de liberté tirera donc un grand profit de la lecture de ce volume.

Blandine HUERE
Université Paris Nanterre

Alexander J. MAZUR, *The Platonizing Sethian Background of Plotinus's Mysticism*, revised edition by Dylan M. Burns, with Kevin Corrigan, Ivan Miroschnikow, Tuomas Rasimus, and John D. Turner, Leiden / Boston, Brill (coll. Nag Hammadi and Manichaean Studies 98), 2021, 25 cm, XVII-337 p., 141 €, ISBN : 978-90-04-44167-5.

Le livre d'Alexandre (Zeke) Mazur [= AZM] est une édition posthume de sa thèse de doctorat soutenue en 2010 à l'Université de Chicago. Cette publication était très attendue, car, bien avant que la soutenance ait eu lieu, les vues originales d'AZM sur la mystique plotinienne attiraient l'attention des spécialistes. Dans les années

2003-2004, le jeune chercheur a fait une entrée remarquée dans le débat universitaire, en publiant un long article en deux parties : « Unio Magica, Part 1 : On the Magical Origins of Plotinus' Mysticism », *Dionysius* 21 (2003), p. 23-52 et « Unio Magica, Part 2 : Plotinus, Theurgy, and the Question of Ritual », *Dionysius* 22 (2004), p. 29-56. Cet article s'est attiré une vive critique de la part de Werner Beierwaltes, « Plotins philosophische Mystik und ihre Bedeutung für das Christentum », dans P. Schäfer (éd.), *Wege mystischer Gotteserfahrung*, Munich, 2006, p. 81-95, à quoi AZM a répondu de façon non moins vigoureuse dans « Unio Intellectualis ? A Response to Professor Werner Beierwaltes on Unio Magica », *Dionysius* 26 (2008), p. 193-200. Rétrospectivement, la violence du débat sur un tel sujet peut étonner.

Les premières publications d'AZM annonçaient déjà l'originalité et l'audace de son travail postérieur. En effet, son postulat fut de reconsidérer l'enseignement de Plotin sur l'union mystique avec l'Un, en tenant compte des sources de cet enseignement. De prime abord, cette proposition paraît anodine. Cependant, selon AZM, elle implique de se tourner vers des pratiques spirituelles connues au temps de Plotin. L'analyse de la conception plotinienne de l'union mystique conduit AZM à constater que celle-ci est essentiellement une expérience qui demande le dépassement de la distinction intellectuelle entre le sujet et l'objet, entre l'humain et le divin. La contemplation ne serait pas une sorte de processus intellectuel, mais une transformation réalisée en passant par plusieurs étapes de connaissance non-discursive. Pour étayer son propos, AZM se tourne vers la théurgie et ses pratiques, notamment vers les rituels magiques. Cette perspective est annoncée par le titre provocateur de son premier article : *unio magica* censée corriger voire remplacer l'interprétation habituelle de l'*unio mystica* plotinienne. En décrivant ainsi l'union mystique, AZM cherchait à affranchir la pensée plotinienne de ses lectures usuelles, qu'il considérait anachroniques, tributaires en particulier de la mystique chrétienne. Sans surprise, cette proposition a suscité un débat qui ne risque pas de s'arrêter de sitôt.

Pour compléter l'inventaire des publications notables d'AZM, il faut signaler sa traduction commentée du *Traité* 33 (II.9) de Plotin, *Contre les gnostiques*. L'édition posthume de ce travail a été préparée par les amis et collaborateurs d'AZM en 2019, tandis que sa traduction française (par Jean-Marc Narbonne) est parue en 2021 : *Introduction and Commentary to Plotinus's Treatise 33 (II.9) 'Against the Gnostics' and Related Studies*, ed. by F. Lacroix & J.-M. Narbonne, Laval, Presses de l'Université Laval, 2019 ; *Traité* 33 (II.9), trad. par J.-M. Narbonne, introd. par Z. Mazur, notes par L. Ferroni, Z. Mazur & J.-M. Narbonne, avec une note complémentaire par M. Pagotto Marsola, dans Plotin, *Œuvres complètes. Traité 30 (III 8), Traité 31 (V 8), Traité 32 (V 5), Traité 33 (II 9)*, sous la direction de L. Ferroni et J.-M. Narbonne, (CUF) Paris, Les Belles Lettres 2021, p. 159-266 et 436-583. Cet ouvrage mérite l'attention, car ce traité par excellence antignostique met à l'épreuve le fondement même de la théorie d'AZM concernant la proximité entre Plotin et les gnostiques séthiens.

Le livre *The Platonizing Sethian Background of Plotinus's Mysticism* est un exposé magistral de l'ensemble de thèses d'AZM, divisé en trois grands chapitres, accompagnés d'une introduction et d'une conclusion qui méritent un commentaire à part. Le premier chapitre est consacré à la structure de l'ascension qui conduit à l'union mystique avec l'Un (« The Structure of Plotinus's Ascent to Mystical Union with the One », p. 26-62). En plus de l'information de Porphyre sur l'importance du *Banquet* de Platon pour la vie spirituelle de Plotin (*VP* 23), AZM choisit dix-huit passages plotiniens (ajoutés en forme d'Appendix A, p. 274-292), provenant des traités 1 (I.6), 6 (IV.8), 9 (VI.9), 30 (III.8), 31 (V.8), 32 (V.5), 38 (VI.7) et 39 (VI.8), qu'il considère comme essentiels pour son analyse. Il met en évidence l'importance du vocabulaire érotique dans la structure très complexe de la mystique plotinienne, sommairement divisée en cinq étapes. Pour préciser cette division, l'auteur ajoute quelques subdivisions et excursus explicatifs. Le chapitre suivant est consacré à la dynamique de l'union de l'Intellect avec l'Un (« The Identity of Prenoetic and Hypernoetic Subjects in Plotinus », p. 63-138) ; et il est complété par un recueil de quatorze passages plotiniens (Appendix B, p. 293-302). AZM aborde la difficile question de l'ontogenèse – de l'origine de l'Intellect/Être à partir de sa relation avec l'Un –, en mettant en évidence les liens entre les textes plotiniens et certains traités de Nag Hammadi (*Zostrien* et *Allogène* en particulier). Le rapprochement avec le corpus gnostique séthien est poursuivi et approfondi dans le chapitre 3 (« 'The Way of Ascent is the Way of Descent' : The Mechanism of Transcendental Apprehension in Platonizing Sethian Gnosticism », p. 139-230). AZM se garde de faire dépendre la mystique plotinienne de celle des traités séthiens, bien qu'il dresse de nombreuses parallèles entre les deux corpus. Les tableaux comparatifs joints aux textes dans l'Appendix C (p. 303-314) soutiennent cette lecture. L'analyse est complétée par des références aux écrits issus des autres tradition gnostiques, notamment de l'hermétisme et du valentinisme. Indubitablement, cette démonstration des ressemblances, perceptibles autant au niveau du vocabulaire que du raisonnement, est très persuasive. AZM expose et défend une thèse au sens fort du terme : l'ascension et l'union avec l'Un plotinien ressemble – et cela en de nombreux points – à l'ascension mystique décrite par les gnostiques séthiens.

À plusieurs reprises, AZM discute les limites de sa proposition, en faisant preuve de lucidité par rapport à son caractère novateur et provocateur. Malgré cela, dans les parties par excellence méthodologiques (« Introduction : The Gnostic Background of Plotinus's Mysticism », p. 1-25 et « Conclusion : Dissolving Bouandries », p. 231-273) l'auteur a du mal à ne pas considérer la rencontre de Plotin avec les gnostiques séthiens comme une solution ultime à tous les problèmes d'interprétation de la mystique plotinienne. On peut difficilement contester la démarche consistant à « comprendre la pensée mystique de Plotin en elle-même » et à « la situer dans son propre contexte religieux et historique » (p. 25). Mais on peut néanmoins se demander si le contact avec les séthiens épuisent un tel problème. Pour ne pas chercher très loin : les débats à l'intérieur de l'école platonicienne et avec d'autres écoles philosophiques ne faisaient-ils pas partie, eux aussi, de ce « contexte propre » de la pensée plotinienne ? N'appartenaient-ils pas à l'environnement intellectuel et spirituel de Plotin ? Il y a peut-être ici une piste permettant de prolonger et compléter les vues d'AZM.

Il faut reconnaître l'importance d'une meilleure prise en compte des doctrines gnostiques dans l'étude du néoplatonisme. Les études du médio- et du néoplatonisme ont été impactées par la découverte de la bibliothèque de Nag Hammadi et la publication des traités appartenant à un courant fortement platonisant du gnosticisme en tant que manifestation du platonisme non-scolaire, voire « non-orthodoxe » (pour reprendre la terminologie popularisée par P. Athanassiadi). Par ce biais-là, le gnosticisme, en tant que courant à la fois philosophique et religieux, peut désormais plus facilement retrouver sa place dans l'histoire de la philosophie ancienne. Mais ce type d'études reste encore problématique pour plusieurs raisons, signalées d'ailleurs par AZM. À cause de l'état fragmentaire et du caractère polémique des sources littéraires, il est très difficile d'inscrire les doctrines gnostiques dans le temps et l'espace. Ainsi, la chronologie des traités séthiens (p. 17-25), tout comme les conditions historiques de la rencontre de Plotin avec les gnostiques (p. 250-260) constituent deux points fragiles de l'interprétation de la mystique plotinienne, proposée par AZM. Bien qu'il s'agisse de questions de chronologie, qui ne changent rien ou pas grand-chose à la pertinence des analyses d'AZM, elles dévoilent la part de l'arbitraire desdites analyses. Pour dresser un meilleur cadre historique, on pourrait tenir compte d'une autre forme encore du platonisme non-scolaire, à savoir du platonisme chrétien. Par exemple, John Turner (*Sethian Gnosticism and the Platonic Tradition*, 2001) a su en tirer profit pour établir la chronologie relative du séthianisme. Les écrits chrétiens sont eux aussi susceptibles de transmettre les mêmes concepts et idées platoniciennes que l'on retrouve dans des écrits issus de différents milieux gnostiques. Et – *at last but not least* – il faudrait également tenir compte des très nombreuses références bibliques dont les auteurs gnostiques se servent pour étayer leurs propos, en les comparant avec le vocabulaire et les concepts platoniciens. Pour cela, le livre d'AZM s'avère extrêmement utile, car il indique une voie à suivre pour mieux interpréter toutes les formes du platonisme non-scolaire.

IZABELA JURASZ
Humboldt Universität, Berlin

Anne-Isabelle BOUTON-TOUBOULIC (éd.), Augustin, *Contre les Académiciens* = *Contra Academicos*, Paris, Institut d'études augustiniennes, 2022 (Bibliothèque augustinienne, 4/3), 660 p., ISBN : 978-2-85121-316-7.

La prestigieuse collection de la *Bibliothèque Augustinienne* (BA) s'enrichit d'un nouveau volume entièrement dédié à l'un des tout premiers dialogues philosophiques d'Augustin, consacré à la question du scepticisme, le *Contra Academicos*. L'édition ancienne et minimaliste de René Jolivet (1939, BA 4/1) rendait cette nouvelle édition nécessaire. Anne-Isabelle Bouton-Touboulic (dorénavant ABT) livre ici un volume particulièrement complet : l'édition du texte latin et sa traduction (p. 265-535) sont précédées d'une longue introduction (p. 5-225), du plan détaillé du texte (p. 219-226), d'une riche bibliographie (p. 227-257) ; en fin de volume on trouvera les fameuses « notes complémentaires » (29 N.C. p. 539-627) qui sont comme de petits dossiers d'études dont tout lecteur de la BA connaît la valeur et l'utilité, et enfin deux index, un index biblique et un *index locorum*.

Le premier chapitre de l'introduction « La nouvelle Académie et la polémique anti-académicienne du *Contra Academicos* » rappelle l'histoire de la Nouvelle Académie et plus généralement l'histoire du scepticisme telle qu'elle apparaît dans le *Contra Academicos* par la médiation notamment (mais peut-être pas uniquement comme en témoigne la N.C. 6 sur certaines positions scepticisantes de Porphyre) des *Academica* de Cicéron. La lecture comparée des deux œuvres donne lieu dans la note 19 à un tableau récapitulatif (p. 602-605) des arguments similaires dans le *CA* et les *Academica* de Cicéron, très utile pour initier une comparaison systématique des arguments. Le deuxième chapitre (« Le scepticisme dans l'itinéraire d'Augustin et l'intention du *Contra Academicos* ») est particulièrement important parce qu'il affronte la question centrale de la nature de l'expérience sceptique qu'Augustin relate dans les *Confessions* et qui donne sens au *Contra Academicos*. Isabelle Bouton-Touboulic insiste sur « la profondeur de cette crise sceptique » que « la composition même du *Contra Academicos* suffit à attester » (p. 36) tout en rappelant les différents lieux augustiniens où les académiciens sont discutés, notamment le témoignage central des livres V et VI des *Confessions*. La lecture d'ensemble de l'« intention d'Augustin dans le *CA* » fait ainsi apparaître deux aspects essentiels. D'une part on voit clairement le sens de l'usage augustinien du scepticisme qui, de manière paradoxale, réhabilite la croyance (*credere*) soutenue par l'autorité (*auctoritas*). ABT rappelle, notamment au chap. V p. 154-155 (voir aussi p. 124-125), que les trois livres convergent vers « l'énoncé fondamental du livre III » : « Nul ne doute que nous soyons poussés à apprendre sous le double poids de l'autorité et de la raison. C'est donc pour moi une chose bien arrêtée de ne m'écarter sur aucun point absolument de l'autorité du Christ ; car je n'en trouve pas de meilleure (*CA* 3, 20, 43). » La discussion rationnelle des positions sceptiques aboutit ainsi non pas comme le veulent les néo-académiciens à affirmer la nécessité de l'*épochè* mais bien celle de la croyance dans l'autorité du Christ selon un schéma qui s'avérera constant dans l'œuvre augustinienne. A ce titre on pourrait d'ailleurs regretter que l'introduction ne donne pas plus à voir la prégnance de ce thème fidéiste auquel amène la discussion des sceptiques dans l'œuvre postérieure augustinienne, notamment dans la *Cité de Dieu* et surtout dans le *De trinitate.*

D'autre part, l'introduction met en lumière la question de « l'imbrication des portées éthique et épistémologique de la discussion » (p. 92, voir aussi p. 52). C'est cette imbrication qui permet de voir les liens parfois inaperçus entre le livre I et les livres II et III que le chap. IV (« le mouvement du dialogue ») démontre opportunément. Cette imbrication de l'éthique et du gnoséologique est centrale pour comprendre le sens du dépassement augustinien du scepticisme par ce qu'on pourrait appeler dans le *CA* un « mouvement rationnel vers la foi ». Le chapitre V « l'enjeu de l'héritage platonicien » souligne les différentes facettes de la présence du platonisme dans le *CA* qui est un point particulièrement problématique d'histoire des idées. Le platonisme est omniprésent chez Augustin, qu'il s'agisse du néo-platonisme ou précisément de la tradition néo-académicienne. Pour cette raison il importait de souligner le sens de la lecture augustinienne de la position néo-académicienne au sein du platonisme, et notamment de la fameuse interprétation « ésotérique » de la Nouvelle-Académie selon laquelle cette dernière aurait utilisé la voie de l'*épochè* pour dissimuler la transmission des véritables thèses de Platon. ABT, comme la plupart des interprètes actuels, montre comment cette lecture tendancieuse de la Nouvelle Académie correspond à un usage particulier « d'une vision unitaire de l'Académie autour du platonisme dogmatique » (p. 146). On comprend moins, en revanche, en quoi les excellentes pages sur la raison et l'autorité déjà mentionnées sont liées à la tradition platonicienne sinon de manière assez lointaine. Certes, comme le rappelle ABT, Platon dans le *Ménon* avait montré l'utilité pratique de la *doxa.* Mais le déplacement qu'elle souligne, à juste titre, où « loin d'être cantonné à certain objets, le *credere* devient pour Augustin un acte cognitif constitutif de toute activité intellectuelle » (p. 163) constitue à mon sens une déviation radicale vis-à-vis de ce qu'on appelle communément le platonisme et sa propre opposition entre *doxa* et *epistèmè.*

Cette introduction permet ainsi de comprendre comment Augustin comprenait, transposait, interprétait ces textes et ces positions malgré la distance temporelle qui en sépare les différents acteurs, ainsi que les couches interprétatives qui les recouvrent. À cet égard les pages sur la pratique de la dialectique (chap. VI) et plus généralement sur l'usage augustinien de la Nouvelle Académie sont remarquables et témoignent d'un investissement intellectuel considérable dans ce champ d'études.

En ce qui concerne l'édition du texte à proprement parler, elle se présente comme « un texte révisé de W. M. Green (*CCL* 29/2, 1970) » à partir d'un travail sur les principaux manuscrits, qui prend en compte également l'édition récente de Th. Fuhrer (*Bibliotheca Teubneriana* 2017, absente de la bibliographie mais dûment citée en notes). Un tableau (p. 218) recense les 25 variantes textuelles par rapport au texte de Green, chacune est motivée dans les notes courantes du texte ; la plupart correspondent aussi au texte de Fuhrer.

La traduction du *CA* est précédée de celle des *Révisions* I, 1 où Augustin revient sur son texte et en constitue une utile introduction rétrospective. Contrairement à certain passage de l'introduction – où l'éditrice cède parfois à la facilité de ne pas traduire les concepts latins : le *credere,* l'*auctoritas,* le *probabile,* etc. -, la traduction fait des choix conceptuels clairs et cohérents. Il est certainement vain de comparer des traductions qui relèvent de périodes et donc de pratiques très différentes, mais la comparaison de diverses traductions de la simple phrase *Hoc mihi de Academicis interim probabiliter, ut potui, persuasi* (III, 20, 43) montre bien la précision de cette nouvelle traduction. Ainsi ABT traduit cette phrase par « Au sujet des Académiciens, voilà ce dont j'ai pu me persuader pour le moment, comme étant probable » ; cette phrase était traduite par Jolivet par « Voilà les opinions probables que je me suis faites, entre-temps, comme j'ai pu, au sujet des Académiciens » et par Jean-Louis Dumas (Bibliothèque de la Pléiade, 1998) par « voilà ce dont je me suis persuadé, pour le moment, au sujet des académiciens ». Cette simple comparaison montre l'attention à traduire chaque mot et chacune de ses nuances, notamment ici la répétition induite par *probabiliter persuasi* ainsi que la nuance du conatif *ut potui*.

La traduction cherche à respecter les nuances de vocabulaire et porte une attention réelle à ne pas écraser les termes sous des concepts trop généraux ou systématiques. On peut prendre à titre d'exemple la précision sémantique qui amène à traduire *temerariam consensionem* par « acquiescement précipité » (III, 15, 34) plutôt que par « assentiment téméraire » précisément parce qu'Augustin n'utilise pas ici *assensus* ; certes le contexte est celui d'une critique de la doctrine de la suspension de l'assentiment et la différence pourrait être interprétée comme une simple variation. Mais précisément dans ce passage ce qui est en jeu ce n'est pas la critique de la suspension de l'assentiment des académiciens, mais bien plutôt le fait qu'Augustin lui aussi critique une certaine tendance (pas nécessairement académicienne) à consentir de manière précipitée (pas seulement sur des matières épistémologiques mais en général), ce qui ne l'empêche pas pour autant de critiquer la suspension de l'assentiment. Ce n'est pas parce qu'il faut éviter la précipitation, et en général la crédulité, qu'il faut pour autant chercher à se mettre à tout prix à l'abri dans la suspension du jugement.

Parmi les notes complémentaires, on peut relever la note 6 « Licentius et la présentation du point de vue de la Nouvelle Académie au livre I », très développée, qui relève la présence de motifs platoniciens et de thèmes issus de l'*Hortensius* dans la présentation de la Nouvelle Académie par Licentius qui s'appuie sur une distinction marquée entre l'homme et Dieu. L'hypothèse selon laquelle Augustin opposerait ici au « pessimisme » de Porphyre un « optimisme gnoséologique » qui repose sur la « rencontre du corps et de l'intellect divin dans l'Incarnation, [qui] permet *dès cette vie*, [de] surmonter l'obstacle du corps pour se tourner vers la vraie philosophie et trouver la vérité » (p. 550) est développée de manière particulièrement claire et doit être versée au dossier comme on l'a vu complexe du « platonisme d'Augustin ». La note 7 analyse précisément la définition de l'erreur néo-académicienne donnée par Licentius. À cet égard on peut peut-être discuter la traduction d'*opinio/opinari* par un lexique systématiquement lié à l'erreur : comme en témoigne la traduction de *quid, si quisquam nihil quaerat et interrogatus verbi gratia utrumnam modo dies sit, temere statimque noctem esse opinetur atque respondeat, nonne tibi videtur errare ?* (I, 4, 11) par « Mais imagine quelqu'un qui ne cherche rien et à qui on demande par exemple s'il fait jour actuellement ; sans réfléchir, et instantanément, il se hasarde à répondre qu'il fait nuit ? ne te semble-t-il pas dans l'erreur ? » La note ajoute que Cicéron englobe « l'*opinari* dans la catégorie plus large de l'*errare* » (p. 558). Mais je me demande si la traduction ne fausse pas ici le sens du terme *opinio* car ce qui pose problème pour Augustin ne semble pas tant le fait de penser quelque chose sous la forme d'une opinion, mais de le faire « sans réfléchir et instantanément ». En soi *opinari* peut signifier simplement « penser quelque chose » voire « considérer comme vraie une proposition », et pas nécessairement « se tromper » ou « se hasarder à penser ». Si l'on accepte de considérer l'opinion de manière neutre, et pas nécessairement comme une erreur, c'est-à-dire si l'on accepte de sortir du cadre de référence stoïcien qui constitue le point de départ de cette discussion et qui justifie ce choix de traductions, on comprend mieux, à mon avis, non seulement « l'effacement de la frontière entre connaissance et opinion » dont parle ensuite ABT, mais aussi plus généralement l'articulation de la raison et de la *fides* qui découle naturellement de cette nouvelle compréhension de ce que c'est que d'avoir une opinion (*opinari*). Enfin la note 13 (« une double expérience de lecture (2,2,5-6) ») est particulièrement utile pour comprendre la connaissance précise qu'avait Augustin des livres des néo-platoniciens ainsi que ses premières expériences de lectures bibliques.

Il s'agit donc là d'un volume indispensable non seulement pour les lecteurs d'Augustin mais pour tous ceux, chercheurs ou étudiants qui s'intéressent de près ou de loin à l'histoire du scepticisme ancien et plus généralement à l'histoire de la philosophie de la connaissance. Tant la conception intellectuelle que la conception matérielle du volume est impeccable. Il s'agit donc là d'une édition qu'on dirait aujourd'hui « durable » en tout point, la Bibliothèque augustinienne (dont ABT est co-directrice) étant, avec celle de la Pléiade, une des dernières collections en France à publier des volumes reliés avec soin. On sait d'avance que celui-là aura sa place dans toutes nos bibliothèques.

Stéphane MARCHAND
Université Paris 1 Panthéon Sorbonne
UMR 7219 SPHERE - GRAMATA

Véronique BOUDON-MILLOT, *Vieux, un Grec ne peut pas l'être*, suivi de la première traduction française du traité de Galien, *Sur la santé*, livre V, Paris, Les Belles Lettres, 2023, 372 p., ISBN : 978-2-251-45451-1.

Comme l'annonce son titre, emprunté au *Timée* (22b4-5) qui reprend les propos d'un prêtre égyptien pour qui les Grecs demeurent à jamais des enfants, leur savoir n'étant pas ancré dans un passé lointain, l'ouvrage de Véronique Boudon-Millot (désormais l'A.) ne se veut pas un livre sur la vieillesse chez les Grecs. L'esprit antique n'a guère d'intérêt pour la vieillesse prise en elle-même, non parce qu'il vouerait à la maturité un culte démesuré, mais par conscience aiguë de la relativité de cet âge de la vie. Les Grecs promeuvent une vision inclusive de la vieillesse – c'est là le fil conducteur autour duquel s'organise *Vieux, un Grec ne peut pas l'être* –, qui ne saurait se concevoir en dehors de son autre, la jeunesse. En privilégiant le vieillir (le processus) à la vieillesse (l'état figé), les médecins (tout particulièrement les auteurs du *Corpus hippocratique* et Galien), mais aussi les philosophes (Platon, Aristote) contribuent à réinscrire cette phase de l'existence dans la vie.

L'ouvrage traite des enjeux biomédicaux en lien direct avec le vieillissement. Est-il normal ou pathologique ? Peut-on, à défaut de le supprimer, le ralentir ? Quels facteurs sont susceptibles de l'accélérer ? Quelles pratiques peuvent favoriser une « santé sénile » ? Ces pratiques relèvent-elles de la médecine thérapeutique ou du soin ? L'A. aborde aussi certains enjeux éthiques liés au vieillissement, à l'image de la question de la dépendance pouvant survenir durant cette phase de la vie. Après un résumé des livres I à IV et du livre VI du traité de Galien *Sur la santé* (Annexe I), l'A. nous propose une traduction annotée du livre V, basée sur l'édition du texte grec de K. Koch (*Corpus Medicorum Graecorum* V 4, 2, Leipzig et Berlin, 1923, Annexe 2), ainsi qu'un lexique grec-français. Elle nous partage aussi ses traductions inédites d'extraits conséquents du traité galénique *Du Marasme* qui reste encore à ce jour non traduit en français dans son intégralité.

Les Grecs n'en nourrissent pas moins à l'égard de la vieillesse une profonde ambivalence dont on trouve un premier écho dans l'approche qu'en proposent les mythes (chap. 1 « Vieillir : mythes et représentations ») qui la signalent comme indésirable mais indéfectiblement liée à la condition humaine. Toute tentative de s'en émanciper se solde par un échec. En témoigne, entre autres, l'histoire de Tithon (*Hymne homérique à Aphrodite* 218-238), mortel aimé par la déesse Aurore qui demande à Zeus, pour son amant, l'immortalité, mais oublie d'ajouter à sa requête l'absence de vieillesse, le condamnant ainsi au cauchemar d'une vieillesse éternelle. L'expression formulaire « au seuil de la vieillesse » (*gèraos oudos*) qui donne au chapitre 2 son titre, présente, entre autres, chez Homère, Hésiode et Platon, envisage la vieillesse comme admettant une entrée, mais aussi une sortie. L'issue peut correspondre à la mort, bien entendu, mais aussi à cette ultime étape de l'existence qu'est l'extrême vieillesse que l'A. fait coïncider avec la dépendance, pensée comme incapacité « de vaquer à ses occupations habituelles » (p. 33), à l'image du travail des champs pour Laërte, du commandement pour Priam, que les textes se contentent toutefois d'évoquer en creux. Ce dédoublement, qui préfigure notre distinction entre troisième et quatrième âge, a pour effet de resituer la vieillesse « encore verte » (p. 34) plus nettement dans la vie, puisqu'elle n'en constitue pas une version amoindrie. La relativité de la vieillesse se lit aussi dans le rapport des Grecs à l'âge (chap. 9 « Portraits de vieillards »), à la fois approximatif, en l'absence d'état civil, mais aussi sujet à une valorisation hautement symbolique, la longévité, parfois hors norme (voir, entre autres, *DL* IX, 18), étant synonyme de grande sagesse.

Le cœur de l'ouvrage est cependant dédié à la perspective médicale et naturaliste qui s'ouvre au chap. 3 (« Nommer la vieillesse, penser le vieillissement ») sur une mise au point terminologique soulignant la variété, mais aussi une certaine instabilité dans l'usage des termes en lien avec la vieillesse. En témoigne la réversibilité des rapports d'ancienneté entre *presbutès* et *gerontès* dont on peine à traduire la différence, et la non-uniformité des systèmes de classes d'âge, y compris au sein du *Corpus hippocratique*. L'étude se poursuit par une présentation des principaux symptômes dégénératifs de la vieillesse (chap. 4 « La vieillesse : une question d'apparence ? ») qui croise notamment les conceptions hippocratique et aristotélicienne, soulignant au passage ce que la seconde doit à la première. Dans des pages à la fois denses et riches, l'A. compare, au chap. 5 (« Physiologie du vieillissement »), différentes théories physiologiques : celle développée par le Platon du *Timée* (81d3-4) où la vieillesse est définie comme un *pathos* du vivant qui dépérit (*phthinei*) ; celle du *Corpus hippocratique*, partagé entre une conception de la vieillesse comme froide et humide (*Du régime* 32-33 ; *De la nature de l'homme* 12, 6) ou à l'inverse froide et sèche (*Maladie sacrée* 9, 2) ; celle d'Aristote qui démultiplie les modèles pour penser le vieillissement, puisqu'au dépérissement (*phthisis*) présent notamment dans le traité *Du ciel* (III, 6, 305a11), viennent s'ajouter la putréfaction (*GA* V, 4, 784b6-7 ; *Météo*. IV, 1, 379a5) et la consomption (*maransis*) dont l'A. restitue la complexité avec une grande clarté à partir d'extraits des petits traités *De la jeunesse et de la vieillesse* (469b-470b), *De la vie et de la mort* (479a-b) ; et, pour finir, la conception galénique de la vieillesse comme marasme (*Sur les tempéraments* II, 2 ; *Sur le marasme*). L'A. reconstitue une filiation entre le traité *De la nature de l'homme* (12, 6) qui déjà pose une équivalence entre vieillir et se consumer (*marainesthai*), la *maransis* aristotélicienne et le *marasmos* galénique. La « continuité remarquable » (p. 86) que l'A. note entre ces termes issus du verbe *marainô* n'est cependant pas incompatible, selon nous, avec une plus profonde hétérogénéité doctrinale, notamment entre la conception hippocratique pour qui le vieillissement est un processus de régression continue entamé dès la naissance (p. 73) et celle d'Aristote chez qui l'histoire du développement biologique, partagée entre jeunesse, maturité et vieillesse (*Rhét.* II, 12, 1388b36 et 14, 1390b6-13 ; *De la vie et de la mort*, 2, 479a32 ; *GA* IV, 6, 775a13) inviterait davantage à penser la transition vers la vieillesse en terme de rupture progressive dans l'équilibre matériel du mélange qu'est le vivant (*GC* II, 7, 334b8-30). Nous renvoyons sur ce point notamment aux travaux de R. King (*Aristotle on Life & Death*, Londres, Duckworth, 2001, p. 74-80) et de K. Epstein (« Refining Method in Zoology: Aristotle on Aging and Generation », dans S. Föllinger (éd.), *Aristotle's Generation of Animals: A Comprehensive Approach*, Berlin/Boston, de Gruyter, 2022, p. 319-340). En mettant en perspective *maransis* aristotélicienne et *marasmos* galénique, l'A. souligne combien le médecin de Pergame est en dialogue constant avec les traités aristotéliciens dont il s'efforce de résoudre certaines tensions internes : la vieillesse est-elle contre-nature ou naturelle (*Marasme* 2) ? Jusqu'où la vieillesse peut-elle être comparée à une maladie (*ibid.* 1) ? Le chap. 6 (« La vieillesse n'est pas une maladie ») prend une tournure plus prescriptive, puisqu'il s'agit de défaire, principalement avec Galien, l'association entre vieillesse et maladie et de se doter des moyens de penser une « santé sénile » (*Sur la santé*, VI, 2). À la typologie des marasmes finement restituée par l'A. au chapitre précédent (p. 92-101), répond une étude serrée des différents niveaux de santé en contexte galénique (*ibid.*, V, 4) – dont on notera au passage qu'ils empruntent aux stoïciens leurs niveaux du qualifié (*to poion*) qu'on trouve dans un témoignage de Simplicius (*CAG*, 212, 12-23 et 28-30). Ces niveaux de santé sont à leur tour mis en perspective avec les divisions galéniques de la médecine. Sur cette base, l'A. déploie au chap. 8 (« De l'art de la gérocomie ») la thèse selon laquelle le propos de Galien est précisément de promouvoir un art du soin, et non une médecine de la vieillesse qui vaudrait à la condition vieillissante d'être systématiquement identifiée à celle du malade.

Cet ouvrage témoigne de la fécondité des approches non pas diachroniques mais thématiques et transhistoriques qui favorisent des rapprochements entre des textes trop souvent considérés séparément les uns des autres. La perspective que privilégie *Vieux, un Grec ne peut pas l'être* permet en effet de reconstituer, sur un temps long, les polémiques et débats qu'a pu susciter la question du vieillissement chez les médecins et philosophes de l'Antiquité. Elle retrace aussi l'histoire et l'évolution de certains concepts qui voyagent d'une école à une autre, dont la généalogie du marasme que nous propose ici l'A. constitue le meilleur exemple. Elle insiste aussi sur les continuités réelles entre corpus et rappelle au passage, de façon salutaire, que ces auteurs, philosophes et médecins, se lisent les uns les autres (le Galien lecteur d'Aristote est particulièrement bien mis en lumière) et élaborent leur théorie depuis les points de tension repérés chez ceux qui les précèdent.

La thèse défendue par l'A. insiste sur l'inclusion de la vieillesse dans l'existence présentée comme particulièrement une et continue. L'entrée dans la vieillesse ne produit pas de rupture. Au contraire, elle prolonge le processus évolutif normal qu'est la vie. Cette approche, qui invite à une fluidification des transitions menant d'un âge de la vie à un autre promeut une image des sociétés anciennes comme potentiellement moins âgistes que les nôtres, plus enclines à inclure les populations âgées dans une vision dite normale de l'humanité. Mais, et l'A. anticipe cette réserve, cette approche inclusive de la vieillesse vaut d'abord pour la minorité privilégiée, instruite et principalement masculine, à laquelle s'adresse d'ailleurs prioritairement la gérocomie de Galien. Si celle-ci donne à l'hygiène une dimension éthique (p. 213), en proposant, à la façon d'une pratique de soi, un régime adapté à cette période de la vie, la responsabilité de prendre soin de soi durant sa vieillesse incombe aux seuls individus. Or, comme le montre le chap. 7 (« Influences de l'environnement et du mode de vie ») où sont pris en compte les effets sur le vieillissement des conditions économiques et sociales de sociétés anciennes profondément inégalitaires, les populations âgées sont loin de former un ensemble homogène. L'importance de l'âge sur la qualité de vie des individus tend à s'effacer devant celle d'autres facteurs. Comme le souligne l'A. dans son dernier chapitre (« En guise de viatique »), le modèle inclusif que promeut la médecine antique doit être reconsidéré au regard du fait que la probabilité d'atteindre cet âge de la vie constitue, dans les sociétés anciennes, une condition majoritairement non partagée et donc un privilège.

Laetitia MONTEILS-LANG
Université de Montréal

Fosca MARIANI ZINI (éd.), *The Legacy of Aristotelian Enthymeme. Proof and Belief in the Middle Ages and the Renaissance*, London / New York / Oxford / New Delhi / Sydney, Bloomsbury Academic, 2023. viii+224 pages. ISBN : 978-1-350-24880-9.

Qu'il soit défini comme un « syllogisme imparfait », dont il manque une prémisse et qui est incapable de déboucher sur une conclusion valide, ou qu'il soit envisagé comme un « syllogisme défectueux » impliquant une théorie argumentative qui lui est propre, l'enthymème n'a jamais cessé de nourrir les réflexions des lecteurs de la *Rhétorique* et des *Premiers Analytiques*, les deux traités principaux d'Aristote dans lesquels est convoquée cette notion.

En rassemblant dans son livre huit contributions (accompagnées chacune de son apparat de notes et de sa bibliographie), Fosca Mariani Zini propose de mettre en lumière, suivant un ordre chronologique, quelques interprétations particulières qui ont été données de l'enthymème, entre l'Antiquité tardive et la Renaissance. Les questions soulevées par l'héritage de l'enthymème aristotélicien sont aussi larges que diverses : quelle est la relation entre preuve et croyance ? Quels sont les critères de la complétude, et par conséquent, de la validité de l'enthymème ? Dans quelle mesure l'enthymème peut-il être considéré comme un syllogisme – et dans quel sens convient-il alors de prendre cette notion de « syllogisme » ? Comme l'indique l'éditrice du volume, « l'analyse de l'enthymème fournit un point de vue particulier qui nous permet de mettre en lumière les relations entre les critères de validité d'arguments plausibles ou contingents et leur valeur épistémique 'dans la longue durée' » (p. 10).

Dans le premier chapitre, intitulé « The theories of enthymeme between late Antiquity and the early Middle Ages (c. 325-880) » (p. 23-45), Renato de Filippis examine les diverses définitions qui ont été données de l'enthymème chez les auteurs latins, depuis la *Rhétorique à Herennius*, Cicéron et Quintilien jusqu'aux manuels de rhétorique composés entre le IVe et le VIIIe siècle et qui ont été rassemblés par Karl Halm dans le volume des *Rhetores Latini Minores* (Julius Rufinianus, Consultus Fortunatianus, Julius Victor, Isidore de Séville, Cassiodore). L'enthymème, qui est généralement comparé à l'épichérème afin d'en déterminer plus précisément les éléments propres, est envisagé chez ces auteurs de trois façons : soit comme « syllogisme imparfait » ; soit comme démonstration *a contrario* ou *ex repugnantibus* ; soit encore comme *mentis conceptio*.

Sur un peu moins de trente pages, Saloua Chatti (« Enthymemes in al-Fārābī's and Avicenna's systems », p. 47-74) examine la façon dont l'enthymème (ar. *ḍamīr*) a été envisagé par deux des trois principaux *falāsifa*, ces philosophes de langue arabe qui ont repris et poursuivi l'héritage de la philosophie grecque : al-Fārābī et Avicenne. À défaut d'étudier de façon exhaustive la question de l'enthymème – ce qui dépassait bien évidemment le cadre d'un article –, Saloua Chatti a porté son attention exclusive sur le *Kitāb al-Khiṭāba* d'al-Fārābi et sur trois traités d'Avicenne (le *ʿUyūn al-ḥikma*, *Al-Ḥiṭaba* et *Al-Qiyās*) et a choisi d'insister, avec toute la précision requise par l'exercice, sur le contexte dans lequel ces textes ont été produits, avant d'étudier la fonction et le but qu'al-Fārābī et Avicenne confèrent à l'enthymème dans la constellation des types d'argumentation logique qu'ils reconnaissent.

Dans le chapitre 3 (« Argumentum, locus and enthymeme. Abaelard's transformation of the topics into a theory of enthymematic inference », p. 75-97), Christopher J. Martin démontre comment les enthymèmes entendus comme des inférences topiques et conditionnelles ne peuvent pas être réduits à des syllogismes imparfaits, mais désignent des inférences conditionnelles dont les critères de complétude et de validité ne sont pas les règles aristotéliciennes de convertibilité.

Reprenant de façon pédagogique et avec une clarté absolue l'histoire des enthymèmes au XIIIe siècle en décrivant notamment les sources dont disposent les philosophes de l'époque, Julie Brumberg-Chaumont examine, dans le cadre de son article (chapitre 4 : « The logic of enthymemes as (incomplete) syllogisms. Thirteenth-century theories and practices », p. 99-145), la façon dont a été comprise la notion d'incomplétude mobilisée dans la notion d'enthymème et dans celle de syllogisme abrégé ; comment le syllogisme abrégé se distingue de l'enthymème scientifique, constitué de signes nécessaires ; et quel rôle la redécouverte de la *Rhétorique* d'Aristote a joué dans l'éclairage de ces questions, la *Rhétorique* ayant d'abord été connue à travers la seule traduction arabo-latine d'Hermann avant d'avoir été traduite un peu avant 1270 par Guillaume de Moerbeke à partir de l'original grec. L'autrice propose ainsi une description éclairante des différentes interprétations qui ont été avancées de l'enthymème dans la tradition aristotélicienne avant de se concentrer sur le *De ortu scientiarum* et le commentaire aux *Premiers Analytiques* de Robert Kilwardby, qui défend une vision syllogistique des enthymèmes, ainsi que sur le commentaire de Gilles de Rome à la *Rhétorique* d'Aristote, qui, lui, n'offre pas d'analyse logique des enthymèmes – un geste philosophiquement fondé, défend Julie Brumberg-Chaumont : « Giles of Rome, faced with the generally accepted theory of the enthymeme as an incomplete syllogism when he redacted the first Latin commentary on the treatise, reacted to this negative statement by claiming that being an incomplete or even a 'defective' syllogism is 'incidental' to the enthymeme. As a consequence, the very project of a logic of enthymeme falls outside the scope of both rhetoric and dialectic », p. 131.

Deux chapitres sont dédiés au XIVe siècle. Dans le chapitre 5 (« Inference and enthymeme in Ockham », p. 147-167), Paola Müller explique que, même s'il ne propose pas de doctrine spécifiquement dédiée aux enthymèmes, Guillaume d'Ockham traite des enthymèmes en rapport avec la théorie des conséquences et des raisonnements trompeurs en cherchant à relier d'une façon cohérente l'approche sémantique et l'approche syntaxique. Dans le chapitre 6 (« Enthymematic inferences in John Buridan », p. 169-186), Barbara Bartocci reconstruit la théorie de l'enthymème chez Jean Buridan, défini comme un syllogisme imparfait, tant d'un point de vue logique (c'est une conséquence matérielle) que d'un point de vue épistémologique (c'est une inférence). Elle éclaire non seulement la façon dont Jean Buridan comprend les conséquences enthymématiques, mais aussi les arguments qui sont formellement non valides mais qui ont malgré tout quelque valeur dans les discussions du quotidien et dans les disciplines qui ne visent pas des conclusions absolument certaines. Présentant des exemples d'enthymèmes, elle montre comment Buridan les réduit à des syllogismes – syllogismes entendus comme une catégorie qui inclut ici les syllogismes catégoriques et les syllogismes hypothétiques.

Le volume s'achève sur deux contributions relevant désormais de contextes et de questionnements bien différents puisqu'ils sont consacrés à la Renaissance. Dans le chapitre 7 intitulé « The enthymeme from signs and the study of nature in the Renaissance », (p. 187-199), Marco Sgarbi étudie la façon dont les auteurs de l'Italie du XVe et du XVIe siècle, comme Agostino Nifo, Alessandro Achillini, Marcoantonio Zimara, Bernardino Tomitano ou Girolamo Balduino, ont recueilli l'héritage des commentateurs d'Aristote que sont Philopon et Simplicius, qui ont élargi la notion d'enthymème formé à partir de signes nécessaires (ou preuves) à celle de syllogisme concluant de l'effet à la cause, c'est-à-dire comme produisant une inférence, à partir de ce qui est *a posteriori*, de ce qui est *a priori*, alors que ce type de relation causale est clairement absent dans l'enthymème rhétorique aristotélicien. L'enthymème est dès lors interprété à la Renaissance comme une *demonstratio ex signis* et devient l'instrument mis en œuvre dans les recherches naturelles et la connaissance des particuliers fondée sur l'expérience. Dans le dernier chapitre (« The lion's fault: the enthymematic foundation of the signatures », p. 201-213), Marie-Luce Demonet examine l'usage de l'enthymème (entendu comme 'enthymème physiognomonique' ou 'enthymème visuel') dans la théorie de la physiognomonie, à partir du *De humana physiognomonia* (1586) et des *Physiognomonica* (1588) de Della Porta, en soulevant notamment la question de savoir si la physiognomonie du Pseudo-Aristote ouvre la voie à la théorie des signatures étudiée par Michel Foucault. Selon Marie-Luce Demonet, l'enthymème visuel, qui est un syllogisme imparfait, ne se réduit pour ainsi dire jamais à un syllogisme valide ; il se révèle en revanche d'une grande utilité lorsqu'il s'agit de saisir des éléments qui nous étaient jusqu'alors cachés dans l'expérience des natures physiques et humaines.

En choisissant de publier un volume sur un sujet aussi généralement peu considéré que celui de l'enthymème, lequel est défini en effet comme un « syllogisme imparfait », Fosca Mariani Zini est parvenue à rendre ses lettres de noblesses à une forme d'argumentation qui n'est d'habitude reconnue comme majeure que dans le domaine de la rhétorique. En rassemblant des textes divers et d'une grande richesse, touchant à la logique la plus ardue, à la rhétorique, mais aussi à la théologie, l'éthique, la physiognomonie, la médecine ou la science naturelle, ce volume dévoile l'importance que la notion d'enthymème a pu revêtir depuis l'Antiquité jusqu'à la Renaissance, en Europe occidentale ou dans le domaine de la philosophie arabe. Puisse ce geste innovant inspirer d'autres chercheurs et ouvrir la voie à de nouvelles investigations sur l'enthymème !

Frédérique WOERTHER
UMR 8230, CNRS / ENS Ulm

Frédérique ILDEFONSE, *Le Multiple dans l'âme. Sur l'intériorité comme problème*, Paris : Vrin, 2022 (Textes et traditions), 888 p. ISBN 978-2-7116-3073-8.

Dans un livre publié en 2012 aux Presses Universitaires de France, *Il y a des Dieux*, Frédérique Ildefonse (l'A.) raconte la prise de conscience ou plutôt le « pari », ce sont ses termes, qui la conduit à Salvador, sur le *terreiro* abritant des *orixás*, ces saints de la religion afro-brésilienne du candomblé pratiquée par les esclaves en résistance à la domination des Blancs : « Je ne pouvais plus seulement nourrir d'elle-même ma recherche sur les Grecs. J'avais découvert qu'il existe un lien entre le polythéisme et la multiplicité psychique que ne vient intégrer aucune intériorité » (p. 9). L'ouvrage conséquent que l'A. publie chez Vrin dix ans plus tard sous le titre *Le Multiple dans l'âme* en est la réciproque. Le détour par les *orixás* et les rituels du candomblé s'est avéré plus que fécond, puisqu'il rend possible un retour vivant aux Grecs, c'est-à-dire qu'il a rendu l'esprit disponible pour saisir pleinement et intimement la singularité avec laquelle le monde grec antique a problématisé son expérience et la distance qui nous en sépare.

Cette immersion dans le « polythéisme vivant », la familiarité avec les travaux d'ethnologues spécialistes du Brésil (Roger Bastide ou Patricia de Aquino), du Mexique (Perig Pitrou) ou de l'Égypte antique (Jean Sainte Fare Garnot) ainsi qu'avec les travaux d'anthropologues ou de philosophes portant précisément sur les questions de « personne » ou de « moi » (Ignace Meyerson, Marcel Mauss, Philippe Descola, Alain Damasio, Vincent Carraud ou Vincent Descombes et Charles Larmore) donnaient ou redonnaient une acuité toute particulière aux travaux de Jean-Pierre Vernant, cité longuement et tout au long de l'ouvrage, qui en appelait dans « La fabrique de soi » à une « histoire de l'intériorité » qui serait encore à faire à propos de l'Antiquité grecque. Voilà qui sert de contexte et de point de départ à un long travail d'enquête, en dialogue avec un certain nombre de travaux s'intéressant à la manière dont les Grecs ont appréhendé l'identité, dont ils conçoivent ce que nous appelons intériorité, intime, moi et le dialogue qu'il est possible de tisser entre notre monde contemporain et les mondes antiques (Ruth Padel, Françoise Frontisi, Christopher Gill, Marion Bourbon). L'enquête se traduit concrètement par une série d'articles, de contributions au programme de l'EHESS sur le comparatisme, et par la co-fondation d'un séminaire « En-deçà du sujet », qui vont être autant de milieux et de jalons nécessaires à l'élaboration du travail que constitue le présent ouvrage. Jalons auxquels il faudrait ajouter l'ouvrage collectif co-dirigé avec Gwenaëlle Aubry, *Le moi et l'intériorité*, paru chez Vrin en 2008. Le travail de recherche qui nous est proposé dans le *Multiple dans l'âme* se revendique donc d'un triple ancrage qui est loin d'être anodin : le polythéisme vivant du candomblé, une approche de l'Antiquité chère à Vernant qui se fait fort de tenir ensemble philosophie et anthropologie, tout particulièrement les aspects ayant trait au sacré, au divin, au rituel (Louis Gernet, Marcel Detienne, Eric R. Dodds, Claude Calame, Alain Petit), ainsi qu'une expérience collective de la recherche qui implique notamment les travaux de Catherine Darbo-Peschanski (la notion d'acte réparti) et de Jean-Louis Durand (l'idée d'une articulation de l'un et du multiple) à qui est dédié l'ouvrage.

Dans *Le Multiple dans l'âme*, l'A. se propose donc d'instruire, à partir d'un corpus qui va d'Homère à Plotin, une « histoire des problématisations de l'intérieur », formule et démarche qui font écho à un concept élaboré par Michel Foucault, à qui l'A. fait très explicitement référence en abordant de façon précise les thèses développées dans les derniers travaux du philosophe ainsi que les critiques dont ces thèses ont fait l'objet de la part des antiquisants (II 3 ; IV 2). L'A. se propose en réalité de pousser jusqu'au bout et par-delà Foucault lui-même la démarche de problématisation, cherchant « en amont » du « souci de soi » et rompant par exemple avec l'idée foucaldienne que le δαίμων serait « un sujet dans le sujet ». En effet, ce sont précisément ces concepts – soi, sujet, mais aussi individu, personne, moi – dont l'A. refuse d'admettre qu'ils préexistent et dont elle interroge la pertinence tout au long de l'ouvrage, et ce d'une façon plus radicale que les travaux, qu'elle discute, qui admettent pourtant l'historicité des notions de sujet ou de personne. Il n'est plus question en effet de se contenter de considérer ces catégories comme des approximations indispensables que l'on serait « forcé » d'utiliser, pour traduire les textes par exemple. Pas même – surtout pas – celle d'intériorité qu'utilise par exemple Philippe Descola comme une catégorie valide pour élaborer ses quatre ontologies. Dans la perspective développée par l'A., l'intériorité – comprise comme « la caractéristique d'un vivant humain qui s'approprie les phénomènes psychiques qui se produisent en lui, considère les phénomènes intérieurs comme siens ou encore s'identifie à ses états intérieurs » (p. 11) – n'est que l'une des manières, récente et culturellement située, de problématiser l'intérieur. L'intériorité ne saurait être une structure invariante, une catégorie universelle de l'esprit humain qui serait remplie ou incarnée de différentes manières. L'intériorité doit être comprise comme un « problème », c'est-à-dire comme une manière particulière de problématiser l'intérieur dont il s'agirait en outre de repérer et de comprendre les conditions d'émergence et la portée.

Retrouver sous nos habitudes de penser d'autres catégories, d'autres partages en lieu et place des oppositions tranchées qui nous sont habituelles (entre extérieur et intérieur, entre un et multiple, entre concentration sur « soi » et ouverture sur le monde) impliquait une attention toute particulière au détail du texte grec afin d'éviter les effets de familiarité auxquels nous ont habitués des traductions certes très confortables et très justes, puisqu'elles s'adaptent au mieux à nos manières de voir, mais dommageables en ce qu'elles masquent d'emblée une hétérogénéité qui nous serait en effet difficilement intelligible au premier abord et qui nécessite, pour être saisie, une véritable ascèse de la pensée à quoi nous convie et nous aide l'ouvrage, notamment en discutant minutieusement les choix de traduction, en français ou en anglais, pour les très nombreux passages significatifs étudiés. Le gain n'est pas mince. « Pourvu que l'on suspende la tendance à traduire les textes anciens en utilisant de façon quasi automatique les concepts modernes, de moi, de sujet, de personne, ou même de soi et d'individu, d'autres termes peuvent apparaître, qui ont été peu investis par la conceptualité philosophique et dont l'analyse est pourtant éclairante. C'est le cas d'ἕκαστος, 'chacun', 'chaque' » (p. 729). La longueur de l'ouvrage trouve toute sa légitimité dans cet indispensable travail de relecture du texte grec.

Outre une critique de ces traductions « parlantes » pour nous mais qui masquent ce dont il est en réalité question, l'A. met en garde contre une tendance fréquente qui consiste à « transformer un pronom en concept » (p. 32). On ne saurait induire à partir d'un pronom de première personne qu'il existe quelque chose comme un sujet, un moi renvoyant à une entité séparée et souveraine ou à de l'intime, ni faire d'une tournure réflexive un argument en faveur d'une réflexivité qui engagerait quelque chose comme un « soi-même » ou un « rapport de soi à soi ». L'expression de « retour à soi » ou « en soi » existe bel et bien, mais elle ne renvoie pas à ce que nous appelons « soi » (p. 55-56), puisque cette concentration sur soi implique dans le même mouvement, qui nous apparaît contradictoire, l'ouverture au monde. « Le retour à soi-même ou en soi-même n'est pas une étape ultime : il faut y lire une forme de concentration qui va de pair avec une ouverture. Le retour à soi-même apparaît moins comme un retour chez soi ou en soi que comme un sas qui permet l'accès et le passage à l'ordre structurant du monde » (p. 712).

La structure de l'ouvrage répond quant à elle à différentes logiques. L'ouvrage se lit de plusieurs façons. On peut distinguer en effet, comme nous y invite l'A., une première partie « critique » (analysant la pertinence des concepts de « personne », que l'on rattache assez systématiquement au πρόσωπον au point de négliger la spécificité de ce dernier, et de « moi », à quoi l'on assimile parfois l' ἴδιον ἡγεμονικόν stoïcien) et trois autres parties plus « positives », qui analyseraient les manières dont les Grecs – en tout cas Homère et les philosophes, car c'est sur les textes philosophiques, en plus des textes homériques, que se fonde presque exclusivement l'analyse – problématisaient l'intérieur. Mais les deux aspects s'entremêlent malgré tout nécessairement. Critiquer la pertinence des notions de « personne » et de « moi » dans l'Antiquité conduit en effet à analyser le sens à donner à l' ἴδιον ἡγεμονικόν stoïcien qui est une manière de problématiser l'intérieur. Réciproquement, prendre au sérieux l'idée de multiplicité intérieure, insister sur les conditions d'impossibilité de la réflexivité telle que nous l'entendons, souligner l'ouverture radicale du vivant humain sur l'extérieur, la primauté du commun et du rapport ainsi que l'importance cruciale de l'ancrage cosmique, analyser la spécificité du sens à donner aux pronoms αὐτός (II) et ἕκαστος (IV), reprendre à nouveaux frais les notions de συναίσθησις et d'οἰκείωσις (III) ou encore de δαίμων (IV) conduit à invalider la pertinence des notions de « soi » et de « souci de soi » (II), de « conscience » et de « perception de soi » (III), d' « individu » et de « sujet » (IV) qui nous sont si familières et sans lesquelles il nous est bien difficile de penser notre expérience. Peut-être faudrait-il réserver malgré tout un sort particulier au concept d'individu, comme semble d'ailleurs le laisser penser l'A., sans toutefois se référer à l'ouvrage collectif dirigé par Sandra Boehringer et Violaine Sebillotte Cuchet (*Des femmes en action. L'individu et la fonction en Grèce antique*, Paris-Athènes, Éditions de l'EHESS, 2013), qui met au jour la fécondité heuristique de cette notion, qui n'a rien d'une approximation quand elle se trouve articulée avec le concept de fonction.

Outre la complémentarité méthodologique entre du « critique » et du « positif », dont on voit qu'ils s'entremêlent tout au long de l'ouvrage, la véritable tension conceptuelle réside dans le passage entre une question initiale et une question essentielle. « L'enquête initiale sur les différentes manières de problématiser l'intérieur s'avère être une enquête préalable qui ouvre sur une seconde enquête portant sur de l'un et du multiple dans l'âme ainsi que dans le rapport aux dieux » (p. 116). L'ouvrage nous conduit donc à passer d'une formulation approximative (dans les termes de l'intérieur) à une formulation idoine (dans les termes du multiple), qui ne peut être conquise que dans le cours même du déploiement de l'analyse. Le titre de l'ouvrage rend compte de ce passage d'une question relative à l' « intériorité comme problème » à une réflexion – qui devient majeure et centrale – autour de l'idée de multiplicité comprise dans sa radicalité : « du multiple dans l'âme et non un moi multiple ou une intériorité multiple » (p. 115). Celle-ci devient, dès la deuxième partie, dès que l'on aborde les manières dont les Grecs, d'Homère à Plotin, formulent leur problématisation de l'intérieur, le fil directeur de l'enquête. Le prisme du multiple permet en outre d'identifier un sol commun entre multiplicité de l'âme et multiplicité divine, d'articuler l'idée d'une multiplicité intérieure avec une conception polythéiste, coïncidence que l'A. découvrait également dans la culture afro-brésilienne. Aussi la notion d' « hospitalité psychique » s'avère-t-elle centrale. Elle renvoie à l'idée que l'esprit est accueilli à l'intérieur, ou que l'intérieur est accueil d'un autre. La confrontation avec les textes antiques nous révèle en effet que l'idée qui nous est si familière aujourd'hui, selon laquelle l'esprit serait « à l'intérieur » ou « intérieur » était alors « dénoncée par Plutarque et Épictète » comme une « illusion » dont il fallait « se défaire » (p. 13). « L'hospitalité psychique » propre au contexte antique consiste en revanche « dans le fait d'héberger à l'intérieur de nous une instance divine dont nous avons avantage, si possible, à ce qu'elle nous gouverne de l'intérieur de nous. » (p. 724-725).

L'ouvrage ne propose pas une approche chronologique mais privilégie une approche conceptuelle. Et cette approche problématisée permet, pour chacune des pistes développées, de souligner les infléchissements, les innovations, les parentés ou les retours entre les différents auteurs ou chez un même auteur. L'A. souligne l'importance du renversement opéré par le mythe d'Er, l'importance également, peu soulignée et négligée par Foucault, des développements aristotéliciens sur l'amitié dans une analyse de la subjectivation antique. Et elle insiste tout particulièrement sur les infléchissements que représente le stoïcisme, notamment impérial, à travers ce qu'elle appelle une « injonction à l'unité », l'option du monisme psychique, l'élaboration de l'οἰκείωσις ou une compréhension intérieure du δαίμων. Les différents aspects semblent dessiner, même si l'auteur ne le formule pas ainsi, trois axes de l'expérience, à partir de et par-delà Foucault : un vivant humain qui est toujours dans une situation de dialogue initial (le rapport à l'autre), un vivant humain ouvert sur des sensations qui le traversent (le rapport à la nature), un vivant humain qui héberge en lui un démon et qui s'inscrit dans le cycle des incarnations successives (le rapport au divin, l'ancrage cosmique). On ne parlerait évidemment pas d'un rapport « de soi » aux autres, à la nature ou au divin, mais on comprendrait plutôt qu'être quelqu'un, ou plutôt quelque un, autrement dit un parmi les autres (ἕκαστος) se constitue dans ce tissu de relations qui articule sans les opposer l'intérieur et l'extérieur, l'un et le multiple, la concentration et l'ouverture. Sans oublier la dimension normative qui caractérise la subjectivation antique et qui permet de l'assimiler à une éthique de l'*optimum* dont αὐτός porterait la charge : « Si [...] αὐτός qui apparaît comme la visée de l'éthique grecque est le garant d'une vie réussie [...], ce qui nous fait n'est pas profondément notre vie, en tant qu'elle serait l'ensemble de ce que nous éprouvons, traversons, aussi bien qu'elle serait faite de nos actions, mais bien plutôt la manière dont nous orientons la part divine en nous » (p. 646).

Outre un gain significatif quant à la compréhension d'un aspect majeur de la pensée antique, outre une relecture neuve et stimulante d'un certain nombre de textes qui étaient devenus presque trop familiers, il faudrait souligner le soin accordé à une bibliographie ramassée relativement à l'ampleur de l'ouvrage ainsi que la présence d'index très utiles des noms et des passages cités – même si l'on peut regretter l'absence d'un index des notions, remplacé par un glossaire – qui font de l'ouvrage le support et le relai explicite vers d'autres travaux passés et à venir, une modestie et une générosité qui, adossées à la compétence scientifique et à la critique honnête et franche, constituent la condition d'un véritable dialogue, comme le suggérait déjà Platon dans le *Gorgias*. De par sa dimension heuristique qui rend à sa contingence notre manière de concevoir l'intérieur, l'esprit et la pensée tout en suggérant en creux les conditions nécessaires à une problématisation de l'intérieur en termes d'intériorité – la perte d'un ancrage cosmique, la recherche d'une stabilité, l'effroi face à la multiplicité, une certaine « vacance » rituelle, une certaine solitude aussi – *Le Multiple dans l'âme* est donc un texte pleinement philosophique, et par conséquent politique. En plus de nous apprendre beaucoup, il nous donne autant à penser, en tant que chercheurs et chercheuses, citoyens et citoyennes du monde, en tant qu'occidentaux aussi dans un monde qui hérite, quoi qu'on en dise, de l'impérialisme qu'a longtemps exercé l'Occident, et donc de la relégation dans laquelle ont été tenues d'autres manières de problématiser l'expérience, la manière même dont une expérience se conçoit et se vit, les conséquences concrètes qui en résultent. Autre gain et non des moindres : en insistant sur l'inadéquation des concepts de soi, de travail sur soi, de conscience, plutôt que sur la proximité ou sur le rôle de jalons que certains textes représentent indéniablement pour l'élaboration ou la genèse des concepts de « personne » ou d' « individu », l'ouvrage rend impossible un certain nombre d'usages contemporains, réducteurs et politiquement discutables, des textes antiques.

Sandrine ALEXANDRE
IRePh - Université Paris Nanterre

Bulletin Bibliographique

Éditions, traductions et commentaires

– Th. Auffret, J. Barnes and M. Rashed, *Alexander of Aphrodisias. On the Conversion of Propositions*, Berlin, De Gruyter, Scientia Graeco-Arabica, 2024.

– P. Golitsis and Ph. Hoffmann, *Simplicius de Cilicie. Commentaire à la* Physique *d'Aristote : Digressions sur le lieu et sur le temps*, édition critique avec introduction et traduction, Berlin, De Gruyter, Commentaria in Aristotelem Graeca et Byzantina – Series academica, 2024.

– R. Lefebvre, *Sextus Empiricus. Contre les moralistes*, texte introduit, traduit et commenté, Paris, Les Belles Lettres, La Roue à livres, 2024.

– J.-F. Pradeau, *Porphyre. Lettre à Marcella*, édition critique, traduction française, introduction et notes, Leiden-Boston, Brill, Philosophia antiqua, 2023.

Études

– U. Chaintreuil, *L' Unité de la Forme. L' Ontologie d'Aristote et le défi de la complexité*, Paris, Classiques Garnier, Les Anciens et les Modernes - Études de philosophie, 2024.

– E. Cagnoli Fiecconi, *Ethics for Rational Animals. The Moral Psychology at the Basis of Aristotle' s Ethics*, Oxford University Press, 2024.

– D. Machek, *The Life Worth Living in Ancient Greek and Roman Philosophy*, Cambridge University Press, 2024,

– J.-M. Narbonne, *Protagoras premier penseur de la démocratie. Une relecture philosophique et historique*, Paris, Vrin / Presses de l'Universite Laval, Zetesis, 2024.

– L. Saudelli, *Penser les contraires*, Paris, Vrin, Textes et Traditions, 2024.

– S. Sierksma-Agteres, *Paul and the Philosophers' Faith*, Brill, 2024, ouvrage en accès ouvert sur le site de l'éditeur à partir de juillet 2024 (https://brill.com/display/title/65088)

Recueils

– O. Boulnois, Ph. Hoffmann, C. Lafleur et J.-M. Narbonne, avec la collaboration de J. Carrier, *L'Esprit critique dans l'Antiquité II. La Naissance de la théologie comme science*, Paris, Belles Lettres, 2024.

– G. Guyomarc'h, F. A.J. de Haas (dir.). *Studies on Alexander of Aphrodisias'* On Mixture and Growth, Leiden-Boston, Brill, Philosophia Antiqua, 2024.

– J. Jouanna, *Médecine et tragédie en Grèce antique. Scripta minora 1961-2023*, édition établie par Antonio Ricciardetto, introduction par Caroline Noirot et Antonio Ricciardetto, Paris, Les Belles Lettres, 2024.

Achevé d'imprimer en novembre 2024
sur les presses de
La Manufacture - Imprimeur – 52200 Langres

Tél. : (33) 325 845 892

N° imprimeur : 240897 - Dépôt légal : novembre 2024
Imprimé en France